Microsoft®
Publisher 98
by Design

Luisa Simone

***Microsoft* Press**

PUBLISHED BY
Microsoft Press
A Division of Microsoft Corporation
One Microsoft Way
Redmond, WA 98052-6399

Library of Congress Cataloging-in-Publication Data
Simone, Luisa, 1955-
    Microsoft Publisher 98 by Design / Luisa Simone.
      p.   cm.
    Includes index.
    ISBN 1-57231-641-1
    1. Microsoft Publisher.   2. Desktop publishing.   I. Title.
Z253.532.M53S57   1998
686.2'25445369--dc21   97-51966
                                           CIP

Printed and bound in the United States of America.

1 2 3 4 5 6 7 8 9   QEQE   3 2 1 0 9 8

Distributed to the book trade in Canada by Macmillan of Canada, a division of Canada Publishing Corporation.

A CIP catalogue record for this book is available from the British Library.

Microsoft Press books are available through booksellers and distributors worldwide. For further information about international editions, contact your local Microsoft Corporation office. Or contact Microsoft Press International directly at fax (425) 936-7329. Visit our Web site at mspress.microsoft.com.

Acquisitions Editor: Kim Fryer
Project Editor: Patricia Draher
Manuscript Editor: Anne Owen
Technical Editors: Bill Kilcullen and Ellen Loney
Interior Graphic Designer: Amy Peppler Adams
Cover Designer: Patrick Lanfear
Compositor: Claudia Bell
Proofreader: Phil Worthington

To J.V.S.—otherwise known as Mom

Contents

Acknowledgments

Quite simply, this book would not exist if not for the combined efforts of many people. In particular, I'd like to thank Andrew Adams and Amy Peppler Adams of designLab, who supervised the design and production of this fifth edition. They handled the inevitable snags—including text revisions, layout changes, and missed deadlines—with aplomb. Thanks also to my editor, Anne Owen, and technical editors, Bill Kilcullen and Ellen Loney, who corrected, double-checked, and otherwise tweaked the copy into its present readable form.

Working with beta software is never easy, but the Microsoft Publisher 98 support team—especially Dennis Campton, Nancy Jacobs, and Mike Schackwitz—were always available to share their knowledge about the inner workings of Publisher 98.

Finally, I must thank several guardian angels at Microsoft Press—namely Kim Fryer, Patricia Draher, and Kim Eggleston—who provided invaluable guidance and support during the planning and production stages of this book.

Introduction

At first glance, Microsoft Publisher 98 looks virtually unchanged. It still combines powerful desktop publishing functions with an easy-to-use interface. And it still provides Wizards to help even novice designers create professional-looking publications. The instant text effects generated by the WordArt module and the preformatted objects in the Design Gallery can add a special touch to a document at the click of a button.

Publisher still generates a broad range of publications, including books, posters, and mail merge documents. And producing the final version of a publication remains blissfully simple, regardless of whether you are using a standard desktop printer, sending a file to a commercial printing service, or generating an HTML document for the World Wide Web.

But in proof of the old adage, Publisher 98's looks are deceiving. A host of new and improved features have been seamlessly integrated into this familiar program.

What's New in Publisher 98

Publisher's most basic function—its capability to edit and format text—has been updated to support multiple languages and the international character set, so you can disseminate your documents globally. And adjusting your copy to work with a layout has never been easier, thanks to the new Copyfit Text command that can enlarge or reduce the point size of text automatically. Finally, new vertical alignment options and a more sophisticated implementation of the line-spacing, kerning, and tracking controls let you fine-tune the position and density of your text.

Enhanced Web Publishing Tools

Over the past year, the World Wide Web community has become more diverse and sophisticated. Publisher lets you graduate to the next higher level of Web publishing with several new tools. Using simple dialog boxes, you can add background music to a Web page, assign keywords to help readers find your site using standard Web search engines, and specify the character set and HTML version your audience will be using. With the new Form Control tool, you can add Internet objects, such as option buttons, check boxes, text boxes, and drop-down lists, to a Web page. When viewed in a Web browser, these objects are fully functional and allow your reader to complete and submit a form electronically.

More ambitious Web designers can bypass Publisher's few remaining limitations by inserting HTML code fragments into a document. As an example, Publisher converts all imported images to the GIF picture format. But by using a code fragment, you can display in-line JPEG pictures instead. You can even animate your Web site by inserting animated GIF files or incorporating Dynamic HTML code into your Web page.

More Powerful Wizards

Previous versions of Publisher provided Wizards to help you create documents and partial-page elements (like a masthead or calendar). The Wizards in Publisher 98 can create a broader range of documents. In fact, there are so many Wizard-based designs available that Publisher categorizes them in two different ways: by type and by style. You can choose to view all the variations of one particular type of publication, such as a newsletter or flyer. Or you can choose to view a variety of publications that share a common style, like the Blend or Waves design sets.

Best of all, Publisher's Wizards remain linked to the documents they create. Wizards are also associated with many of the objects in the Design Gallery. This live link allows you to invoke a Wizard at any time in order to modify or restore the original design. Wizards can even help you convert a paper-based publication to a layout that is suitable for the Web.

Synchronized Information and Coordinated Colors

Publisher 98 can help you maintain a higher level of consistency in your documents. Publisher can keep track of certain key pieces of information about you or your company, such as your name, address, and telephone number. These elements—called Personal Information components—are synchronized with one another. So, if you change one instance of a personal information component containing your address, all similar components in the current publications are automatically updated with the new information. In addition to personal information components, Publisher can update the date and time, or synchronize elements found in the Design Gallery (such as Web site navigation bars or the dates in a calendar).

Publisher also provides over 60 predefined color schemes to help you manage color in your documents. Each color scheme contains six colors that complement each other. The current color scheme appears on the cascading menu for fill and line color, making it easy to apply color consistently throughout a document. And because Publisher maintains a link between the objects in your publication and the color scheme itself, choosing a different scheme automatically updates the objects with new hues.

Why This Book Is Easy to Use

This book is not a manual, but it does contain valuable reference material. The first part of the book, "Publisher 98 Fundamentals," provides a guide to the features and tools Publisher offers. Each chapter in this section focuses on a related group of tools. For example, Chapter 3, "Layout Tools," discusses the functions needed to build a cohesive page design, such as object positioning, grouping, alignment, and rotation. Whenever appropriate, these chapters also include technical information to help you understand how Publisher functions within the context of other computer-based graphics applications. For example, Chapter 12, "Creating Documents for the World Wide Web," explains why and how Publisher's wide range of formatting options must be restricted to produce well-behaved HTML documents for the Web.

The second part of the book, "Design Projects," illustrates essential desktop publishing concepts, teaches fundamental skills, and elucidates the elements of good design. The sample publications have been designed to showcase Publisher's wide-ranging capabilities. They include Web documents, an advertisement, a newsletter, a flyer, and a three-fold brochure. If there is a faster or smarter way to accomplish a task in Publisher 98, the design projects take advantage of it. Small businesses, families, nonprofit organizations, and individuals will find all of these projects inspiring—whether used as step-by-step blueprints or as the starting point for original designs.

The projects give you the opportunity to put design theory into practice and illustrate, in a way that no description can, the synergy among Publisher's various functions. To show you how content drives design, each project contains text and pictures that reflect real-life business and personal situations. You can duplicate the design projects exactly as they appear in this edition. All of the images and multimedia files (including a background soundtrack and an animation) are part of Publisher's Clip Gallery. The full text for each project is provided in Appendix B. But if you don't want to retype the copy, you can download word processing files directly from the Microsoft Press Web site at http://mspress.microsoft.com/mspress/products/1426/.

Appendix A details the new, more robust drawing tools offered by Microsoft Draw 98—a graphics program that ships with Publisher. Using Draw you can create original art, modify existing pictures, and produce even more spectacular WordArt effects.

A Graphical Approach to Explaining Application Features and Design Concepts

Even a cursory inspection will reveal that *Microsoft Publisher 98 by Design* is chock-full of illustrations. This visual presentation of information not only is aesthetically appealing but also stresses the procedural nature of much of the book. For example, instead of simply telling you how to use a dialog box, this format *shows* you how to use a dialog box by annotating an illustration of the computer screen with numbered steps. You can use this book as a step-by-step instructional guide to Publisher's tools and functions. But it is also designed to be used as a reference book that explains computer graphics concepts and technology, and as a design tutorial for a wide variety of publications.

Much of the ancillary information appears in a separate Tip column in the left-hand margin of the page. This allows the step-by-step instructions to proceed uninterrupted and lets you more easily find certain types of information by looking for these icons:

Power Tips give you the inside scoop on advanced functions or shortcuts in the program. Within the project chapters, Power Tips offer design advice.

Troubleshooting Tips answer frequently asked questions and warn you about potential problems.

Cross References point you toward more information on a given topic.

Keyboard Shortcuts provide the keystroke equivalents for frequently used commands.

What You Need to Begin Using Microsoft Publisher 98

To use Publisher 98, you need to be running Microsoft Windows 95 or Microsoft NT version 4.0 or later. The absolute minimum hardware requirements include the following:

- 486 processor
- 8 MB of memory (12 MB for NT)
- Hard disk with 24 MB of free disk space
- VGA monitor
- Mouse
- CD-ROM drive

If you plan to create large documents, or if you want Publisher 98 to perform quickly, you'll need more processing power. That translates to a Pentium or Pentium II processor, 16 MB of memory (preferably more), a 256-color or 24-bit color monitor and video adapter, and *lots* of hard disk space. The typical installation of Publisher 98 requires 109 MB of hard disk space. Of course, you'll also need a graphics-capable printer, though color output is optional. And you'll need a Twain 32–compliant scanner or digital camera if you want to capture original images.

To get the most out of this book, you should also have a working knowledge of the Windows operating environment. The instructions assume that you understand how to locate files stored in folders on your hard disk, and that you know the difference between clicking, dragging, and double-clicking mouse buttons. If these concepts are not familiar, you should refer to the Windows 95 or Windows NT online help system for more information.

A Desire to Experiment

I've said it before, and it's still true: to become a competent designer, you need a little something more than hardware and software—you need the willingness to experiment. You can rely on Wizards, the Design Gallery, and special effects such as BorderArt and WordArt to jump-start the design process and to serve as a source of visual inspiration, but Publisher's powerful tools ultimately let you develop your own design ideas. Luckily, the tools are so easy to use that the experimentation often feels more like play than work.

This book encourages you to exercise your creativity and develop confidence in your own aesthetic judgments. By the time you've finished reading this book, you'll look at the publications that surround you with new eyes—as designs that you too can create.

PART 1

Publisher 98 Fundamentals

1 Becoming Familiar with Microsoft Publisher

Can I run Publisher 98 with Windows 3.1? No. If you want to run Publisher 98 (or Publisher 97), you must upgrade to Windows 95. Publisher 98 won't work with earlier versions of Windows.

The keyboard is faster than a mouse. You can also operate Publisher using the keyboard. Keyboard equivalents are shown to the right of the command names on the menus that drop down from the menu bar. Keystrokes are often faster than the mouse if your hands are already on the keyboard or if you must perform repetitive tasks. For example, you can quickly save a file by holding down the Ctrl key and typing *s* (Ctrl-S).

Microsoft Publisher is easy to use. When you master a few basic concepts and skills, you can create sophisticated and professional-looking publications. Taking a few minutes now to familiarize yourself with Publisher's interface and its unique approach to document creation will save you valuable time later and enable you to turn out products with a minimum of confusion and frustration.

A Quick Tour of Publisher's Interface

You interact with Publisher as you do with most Windows-based applications by using menu commands, toolbars, and dialog boxes. Publisher is Microsoft Office-compliant, which means that it shares many interface conventions with popular programs like Microsoft Word and Excel.

Menus and Toolbars

Menus and toolbars are actually quite similar because they both let you issue commands using a mouse. But where menus use words to describe commands, toolbars use icons—or pictures—to represent the program's functions.

Access shortcut menus.
Right-clicking on any object in the Publisher window invokes a shortcut menu containing commands that are specific to that element. For example, if you right-click a picture frame, the shortcut menu lets you insert an image file. Right-clicking a text frame instead brings up commands to change hyphenation options or to run a spell check.

Format toolbars, which appear under the Office toolbar, change depending on which tool or object is active. For example, when the text tool is active, the toolbar contains text formatting functions.

The Office toolbar appears along the top of the window right under the menu bar. It contains frequently used functions, such as starting a new file or Undo/Redo.

Think of the menu bar as the top level of an outline, with related commands appearing on a drop-down list under each title. A command is executed when you click it.

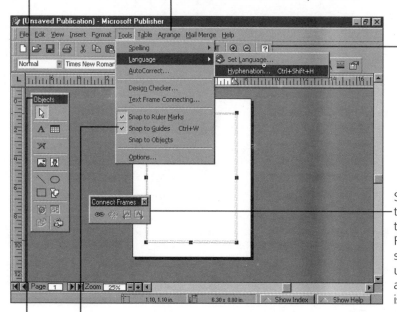

Special function toolbars, such as the Connect Frames toolbar shown here, pop up when the appropriate object is selected.

Menu commands can be preceded by a check mark (which signifies that the command is currently active), followed by a triangle (which opens a cascading menu containing more choices), or followed by an ellipsis (which indicates a dialog box will open when you choose the command).

The main toolbar, located along the left-hand side of the screen, provides the tools to create and select objects, such as text or picture frames.

Why can't I find the dialog box options I need?
The options you want might be in distinct but related dialog boxes. Windows 95 organizes these dialog boxes with tabs. Click a tab to bring it to the front of the stack and to reveal a new set of options.

Use the interactive status readout when drawing or resizing frames. Publisher's status line reports the size of a frame to the nearest 1/100 of an inch. You can use this information, which is instantly updated, to increase your precision as you draw or resize a frame.

Dialog Box Options

Whenever Publisher needs information from you to complete a command, it presents you with a window called a dialog box.

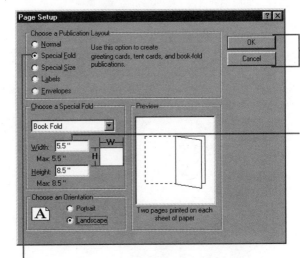

You must select a command button in the dialog box to submit the information, cancel the operation, or call up additional options before you can return to the main program.

In some cases, you can type information directly into a text box.

You provide information by selecting radio buttons, check boxes (not shown), or items from drop-down list boxes.

Getting Feedback from Publisher's Interface

Publisher's tools are designed to provide valuable feedback on the currently selected object or operation. You can work more efficiently and more accurately if you learn to "read the screen."

Float or dock the toolbars. Publisher lets you rearrange your desktop by floating or docking the various toolbars. To float a toolbar, double-click a docked toolbar's Move icon (the double gray bars at the left). You can move and even change the shape of a floating toolbar. To dock a toolbar, double-click a floating toolbar's title bar. The toolbar will be locked in position along the top or bottom of the workspace.

Reset tippages to reappear. Tippages are learning tools that appear on screen the first time you use a particular function, such as text frame linking or grouping. You can force tippages to appear for features you have used previously by clicking the Reset Tips button found on the Editing and User Assistance tab in the Options dialog box (on the Tools menu).

The Format toolbar displays different functions depending on whether the currently selected object is a text frame, picture frame, or a WordArt frame. For example, picture formatting options appear only when a picture frame is selected.

Menu commands that can't be executed at the current time appear as gray (rather than black) text.

Reminders, tippages (pronounced "tip page"), and alert boxes are messages that pop up in response to specific situations. For example, if you do something illogical, like attempt to type into a rectangle that isn't truly a text frame, Publisher reminds you that you can insert text only into a text or table frame.

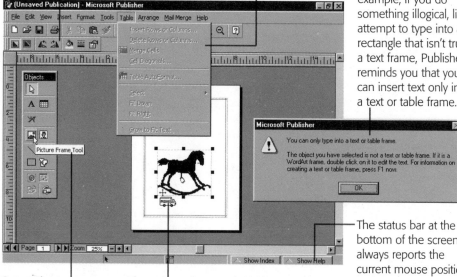

ScreenTips appear whenever the mouse pointer is positioned over a screen element for a few seconds.

The pointer changes shape in response to the action you are performing. For example, the Move pointer lets you reposition objects. Publisher also displays distinct pointers for editing text or selecting, drawing, cropping, and adjusting objects.

The status bar at the bottom of the screen always reports the current mouse position and the size of the selected object.

Customizing Publisher's Interface

Like other Microsoft Office products, Publisher offers configuration options to display or hide—and even animate—many elements of the interface. Publisher ships with all interface elements displayed and the animation features turned off. But you can reconfigure the interface the suit your own workstyle.

Customize Interface Elements	
To take this action...	**Do this...**
Hide the Standard toolbar	Choose Toolbars on the View menu. Deselect Standard on the cascading menu.
Hide the formatting toolbars	Choose Toolbars on the View menu. Deselect Formatting on the cascading menu.
Hide the status bar	Choose Toolbars on the View menu. Deselect Status Bar on the cascading menu.
Switch from normal to large icons	Choose Toolbars on the View menu and then choose Options from the cascading menu. Select Large Icons. Click OK.
Hide ScreenTips on toolbars or objects	Choose Toolbars on the View menu and then choose Options from the cascading menu. Deselect Show ScreenTips On Toolbars or Show ScreenTips On Objects. Click OK.
Hide shortcut keys in ScreenTips	Choose Toolbars on the View menu and then choose Options from the cascading menu. Deselect Show Shortcut Keys in ScreenTips. Click OK.
Animate menus as they open or close	Choose Toolbars on the View menu and then choose Options from the cascading menu. Open the Menu Animations drop-down list and choose Random, Unfold, or Slide. Click OK.
Turn off Publisher's Helpful pointers and use the standard Windows 95 pointers instead	Choose Options on the Tools menu. Click the General tab and then deselect the Use Helpful Pointers check box.
Turn off tippages	Choose Options on the Tools menu. Click the Editing And User Assistance tab and then deselect the Show Tippages check box.
Turn off reminders	Choose Options on the Tools menu. Click the Editing And User Assistance tab and then deselect the Remind To Save Publication check box.

 **Use the Office help assistant.** Publisher 98 contains the Office help assistant. This entertaining cartoon animation allows you to type an English-language statement about your current question or problem. The results of your search are displayed in a list at the top of the dialog box. Clicking an item opens Publisher's standard help window and displays the appropriate information.

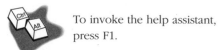

To invoke the help assistant, press F1.

Access Publisher's electronic demos. Publisher's Help system gives you instant access to 15 demonstrations of specific functions, such as layering and the background. Simply open the help index and type the word *demo* into the keyword text box. Publisher displays a list of all available demos. Select an arrow button to display the demo of your choice.

Getting Answers from Publisher's Help System

Your document and Publisher's help tools can be on screen simultaneously, so you can get answers to your questions without interrupting your work session. Publisher's help system is divided into two windows: one for an index and one for detailed information.

The Question Mark icon identifies the Help button and gives you quick access to the Office help assistant. Within dialog boxes, you can use a special question mark cursor to click an item for context-sensitive help.

3 Click the How To tab to display step-by-step instructions, or click the More Info tab to display background information.

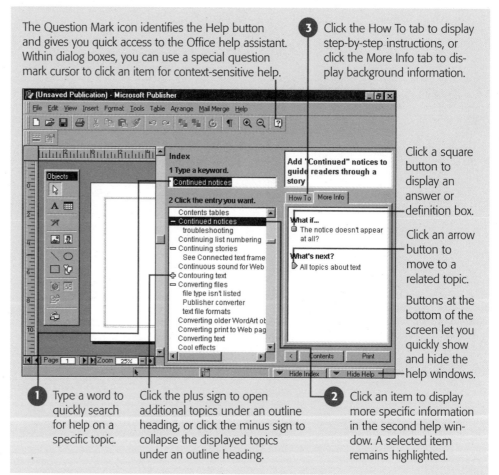

Click a square button to display an answer or definition box.

Click an arrow button to move to a related topic.

Buttons at the bottom of the screen let you quickly show and hide the help windows.

1 Type a word to quickly search for help on a specific topic.

Click the plus sign to open additional topics under an outline heading, or click the minus sign to collapse the displayed topics under an outline heading.

2 Click an item to display more specific information in the second help window. A selected item remains highlighted.

Visit Publisher's Web site. Clicking the Microsoft Publisher Web Site command on the Help menu invokes your Web browser and connects you to Publisher's World Wide Web site. Once you're on line, you can learn about special offers, download free software and clip art, and access Microsoft's extensive help database.

Quick Access to the Undo and Redo commands. Click the Undo button on the Standard toolbar to reverse the last action you performed. Click the Redo button on the Standard toolbar to reverse the last Undo action you performed.

To undo your last action, press Ctrl-Z. To redo the last undo action, press Ctrl-Y.

Reversing a Mistake with the Undo and Redo Commands

Don't worry if you click the wrong menu item, inadvertently resize a frame, or accidentally move an object while working on a design. You can easily correct these and many other common mistakes by issuing the Undo command from the Edit menu. You can even reverse the Undo action itself by issuing the Redo command from the Edit menu. Publisher can undo or redo the last 20 actions you performed.

But be warned: some actions, like choosing a new data source for a mail merge publication, can't be undone. You'll also find that once you've interrupted the Undo or Redo sequence, you can't continue to undo or redo previous actions.

The Redo command tells you exactly what Undo operation it will reverse; in this case, a move.

The Undo command tells you exactly what operation it will reverse, in this case filling an object with color.

The Building Blocks of Documents: Text, Pictures, Drawn Elements, and OLE Objects

Publisher treats words, pictures, and everything else in a document as objects. A document is simply a collection of different kinds of objects. Understanding

How does desktop publishing differ from word processing? Word processing documents are linear: one character leads to the next, lines of text are sequential, and pages follow each other in a predictable order. Desktop publishing documents are nonlinear. You use text and pictures as building blocks to construct a page design in any order you want.

Publisher is a desktop publishing application—not a word processing application. Although Publisher provides some word processing features (including a spelling checker and a find-and-replace feature), it is not intended to function as a true word processing application.

object attributes and how objects behave and interact with one another is the key to working with Publisher. A Publisher document can contain four basic kinds of objects, as shown in the following table.

Types of Objects in Microsoft Publisher		
Object Type	**Content**	**Description**
Text or table	Words	Text that is typed directly into a Publisher document or imported from a word processing file
Picture	Any visual material imported from an external source	Scanned photographs, technical diagrams, clip-art images, charts, and other graphics
Drawn	Visual elements you create in Publisher	Rules, decorative borders, and geometric shapes such as boxes, ovals, and ploygons
OLE	Objects that are created by other programs	Any kind of computer-based data: cells from a spreadsheet, text from a word processor, pictures from a drawing application, or fields from a database

Components of Objects

In a Publisher document, each object consists of the content, the frame, and the formatting attributes.

Frames versus Content

Despite their very close relationship, you must learn to see a frame and the content it contains as separate aspects of the same object.

Think of the content of an object as its meaning. For example, the content of a picture object is the picture itself, and the content of a text object is the words. You can change the formatting attributes, such as the size, shape, position, or color of an object, without altering its content.

In your own home, picture frames contain pieces of art and allow you to position that art on the wall anywhere you please. Publisher's frames contain words, pictures, drawn elements, or other objects, and allow you to size and position those objects on the publication page. The composition of frames on the page is called a layout.

Is a border the same as a frame? No. These two terms should not be used interchangeably. A frame is the rectangle that defines an object's boundary. A border is a formatting attribute, such as a 1-point black line, that can be applied to a frame.

Formatting Attributes

We often define objects by describing their properties or attributes. For example, a balloon can be red or blue, a chair can be straight-backed or cushioned, and a person can be tall or short. All objects in Publisher also have attributes, and you can alter the appearance of objects by changing their attributes. This alteration process is called formatting.

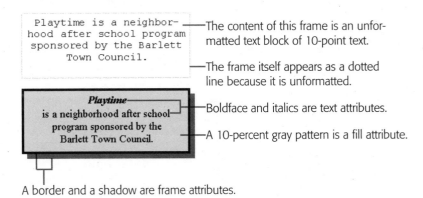

Playtime is a neighborhood after school program sponsored by the Barlett Town Council.

—The content of this frame is an unformatted text block of 10-point text.

—The frame itself appears as a dotted line because it is unformatted.

Playtime is a neighborhood after school program sponsored by the Barlett Town Council.

—Boldface and italics are text attributes.

—A 10-percent gray pattern is a fill attribute.

A border and a shadow are frame attributes.

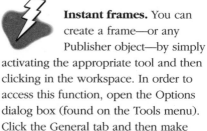

Instant frames. You can create a frame—or any Publisher object—by simply activating the appropriate tool and then clicking in the workspace. In order to access this function, open the Options dialog box (found on the Tools menu). Click the General tab and then make sure a check mark appears next to Single-Click Object Creation. One word of warning: the frames you create in this way appear on the page in a standard size. You must then resize each frame.

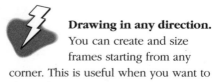

Drawing in any direction. You can create and size frames starting from any corner. This is useful when you want to align a frame with other elements or guides on the page.

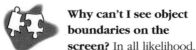

Why can't I see object boundaries on the screen? In all likelihood, you have hidden the object boundaries. To display them, open the View menu and choose the Show Boundaries And Guides command, or use the keyboard shortcut Ctrl-Shift-O.

Creating a Frame

Before you can type text, import a picture, design WordArt, or insert an OLE element, you must draw the appropriate frame for that type of object.

Draw a Frame

1 Activate the toolbar tool that will create the kind of object you want. The pointer changes into a crossbar.

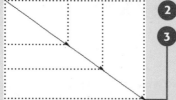

2 Position the crossbar on the page.

3 Holding down the mouse button, drag the mouse diagonally. The frame boundary will look like a square or a rectangle. Essentially, you are drawing from one corner to the opposite corner of the object.

4 When the shape and size of the frame are to your liking, release the mouse button.

Identifying and Selecting an Object

Publisher helps you see where one object ends and another object begins by displaying a dotted line—called an object boundary—around each object.

The Martin Krump Trio

If an object has a border, such as the black rule shown here, it exactly follows the object boundary and obscures that border from view.

This dotted line represents an object boundary. Although you can see object boundaries on the screen, they never print.

Before you can modify or format any object, you must select it. You can tell that an object has been selected because selection handles appear on the frame surrounding the object.

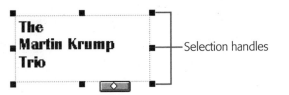 Selection handles

 Learn the difference between a multiple selection and a group.
A multiple selection is a temporary group that's created when you select more than one object at a time. As soon as you de-select the elements, they are once again treated as individual objects. Publisher allows you to convert a multiple selec-tion to a permanent group of objects that are "glued" together until you ungroup them. Grouped objects offer you flexi-bility because you can treat them like a single object while you design your publication.

 For more information about working with grouped objects, see Chapter 3.

 Mix and match selection tools. You can work more efficiently by using the various selection tools in combination. For example, if you want to select every element on a page but one, use the Select All command and then use the Shift key to deselect a single object.

Select and Deselect an Object

1 If the pointer is not an arrow, click the Pointer tool on the toolbar.

2 Using the pointer, click an object. The object remains selected until you click another object or any blank area of the screen.

3 Click away from the selected object to deselect it.

Multiple Selections

Sometimes it is efficient to work with more than one object at a time, particularly when you want to move or delete them. Publisher lets you select several objects simultaneously in what is known as a multiple selection.

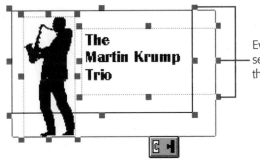 Every currently selected object in a multiple selection is displayed with gray (rather than the usual black) selection handles.

You can select more than one object in several ways, as explained in the table on the next page.

Methods of Creating a Multiple Selection	
To select...	**Do this...**
Every object on the page	Choose the Select All command on the Edit menu.
Objects that are not close to each other on the page or to exclude objects from the current multiple selection	Holding down the Shift key, use the Pointer tool to click a series of objects.
Objects that are adjacent to one another on the page	Use the Pointer tool to draw a special boundary—called a selection box or a marquee selection—around all the objects you want to select.

Previewing Your Layout

Publisher's WYSIWYG (What You See Is What You Get) display always attempts to show you how the final printed page will look. You can enhance the appearance of Publisher's WYSIWYG display by hiding layout guides and nonprinting characters (like paragraph markers and spaces).

A screen image with guides, boundaries, and special characters displayed

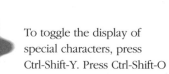

To toggle the display of special characters, press Ctrl-Shift-Y. Press Ctrl-Shift-O to toggle the display of boundaries and guides.

For more information on layout tools, see Chapter 3.

A screen image with guides, boundaries, and special characters hidden, accurately representing the final printout

Make use of dialog box previews. Many of Publisher's dialog boxes contain a preview area that lets you see how the current settings will affect your publication. For the most part, dialog box previews are not WYSIWYG but instead represent your design decisions with simple schematic drawings that are nevertheless accurate. Taking a few extra seconds to examine the preview can help you discover and correct mistakes quickly—and ultimately save you time.

Preview Your Document

1 Open the View menu and select Hide Special Characters and/or Hide Boundaries and Guides.

2 To redisplay special characters, object boundaries, and guides, click the Show Special Characters and Show Boundaries And Guides commands on the View menu.

Beginning Work on a Publication

Just like conventional paper documents, Microsoft Publisher documents contain pages—albeit electronic ones. Instead of stacking and shuffling sheets of paper, however, you use Publisher's commands to manage and move around in your electronic documents.

For instructions on installing the Microsoft Publisher application, see *Microsoft Publisher 98 Companion*.

Circumvent the Catalog dialog box. You can choose to bypass the Catalog dialog box when you open Microsoft Publisher. Choose Options on the Tools menu. In the Options dialog box, deselect the check box labeled Open Publications Catalog At Startup. Publisher will start with a blank, full-page document.

Starting Publisher

Using the Microsoft Windows 95 Start button is the simplest way to load Publisher, but you can also double-click the program icon found in the Microsoft Publisher folder or create shortcut icons to start Publisher directly from the desktop.

Open the Microsoft Publisher Application

1. Install Microsoft Publisher on your hard disk.

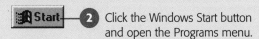 2. Click the Windows Start button and open the Programs menu.

3. Click the icon for Microsoft Publisher. If this is the first time you've run Publisher, the Introduction To Publisher screen will appear. You can choose to read the introduction or click the Cancel button to invoke Publisher's Catalog startup dialog box.

Why can't I find a Templates tab in the Catalog dialog box? Publisher 98 doesn't create a Templates tab. To access a template you previously created, click the Existing Publications tab, and then select the Templates button at the bottom of the dialog box. Even if you are upgrading from an older version of Publisher and have templates stored on your hard disk, you can access them by using the new Templates button.

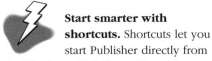

Start smarter with shortcuts. Shortcuts let you start Publisher directly from the Windows 95 desktop. To work most efficiently, create a shortcut to an actual publication file. When you double-click the icon representing the publication file, Windows automatically starts Publisher, loads the file, and uses the folder where the file is stored as Publisher's working directory.

Creating a shortcut is easy. Using Windows Explorer, find the publication file you want to use as a shortcut. Right-click the filename and choose Create Shortcut from the pop-up menu. Windows will place the shortcut in the current folder. Drag the shortcut icon from Windows Explorer to the desktop. Double-click the shortcut icon to start Publisher and load the file simultaneously.

Open the Microsoft Publisher Application *(continued)*

4 Click one of the four tabbed options.

Wizards create formatted documents for you.

The Blank Publications tab lets you build an original design.

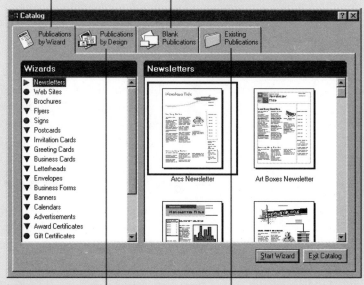

Publications By Design also employs Wizards but offers a set of documents with a consistent look.

The Existing Publications tab lets you retrieve a publication file or a template you previously stored on disk.

To start a new publication, press Ctrl-N.

Quick access to common commands. The standard Microsoft Office toolbar contains icons to quickly create, open, and save publications. If you've used other Office products, such as Word or Excel, these icons (shown below) will be familiar to you. The Page icon starts a new blank publication. The Folder icon opens an existing publication. And the Diskette icon saves the current publication.

Page icon — Diskette icon

Folder icon

For more information about these and other page layout options, see Chapter 2.

Starting a Publication from Scratch

Whenever you begin a new publication with a blank page, Publisher provides 11 predefined page layouts.

Begin Designing a New Publication

1 If it is not already active, click the Blank Publications tab along the top of the Catalog dialog box.

Thumbnail sketches show you how each page layout option relates to standard 8.5-by-11-inch paper.

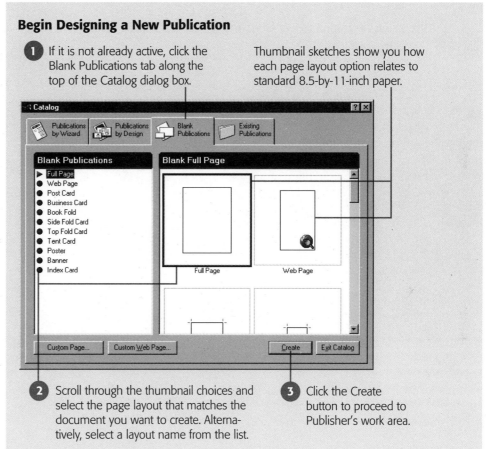

2 Scroll through the thumbnail choices and select the page layout that matches the document you want to create. Alternatively, select a layout name from the list.

3 Click the Create button to proceed to Publisher's work area.

To open an existing file, press Ctrl-O and select the file using the Open Publication dialog box.

 Open a publication directly from the File menu. At the bottom of the File menu, you'll find a list of the last four publications you worked on. Clicking on a filename, or typing the number that precedes the filename, circumvents the Catalog dialog box and opens the file immediately.

 Organizing files. Depending on the software installed on your system, Publisher will attempt to store your documents in the Personal folder (found in the Windows folder) or the My Documents folder. You can work more efficiently by choosing or creating a new folder for each design project.

Opening an Existing Publication

The Catalog dialog box appears whenever you choose the Open command from the File menu. It provides easy access to recently used files.

Open a Recently Used File

Like the File menu, this list box displays the filenames (and paths) of the last four files you worked on.

1 In the Catalog dialog box, select the Existing Publications tab.

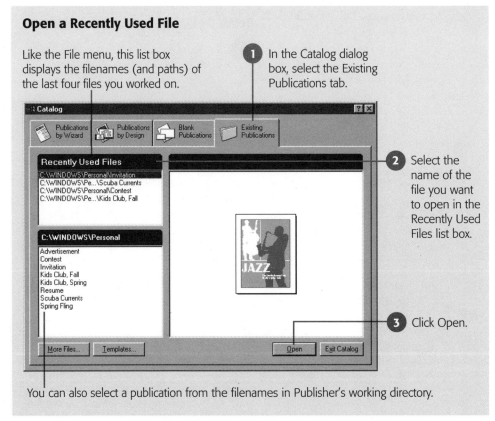

2 Select the name of the file you want to open in the Recently Used Files list box.

3 Click Open.

You can also select a publication from the filenames in Publisher's working directory.

Save a publication file from inadvertent changes.

If you want to review a file and safeguard it from any changes, click the Open As Read-Only option at the bottom of the Open Publication dialog box. Publisher will display the file on screen but will prevent you from saving the file with the same filename.

Finding an Older File

If you don't see the name of the publication in the Catalog dialog box, you can use the Open Publication dialog box to browse or search for a specific file.

Browse for an Existing File

1 In the Catalog dialog box, select the Existing Publications tab.

2 Select the More Files button. The Open Publication dialog box appears.

3 In the Look In drop-down list box, browse the drives and individual folders to locate the file you want.

> If a check mark appears in the Preview File check box, Publisher displays a thumbnail sketch to help you identify the file visually.

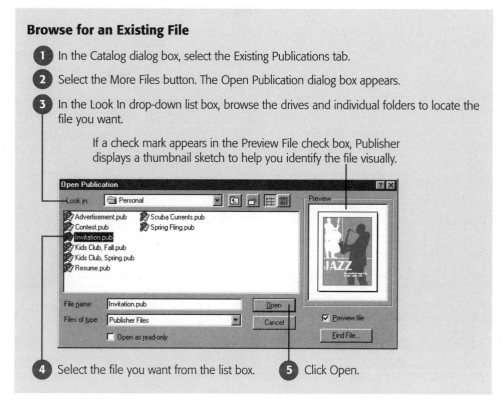

4 Select the file you want from the list box.

5 Click Open.

Wildcard symbols. Use the standard wildcard symbols, the asterisk (*) and the question mark (?), for the parts of the filename you are not going to specify in the Find This File text box.

Search for an Existing File

1 Click the Find File button in the Open Publication dialog box. The Find File dialog box appears.

2 Specify the type of file you want to find. For example, *.pub locates only Publisher files.

3 Alternatively, select Find This File and specify the particular filename you want to find.

4 Specify the drive you want Publisher to search.

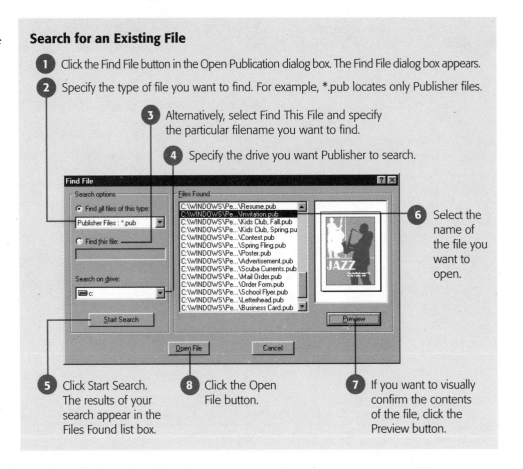

6 Select the name of the file you want to open.

5 Click Start Search. The results of your search appear in the Files Found list box.

8 Click the Open File button.

7 If you want to visually confirm the contents of the file, click the Preview button.

You choose a paper size in the Print Setup dialog box, which is described in Chapter 16.

How are the layouts in the Page Setup dialog box different from the layouts in the Catalog dialog box? The predefined layouts in the Catalog dialog box and the Page Setup dialog box are identical. If you are creating a completely standard publication, you can choose a page layout directly from the Catalog dialog box. The Page Setup dialog box offers advanced options that allow you to customize the size and orientation of your publication page.

Setting Up the Publication Page

The page layout determines the general size and orientation of your publication and affects how the pages will be arranged at print time. The key to setting up a publication properly is understanding that paper size and Publisher's page size are not necessarily the same thing.

Paper size refers to the physical dimensions of the paper in your printer. Minimum and maximum paper sizes are determined by the capabilities of your printer. Most desktop printers use a standard 8.5-by-11-inch sheet of paper.

Publisher's page size refers to the dimensions of your publication, which can be the same, smaller, or larger than the paper size. In Publisher, the smallest allowable page size is 0.25 by 0.25 inch, and the largest is 240 by 240 inches (that's 20 feet by 20 feet).

Publisher assumes four possible relationships between page size and paper size:

- The page size can equal the paper size.

- The page size can be smaller than the paper size. In this case, the page size is the trim size of your document.

- Two or more pages can fit on a single sheet of paper. Publisher can arrange the pages so that they can be folded to become a card or a book.

- A single page can be larger than a single sheet of paper. Publisher can print the page across several sheets of paper, as in a banner.

Creating a Publication Page Equal to the Paper Size

You will often want to create 8.5-by-11-inch pages on 8.5-by-11-inch pieces of paper, which is the standard size of paper used for business correspondence in the United States.

Is the Normal setting synonymous with letter-sized paper? No. When you choose the Normal option, Publisher assumes that the page size and paper size are equal. If you have chosen a paper size other than 8.5 by 11 inches in the Print Setup dialog box, such as legal length (8.5 by 14 inches) or ledger size (11 by 17 inches), the Normal option in the Page Setup dialog box will reflect the size of the chosen paper.

 For more information about Print Setup options, see Chapter 16.

Create a Page Size That Matches the Size of Your Paper

1 Choose Page Setup on the File menu, or click the Custom Page button on the Blank Publications tab in the Startup dialog box. The Page Setup dialog box appears.

2 Select Normal.

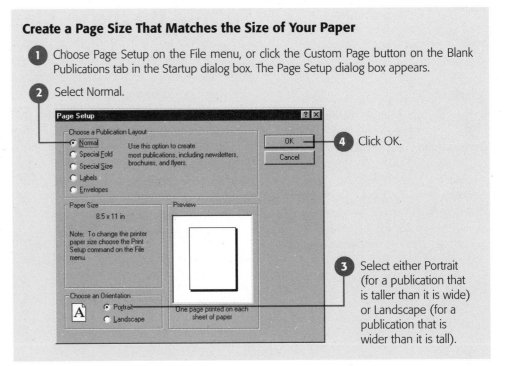

4 Click OK.

3 Select either Portrait (for a publication that is taller than it is wide) or Landscape (for a publication that is wider than it is tall).

Creating a Publication Page Not Equal to the Paper Size

Publisher allows you to create document pages that are larger or smaller than the paper installed in your printer. Publisher can crop down to small pages, tile the paper together to create large pages, and arrange pages into book form.

Special-Sized Publications

Whether you are creating small documents, such as index cards and business cards, or oversized documents, such as banners and posters, Publisher always figures out the best way to position the page on the paper.

Orientation of special-sized publications. When planning a special-sized publication, choose the Portrait or Landscape paper orientation carefully. The orientation for small publications, like business cards, will determine how many copies you can fit on a single page. Larger publications are also affected. For example, the paper orientation determines the height of a banner: in Portrait mode, banners are 11 inches tall, but in Landscape mode, banners are only 8.5 inches tall.

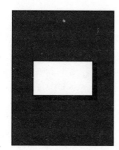

For small documents, Publisher centers a single page on the paper.

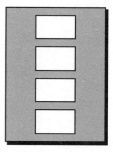

Publisher can print multiple copies of a small document on a single sheet of paper to avoid waste.

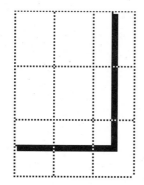

For oversized documents, Publisher prints your design across several sheets of paper.

Create a Document Larger or Smaller Than the Paper Size

1 Choose Page Setup on the File menu, or click the Custom Page button on the Blank Publications tab in the Catalog dialog box. The Page Setup dialog box appears.

2 Select the Special Size option.

3 Open the Choose A Publication Size drop-down list box and select one of the predefined options. Alternatively, choose the Custom or Custom Banner option.

4 If you chose the Custom or Custom Banner, enter values from 0.25 inch through 20 feet into the Width and Height text boxes.

5 Select either Portrait or Landscape.

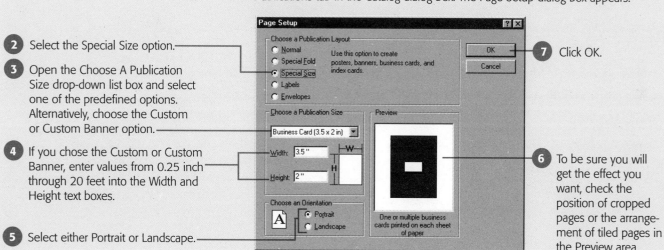

7 Click OK.

6 To be sure you will get the effect you want, check the position of cropped pages or the arrangement of tiled pages in the Preview area.

Why won't Publisher allow me to change the size of a predefined publication size? When you choose a predefined publication size, Publisher displays fixed dimensions in the Width and Height text boxes. These sizes, shown in the following list, are fixed. If you want to enter different values in the Width and Height text boxes, you must choose the Custom or Custom Banner option.

- ❷ Banner (5 feet)
- ❷ Banner (10 feet)
- ❷ Banner (15 feet)
- ❷ Business Card (3.5 by 2 inches)
- ❷ Index Card (5 by 3 inches)
- ❷ Post Card (3.94 by 5.83 inches)
- ❷ Post Card (5.5 by 4.25 inches)
- ❷ Post Card (5.83 by 4.13 inches)
- ❷ Poster (18 by 24 inches)
- ❷ Poster (24 by 36 inches)
- ❷ Printer Sheet Size

Folded Publications

Folded publications include books and cards. Although a folded document may seem simple to create, some pages might need to be printed out of order—or upside-down—for the publication to be ordered and oriented correctly after the paper is folded. The following illustrations show you the four predefined ways Publisher can arrange the individual pages on each sheet of paper. Each arrangement is called an imposition (the technical term for how multiple pages are placed on a single sheet of paper).

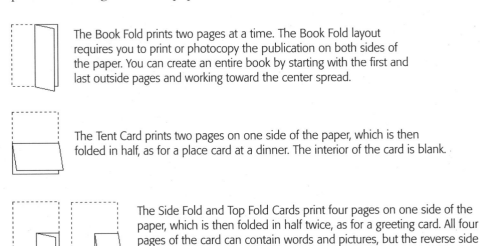

The Book Fold prints two pages at a time. The Book Fold layout requires you to print or photocopy the publication on both sides of the paper. You can create an entire book by starting with the first and last outside pages and working toward the center spread.

The Tent Card prints two pages on one side of the paper, which is then folded in half, as for a place card at a dinner. The interior of the card is blank.

The Side Fold and Top Fold Cards print four pages on one side of the paper, which is then folded in half twice, as for a greeting card. All four pages of the card can contain words and pictures, but the reverse side of the folded card (the side of the paper you can't see) is left blank.

Will my older printer be able to print the folded layouts? The Book Fold layout requires that pages be printed on both sides of the paper (duplex printing). If your printer can't do this, photocopy the pages back to back and then fold, collate, and staple the pages into your book.

The Top Fold and Side Fold Card layout options require that two of the four pages be printed upside-down, and the Tent Card option requires that the second page be printed upside-down. Some older laser printers or dot matrix printers might have difficulty printing inverted text. To solve this problem, use Publisher's WordArt tool to create the text.

Create a Folded Document

1 Choose Page Setup on the File menu, or click the Custom Page button on the Blank Publications tab in the Catalog dialog box.

2 Select Special Fold.

3 Open the Choose A Special Fold drop-down list box and select one of the predefined layouts. Publisher computes the maximum page size and displays the values in the Width and Height text boxes.

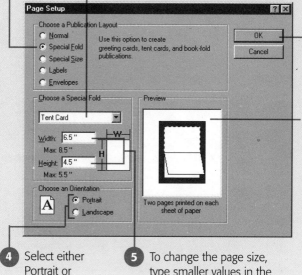

6 Click OK.

Notice that the Preview area changes to reflect your choices. If you decide to create smaller pages, Publisher will show you approximately how much paper will be trimmed (indicated by a gray tint). If you change the width or height, click another active area in the dialog box to change the preview before you click OK.

4 Select either Portrait or Landscape.

5 To change the page size, type smaller values in the Width and Height text boxes.

Why won't Publisher allow me to create an envelope that is 3-by-3 inches? Publisher cannot print envelopes that are smaller than 3-by-5 inches or larger than 8.5-by-11 inches.

Creating Publications for Special Papers

Most of today's desktop printers can accommodate specialty papers, such as pre-scored brochures or perforated business cards. Publisher provides page layout options for two of the most common specialty items: envelopes and adhesive labels.

Create an Envelope

1 Choose Page Setup on the File menu, or click the Custom Page button on the Blank Publications tab in the Catalog dialog box.

2 Select Envelopes.

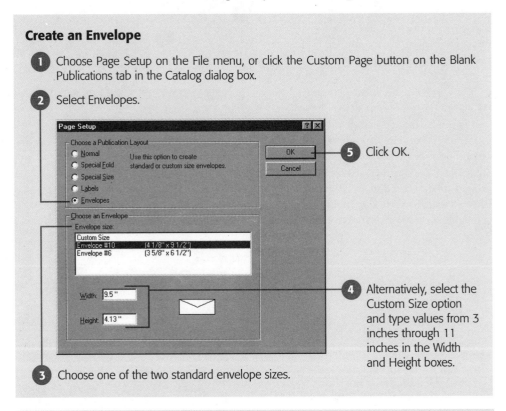

5 Click OK.

4 Alternatively, select the Custom Size option and type values from 3 inches through 11 inches in the Width and Height boxes.

3 Choose one of the two standard envelope sizes.

Create Labels

1 Choose Page Setup on the File menu, or click the Custom Page button on the Blank Publications tab in the Catalog dialog box.

2 Select Labels.

How can I get different information to print on each label? When you choose a predefined label page layout, Publisher creates a page size equivalent to a single label. If you use normal text frames, the same information will print on every instance of the label. To print different information on each label, you must use Publisher's Mail Merge and Print Merge functions.

 For more information about Publisher's mail merge functions, see Chapter 13. The Print Merge command is discussed in Chapter 16.

Create Labels *(continued)*

Publisher also reports the row and column arrangement of the labels and the total number of labels per sheet.

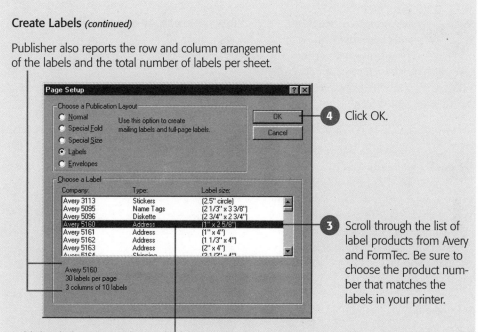

4 Click OK.

3 Scroll through the list of label products from Avery and FormTec. Be sure to choose the product number that matches the labels in your printer.

Publisher helps you to identify the label product by providing information on the manufacturer, product number, purpose of the label, and the size of individual labels.

Changing Your View of Publication Pages

Publisher allows you to change your view of the pages in a document. You can view the pages in your document singly or by spreads. A spread mimics the layout of a book or magazine that is lying open in front of you, where two pages face each other.

You can also switch among various magnification levels. Viewing the page at a reduced size allows you to see an overview of your design. Zooming in on the page makes type legible and provides a higher degree of accuracy when creating or positioning frames.

Advantages of working with spreads. Work with spreads when you plan to have rules or other elements print across facing pages, or when you want an overview of your design.

 Magnify a particular element. You can zoom in on a specific object by selecting it before you change the magnification level. Publisher always keeps the selected object in the center of your window. Choosing Zoom to Selection will automatically enlarge the object to the edges of the window.

 Toggle back and forth between Actual Size and the current magnification level by pressing the F9 key.

 Use a menu to change zoom levels. You can also use menu commands to choose a magnification level. Select Zoom on the View menu. From the cascading menu, select one of 13 magnification levels.

View a Spread or a Single Page

1 Open the View menu and choose Two-Page Spread.

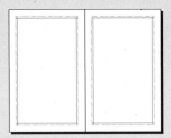

Now every time you turn a page, you will see the two facing pages in the work area.

The left-hand page is always an even-numbered page, and the right-hand page is always an odd-numbered page.

2 Choose Single Page on the View menu to return to single-page view.

Change the Magnification of a Page

1 Click the Zoom Indicator box to display Publisher's 13 magnification choices.

2 Select a zoom level.

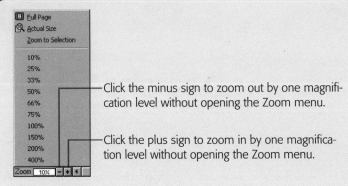

Click the minus sign to zoom out by one magnification level without opening the Zoom menu.

Click the plus sign to zoom in by one magnification level without opening the Zoom menu.

How do I insert pages into a spread? If you already have more than one page in your document and are working with a two-page spread, Publisher modifies the Insert Page dialog box slightly, allowing you to insert pages before the left page, after the right page, or between the pages of the spread. If you indicate that you want to insert an odd number of pages in the middle of a spread, Publisher asks, with an alert box, if you want to change the way the pages are paired.

Inserting and Deleting Pages

You can add one page—or multiple pages—to your publication at any time during the design process. However, you can delete only one page or one spread at a time.

Add Pages to Your Document

1 Move to the page that falls before or after where you want to insert the new page.

2 Choose Page on the Insert menu.

3 Type the number of pages you want to add to the publication.

4 Indicate the location of the new pages.

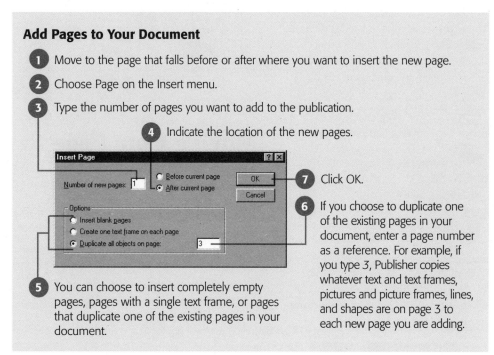

7 Click OK.

6 If you choose to duplicate one of the existing pages in your document, enter a page number as a reference. For example, if you type 3, Publisher copies whatever text and text frames, pictures and picture frames, lines, and shapes are on page 3 to each new page you are adding.

5 You can choose to insert completely empty pages, pages with a single text frame, or pages that duplicate one of the existing pages in your document.

Delete Pages from Your Document

1 Check to make sure that the page you want to delete is the current one.

2 Choose Delete Page on the Edit menu. If you are working in single-page view, Publisher deletes the page and renumbers the remaining pages.

What happens to my text and pictures when I delete a page? When you delete a page, you also delete all the pictures and text frames on that page. The text itself will be deleted if the text frames are not linked to other frames. If links do exist, the text will reflow to other pages in the document.

 For more information about linking text frames, see pages 66 through 67 in Chapter 4.

 Access the Go To Page dialog box. Clicking the Go To Page command on the View menu also opens the Go To Page dialog box (shown below). The Go To Page dialog box is especially useful when you want to jump to nonadjacent pages in a long document.

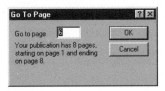

 Press F5 to open the Go To Page dialog box.

Delete Pages from Your Document *(continued)*

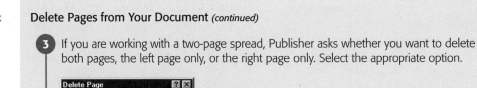

③ If you are working with a two-page spread, Publisher asks whether you want to delete both pages, the left page only, or the right page only. Select the appropriate option.

④ Click OK.

Moving from Page to Page

You can move forward or backward through the pages of your document with a set of page controls at the bottom of the work area, as shown here.

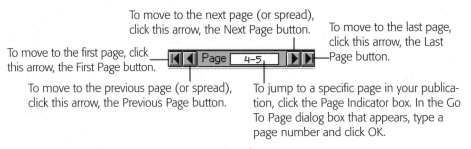

To move to the next page (or spread), click this arrow, the Next Page button.

To move to the last page, click this arrow, the Last Page button.

To move to the first page, click this arrow, the First Page button.

To move to the previous page (or spread), click this arrow, the Previous Page button.

To jump to a specific page in your publication, click the Page Indicator box. In the Go To Page dialog box that appears, type a page number and click OK.

The Background and Foreground Relationship

Whenever you start a new design, Publisher automatically creates a blank background for your document. All the pages or spreads in a publication share the same background, so it is the ideal place on which to position elements that should appear on every page of the document. In contrast, the foreground contains text and design elements that are specific to an individual page.

How can I distinguish the background from the foreground? At times you might find it difficult to distinguish the background from the foreground. When they are empty, they look identical. Publisher identifies the background by replacing the page controls located at the lower left-hand corner of the window with a symbol that represents the background. When you have different backgrounds for the right-hand and left-hand pages, Publisher displays two background indicators, as shown in the following illustration.

Left   Right

 To switch between the background and the foreground, press Ctrl-M.

 Why can't I find the Go To Background command? In all likelihood, you are already on the background. When you move to the background, the View menu changes to display the Go To Foreground command.

The repetitive text and graphics you place on the background, such as rules or a logo, show through the foreground overlay and appear on every page in your publication.

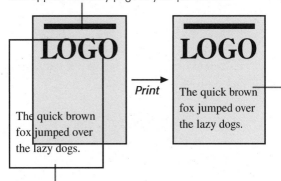

You work on the background and foreground separately, but when you look at a page on the screen or print it, Publisher combines the two into a complete layout.

Think of the foreground as a transparent surface on which you place the text and graphics for the current page. These elements float over the background as if they were on a clear overlay.

Moving Between the Background and Foreground

You work with the background and foreground in exactly the same way. You must draw text frames to add words and picture frames to add pictures. But you can't work on the background and foreground *simultaneously*. For example, when you are on the foreground, you can't select background objects. You must explicitly move to the background in order to create or edit objects that appear on every page of your publication.

Move to the Background or Foreground

1 Choose Go To Background on the View menu.

2 To return to the foreground, choose Go To Foreground on the View menu.

Send objects from the foreground to the background. You can send an object from the foreground to the background while remaining on the foreground page. First select the object, and then select the Send To Background command from the Arrange menu. Publisher will display a dialog box alerting you to the fact that the object is now on the background. Click OK.

Why are mirrored guides useful? Mirrored guides allow you to create symmetrical designs. In many cases, you'll find that symmetry makes documents more readable. For example, you can place page numbers on the outside edges of the page—meaning the extreme left and extreme right of a two-page spread—where they are easier to find. Mirrored guides also let you adjust the interior margins (called the gutters) for book layouts, creating a safety zone for staples or spiral binding.

For more information about layout guides, see Chapter 3.

Creating Different Backgrounds for Left-Hand and Right-Hand Pages

A publication might need similar but slightly different backgrounds for its left-hand and right-hand pages. You can create completely different designs for the left-hand and right-hand background pages manually, but Publisher also offers mirrored guides so that the left-hand page background is a reflection of the right-hand page background.

Use Mirrored Layout Guides

1 Open a new, one-page document.

2 Choose Go To Background on the View menu.

3 Design the single background page as the right-hand page. Position the elements you want to appear on *both* pages of a spread, such as the page number.

4 Choose Layout Guides on the Arrange menu.

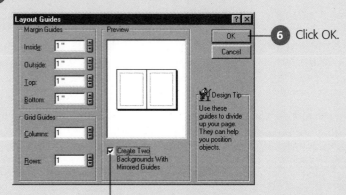

6 Click OK.

5 Click the Create Two Backgrounds With Mirrored Guides check box if it isn't already selected. Notice that the names for the margin guides change from Left and Right to Inside and Outside—the appropriate labels for a mirrored layout.

What happens when I turn off the background?
When you turn off the background, all of the elements positioned on the background disappear from the current page. They have not been deleted; they are hidden from view and will not print. The background elements will continue to appear on all the other pages in the document, including on any new pages you insert.

Can I change the appearance of the page number?
Yes, you can use any of Publisher's standard text formatting commands to change the attributes (such as font or point size) of a page number. Remember to highlight the page number (or the number sign) before you choose new formatting attributes.

For more information about text formatting attributes, see Chapter 6.

Accommodating Unique Pages in a Multipage Document

No matter how hard you strive for consistency, every publication contains a few unique pages. For example, title pages rarely contain page numbers or running heads. You can accommodate these pages by turning off the background.

Turn Off the Background

1 Be sure that you are on the foreground of the page whose background you want to suppress.

2 Choose Ignore Background on the View menu.

3 If you are on a spread, the Ignore Background dialog box appears. Specify the left or right page, and then click OK.

Adding Page Numbers

You can insert automatic page numbers on either the foreground or the background page. Publisher automatically adjusts the page numbering whenever you add or delete pages.

Insert Automatic Page Numbers

1 Select the Text tool from the toolbar. Draw a text frame and position it where you want the page number to appear on the page.

2 Select Page Numbers on the Insert menu.

 If you insert the page number on the foreground, Publisher displays the actual page number.

 If you insert the page number on the background, Publisher displays a number sign. The number sign will be replaced by the correct page number on each foreground page.

Follow page numbering conventions. If you plan to bind your publication as a book, remember to design it so that right-hand pages are always odd and left-hand pages are always even. This means that you should always enter an odd number into the Start With Page text box, because Publisher always begins multiple-page documents with a single right-hand page.

Save files faster. You can decrease the amount of time it takes to save a file to disk by deselecting the Backup and Preview check boxes in the Save As dialog box.

Take advantage of Windows 95 file naming conventions. Windows 95 lets you type a long, descriptive filename. Use it to truly describe the contents of the document and more easily identify your publications. A filename like *Newsletter July 98*, for example, is much more informative than an abbreviated name like *News01*.

Changing the Starting Page Number

Sometimes you might want to begin your publication with a page number other than 1. For example, your document might be a section of a long report or a chapter of a book.

Specify the Starting Page Number

1 Click Options on the Tools menu.

2 On the General tab, type the number you want to assign to the first page of your document in the Start Publication With Page text box. The starting page number must be between 1 and 16,766.

Saving a Document

After you have created or changed a document, you must save it on a disk if you want to use it again. The way you save your document depends on whether you are working in a new document or one that has been saved before.

Save a New Document

1 Choose either Save or Save As on the File menu. In either case, the Save As dialog box appears.

For more information about using and saving templates, see Chapter 14. For more information about Publisher's capability to import and export word processing formats, see Chapter 5.

How can I retrieve the backup file if my original file is lost or corrupted? Publisher always saves the backup file in the same directory as the original and adds the prefix "Backup of" to the original filename. For example, the backup file for XXX.pub appears in the file list as "Backup of XXX.pub." To retrieve the backup, open it as an existing publication by using the Open Publication dialog box.

To save your document, press Ctrl-S.

What is the difference between the Save and the Save As commands? The Save command simply stores the current file on disk, using the filename and the file options you selected when you first saved the document. The Save As command opens a dialog box that allows you to type a new filename and to choose new options.

Save a New Document *(continued)*

Turning on Save All Text As File lets you export text in a standard word processing format. If you have highlighted a block of text, the check box will be labeled Save Selection as File.

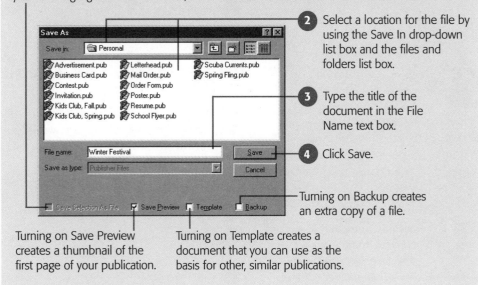

2 Select a location for the file by using the Save In drop-down list box and the files and folders list box.

3 Type the title of the document in the File Name text box.

4 Click Save.

Turning on Backup creates an extra copy of a file.

Turning on Save Preview creates a thumbnail of the first page of your publication.

Turning on Template creates a document that you can use as the basis for other, similar publications.

Save an Existing Document

1 Choose the Save command on the File menu. Publisher saves the file under the current name by overwriting the previous version of the file stored on disk.

Discarding Changes Made to a Document

Publisher also lets you close your publication without saving your edits. Use this feature if you don't like the changes you have made to your publication and want to revert to the most recently saved version of the document.

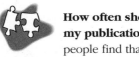

How often should I save my publication? Most people find that an interval of 10 to 15 minutes between saves guarantees that they have the most current version of the publication stored on disk, even if they experience a power outage or a system failure.

Disable Autosave. If you do not want to be reminded to save your file, deselect the Remind To Save Publication check box in the Options dialog box.

Using Autosave As a Reminder

The Autosave feature can remind you to save your publication. The Autosave alert box appears on your screen at predetermined intervals. In the alert box, click Yes to save the current version of your publication. If you click No, you will return to the current document without saving the changes you have made.

Use Autosave As a Reminder

1 Choose Options on the Tools menu.

2 On the Editing And User Assistance tab, make sure that a check mark appears next to Remind To Save Publication.

3 In the Minutes Between Reminders text box, enter a value between 1 and 999 minutes.

4 Click OK.

Layout Tools

Professional art directors and designers use specialized tools, such as rulers, T-squares, and proportion wheels, to create neat and precise layouts. Microsoft Publisher provides these same tools in an electronic form that makes them easy to access and easy to use.

Rulers

Publisher's rulers lie along the left and top sides of the work area. You use these rulers to measure and position objects in relation to each other and in relation to the edges of your publication page. You can move the on-screen rulers, reposition the zero point, change the unit of measurement they display, and even mix different units of measure in a single publication.

Turn rulers off. You can choose to turn off the display of rulers—and increase the size of your workspace in the bargain. To do so, open the View menu and deselect Rulers. You can also right-click any portion of the work area to invoke a shortcut menu, shown in the following illustration, from which you can select or deselect the rulers.

For more information about creating indents and tabs, see Chapter 6.

A movable box designates the intersection of the vertical and horizontal rulers.

A special indents and tabs ruler appears on the horizontal ruler whenever you select a text frame.

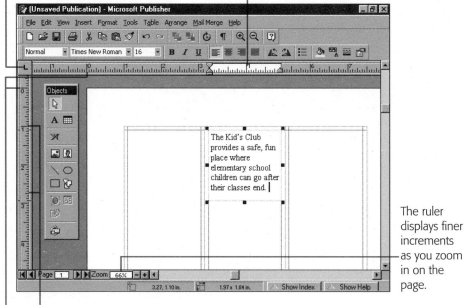

The ruler displays finer increments as you zoom in on the page.

The ruler always displays tick marks measuring the width and height of the currently selected object.

The zero points on the rulers align with the upper left corner of your document's page, not with the corner of the work area.

Why don't my rulers display points? If you choose points as a unit of measurement, Publisher shows inches on the rulers because points are too small to be displayed clearly. However, Publisher divides each inch into 24 equal segments of 3 points each, for a total of 72 points per inch. In addition, the status line at the bottom of the work area uses points as the unit of measurement to report the size and position of objects.

 Why would I want to mix different units of measurement within a publication? Key elements of a design are often associated with a specific unit of measurement. For example, margins are typically specified in inches, and paragraph indents are typically measured in picas.

 Use abbreviations to designate the unit of measurement. Use the following abbreviations whenever you override the default unit of measure in a dialog box:

@ *in* or a double quote (") for inches

@ *cm* for centimeters

@ *pi* for picas

@ *pt* for points

Change the Default Unit of Measurement

1 Choose Options on the Tools menu. The Options dialog box appears.

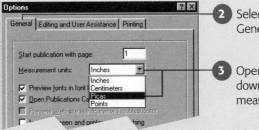

2 Select the General tab.

3 Open the Measurement Units drop-down list box and select a unit of measurement from the list.

4 Click OK.

Override the Default Unit of Measurement

1 Open any Publisher dialog box that requires numeric input, such as the Indents And Lists dialog box shown here.

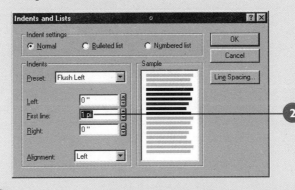

2 Enter a numerical value followed by the abbreviation for your preferred unit of measurement.

3 Publisher will automatically convert your entry to the default unit of measurement. If you enter *1 pi*, for example, and the default unit of measurement is inches, Publisher will display *0.17"* (or 1/6 of an inch).

Layout Tools

Reposition the rulers and zero points simultaneously. You can save yourself a few mouse clicks by moving the rulers and the zero points in one operation. Simply place the pointer in the box where the two rulers intersect. When the pointer changes to a double-headed arrow, hold down the Ctrl key and using the *left* mouse button, drag the rulers to the new location. The zero point will now indicate the upper left corner of an object, not of the page.

Reposition Both Zero Points

1 Position the pointer in the box where the rulers intersect at the upper left corner of the work area. The pointer changes to a double-headed arrow.

2 Hold down the Shift key, use the right mouse button, and drag the pointer to the new position on the document page, next to the object you want to measure. The zero points on the rulers reflect this new location.

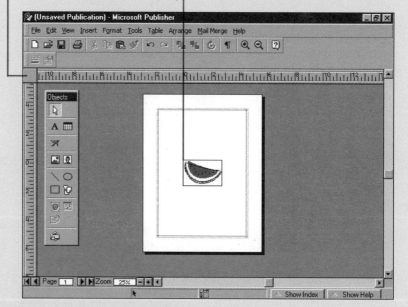

3 To return the zero points to their original positions, double-click the left mouse button on the box at the intersection of the vertical and horizontal rulers.

Set One Zero Point

1 Position the pointer on the ruler that contains the zero point you want to move. Make sure that the pointer is positioned at the exact location where you want the zero point to appear.

Zoom in before moving the rulers. If you move the rulers and then zoom in on a portion of the page, you'll find that Publisher can't reposition the rulers automatically. If you want to keep the rulers and the object you are measuring in sync, first zoom in on the object and then move the rulers.

 For more information about Publisher's magnification tools, see pages 29 through 30 in Chapter 2.

Set One Zero Point *(continued)*

2 When the two-headed arrow appears, hold down the Shift key and click the *right* mouse button. The zero point moves to the new position.

3 To return the zero point to its original location, double-click the left mouse button on the box at the intersection of the vertical and horizontal rulers.

Reposition One or Both Rulers

1 To reposition a single ruler, place the pointer on the vertical or the horizontal ruler. To reposition both rulers, place the pointer in the box where the two rulers intersect. The pointer changes to a double-headed arrow.

2 Using the left mouse button, drag the ruler to the new location. The ruler remains in its new position until you drag it back to its original location.

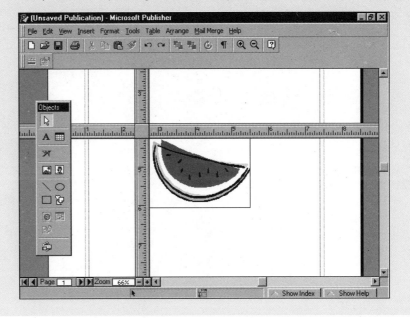

Layout Tools

Why can't I see the ruler guides when I move to another page? Ruler guides are part of the page on which they are created. Normally, you create unique ruler guides for each page in a publication. If you want identical ruler guides to appear on all the pages in your publication, either create ruler guides on the background page, or you can use layout guides instead.

Use menu commands to create ruler guides. To create ruler guides using menu commands, select Ruler Guides on the Arrange menu. On the cascading menu, click either Add Horizontal Ruler Guide or Add Vertical Ruler Guide. When you create a ruler guide using the menu command Publisher places a single guide in the center of your screen. You must then move the ruler guide to the desired location.

Deleting all ruler guides. You can quickly delete all the ruler guides on a page. Choose the Ruler Guides command on the Arrange menu. On the cascading menu, select Clear All Ruler Guides.

To switch between hiding and showing boundaries and guides, press Ctrl-Shift-O.

Ruler Guides

Instead of moving the rulers themselves, you can create ruler guides, which are more flexible than the rulers. You can create ruler guides interactively or by selecting menu options. You can continue to adjust the position of ruler guides as you work.

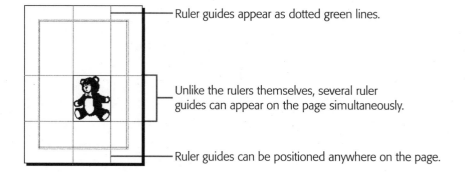

Ruler guides appear as dotted green lines.

Unlike the rulers themselves, several ruler guides can appear on the page simultaneously.

Ruler guides can be positioned anywhere on the page.

Drag a Guide from the Ruler

1. Holding down the Shift key, position the pointer over either the horizontal or vertical ruler. The pointer changes to the Adjust pointer.

2. Press the left mouse button and drag a ruler guide to any position on the page.

Move and Delete Individual Ruler Guides

1. Holding down the Shift key, position the pointer over the ruler guide you want to move or delete. The pointer changes to the Adjust pointer.

2. Drag the ruler guide to a new location on the page, or delete it by dragging it off the page entirely or back to the ruler with which it is parallel.

Colors indicate guide status. When you move an object, Publisher confirms that the object boundary has correctly aligned with the guide by displaying the overlap between the guide and the object boundary in reverse video. That means the pink margin guides turn bright green, the light blue layout guides turn orange, and the green ruler guides turn red.

Why can't I find my layout guides? Layout guides (and ruler guides) are obscured by opaque objects, such as a text or picture object with a solid or tinted background. If you want to see the layout guides at all times, you must make any opaque objects transparent. Select the object and then press Ctrl-T.

Create a drawing grid. You can create a precise drawing grid with layout guides to help you develop detailed designs, charts, or diagrams. For example, you could create the electronic equivalent of 0.25-inch graph paper by dividing an 8.5-by-11-inch sheet of paper into 34 columns and 44 rows, without margins. If you use Publisher's layout guides as drawing paper, draw objects to align with the pink margin guides, which represent the precise page divisions. The blue guides include a safety margin (or gutter allowance) of 0.1 inch.

Layout Guides

Layout guides are visual guidelines that appear on every page of your electronic document but never on the printed output. They function purely as an internal tool that helps you position objects accurately and maintain a consistent look from page to page.

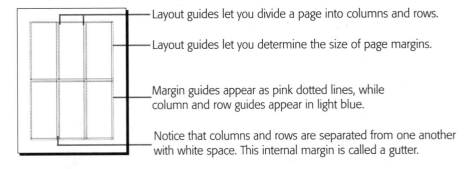

Layout guides let you divide a page into columns and rows.

Layout guides let you determine the size of page margins.

Margin guides appear as pink dotted lines, while column and row guides appear in light blue.

Notice that columns and rows are separated from one another with white space. This internal margin is called a gutter.

Create Margins, Columns, and Rows on Every Page

1 Choose Layout Guides on the Arrange menu.

2 Set the margin guides by entering values in these text boxes.

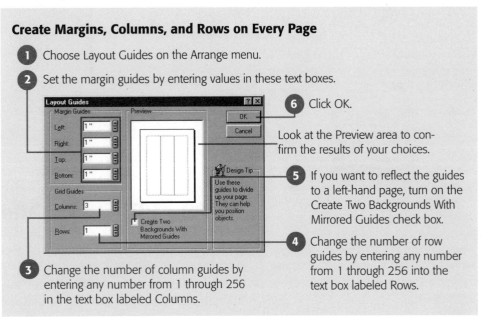

6 Click OK.

Look at the Preview area to confirm the results of your choices.

5 If you want to reflect the guides to a left-hand page, turn on the Create Two Backgrounds With Mirrored Guides check box.

4 Change the number of row guides by entering any number from 1 through 256 into the text box labeled Rows.

3 Change the number of column guides by entering any number from 1 through 256 in the text box labeled Columns.

Hide ruler and layout guides. Layout guides, although helpful, are sometimes distracting. Turning off the display of ruler guides, layout guides, and object boundaries gives you an accurate screen preview of the printed page. To hide the guides, choose Hide Boundaries And Guides on the View menu. To display guides and object boundaries, choose Show Boundaries And Guides from the View menu.

 Return column and row guides to standard positions. After you have created custom positions for column and row guides, you can easily return to a standard layout with evenly spaced columns and rows. Select Layout Guides on the Arrange menu to open the Layout Guides dialog box.

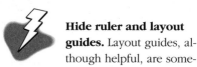

Two new check boxes appear in this dialog box, allowing you to choose Reset Even Spacing under Columns and Rows. Turn on one or both of the check boxes. When you click OK, Publisher will move the column and row guides to standard positions.

Customizing the Position of Layout Guides

When you first create layout guides, Publisher divides the page into columns of equal width and rows of equal height. Your page design, however, may require irregularly sized columns and rows.

Move Column and Row Guides to New Custom Positions

1 Create the appropriate number of column and row guides by following the preceding procedure entitled "Create Margins, Columns, and Rows on Every Page."

2 Go to the background page. The background page will display the column and row guides.

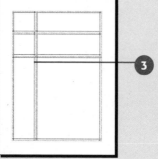

3 Holding down the Shift key, position the pointer over a column or row guide you want to move. The pointer changes to the Adjust pointer.

4 Drag the column or row guide to a new location.

5 Go to the foreground page. The new custom arrangement of columns and rows will appear on every page.

Using Publisher's Snap To Functions

You can create and position objects by eye, using Publisher's rulers and guides as a purely visual guide, but you'll produce tighter layouts if you take advantage of Publisher's various Snap To functions. When the Snap To function is in effect, Publisher will force any frame you draw, move, or resize to align with the closest ruler mark, guideline, or object. Objects already placed

Use Snap To Ruler Marks to position guides. When Snap To Ruler Marks is turned on, everything you move—including ruler guides and layout guides—snaps into precise alignment with the ruler. This can help you create accurate layouts.

Why don't objects snap to the ruler guides when Snap To Ruler Marks is turned on? Ruler guides are pulled down from the rulers. But once created, they function like layout guides. In order to have ruler guides exert a magnetic pull, turn on the Snap To Guides command in the Tools menu.

To toggle Snap To Guides on or off, press Ctrl-W.

Why are my objects snapping around the page if the guides are not displayed? Even though you have turned off the display of guides, the guides still exist and continue to exert a magnetlike pull on objects as long as Snap To Guides is turned on.

on a page will not move, but new objects you add will be affected by the Snap To functions. The pointer will also snap to the ruler marks or guides as you move it around the publication page.

Publisher's Snap To functions work at all magnification levels and allow you to position objects accurately, even when you are working in a zoomed-out view of the document, such as Full Page view.

Turn Snap To Functions On and Off

1 Open the Tools menu.

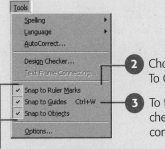

2 Choose Snap To Ruler Marks, Snap To Guides, or Snap To Objects.

3 To toggle these commands off (and remove the check mark), open the Tools menu and select a command that is preceded by a check mark.

Snap To functions are invoked with a toggle command.
A check mark indicates that the command is active.
All three Snap To functions can be active at the same time.

Object Groups

Every time you select two or more objects, you automatically create a temporary group, or multiple selection. Publisher always gives you the option of converting a multiple selection into a permanent group. You can think of a group as a collection of objects that are "glued" together. A true group gives you a lot of layout and design flexibility because you can do the following:

@ Copy, move, rotate, resize, or delete a group as though it were a single object.

@ Subselect any element within the group to change its formatting attributes.

Layout Tools

Why won't objects align with each other even when I have Snap To Objects turned on? Snap To Objects might not work as you expect for two reasons:

 You didn't move the objects close enough to one another. The objects must be within 0.125 (1/8) inch of each other for Snap To Objects to work properly.

 You've turned on Snap To Ruler Marks or Snap To Guides. These snap modes can interfere with Snap To Objects. It's best to toggle them off before using Snap To Objects.

 For more information about linking text frames, see pages 62 through 64 in Chapter 4. For more information on multiple selections, see Chapter 1.

 Use the Group/Ungroup command. You can also choose Group Objects or Ungroup Objects on the Arrange menu.

To group or ungroup objects, press Ctrl-Shift-G.

Select all the elements in a group to apply new formatting attributes to all elements equally.

Type or import text into text objects within the group, and link text frames.

Group groups. You can create 18 levels of groups within groups.

Keep objects together even when you deselect a group. The elements remain together until you ungroup them.

In a multiple selection, selection handles (in gray instead of black) surround each object.

A Group button appears at the bottom right of the selection box containing two or more objects. Click the Group button to "lock" the two parts of the icon together.

A single set of selection handles surrounds the whole group. Individual object boundaries, however, are maintained.

You can subselect objects within a group. A subselected object within a group is indicated by a pink outline (or another color if the background is colored).

Clicking the locked Group button again will ungroup the objects and return them to a multiple selection.

Move an object using horizontal and vertical coordinates. You can move an object or a group to an exact location on a page using the Size And Position dialog box. With the object or group selected, choose Size And Position on the Format menu. Enter values that correspond to the horizontal and vertical rulers. For example, a value of 2 inches in the Horizontal text box places the left side of an object at the 2-inch mark on the horizontal ruler. Publisher updates the location of the object as you change the values in the dialog box.

For more information about the Size and Position dialog box, see page 53.

Move objects in a perfectly straight line. You can move an object, a multiple selection, or a group in a perfectly straight line by holding down the Shift key as you drag the mouse. Your movement will be constrained to either vertical or horizontal movement.

Moving and Copying Objects

Publisher makes it easy to move and copy individual objects, a multiple selection, or a group of objects on the same page or from page to page. You can also move an object up and down or left and right in very small increments by using the Nudge command.

Move a Single Object, a Multiple Selection, or a Group

1 Select the object or objects you want to move.

2 Position the pointer along the edge of an object. The pointer changes to the Move pointer.

3 Drag the object or objects to the new position and release the mouse button.

Whenever you move a single object, a multiple selection, or a group, Publisher displays the object boundary of each individual object. This can help you position both multiple selections and grouped objects more precisely in relation to other objects on the page. When you release the mouse button, the entire object is redrawn in its new location.

Move and Copy Objects Simultaneously

1 Select the object or objects you want to move and copy.

2 Holding down the Ctrl key, drag the object to a new location on the page, to the scratchboard, or to another application that supports drag-and-drop editing.

3 Publisher leaves the original object in its previous position and draws a copy of the object in the new location.

Why can't I move more than one object at a time? You can move all the objects in a multiple selection or group at the same time. But you must be sure to position the Move pointer over one of the objects. If you click on the background (even if the area seems to be included in the multiple selection or group box), you will deselect the objects instead of moving them.

What happens to objects in the scratch area? If you leave objects in the scratch area, they will be saved along with the publication file, although they will not print because they fall outside the page boundaries.

Move Objects from Page to Page

1 Select the object or objects you want to move.

Page boundaries are indicated with a solid black border and a drop shadow. Objects outside this area do not print.

2 Drag the selected object completely off the page onto the scratch area.

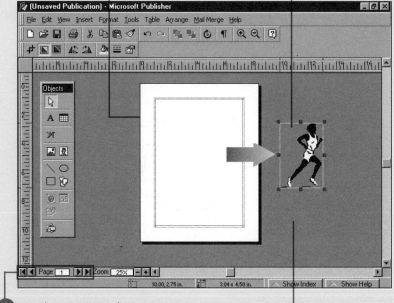

3 Use the page controls to turn to any other page in your document.

The scratch area, or Pasteboard, refers to the gray area outside the page. This is a temporary holding area for objects.

4 Drag the object from the scratch area onto the current page.

Use Drag-and-Drop editing to move or copy objects between publications. You can easily move objects between two different Publisher documents, thanks to the drag-and-drop capabilities of Windows 95. Technically, Publisher doesn't allow you to have more than one publication open at the same time. However, you can run two copies of the Publisher program in order to display two publications side by side. With two publications open side by side, select the object you want to move or copy. To move the object, drag it from the first window to the second window. To copy the object, hold down the Ctrl key while dragging it from the first window to the second window. Release the mouse button only when the Drop pointer is displayed.

If you drag the object to an area of the screen where it cannot be moved or copied, Windows 95 displays the Unavailable pointer (a cancellation symbol) to indicate that the move or copy operation will be aborted.

To move the selected object 1 pixel at a time (or whatever amount you specified in the Nudge By text box), hold down the Alt key and press any of the direction keys on your keyboard.

Nudge an Object into Place

1 Select the object you want to move.

2 Choose Nudge on the Arrange menu. The Nudge dialog box appears.

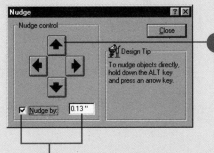

4 Click the appropriate Nudge Control arrow to move the selected object up, down, left, or right. If you did not specify a value in the Nudge By text box, Publisher will move the object 1 pixel at a time.

3 If you want to specify the increments by which the object will move, turn on the Nudge By check box and either accept the value Publisher suggests or type a new value from 0 through 2 inches in the text box.

Resizing Objects

Often you must reduce or enlarge the size of individual elements to create a balanced, visually pleasing layout. Publisher allows you to resize an object by using numerical values or interactively using selection handles. Depending on the handle you select, you can resize only the height, only the width, or both the height and the width simultaneously. When you resize an object, it is often important to maintain the object's proportions, as the following example shows.

What is the smallest amount that I can nudge an object? If you uncheck the Nudge By text box, Publisher will move an object by 1 pixel increments. But be warned: a pixel represents a different distance depending on the resolution of your screen and the current magnification level. For the smallest possible nudge, zoom in to 100 percent view or higher.

 Resizing an object from its center. Holding down the Ctrl key as you move a selection handle enlarges or reduces an object from its center. This can help you keep objects in a complex layout properly aligned.

 Can I maintain the aspect ratio of text frames, table frames, drawn shapes, and Design Gallery objects when I resize them? Yes, you can maintain the aspect of these objects, but you must hold down the Shift key as you drag the corner selection handle. If you neglect to hold down the Shift key, you will resize the height and the width simultaneously and disproportionately.

The relationship between an object's width and its height is called its aspect ratio.

If you don't maintain an object's aspect ratio (its original proportions) the object will be distorted when you resize it.

Using a corner selection handle to resize a picture changes its width and height by the same percentage. This maintains the original aspect ratio.

Resize an Object Using Selection Handles

1 Select the object.

Grab a selection handle on either side of an object to change only its width.

Grab a selection handle at the top or bottom of an object to change only its height.

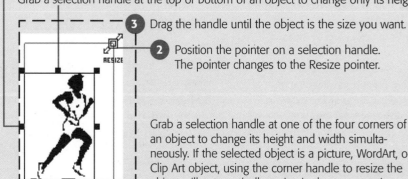

3 Drag the handle until the object is the size you want.

2 Position the pointer on a selection handle. The pointer changes to the Resize pointer.

Grab a selection handle at one of the four corners of an object to change its height and width simultaneously. If the selected object is a picture, WordArt, or Clip Art object, using the corner handle to resize the object will automatically maintain the aspect ratio.

Resize pictures by percentages. If you are working with a picture, a WordArt object, or an OLE object (but not text objects, tables, or drawn shapes), you can use the Scale Picture or Scale Object command on the Format menu to specify the exact size of the object as a percentage of its original size.

For more information about the Scale Object dialog boxes, see Chapter 1.

Can I change the stacking order of grouped objects? You can change the stacking order of grouped objects only in relation to other objects on the page. Publisher moves the whole group of objects up or down in the stacking order. But within the group, the objects maintain their order relative to one another. If you want to change the stacking order within a group, you must ungroup the objects.

Resize an Object Numerically

1 Select the object you want to resize.

2 Select Size And Position on the Format menu.

3 Enter values in the height and width text boxes.

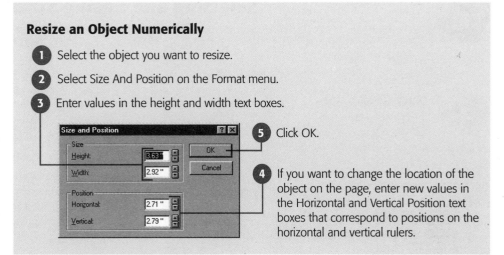

5 Click OK.

4 If you want to change the location of the object on the page, enter new values in the Horizontal and Vertical Position text boxes that correspond to positions on the horizontal and vertical rulers.

Layering Objects

In a complex design, objects frequently overlap. The sequence in which objects overlap is called the stacking order. Though layering works identically on the foreground and background pages, Publisher treats objects on the foreground and background as two separate stacks. Objects on the background always appear below objects on the foreground.

By default, Publisher always stacks objects in the order you create them, but you can change the stacking order at any time.

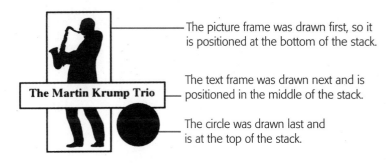

The picture frame was drawn first, so it is positioned at the bottom of the stack.

The text frame was drawn next and is positioned in the middle of the stack.

The circle was drawn last and is at the top of the stack.

To bring an object to the front of a stack, press F6. To send an object to the bottom of a stack, press Shift-F6.

Quick access to the layering commands.

Although it doesn't provide as many options as the Arrange menu, the Standard toolbar does give you two quick ways of changing the stacking order of objects.

Click here to bring the currently selected object to the top of the stack.

Click here to send the currently selected object to the bottom of the stack.

Selecting and Seeing Stacked Objects

Sometimes it is difficult to understand the stacking order, and especially difficult to select objects lower in the stack. The following illustrations explain how to identify and select objects in a stack.

A large opaque object hides any smaller objects and guides layered beneath it in the stack. Clicking selects only the topmost object.

You can select all the objects in the stack by drawing a selection box around the elements. Then Shift-select the topmost object to deselect it.

To see and select only the objects lower in the stack, you can make the topmost object transparent by selecting it and pressing the Ctrl-T keyboard shortcut.

Rearrange the Stacking Order

1 Select an individual object, a multiple selection, or a group.

2 Choose one of the four layering commands on the Arrange menu.

Send To Back: moves the object to the bottom of the stack.

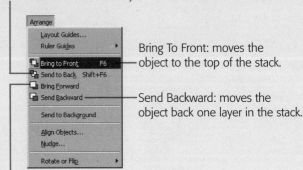

Bring To Front: moves the object to the top of the stack.

Send Backward: moves the object back one layer in the stack.

Bring Forward: moves the object up one layer in the stack.

Can I change the stacking order of objects on the background after I use the Send To Background command? After you use the Send To Background command you will still be working on the foreground. Therefore you cannot select or change the stacking order of objects on the background. Move to the background to select background objects or change their stacking order.

 For more information about the background and foreground, see Chapter 2.

 Rotate in 15-degree increments. You can rotate objects in 15-degree increments by holding down the Ctrl and Alt keys as you rotate an object.

Send Objects to the Background

1 Make sure that you are on the foreground.

2 Select the object or objects you want to send to the background.

3 Choose the Send To Background command on the Arrange menu. Publisher will place the selection on the background page. The object (or objects) will be layered on top of any object already on the background.

Rotating Objects

You can add visual interest to a page design, or simply make elements fit together better, by rotating objects. You can experiment with the orientation of an object by dragging a selection handle. You can also rotate objects by specifying an exact numerical value in the Rotate Objects dialog box or by using shortcut commands to rotate objects by a standard amount.

Rotate an Object Using a Selection Handle

1 Select the object you want to rotate.

2 Holding down the Alt key, position the pointer over a selection handle. The pointer changes to the Rotate pointer.

3 Continue to press the Alt key and drag the pointer in a circular path to rotate the object.

Quickest rotation. To display the Rotate Objects dialog box, click the Rotate icon located on the Standard toolbar.

To rotate objects clockwise in 5-degree increments, press Ctrl-Alt-right arrow key. To rotate objects counterclockwise in 5-degree increments, press Ctrl-Alt-left arrow key.

Use Publisher's toolbar to rotate or flip an object by a standard amount. Icons found on the Format toolbar let you rotate or flip the selected object easily.

Click here to rotate an object 90 degrees to the left (counterclockwise).

Click here to flip a drawn object vertically (top to bottom).

Click here to rotate an object 90 degrees to the right (clockwise).

Click here to flip a drawn object horizontally (left to right).

Why are the Flip Vertically and Flip Horizontally commands unavailable?
Publisher flips only drawn objects. Publisher cannot create a mirror image of text, picture, WordArt, or OLE objects.

Specify the Rotation Angle

1 Select the object you want to rotate.

2 Open the Arrange menu and select the Rotate/Flip command.

3 Select the Custom Rotate option on the cascading menu. The Rotate Objects dialog box appears.

4 Click either the clockwise or counterclockwise rotation button, as many times as necessary, to rotate the object in increments of 5 degrees. Or type a rotation value from 0 through 359 degrees.

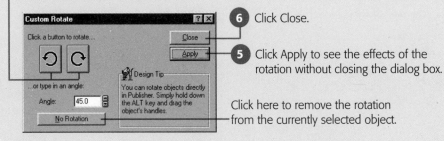

6 Click Close.

5 Click Apply to see the effects of the rotation without closing the dialog box.

Click here to remove the rotation from the currently selected object.

Rotate or Flip an Object by a Standard Amount

1 Select the object you want to rotate.

2 Open the Arrange menu and select the Rotate/Flip command.

3 On the cascading menu, choose one of the following commands:

- Rotate Left turns an object counterclockwise by 90 degrees.

- Rotate Right turns an object clockwise by 90 degrees.

- Flip Vertically inverts a drawn object, bottom to top. It creates an up-down mirror image and is not the same as rotating an object by 180 degrees.

- Flip Horizontally inverts a drawn object left to right. It creates a left-right mirror image and is not the same as rotating an object by 180 degrees.

Center an object on the page. The Align Objects dialog box doesn't contain an explicit command to center an object on the page, but you can do that. Choose the Centers option for both the Left To Right and the Top To Bottom alignments, and then select Align Along Margins. Making these three selections for a group of objects stacks the objects concentrically in the middle of the page.

Quick access to Clipboard commands. You can quickly cut, copy, and paste objects or text by clicking the appropriate icons on the Standard toolbar.

Alternatively, you can right-click on an object or highlighted text. The shortcut menu that pops up contains all the Clipboard commands.

Aligning Objects

To align objects with each other or with the page margins, use the Line Up Objects command.

Align Objects

1 Select the objects you want to align by drawing a selection box around them or by Shift-selecting each object.

2 Choose Align Objects on the Arrange menu. The Align Objects dialog box appears.

3 In the Align Objects dialog box, select the options you want for Left To Right alignment and Top To Bottom alignment. Publisher aligns the selected objects in the direction you choose.

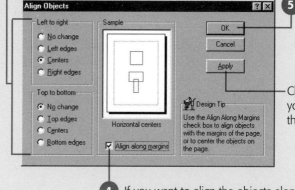

5 When the Sample area displays the arrangement you want (such as the horizontally centered option shown here), click OK.

Click Apply to align objects in your document without closing this dialog box.

4 If you want to align the objects along the margin guides you specified for your publication, turn on this check box.

The Clipboard

You can temporarily store text, numbers, and pictures on the Windows 95 Clipboard. You can then paste any of these elements within the same publication, in different publications, or in different Windows-based applications.

Why can't I cut or delete a text frame? When a text frame contains text, the Del or Backspace key deletes the text only—not the text frame. In the same way, if you have highlighted text in a text frame, the Cut command cuts only the text. If you want to remove the text frame, choose Delete Object on the Edit menu, or Press the Shift-Del keys.

 All Clipboard operations have keyboard shortcuts.

@ Ctrl-C copies objects.

@ Ctrl-X cuts objects.

@ Ctrl-V pastes objects.

@ Del or Backspace deletes objects.

 Can I paste text into an existing text frame? Yes. Select the text frame before you choose the Paste command on the Edit menu. Publisher will insert the text from the Clipboard at the location of the Text Insertion pointer.

Copy, Cut, or Delete an Object or Text

1 Select an object or highlight text.

2 Choose one of the following Clipboard commands on the Edit menu.

Select Cut to remove the object or text from the current publication and place it on the Clipboard.

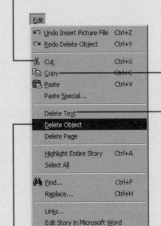

Select Copy to place a duplicate of the object or text on the Clipboard. The original text or object remains in the publication.

Select Delete Text to remove text from the publication. Only the highlighted words or paragraphs are deleted; the text frame itself remains in the publication. No copy of the text is placed on the Clipboard. This command appears on the Edit menu only if you highlighted text.

Select Delete Object to remove the object from the publication. No copy is placed on the Clipboard.

Paste an Object or Text from the Clipboard

1 With no object selected, choose Paste on the Edit menu. Depending on the magnification level, Publisher places the object in approximately the original position or in the center of the window. If you are pasting text, Publisher creates a new text frame.

2 You can continue to paste multiple instances of the object or text into your document, because a copy remains on the Clipboard until you cut or copy something else.

Make a mock-up. The best way to proof your design is to print it on paper. A sample printout created for proofing purposes is referred to as a dummy or mock-up. Seeing the publication trimmed to the final size is the only way to determine whether the design really works and to spot errors or omissions.

The Design Checker

To check the final document for layout problems before you print it, use the Design Checker.

Check Your Design for Errors

1 Choose Design Checker on the Tools menu. The Design Checker dialog box appears.

2 To check every page in your publication, select All. To check a specified range of pages, select Pages and type the starting and ending pages in the From and To text boxes.

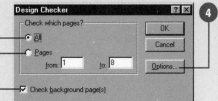

4 Click Options to display a dialog box where you can choose to have Publisher look for all possible problems in a document, or for one or more of six specific errors.

3 To check the background as well as the foreground, turn on this check box.

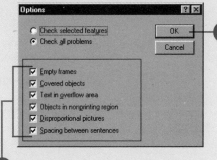

6 Click OK to close each dialog box. Publisher begins checking the layout.

5 Choose the type of error you want to find.

Layout Tools

The power of modeless dialog boxes. The Design Checker uses a special kind of window called a modeless dialog box. That means you don't need to close the Design Checker dialog box while you work on your document. Simply move it out of your way by dragging the title bar.

Use the Design Checker for your Web documents. Publisher can also check for potential problems in your Web documents. Instead of searching for potential printing problems, however, Publisher searches for problems specific to publishing documents on the Internet. For example, Publisher looks for Web pages that can't be reached by hyperlink and for images that will take a long time to download.

For information about creating Web documents, see Chapter 12.

Check Your Design for Errors *(continued)*

7 If Publisher finds a problem, it describes it in a dialog box and suggests ways to fix it. As shown here, the Design Checker has found an empty text frame and suggests deleting it. Click the button that corresponds to the action you want to take.

@ You can take Publisher's suggestions and fix each problem before you continue with the design check. Publisher also allows you to ignore the current instance or all instances of the problem.

@ If you don't understand how to fix the problem, click the Explain button. Publisher provides instructions for analyzing the problem and helping you fix it.

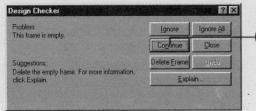

8 Click Continue to proceed with checking your document.

9 When Publisher finishes checking the layout (or if Publisher finds no problems), it displays an alert box advising you that the design check is complete.

Text Frames

One of the most basic rules in Microsoft Publisher is that you cannot type or manipulate text unless the text is inside a frame. Text frames allow you to position blocks of text on the page.

Copyfit Mode versus Text Overflow Mode

Publisher's copyfitting function can automatically adjust the size of the text to fit the frame.

How can I display text that is hidden in the overflow area? As the following illustration shows, Publisher preserves all the text you have typed or inserted. It simply hides it from view by storing it in the overflow area. To display text in the overflow area, either enlarge the text frame or connect it to an empty text frame.

> With an excellent balance of fresh ripe cherries and soft tannins, this ruby wine is ready to to drink right now. But, this full bodied wine also be cellared for the next 3 to 5 years and will only improve with age.

This text (shown in light gray) is normally hidden in the overflow area.

Publisher's text frame connection tools are explained on pages 62 through 64.

> With an excellent balance of fresh ripe cherries and soft tannins, this ruby wine is ready to drink right now. But, this full bodied wine can also be cellared for the next 3 to 5 years and will only improve with age.

The Best Fit copyfitting option enlarges or reduces the size of the text to fill the text frame.

> With an excellent balance of fresh ripe cherries and soft tannins, this ruby wine is ready to drink right now. But, this full bodied wine can also be cellared for the next 3 to 5 years and will only improve with age.

The Shrink Text On Overflow copyfitting option reduces the size of the text to make it fit in the text frame. It will not enlarge the size of the text.

When copyfitting is turned off, Publisher stores any text that can't fit into the text frame in the overflow area. In overflow mode, changing the size or the shape of a text frame changes the amount of text displayed.

> With an excellent balance of fresh ripe cherries and soft tannins, this ruby wine is ready to drink right now.

> With an excellent balance of fresh ripe cherries and soft tannins, this ruby wine is ready to drink right now. But, this full bodied wine can also be cellared for the next 3 to 5 years and will only

> With an excellent balance of fresh ripe cherries and soft tannins, this ruby wine is ready to drink right now. But,

Enlarging or shrinking the text frame changes how much text can fit into it.

Changing the shape of a text frame (short and wide versus tall and skinny) changes how the text flows within the frame.

Why can't I see the text flow buttons on a text frame? The Overflow and Frame Jump buttons appear only when the text frame is selected.

Why can't I see the Connect Frames toolbar? There are three possibilities.

- You may not have a text frame selected. The Connect Frames toolbar appears on screen only when a text frame is active.

- You may have docked the toolbar at the bottom of the work area. To undock the toolbar and have it float in the work area, double-click the move handle.

- You may have closed the toolbar (by clicking the X icon in the upper-right corner). Reopen the toolbar by choosing Text Frame Connecting on the Tools menu.

Text Flow Between Text Frames

You can control the way the stories flow in your publications by using the Connect Frames toolbar or the Autoflow option. You can link and unlink frames that are adjacent to each other on the same page or that fall on different pages. Special text frame buttons appear when text is in the overflow area or when two or more text frames are linked in a chain.

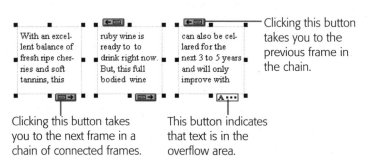

Clicking this button takes you to the previous frame in the chain.

Clicking this button takes you to the next frame in a chain of connected frames.

This button indicates that text is in the overflow area.

Draw multiple text frames. Normally after you draw a text frame, the crosshair pointer reverts to the arrow pointer. You can keep the crosshair pointer active and continue to draw text frames by Ctrl-clicking the Text tool on the toolbar. After you've drawn a series of text frames, select another tool on the toolbar to return to normal selection mode.

What is the difference between the upright pitcher pointer and the tilted pitcher pointer? The upright pitcher indicates that the pointer is not positioned over a text frame and that Publisher cannot flow text. The tilted pitcher indicates that the pointer is over a text frame. But be warned: if the frame already contains text, an alert box appears stating that the text frame must be empty.

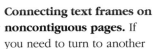

Connecting text frames on noncontiguous pages. If you need to turn to another page, position the pointer over the page controls; the pitcher pointer becomes the standard pointer. Go to the page that contains the next text frame you want to add to the chain. When you move the pointer over a text frame, the tilted pitcher will reappear.

Connect Text Frames

1 Using the Text tool, create any number of text frames on the same page or on different pages in your publication.

2 Select the text frame that will be the first in the chain. This frame can be empty, or it can contain text. The Connect Frames toolbar will appear.

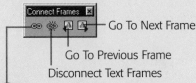
Go To Next Frame
Go To Previous Frame
Disconnect Text Frames

3 Select the Connect Text Frames tool. The pointer changes into an upright pitcher.

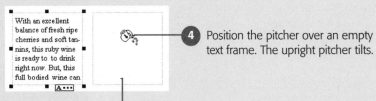

4 Position the pitcher over an empty text frame. The upright pitcher tilts.

5 Click the empty text frame to connect the two frames. If the overflow area of the first frame contains any text, the overflow text will flow into the newly connected text frame. If all of the overflow text does not fit into the newly created text frame, continue to add more text frames to the chain.

Disconnect a Text Frame

1 Select the text frame that immediately precedes the point at which you want to break a chain of text frames.

2 Click the Disconnect Text Frames button. The text from the disconnected text frame and all subsequent frames in the chain flows into the overflow area for the currently selected frame.

What happens to the text when I delete a text frame from a chain of frames? You delete only the frame. The text itself flows into the remaining text frames in the chain.

 What happens when I delete text frames along with a page? If you delete a page that contains unconnected text frames, Publisher deletes the frames and their text along with the page. If you delete a page that contains connected text frames, however, Publisher deletes only the text frames with the page. The text itself flows into the remaining connected frames in the chain or into the overflow area for the previous text frame.

 Inserting text into a text frame from an externally stored file is covered in Chapter 5.

 What happens if I click No in the Autoflow dialog box? If you click No when presented with the Autoflow dialog box, Publisher simply places all the remaining text in the overflow area. You can then create and connect text frames manually.

Delete a Text Frame from a Chain

1 Select the frame you want to delete.

2 Choose Delete Object on thè Edit menu.

Flowing Text Automatically

Publisher's Autoflow function is available only when you insert a text file. If the story is too long for the selected text frame or text frame chain, a dialog box asks whether you want to use the Autoflow feature.

Flow Text Automatically

1 Select an unlinked text frame or the first frame in a linked chain and insert a text file. The following dialog box appears.

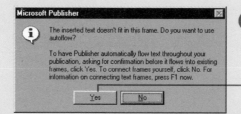

2 Click Yes to have Publisher flow text into frames that already exist in your publication. The following dialog box appears.

Publisher displays this dialog box for each preexisting text frame regardless of whether the frames are connected.

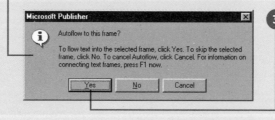

3 Click Yes to have Publisher automatically connect a frame during the Autoflow process, or click No if you want Publisher to skip to the next frame. If you still have text remaining, Publisher prompts you to create new text frames.

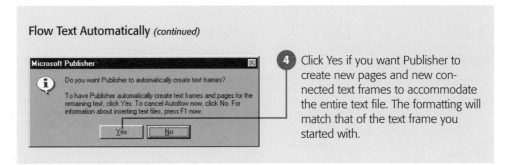

Flow Text Automatically *(continued)*

Microsoft Publisher

Do you want Publisher to automatically create text frames?

To have Publisher automatically create text frames and pages for the remaining text, click Yes. To cancel Autoflow now, click No. For information about inserting text files, press F1 now.

Yes   No

4 Click Yes if you want Publisher to create new pages and new connected text frames to accommodate the entire text file. The formatting will match that of the text frame you started with.

Text margins affect how text wraps around artwork. The text frame margins you create affect how text appears next to the art in your publication. If you create narrow margins—or none at all—in your text frames, the body copy prints very close to the picture frame.

With an excellent balance of fresh ripe cherries and soft tannins, this ruby wine is ready to drink right now. But, this full bodied wine can also be cellared for the next 3 to 5 years and will only improve with age.

If you create wide margins in your text frames, your layout is more open because the pictures have a wide berth.

With an excellent balance of fresh ripe cherries and soft tannins, this ruby wine is ready to drink right now. But, this full bodied wine can also be cellared for the

Formatting a Text Frame

You can change the appearance of a text frame with formatting attributes. You can add a border, choose a fill, or create a shadow for a text frame. Certain key formatting attributes, specifically margins, columns, continued notices, and text wrap, help you to control the flow of text within a text frame.

Text Frame Margins

Publisher defines margins for all four sides of a text frame by using whatever unit of measurement you selected in the Options dialog box. If you selected inches as the unit of measurement, the default text frame margin is 0.04 inches.

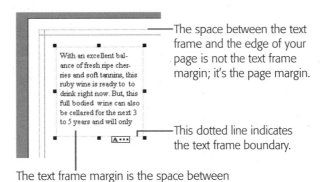

The space between the text frame and the edge of your page is not the text frame margin; it's the page margin.

With an excellent balance of fresh ripe cherries and soft tannins, this ruby wine is ready to to drink right now. But, this full bodied wine can also be cellared for the next 3 to 5 years and will only

This dotted line indicates the text frame boundary.

The text frame margin is the space between the actual type and the text frame.

For more information about selecting the default unit of measurement by using the Options dialog box, see page 41 in Chapter 3.

Use the formatting toolbar to access the Text Frame Properties dialog box.

Instead of using menu commands, you can click an icon on the text formatting toolbar (shown in the following illustration) to open the Text Frame Properties dialog box.

Change the Text Frame Margins

1 Select the text frame whose margins you want to set.

2 Choose Text Frame Properties on the Format menu. The Text Frame Properties dialog box appears.

3 Enter any value from 0 through 16 inches for the text frame margins into the Left, Right, Top, and Bottom text boxes.

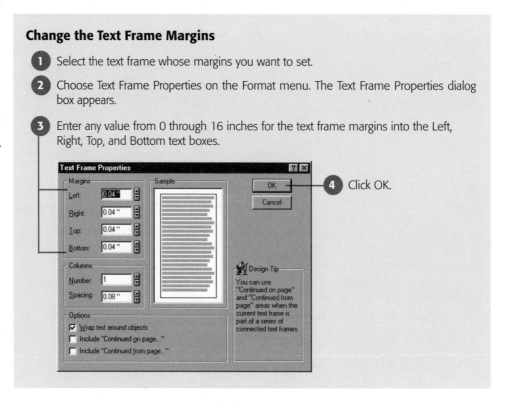

4 Click OK.

Multiple Columns Within a Text Frame

In addition to margins, the Text Frame Properties dialog box lets you set up your text in columns. Columns automatically adjust the alignment and flow of your text.

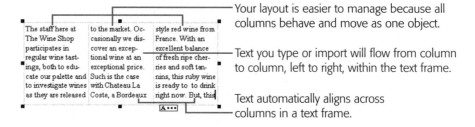

Your layout is easier to manage because all columns behave and move as one object.

Text you type or import will flow from column to column, left to right, within the text frame.

Text automatically aligns across columns in a text frame.

Forcing a column break.
If you want type to appear in the next column even if it has not yet filled the current column, press Ctrl-Shift-Enter to force a column break. If you want type to appear in the next linked text frame even if it has not yet filled the current frame, press Ctrl-Enter.

Format the Text Frame As Two or More Columns

1 Select the text frame.

2 Choose Text Frame Properties on the Format menu.

3 Enter any value from 1 through 63 to indicate the number of columns you want for your text.

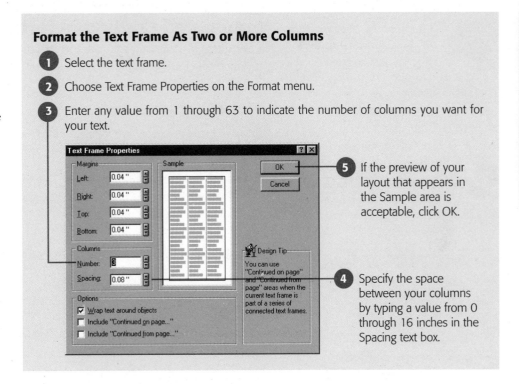

5 If the preview of your layout that appears in the Sample area is acceptable, click OK.

4 Specify the space between your columns by typing a value from 0 through 16 inches in the Spacing text box.

Wrapping Text Around Other Elements

You can create a more integrated design by wrapping text around other elements, such as a picture, WordArt, a table, an OLE object, or even another text frame.

Turn On Text Wrap

1 Select a text frame.

2 Open the Text Frame Properties dialog box.

3 Select Wrap Text Around Objects and click OK.

Can I change the contents of the Continued notices?
Yes, but you must edit each Continued notice individually by using Publisher's standard text editing features; there is no way to change the automatic wording globally.

Changing the text style of all Continued notices within a document. When Publisher creates Continued notices, it also defines two separate text styles, called Continued-From Text and Continued-On Text. You can change the formatting of all the Continued notices in your document by editing these text styles.

For more information about editing text styles, see Chapter 6.

Automated Continued Notices

A good text layout makes it easy for the reader to follow a story from page to page, in part by including elements such as Publisher's automated Continued notices.

Insert a Continued Notice

1 Select the text frame in which you want to add a Continued notice.

2 Open the Format menu and choose Text Frame Properties.

3 Select one or both of the Include "Continued On Page" and Include "Continued From Page" check boxes. Publisher automatically applies a standard format to Continued notices as shown below:

The "Continued From Page" notice appears at the upper-left corner of the text frame.

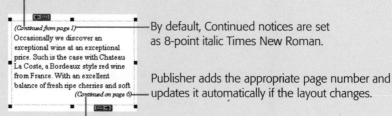

By default, Continued notices are set as 8-point italic Times New Roman.

Publisher adds the appropriate page number and updates it automatically if the layout changes.

The "Continued On Page" notice appears at the lower-right corner of the text frame.

4 Click OK.

Inserting and Editing Text

Microsoft Publisher allows you to insert text by typing directly into a text frame or by importing a word processing file. Publisher's text editing tools give you the power to fine-tune the content of your publications. And specialized text functions, such as the ability to add symbols or typographic characters, give your publications a professional, typeset look.

Publisher's Text Editing Modes

Typing directly into a text frame is the most efficient way to add small amounts of text, such as headlines and captions, to your publications. But you'll find that it is often necessary to revise longer stories to make them work with your design. Publisher lets you type and edit text in several different ways, and offers options to help you select and alter text more easily. You can switch between the different editing functions, described in the following table.

What is the difference between Highlight Entire Story and Select All on the Edit menu? The Highlight Entire Story command on the Edit menu selects all the text in a story, even if the text is placed in multiple text frames across different pages; however, it does not select the text frames. Select All on the Edit menu selects all the *objects* on the current page or spread, which means that it selects the text frames as well as the text they contain.

Ctrl-A highlights all the text in a story.

For more information about the Windows 95 Clipboard, see Chapter 3.

What happens if I drag text and drop it outside of a text frame? If you drop text outside of a text frame, Publisher automatically creates a new text frame to hold the copy.

Methods of Typing and Editing Text	
Method	**Directions for Use**
Insertion mode	Create or select a text frame and begin typing normally. Publisher adds the new text at the location of the insertion point. If the text frame already contains text, you can reposition the insertion point anywhere in the text block by using the arrow keys or the mouse.
Replacement mode	Highlight the text you want to replace and begin typing. Publisher replaces the highlighted text with new text you type, saving you the step of deleting it first.
Drag-and-drop editing	Highlight the text you want to move and drag it to a new location in the same or a different text frame. Holding down the Ctrl key as you press the left mouse button moves a copy of the highlighted text.
Windows Clipboard	Use the Cut or Copy commands to place highlighted text on the Clipboard. Position the text insertion point in a text frame on the same page, a different page, or in a different publication before issuing the Paste command.
Microsoft Word	To activate Word, select a text frame and choose Edit Story In Microsoft Word from the Edit menu. Or right-click the text frame and select Edit Story In Microsoft Word from the Change Text cascading menu. To take advantage of this feature, you must be using Publisher 97 or later and Word 6 or later.

What are the advantages of using Microsoft Word as my text editor? When you choose to use Microsoft Word as your text editor, you can utilize Word's robust editing tools, such as the grammar checker. In addition, you can edit a nonlinear design (with text placed in multiple text frames on different pages) in a linear and logical fashion because Word presents the text as a normal word processing document.

 Can I import a Microsoft WordPad file into a text object? Yes. Because WordPad is compatible with Microsoft Write, you can choose Microsoft Write when you import the file.

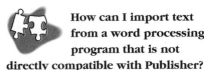 **How can I import text from a word processing program that is not directly compatible with Publisher?** In your word processing program, export one of the two generic file formats that Publisher supports. The Rich Text Format (RTF) contains formatting information that Publisher will preserve. The Plain Text format is a universal file type that you can export from word processors, databases, and spreadsheets. Publisher accepts Plain Text and Plain Text (DOS). Because Plain Text files contain no formatting information, Publisher applies its default Normal style.

Enable Text Editing Assistance

1 Click Options on the Tools menu.

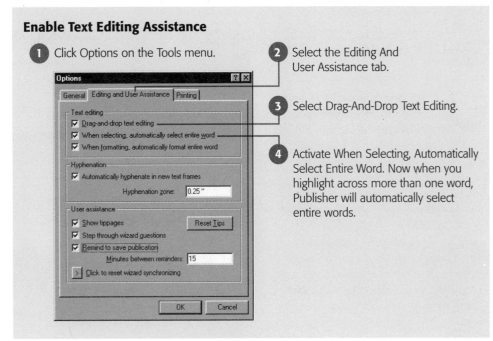

2 Select the Editing And User Assistance tab.

3 Select Drag-And-Drop Text Editing.

4 Activate When Selecting, Automatically Select Entire Word. Now when you highlight across more than one word, Publisher will automatically select entire words.

Inserting a Text File

Publisher can import and read text files from many word processing applications. When you import a file from one of the following applications, Publisher usually retains any text formatting you've used, such as font and point size, italics and boldface, paragraph indents, customized line spacing, and defined text styles:

- @ Microsoft Word versions 2, 6, 97, and 98
- @ Microsoft Works versions 3 and 4
- @ WordPerfect versions 5 and 6
- @ Microsoft Write
- @ Microsoft Publisher, all versions

The Find File dialog box is covered in Chapter 2.

 Sharing import filters with other Microsoft products.

Publisher can use text import filters that other Microsoft products have installed on your computer system. For example, some applications include a filter for Excel worksheet files. Publisher can take full advantage of this filter, allowing you to select individual worksheets within the spreadsheet file, and individual named ranges within the worksheet (as shown below). Provided that you've structured the spreadsheet properly, this feature allows you to extract only the data you need from a larger Excel file.

 Press Ctrl-F to access the Find dialog box.

Import a Text File Created in a Word Processing Application

1 Select the frame into which you want to import text.

2 Open the Insert menu and choose Text File. The Insert Text File dialog box appears.

3 Open the drop-down list box to select a file type.

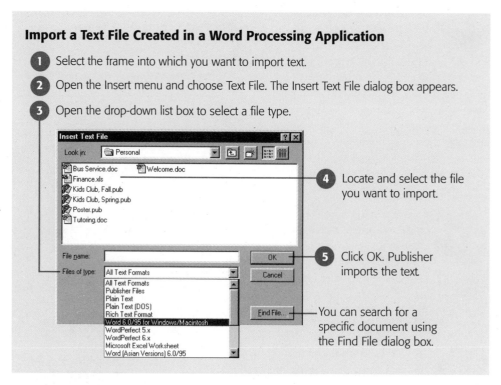

4 Locate and select the file you want to import.

5 Click OK. Publisher imports the text.

You can search for a specific document using the Find File dialog box.

Finding and Replacing Text

Using the Find command, you can locate specific words or phrases anywhere in your document. With the Replace command, you can simultaneously find text and change it. The Replace command is particularly helpful when you edit long documents. For example, if you discover that you've misspelled a client's name in your marketing materials, you can search for each occurrence of the incorrect spelling and replace it with the correct spelling.

Refine the search criteria. You can help Publisher find the exact instance of the word or phrase for which you are searching. Click Match Whole Word Only to find the text only where it appears as a whole word and ignore where it is part of another longer word. For example, if you search for the whole word *dent*, Publisher will not highlight *accident*, *correspondent*, or *dentist*. Click Match Case if you want to find the text only if it uses the same capitalization (for example, all uppercase) as the word in the Find What text box.

Searching for misspelled words. Publisher can search for a word even if you're not sure of the spelling. Simply substitute a question mark character (?) for each letter you are unsure of. For example, you could type *p?tch* to search for *patch* or *pitch*.

Press Ctrl-H to access the Replace dialog box.

Find Text

1 Click the I-beam pointer anywhere in a text frame to set the insertion point. It's best to start at the beginning or the end of a story.

2 Choose Find on the Edit menu. The Find dialog box appears.

3 Type the text you want to find in the Find What text box.

6 Click Find Next to begin the search. When Publisher finds the text, it highlights it.

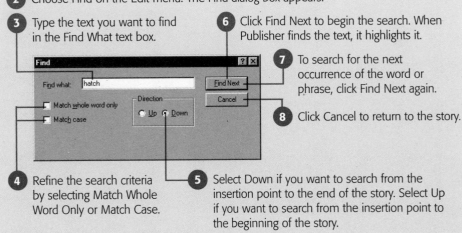

7 To search for the next occurrence of the word or phrase, click Find Next again.

8 Click Cancel to return to the story.

4 Refine the search criteria by selecting Match Whole Word Only or Match Case.

5 Select Down if you want to search from the insertion point to the end of the story. Select Up if you want to search from the insertion point to the beginning of the story.

Replace Text

1 Click the I-beam at the beginning or end of a text frame to set the insertion point.

2 Choose Replace on the Edit menu. The Replace dialog box appears.

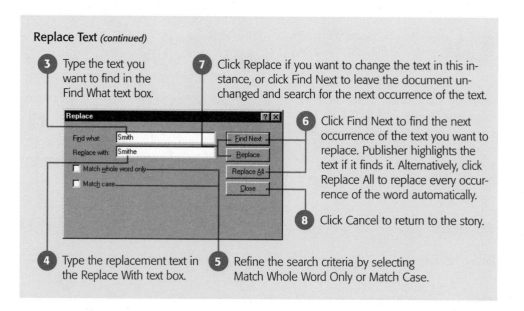

Replace Text *(continued)*

3 Type the text you want to find in the Find What text box.

7 Click Replace if you want to change the text in this instance, or click Find Next to leave the document unchanged and search for the next occurrence of the text.

6 Click Find Next to find the next occurrence of the text you want to replace. Publisher highlights the text if it finds it. Alternatively, click Replace All to replace every occurrence of the word automatically.

8 Click Cancel to return to the story.

4 Type the replacement text in the Replace With text box.

5 Refine the search criteria by selecting Match Whole Word Only or Match Case.

Use Find and Replace to convert typewriter-style documents to typeset documents. Many of the rules you learned in typing class don't apply when you are using a desktop publishing program. For example, two spaces after a period is good typing style, but the spaces will look too wide when the document is typeset.

If you import a long text file into Publisher, you should remove the typewriter-style characters. Instead of manually scrolling through a long document to remove characters like extra spaces or unnecessary tabs, you can use the Replace command to search for and delete them.

Finding and Replacing Special Characters

In addition to searching for standard letters and punctuation marks, you can use the Find command to search for special characters such as tabs and spaces. You can use the Replace command to insert such characters into your text.

The codes in the following table show some of the most common special characters you'll want to find or replace. Type the codes into the Find What and Replace With text boxes just as you would normal text.

Commonly Used Special Character Codes	
Type this code	**To find or replace**
Spacebar	A space.
^	A caret.
^?	A question mark.

Viewing special characters on screen. Publisher can display special characters as part of a text block. This is purely a convenience feature that can help you keep track of tabs and end-of-paragraph markers. To display special characters, select Show Special Characters on the View menu. To preview your text as it will print, select Hide Special Characters on the View menu.

To toggle the display of special characters on and off, press Ctrl-Shift-Y.

Can Publisher translate English text into other languages? No. Publisher's capability to designate text as a foreign language relates only to spell checking and hyphenation functions. Publisher does not offer automatic translation functions.

Exclude words from the spell check. You can use the Set Language command to exclude technical or unusual words from the normal spell check. First highlight the word you don't want to spell check. In the Mark Selected Text As box (found in the Language dialog box), select the (no proofing) option.

Type this code	To find or replace
^_	A manual hyphen.
^~	A nonbreaking hyphen.
^m	The contents of the Find What text box plus the contents of the Replace With text box. For example, if the Find What text box contains the word *leap* and the Replace With text box contains the command ^ming, Publisher creates the word *leaping* every time it finds *leap*.
^n	A line break.
^p	The end of a paragraph.
^s	A nonbreaking space.
^t	A tab.
^w	Any blank space between characters, including spaces and tabs.

Working with Publisher's Spell Check Features

On the simplest level, Publisher's spelling checker catches misspellings in your documents. On a more advanced level, a number of customization options let you choose exactly how the spell checker works.

Configuring the Spell Checker

Publisher lets you determine the language, the kinds of mistakes the spell checker looks for, and whether it corrects mistakes as you type. You can designate unusual, technical, or all uppercase words as exceptions to normal spelling rules.

If your company is named AA Electric, you can prevent Publisher from flagging the two capital *A*'s as a misspelling.

You can have Publisher flag possible errors with red underlining.

Can Publisher check foreign language spellings? Yes, Publisher can check the spelling of foreign language words, but only if you have installed a foreign language dictionary. To purchase a foreign language dictionary, contact your local Microsoft subsidiary or Alki Software Corporation. Alki Software Corporation produces dictionaries that are compatible with Publisher; in the U.S., call 800-669-9673. If you live outside the U.S., call 206-286-2600.

Turn off the display of wavy red underlining.
If you find Publisher's method of alerting you to possible spelling errors annoying, you can turn off the display of wavy red underlining. Select Spelling on the Tools menu. From the cascading menu, select Hide Spelling Errors. This command will be available only if you have selected Check Spelling As You Type in the Spelling Options dialog box.

Publisher will correct misspellings listed in the AutoCorrect dialog box, but you will no longer see the wavy red underlining. Publisher continues to keep track of the possible errors in your publication, however. To view them, open the Spelling cascading menu and select Show Spelling Errors.

Choose a Language

1 Highlight text.

2 Select Language on the Tools menu. Select Set Language on the cascading menu. The Language dialog box appears.

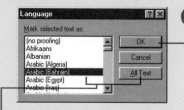

4 Click OK. Now when Publisher checks your English-language document, it will ignore any text designated as a foreign language.

3 Select one of the 94 languages and language variations from the list. Alternatively, click the All Text button, which assigns the language to all text in the entire publication.

Set Spelling Options

1 Select Spelling on the Tools menu.

2 Click Spelling Options on the cascading menu. The Spelling Options dialog box appears.

3 Select the options you would like to activate.

4 Click OK.

Ignore Words In Uppercase omits words containing only capital letters from the spell check.

Flag Repeated Words marks double words with a wavy red underline. The red underline appears instantly only if you have also selected Check Spelling As You Type. If you have de-selected Check Spelling As You Type, the underlining will appear during a normal spell check.

Check Spelling As You Type instantly corrects misspellings listed in the AutoCorrect dialog box and marks possible errors with a wavy red underline.

Add and Delete Words from Publisher's AutoCorrection List

1 Select AutoCorrect on the Tools menu. The AutoCorrect dialog box appears.

2 Select the AutoCorrect tab.

3 Select the types of mistakes you would like Publisher to correct.

Click here to change two consecutive uppercase letters to an uppercase and lowercase letter.

Click here to automatically capitalize words that start a sentence (and follow a period).

Click here to capitalize days of the week.

Click here to correct reversed capitalization, such as mONEY.

Click here to replace text listed in the left column with text listed in the right column.

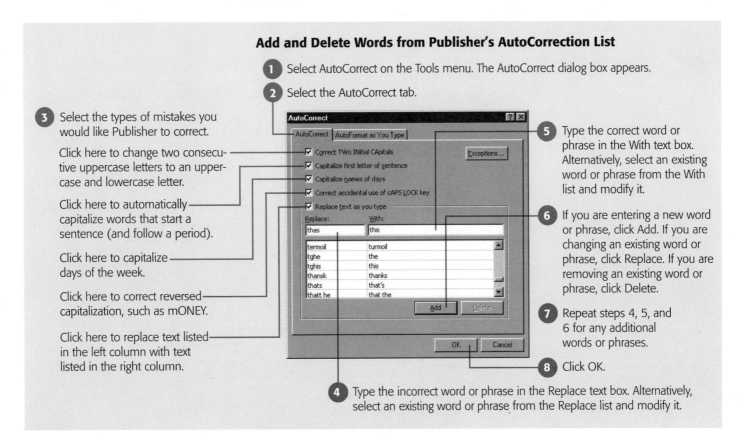

5 Type the correct word or phrase in the With text box. Alternatively, select an existing word or phrase from the With list and modify it.

6 If you are entering a new word or phrase, click Add. If you are changing an existing word or phrase, click Replace. If you are removing an existing word or phrase, click Delete.

7 Repeat steps 4, 5, and 6 for any additional words or phrases.

8 Click OK.

4 Type the incorrect word or phrase in the Replace text box. Alternatively, select an existing word or phrase from the Replace list and modify it.

Inserting and Editing Text

Exempt words and phrases from automatic correction. If you click the Exceptions button in the AutoCorrect dialog box, you can view a list of abbreviations that Publisher will not capitalize. Click the First Letter tab to add or delete entries from the list. Click the Initial Caps tab to create your own list of words with unusual capitalizations.

Checking Spelling

Publisher's default dictionary can spell check English-language documents. If you've been working with Check Spelling As You Type turned on, the spelling check will attempt to correct all the possible errors highlighted with a wavy red underline.

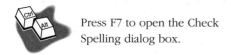

Press F7 to open the Check Spelling dialog box.

Check the Spelling in a Publication

1 Select a text frame.

2 Choose Spelling on the Tools menu. Select Check Spelling from the cascading menu. One of three things will happen:

- ❧ If Publisher finds no questionable words, it returns you to the document.

- ❧ If your document contains more stories and the Check All Stories check box is turned off, Publisher asks whether you want to check the rest of your publication. (Clicking Yes will automatically turn on Check All Stories.)

- ❧ If Publisher finds a word not in its dictionary or a word with a capitalization error, it displays the Check Spelling dialog box.

Publisher shows the misspelled word in the Not In Dictionary text box and also highlights it in your publication.

If the word has a capitalization error, Publisher displays it in the Error In Capitalization text box, which replaces the Not In Dictionary text box.

Click Ignore to leave the word alone. Or click Ignore All to ignore every instance of the word throughout the story.

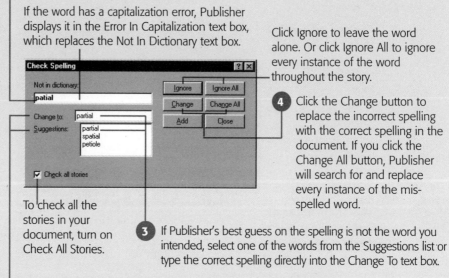

4 Click the Change button to replace the incorrect spelling with the correct spelling in the document. If you click the Change All button, Publisher will search for and replace every instance of the misspelled word.

To check all the stories in your document, turn on Check All Stories.

3 If Publisher's best guess on the spelling is not the word you intended, select one of the words from the Suggestions list or type the correct spelling directly into the Change To text box.

Publisher shows its best guess for the correct spelling or capitalization in the Change To text box. Other possible spellings appear in the Suggestions list box.

Add new words to the dictionary. You can prevent the spell checker from seeing unusual or technical words as errors. Make sure that the word is correctly entered into the Change To text box, and then click the Add button to permanently enter the word in Publisher's dictionary.

Checking the spelling of specific words or phrases. You can check the spelling of a single word or a selected text block by highlighting it before you choose the Check Spelling command. If Publisher does not find the word in its dictionary, it presents the usual Check Spelling dialog box.

Alternatively, position the text pointer over a word Publisher has flagged as a possible error and press the right mouse button. A list of alternative spellings appears on the shortcut menu, as shown in the following illustration.

Special Typographic Characters

The standard computer keyboard contains typewriter-style characters. You can make your publications look more professional by substituting or inserting true typographic characters instead. Publisher can automatically create commonly used typographic characters in response to standard keystrokes, as shown in the following table.

Publisher's Automatic Typographic Characters		
To create...	**You type...**	**Publisher substitutes...**
Curly opening and closing double quotes	" "	" "
Curly opening and closing single quotes	' '	' '
Em dash	- -	—
Copyright, trademark, and registered symbols	(c) (tm) (r)	© ™ ®
Ellipsis	. . .	...

You can specify which typographic characters Publisher inserts by configuring options in the AutoCorrect dialog box. In addition, you can use the Symbol dialog box to insert into your document alternate or extended characters, which are all the available letters and symbols that don't appear on your keyboard.

Why are there straight typewriter-style quotation marks and double hyphens in my imported text? The AutoFormat feature works only for text that you type within a Publisher document. Imported text containing straight quotation marks and double hyphens must be edited to convert typewriter-style characters to typographic characters.

 For more information about Publisher's AutoCorrect functions, see page 77. For more information about the Character Map, see Microsoft Windows 95 online help.

Choose AutoFormat Options

1 Choose AutoCorrect on the Tools menu. The AutoCorrect dialog box appears.

Select this check box to substitute straight typewriter-style quotes with curly quotes. Deselect the check box to type straight typewriter-style quotes.

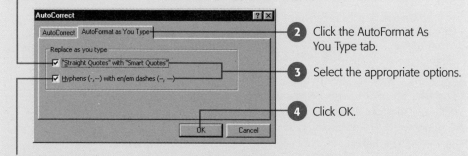

2 Click the AutoFormat As You Type tab.

3 Select the appropriate options.

4 Click OK.

Select this check box to substitute two hyphens with em dash. Deselect this option to type hyphens in all instances.

Insert a Symbol

1 Click to position the insertion point where you want to insert the symbol.

2 Choose Symbol on the Insert menu.

3 Open the Font drop-down list box and choose a typeface.

Use the AutoCorrect function to insert typographic characters. You can use the AutoCorrect function to substitute typographic characters for standard typewriter-style characters. In the AutoCorrect dialog box, make sure that Replace Text As You Type is active. In the Replace text box, enter a combination of standard characters you will use to designate a typographic character. Choose a unique combination of standard letters, numbers, and punctuation that won't ever appear in normal text. As an example, you could use the combination of Y$ to automatically create the typographic character for Yen [¥].

You can enter the typographic character into the With text box in one of two ways. You can press NumLock and then enter the code directly using the number key pad. For example, the code for the Yen symbol is Alt-0165. Alternatively, you can also use the Windows 95 Character Map to place the typographic character on the Clipboard. Then use the Ctrl-V keyboard shortcut to paste the typographic character into the With text box in the AutoCorrect dialog box.

Insert a Symbol *(continued)*

4 Open the Subset drop-down list box and choose a character group, such as Geometric Shapes, Currency, or Mathematical Operators. Alternatively, scroll through the font to find the character you want.

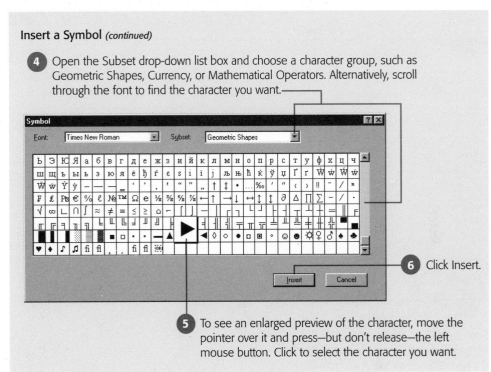

6 Click Insert.

5 To see an enlarged preview of the character, move the pointer over it and press—but don't release—the left mouse button. Click to select the character you want.

Inserting and Updating Information Automatically

There are certain—very specific—types of information that Publisher can insert into your document automatically. They include the date, time, and personal information such as your name and address.

Information components look like standard text frames, but you can identify an information component by placing the pointer over it until a ScreenTip appears.

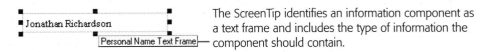

The ScreenTip identifies an information component as a text frame and includes the type of information the component should contain.

For more information about synchronization, see Chapter 14.

Personal Information Components

Personal information components function like the fields in a database, because Publisher can update the information they contain automatically. Your address, for example, often appears in multiple locations within a publication. If you change the text in a single address information component, Publisher instantly propagates the change to all other address information components throughout the document. You can turn this feature—which is known as synchronization—on and off for each personal information component in a publication.

Because we often wear different hats, Publisher provides four personal information sets:

- Primary Business
- Secondary Business
- Other Organization
- Home/Family

Each set contains eight components:

- Personal Name
- Job Title
- Organization Name
- Address
- Tag Line
- Phone/Fax/E-mail
- Logo
- Color Scheme

How do I edit the Logo personal information component? The Logo personal information component is actually a Smart Object that consists of a picture and one or more text frames. You can simply select a text frame and type new text as described in the procedure "Insert and Edit a Personal Information Component" on page 83. To change the picture or the design, click the Wizard button located on the lower-right corner of the Smart Object to invoke the Logo Creation Wizard.

To learn more about the Logo Creation Wizard and Smart Objects, see Chapter 14.

Choose a Personal Information Set

1 Choose Personal Information on the Insert menu.

2 On the cascading menu, choose Select. On the second cascading menu, choose one of the four personal information sets.

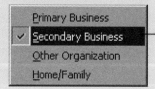

Publisher associates the personal information set you choose with the current publication. You can have only one personal information set associated with a publication.

Insert and Edit a Personal Information Component

1 Select Personal Information on the Insert menu. From the cascading menu, choose the type of personal information component you want to insert. Publisher creates a new personal information component.

Secondary Business Address	1653 Newfield Ave.
Your Address Line 2	Norristown, PA 19401
Your Address Line 3	
Your Address Line 4	

If this is the first time you have created a personal information component, Publisher inserts default information.

If you have previously created a personal information component, Publisher inserts the appropriate information.

2 To change the information, use Publisher's standard editing tools to highlight and change the text.

3 Deselect the frame. If the document contains other instances of this personal information component, Publisher automatically updates them with the new text.

4 Save the publication. The changes are saved in the current personal information set. Publisher will use the new information when creating this personal information component in this and all future documents.

Can I combine a personal information component with normal text or with another personal information component in the same text frame?
No. Each personal information component must remain in its own separate text frame.

Delete or Clear a Personal Information Component

1 Select the personal information component you want to delete or clear.

2 To remove the personal information component without changing the information it contains, select the Delete Object command on the Edit menu or on the shortcut menu.

3 To clear the text from a personal information component, highlight all the text and press the Del or Backspace key. The text will be deleted from this personal information component and from all synchronized components in the document. In the future, when you insert this personal information component, it will be blank.

Turn on synchronization. Even after you've disabled synchronization, you can turn it back on. Open the Options dialog box from the Tools menu. On the Editing And User Assistance tab, click the button labeled Click to Reset Wizard Synchronizing.

Can I change the appearance of a personal information component using Publisher's standard layout and formatting tools? Yes. You can use any of Publisher's tools to change the object's appearance. You can resize the frame, reposition the element on the page, and change the font, point size, text color, fill color, and border of the frame.

But be warned: the formatting changes you make are applied only to the current copy of the personal information component. They are not propagated to other instances of the personal information component in your publication, and they are not saved as part of the personal information set (which means that the formatting changes will not be applied when you create new objects in this or other publications).

Turn Off Synchronization

1 Insert or select a personal information component.

2 Use Publisher's standard editing tools to highlight and change the text.

3 Deselect the frame. If the document contains other instances of this personal information component, Publisher automatically updates them with the new text.

4 Select Undo Propagate Personal Information on the Edit menu.

Date and Time

Publisher always gets the current date and time from your computer's internal clock. You can insert the date and time separately or as a single element. You can also decide whether to insert the information as a standard text element or as an updateable field.

Insert the Date or Time

1 Create or select a text frame. If the text frame contains text, position the insertion point where you want to insert the date or time.

2 Select Date And Time on the Insert menu. The Date And Time dialog box appears.

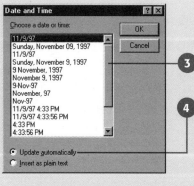

3 Scroll through the list and select one of 17 date/time formats.

4 Select Update Automatically if you want Publisher to revise the date and time whenever you subsequently open or print the publication. Select Insert As Plain Text if you want the current date and time to be preserved.

Why do automatic hyphens appear and disappear? As you change the text by editing, reformatting, or re-sizing the text frame or by rearranging the layout, different words fall in the hyphenation zone and are hyphenated to accommodate the changes. Words formerly hyphenated that move out of the hyphenation zone are closed up again.

Hyphenation Options

You can smooth ragged margins by using hyphens to break words that fall at the ends of lines. Publisher offers several different hyphenation options:

- Automatically hyphenate every story in your publication.

- Turn off hyphenation for a selected story or for all stories.

- Manually approve each of Publisher's suggested hyphens.

- Insert optional hyphens that appear when the word falls at the end of a line.

- Insert nonbreaking hyphens for compound words that are always hyphenated and that you don't want to break between two lines.

When automatic hyphenation is active, Publisher breaks and repositions words based on a number of factors, as shown in the following illustration.

A wider text frame produces longer lines and fewer hyphens.

A narrow text frame produces shorter lines and more hyphens.

Long words that fall in the hyphenation zone are divided between syllables as determined by Publisher's default dictionary.

One-syllable words that are too long to fit are pushed to the next line.

The hyphenation zone defines a region in which Publisher looks for words to hyphenate. The default value is 0.25 inch.

Controlling the number of hyphens in your story. Increase the hyphenation zone to hyphenate fewer words. If the text you're hyphenating is left aligned, increasing the hyphenation zone will create a more irregular, or ragged, right margin. Decrease the hyphenation zone to hyphenate more words and create a more regular right margin.

Press Ctrl-Shift-H to open the Hyphenation dialog box.

Hyphenation in justified text. If the text you're hyphenating is justified (aligned on both the left and right margins), increasing the hyphenation zone will leave more spaces between words, creating unpleasant gaps between the words in your text. Decrease the hyphenation zone setting to hyphenate more words and to give your text a smoother appearance.

Automatically Hyphenate Every Story in Your Publication

1 Choose Options on the Tools menu, and then select the Editing And User Assistance tab.

2 Select Automatically Hyphenate In New Text Frames.

3 Enter a value from 0 through 10 inches in the Hyphenation Zone text box.

4 Click OK to accept the hyphenation settings.

Customize Hyphenation for a Single Story

1 Select the text object that contains the story whose hyphenation you want to modify.

2 Choose Language on the Tools menu. Select Hyphenation from the cascading menu. The Hyphenation dialog box appears.

3 Select the appropriate option.

Deselect this check box to turn off automatic hyphenation for this story.
Or select this check box to turn on automatic hyphenation for this story.

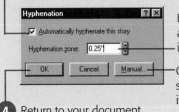

If you've selected automatic hyphenation, enter a value between 0 and 10 inches in 0.01-inch increments in the Hyphenation Zone text box.

Click Manual to review the hyphens that Publisher suggests. You can choose a different hyphenation point if one or more are defined in Publisher's dictionary.

4 Return to your document by clicking OK.

Hyphenate Words Manually

1 Position the insertion point between the two characters where you want Publisher to break the word.

2 Press Ctrl-hyphen.

bi⌐cycle

If Show Special Characters is turned on, Publisher displays a modified hyphen that looks bent.

Viewing optional hyphens. Hyphens that you enter manually are normally printed and displayed only when they fall at the end of a line. If you want to see all these optional hyphens on screen, choose the Show Special Characters command on the View menu.

Insert a Nonbreaking Hyphen

1 Position the insertion point between two characters or between two words if you are creating a compound word.

2 Delete all spaces between the words.

3 Press Ctrl-Alt-hyphen.

Binet⌐Simon·scale

If Show Special Characters is turned on, a nonbreaking hyphen is displayed as a larger-than-standard hyphen.

Text Formats

The fonts and formatting attributes that you apply to the text in a document have subtle yet profound effect on your readers. Well-designed typography can enhance your message and make your publications easier to read. Microsoft Publisher provides character-level, paragraph-level, and document-level text formatting tools.

Character-level formats, such as a drop cap or italicized text, can be applied to selected letters within a larger block of text.

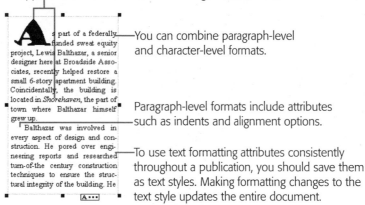

You can combine paragraph-level and character-level formats.

Paragraph-level formats include attributes such as indents and alignment options.

To use text formatting attributes consistently throughout a publication, you should save them as text styles. Making formatting changes to the text style updates the entire document.

Character Formatting

To format characters within a larger block of text, you must first highlight the text. At that point, you can use any of several methods to reformat the selected copy: select a feature from the text toolbar, select options in the Character dialog box, or use Publisher's additional formatting options to create special effects.

Why doesn't the formatting change for words I've already typed? To make changes to a few words in a larger block of copy, you must first highlight the text. If you change the formatting attributes without highlighting the text, you will change only the attributes of the next text you type.

For more information about text frame attributes, see Chapter 4.

Suppress previews in the font drop-down list. You can display a simple list of font names, rather than an actual preview of each font, in the Font drop-down list on the Format toolbar. Doing so enables you to fit more font names into the drop-down list box. To disable the preview, choose Options from the Tools menu. On the General tab, turn off the Preview Fonts In Fonts List check box.

Basic Text Formatting Options: The Format Toolbar

Whenever you create or select a text frame, tools for formatting text appear on the Format toolbar. This toolbar is often the fastest way to change the appearance of text. Although it provides access to only a portion of Publisher's text formatting options, it does include the most frequently used attributes.

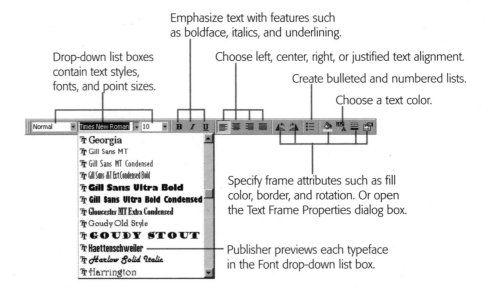

Emphasize text with features such as boldface, italics, and underlining.

Drop-down list boxes contain text styles, fonts, and point sizes.

Choose left, center, right, or justified text alignment.

Create bulleted and numbered lists.

Choose a text color.

Specify frame attributes such as fill color, border, and rotation. Or open the Text Frame Properties dialog box.

Publisher previews each typeface in the Font drop-down list box.

Format Text Using the Frame Toolbar

1 Highlight the text you want to format.

2 Select an option from a drop-down list box or click a formatting button.

Change the size of text by changing the size of its frame. You can interactively resize the point size of text simply by dragging the text frame's selection handle, provided that you have turned on Publisher's automatic copyfitting options for the text frame. With a text frame selected, choose Copyfit Text on the Format menu. Select either Best Fit or Shrink Text On Overflow from the cascading menu.

For more information about copyfitting, see Chapter 4.

Don't change the font style of a decorative typeface. Publisher ships with a number of decorative typefaces. These fonts, which can range from the playful (Goudy Stout) to the forceful (Gill Sans Ultra Bold) to the ethereal (ITC Eras Light) are one-of-a-kind fonts. They do not have true variations, such as italics or boldface, associated with them. If you apply a font-style to these typefaces, Windows 95 attempts to simulate the effect, often with less than desirable results.

The Font Dialog Box

A wider range of text formatting options is available from the Font command on the Format menu. Most of the options—even many of the effects—have legitimate typographic functions. Formatting options such as Superscript, Subscript, Small Caps, and All Caps are traditionally used for footnotes, equations, and time references, as shown in the following illustration. Other effects, such as Outline, Emboss, Engrave, and Shadow, are purely decorative and can be used to create special effects that are similar to those found in WordArt.

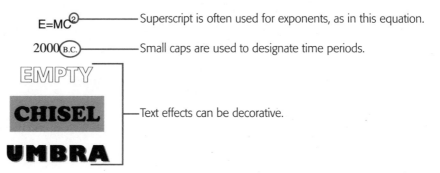

$E=MC^2$ ——— Superscript is often used for exponents, as in this equation.

2000 B.C. ——— Small caps are used to designate time periods.

——— Text effects can be decorative.

Change the Character Formatting of Text

1 Select a text frame. If the frame contains text, highlight the text you want to format.

2 Choose Font on the Format menu. The Font dialog box appears.

3 Select the options you want.

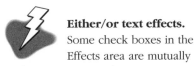

Either/or text effects.
Some check boxes in the Effects area are mutually exclusive. For example, you cannot apply both the Emboss and Outline effects to text.

Change the Character Formatting of Text *(continued)*

Choose a typeface from the Font drop-down list box.

To change the emphasis of your text, open the Font Style drop-down list box and choose Regular, Italic, Bold, or Bold Italic.

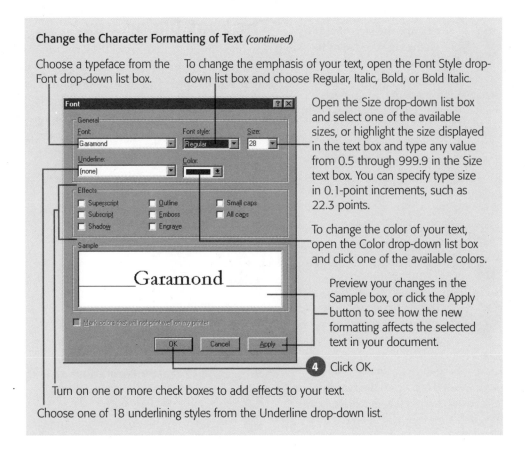

Open the Size drop-down list box and select one of the available sizes, or highlight the size displayed in the text box and type any value from 0.5 through 999.9 in the Size text box. You can specify type size in 0.1-point increments, such as 22.3 points.

To change the color of your text, open the Color drop-down list box and click one of the available colors.

Preview your changes in the Sample box, or click the Apply button to see how the new formatting affects the selected text in your document.

④ Click OK.

Turn on one or more check boxes to add effects to your text.

Choose one of 18 underlining styles from the Underline drop-down list.

Formatting Shortcuts

You can use keyboard shortcuts to quickly change the format of the characters you are *about* to type. For example, if you press Ctrl-I, all of the subsequent text you type will be in italics. You can also use keyboard shortcuts to reformat highlighted text. The same keyboard shortcuts allow you to remove formatting attributes as well. For example, if you highlight a boldface word and press Ctrl-B, the text will return to the normal (or roman) weight. The following table summarizes the most frequently used formatting shortcuts.

Maintain existing text formats. You might select a text block that contains conflicting formatting attributes. For example, a paragraph in the Times New Roman font might contain a few italicized words. When you highlight words or text blocks that contain characters with different formatting, the corresponding drop-down list boxes, check boxes, options, and Sample area in the Character dialog box are empty or not available. You can take advantage of this feature to change one formatting attribute without overriding the settings for other attributes. For example, you can change the font for the entire paragraph but leave any italicized words intact by leaving the drop-down list box for Font Style blank.

Automatically format entire words. You should apply the same formatting to all the letters in a word. For example, the last letter in an italicized word should not print with the Normal font style. You can have Publisher apply formatting changes to the whole word, regardless of whether the whole word is highlighted. Open the Options dialog box from the Tools menu. Click the Editing And User Assistance tab and make sure a check appears next to When Formatting, Automatically Format Entire Word.

Text Formatting Shortcuts	
Keyboard Shortcut	**Attribute**
Ctrl-B	Boldface
Ctrl-I	Italic
Ctrl-U	Underline
Ctrl-Shift-K	Small caps
Ctrl-=	Subscript
Ctrl-Shift-=	Superscript
Ctrl-Spacebar	Remove character formats
Ctrl-Shift-F	Change font
Ctrl-Shift-P	Change point size
Ctrl-]	Increase font size by 1 point
Ctrl-[	Decrease font size by 1 point
Ctrl-Shift->	Increase font size by 0.5 point
Ctrl-Shift-<	Decrease font size by 0.5 point

Character Spacing

You can adjust the spacing of individual characters to fine-tune the legibility of text (especially critical at very small or very large point sizes) and to turn plain text into dramatic graphic elements. Publisher can alter the spacing of the characters themselves by expanding or condensing a font's width. In addition, you can control the spacing between letters by using Publisher's kerning and tracking functions.

What is the difference between automatic and manual kerning? Certain letter combinations, such as *TO* and *AV*, always appear too loose. When you turn on Automatic Kerning, Publisher adjusts the letterspacing for specific letter pairs. You can specify a point size at which automatic kerning kicks in, but you can't specify which letter pairs are kerned, and you can't control the amount of kerning. Manual kerning lets you kern any two letters at any point size. You can move letters closer together or farther apart. And you can specify the exact amount of space to be added or removed.

Specifying the kerning point size to speed up performance. Publisher will kern letter pairs at point sizes greater than or equal to any point size you specify in the Character Spacing dialog box. Deselecting the Kerning check box disables automatic kerning and speeds up Publisher's performance. Typing a size smaller than 14 points can seriously downgrade Publisher's performance.

The visible gap between these letters is an optical illusion caused by the shape of the letters.

As part of a federally funded sweat equity project, Lewis Balthazar, a senior designer here at Broadside Associates, recently helped restore a small 6-story apartment building. Co-incidentally, the building is located in *Shorehaven*, the part of town where Balthazar himself grew up.

Balthazar was involved in every aspect of design and construction. He pored over engineering reports and researched turn-of-the century construction techniques to ensure the

Tracking is applied to larger blocks of text.

You can compensate with automatic or manual kerning, a process that moves letter pairs closer together.

As part of a federally funded sweat equity project, Lewis Balthazar, a senior designer here at Broadside Associates, recently helped restore a small 6-story apartment building. Coincidentally, the building is located in *Shorehaven*, the part of town where Balthazar himself grew up.

Balthazar was involved in every aspect of design and construction. He pored over

Tracking changes of just a few percentage points can dramatically change the amount of text that fits into a text frame.

Change Character Spacing

1 Highlight the text you want to change. If you are manually kerning two letters, place the text insertion point between them.

2 Choose Character Spacing on the Format menu. The Character Spacing dialog box appears.

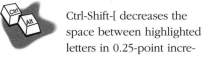

Ctrl-Shift-[decreases the space between highlighted letters in 0.25-point increments. Ctrl-Shift-] increases the space between highlighted letters in 0.25-point increments.

Change Character Spacing *(continued)*

To reduce the width of selected text, enter a percentage from 0.1 percent through 99.9 percent in 0.1-increments. To increase the width of selected text, enter a percentage from 100.1 percent through 600 percent in 0.1-increments.

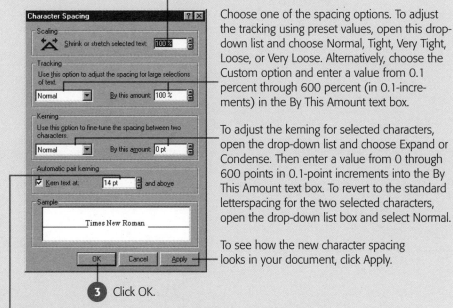

Choose one of the spacing options. To adjust the tracking using preset values, open this drop-down list and choose Normal, Tight, Very Tight, Loose, or Very Loose. Alternatively, choose the Custom option and enter a value from 0.1 percent through 600 percent (in 0.1-increments) in the By This Amount text box.

To adjust the kerning for selected characters, open the drop-down list and choose Expand or Condense. Then enter a value from 0 through 600 points in 0.1-point increments into the By This Amount text box. To revert to the standard letterspacing for the two selected characters, open the drop-down list box and select Normal.

To see how the new character spacing looks in your document, click Apply.

3 Click OK.

Select this check box to turn Automatic Pair Kerning on. Enter a point size from 0.5 through 999.9 points in 0.1-point increments. Publisher will automatically kern any text formatted with this or a larger point size.

Drop Caps

Drop caps (slang for dropped capital letters) and initial caps are common design devices often used to indicate the beginning of a new text unit, such as a chapter. Publisher provides a gallery of preformatted designs for both drop caps and initial caps. You can also create your own unique effects and apply them to a single initial letter, multiple letters, or an entire word.

Text Formats

Can I change or remove drop or initial caps? Yes. Select a paragraph that already contains a drop or initial cap and choose the Change Drop Cap command on the Format menu. In the Drop Cap dialog box, you can choose a different preformatted style, select custom options, or return the drop cap letter to normal by clicking the first style (none) in the gallery (or by clicking the Remove button).

As part of a federally funded sweat equity project, Lewis Balthazar, a senior designer here at Broadside Associates, recently helped restore a small 6-story apartment building. Coincidentally, the building is located in *Shorehaven*, the part of

First letters that share a baseline with the first line of text are called initial caps.

As part of a federally funded sweat equity project, Lewis Balthazar, a senior designer here at Broadside Associates, recently helped restore a small 6-story apartment building. Coincidentally, the building is located in *Shorehaven*, the part of town where Balthazar himself

First letters that hang below the first line of text are called drop caps.

Insert a Preformatted Drop Cap or Initial Cap

1 Select the paragraph where you want to add a drop cap or initial cap.

2 Open the Format menu and choose Drop Cap. The Drop Cap dialog box appears.

3 Select the Drop Cap tab.

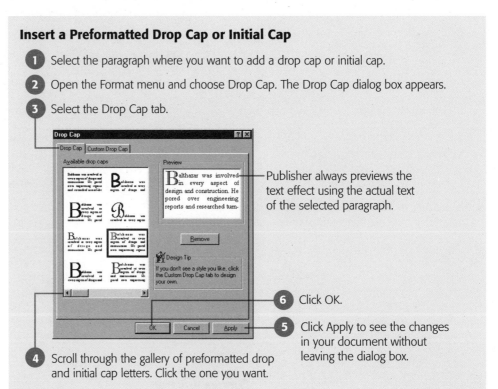

Publisher always previews the text effect using the actual text of the selected paragraph.

6 Click OK.

5 Click Apply to see the changes in your document without leaving the dialog box.

4 Scroll through the gallery of preformatted drop and initial cap letters. Click the one you want.

Create a Custom Drop Cap, Initial Cap, or Lead Word

1 Select the paragraph where you want to add a custom drop or initial cap.

2 Choose Drop Cap on the Format menu.

3 Click the Custom Drop Cap tab.

4 Choose a drop cap, an up (initial) cap, or a custom position. If you choose the custom position, you must enter a value from 0 through 2.

5 Enter a value from 2 through 32 in the Size Of Letters text box. The size of a drop cap is always relative to the height of the remaining text in the paragraph. For example, a size of 4 will produce a drop cap 4 lines tall.

6 If you want to apply the effect to multiple letters or an entire word, enter a value from 1 through 15 in the Number Of Letters text box.

7 Open the Font drop-down list box and choose a typeface. Alternatively, you can pick up the current font from the selected paragraph by clicking Use Current Font.

8 Open the Font Style drop-down list box and choose an emphasis. Alternatively, you can pick up the current emphasis from the selected paragraph by clicking Use Current Font Style.

9 Open the Color drop-down list box and choose an available color. Alternatively, you can pick up the current font color from the selected paragraph by clicking Use Current Color.

10 Click OK. Publisher includes your customized drop cap or initial cap in the gallery. It will be available in this publication only.

Do the math when creating paragraph indents. When you are using the Indents And Lists dialog box (available from the Format menu), you should pay special attention to the values in the Left and First Line text boxes. These values are added to one another to produce the final indented effect for the paragraph.

If you choose a standard paragraph indent with the left indent set at 0.5 inch, typing a value of 0.5 in the First Line text box creates a cumulative effect: the first line indent now measures 1 inch from the margin, as shown in the following illustration.

> As part of a feder-
> ally funded sweat equity
> project, Lewis Balthazar, a
> senior designer here at
> Broadside Associates, re-
> cently helped restore a small
> 6-story apartment building.
> Coincidentally, the building

Use negative numbers in the First Line text box to create a hanging indent. If you set the left indent at 0.5, set the first line indent at –0.25. The first line of text then hangs to the left of the remaining text lines by 0.25 inch, as shown in the following illustration.

> As part of a federally funded
> sweat equity project, Lewis
> Balthazar, a senior designer
> here at Broadside Associ-
> ates, recently helped restore
> a small 6-story apartment
> building.Coincidentally, the
> building is located in *Shore-*

Paragraph Formatting

Publisher defines a paragraph as any amount of text followed by a carriage return, so the formatting applied to paragraphs in Publisher can be as short as one character or as long as the whole publication. Paragraph formats can also be applied to text in a table cell.

Paragraph-level formats—which include attributes such as alignment, indents, and line spacing—determine the shape and density of a multiple-line block of text.

Indents and Lists

Publisher's Indents And Lists dialog box offers numerous preset options to create the most commonly used paragraph formats (shown in the following illustration). In addition, you can create custom paragraph styles.

As part of a federally funded sweat equity project, Lewis Balthazar, a senior designer here at Broadside Associates, recently helped restore a small 6-story apartment building. Coincidentally, the building is located in *Shorehaven*, the part of town where Balthazar himself grew up.

Balthazar was involved in every aspect of design and construction. He pored over engineering reports and

As part of a federally funded sweat equity project, Lewis Balthazar, a senior designer here at Broadside Associates, recently helped restore a small 6-story apartment building. Coincidentally, the building is located in *Shorehaven*, the part of town where Balthazar himself grew up.

Balthazar was involved in every aspect of design and construction. He pored over engineering reports and researched turn-of-the century con-

1. Lewis Balthazar is a senior designer here at Broadside Associates.
2. He recently helped restore a small 6-story apartment building.
3. The building is located in *Shorehaven*, the part of town where Balthazar himself grew up.
4. Balthazar was involved in every aspect of design and construction.
5. He pored over engineering reports.

This is a flush left paragraph with no indent. Blank lines usually separate individual paragraphs. This is a typical format for business correspondence. Notice that the right margin is irregular, or ragged.

Newspapers and magazines typically indent the first lines of second and subsequent paragraphs. The paragraph is justified so that text is flush with both the left and right margins.

Publisher considers each of these numbered items to be a new paragraph because each is followed by a carriage return. Numbered lists often use a hanging indent to offset the numeral from the rest of the text.

Customize the Paragraph Indents

1 Click in the paragraph you want to format. If you want to format more than one paragraph at a time, highlight them all.

2 Choose Indents And Lists on the Format menu. The Indents And Lists dialog box appears.

Quickly change the paragraph alignment. You can assign any of Publisher's standard alignment options to the currently selected paragraph or paragraphs by clicking the Left, Center, Right, or Justified buttons on the Format toolbar.

Control individual line breaks. In addition to choosing alignment options, you can control how individual lines break within a paragraph. This technique is used to improve the rag, the pattern formed by the ends of text lines. To force a line break without starting a new paragraph, press Shift-Enter. To prevent a line break between two words, insert a nonbreaking space by pressing Ctrl-Shift-Space.

Customize the Paragraph Indents *(continued)*

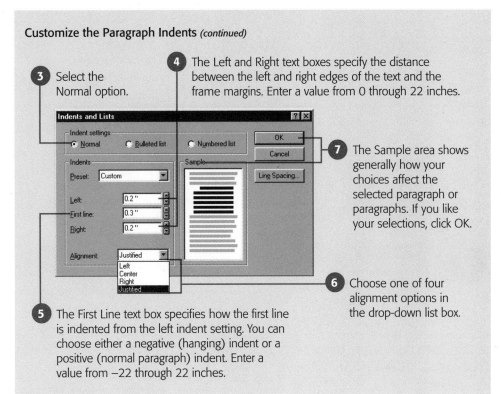

3 Select the Normal option.

4 The Left and Right text boxes specify the distance between the left and right edges of the text and the frame margins. Enter a value from 0 through 22 inches.

7 The Sample area shows generally how your choices affect the selected paragraph or paragraphs. If you like your selections, click OK.

5 The First Line text box specifies how the first line is indented from the left indent setting. You can choose either a negative (hanging) indent or a positive (normal paragraph) indent. Enter a value from −22 through 22 inches.

6 Choose one of four alignment options in the drop-down list box.

Choose a Preset Indent

1 Click in the paragraph you want to format. If you want to format more than one paragraph at a time, highlight them all.

2 Choose Indents And Lists from the Format menu.

3 Select the Normal option in the Indents And Lists dialog box.

Text Formats

Choose a Preset Indent *(continued)*

4 Open the Preset drop-down list box to choose one of five preset indents:

@ Original: makes no changes to the existing indents

@ Flush Left: aligns all of the text with the left margins

@ 1st Line Indent: creates a 0.25-inch indent for the first line only

@ Hanging Indent: indents every line after the first by 0.25 inch

@ Quotation: indents text by 0.5 inch on both the left and right

5 Click OK.

Quick access to bullets.
The Format toolbar contains a Bullet button (shown in the following illustration) that gives you quick access to the most recently used bullets. You can also use the Bullet button to remove a bulleted or numbered format from a paragraph by choosing the None option. Finally, clicking the More option opens the Indents And Lists dialog box.

Bulleted Lists

Bulleted lists draw attention to the important points in your publication and create visual interest by breaking up dense blocks of text. You can add bullets to your text manually, but it's faster to have Publisher create a bulleted list for you.

Format Several Paragraphs As a Bulleted List

1 Select the paragraphs you want to include in the bulleted list. Remember that a paragraph can consist of a character, a single word, or a sentence.

2 Choose Indents And Lists on the Format menu. The Indents And Lists dialog box appears.

3 Choose Bulleted List. The Bullet Type area appears.

The New Bullet dialog box is identical to the Symbol dialog box found on the Insert menu. See Chapter 5.

Better bullets. You can insert decorative bullets into your text by choosing a font like Wingdings in the New Bullet dialog box.

Take advantage of accurate previews. Although the Sample area shows only broad shaded lines for text (referred to as greeked text), it is an accurate preview. Use it to make sure that the carryover lines align under the first character of the first line. For this to occur, the indent you specify in the Indent List By text box must be equal to the amount of space required for the bullet plus the white space between the bullet and the text.

Format Several Paragraphs As a Bulleted List *(continued)*

4 Either choose one of the six bullets displayed or click New Bullet to bring up the New Bullet dialog box, which will appear as one of the six bullet choices in the Bullet Type area.

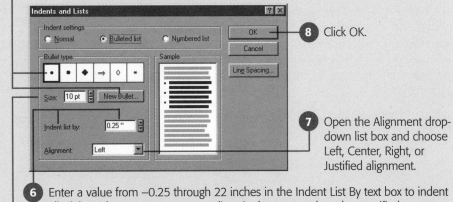

8 Click OK.

7 Open the Alignment drop-down list box and choose Left, Center, Right, or Justified alignment.

6 Enter a value from –0.25 through 22 inches in the Indent List By text box to indent all of the subsequent, or carryover, lines in the paragraph to the specified measurement. To effectively turn this feature off, enter a value of 0.

5 Change the bullet size by typing any value from 0.5 through 999.9 points in the text box.

Numbered Lists

Numbered lists enumerate a series of items or give sequential instructions. When you use the numbered list format, every new paragraph automatically begins with the next higher number or letter in the series.

Set Up a Numbered List

1 Select the paragraphs you want to include in the numbered list.

2 Choose Indents And Lists from the Format menu. The Indents And Lists dialog box appears.

3 Choose the Numbered List option. The Number area appears.

Change the appearance of numbered lists. You can create distinctive formats for your lists by choosing among the options in the Format and Separator drop-down list boxes. The Format drop-down list offers you three choices, and the Separator drop-down list gives you eight options, as shown in the following illustration.

1

b

C

1

2.

3)

4]

5:

(6)

[7]

-8-

For more information about Publisher's Table tool, see Chapter 8.

4 Open the Format drop-down list box and choose one of three options.

5 To specify how you want the numbers separated from the text, open the Separator drop-down list box and choose one of eight options.

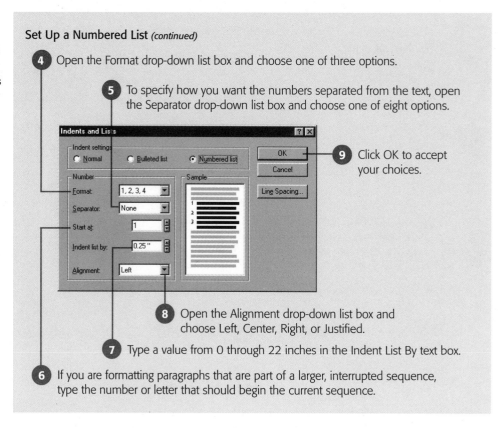

9 Click OK to accept your choices.

8 Open the Alignment drop-down list box and choose Left, Center, Right, or Justified.

7 Type a value from 0 through 22 inches in the Indent List By text box.

6 If you are formatting paragraphs that are part of a larger, interrupted sequence, type the number or letter that should begin the current sequence.

Vertical Alignment

Vertical alignment options let you position text at the top, bottom, or center of a text frame. You can apply Publisher's vertical alignment options to a single text frame, to a text frame containing multiple columns, to connected text frames, and to cells in a table.

Align Text Vertically

1 Select a text frame.

2 Select Align Text Vertically on the Format menu.

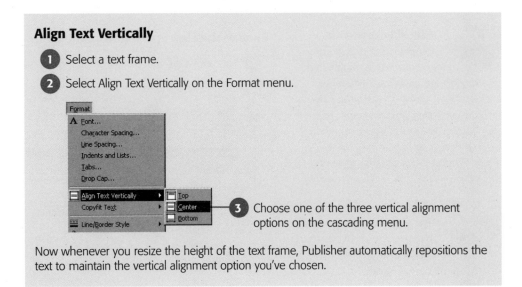

3 Choose one of the three vertical alignment options on the cascading menu.

Now whenever you resize the height of the text frame, Publisher automatically repositions the text to maintain the vertical alignment option you've chosen.

The line spacing changes automatically according to the text point size.

Publisher's default single spacing (1 space) is set at 120 percent of point size. As an example, for 10-point type, the 1 space setting inserts 12 points from baseline to baseline. The advantage of this arrangement is that the line spacing changes automatically when the point size changes. For example, if you decide to format your text at 12 instead of 10 points, the line spacing of 1 space automatically increases to 14.4 points.

Line Spacing

Publisher uses a measurement called line spacing, or leading, to determine the amount of space between the bottom, or baseline, of the characters in one line of text and the baseline of the next line, as shown in the following illustration. To give you even more control over the appearance of your text, you can add extra spacing before and after paragraphs, separately from leading.

As part of a federally funded sweat equity project, Lewis Balthazar, a senior designer here at Broadside Associates, recently helped restore a small 6-story apartment building. Coincidentally, the building is located in *Shorehaven*, the part of town where Balthazar himself grew up.

Increasing the leading of a text block can improve legibility or create a special effect.

As part of a federally funded sweat equity project, Lewis Balthazar, a senior designer here at Broadside Associates, recently helped restore a small 6-story apartment building. Coincidentally, the building is located in *Shorehaven*, the part of town where Balthazar himself grew up.

Decreasing the leading (even by a small increment such as 0.5 point, which is only 1/144 inch) can help you fit more text on a page.

Why did my text disappear? If your text disappears when you change the line spacing, you have probably accidentally entered a very large value into the Between Lines text box. Either you have typed in the wrong numbers, or you have forgotten to add the *pt* abbreviation to indicate that you want to use points as the unit of measurement.

Use points as the unit of measurement. By default, Publisher uses a relative unit of measurement (line spaces) to add spaces between lines of text. You have much more control over line spacing if you use an absolute unit of measure, such as points, instead. To change the line spacing using points, enter a value from 3 through 1,488 points in 0.05-point increments in the Between Lines text box in the Line Spacing dialog box. Remember to add the *pt* abbreviation to specify points.

Add the appropriate spacing between paragraphs. Pressing Enter to add space between paragraphs creates a full blank line space, which can disrupt the text flow. Use the Line Spacing dialog box to add small amounts of white space before or after paragraphs to separate them without disrupting text flow.

Change the Line Spacing from the Default of 1 Space

1 Click anywhere in a paragraph, or highlight the paragraphs you want to reformat.

2 Choose Line Spacing on the Format menu. The Line Spacing dialog box appears.

3 Enter a new value from 0.25 through 124 spaces (sp) in increments of hundredths of a line space.

4 Click OK.

Specify Extra Leading Before and After Paragraphs

1 Click anywhere in a paragraph, or highlight the paragraphs you want to change.

2 Choose Line Spacing on the Format menu.

3 In the Line Spacing dialog box, enter any value from 0 through 1488 points (pt) or between 0 and 124 spaces (sp) in the Before Paragraphs and After Paragraphs text boxes.

4 Click OK if you like the effect as shown in the Sample area.

Using Tabs

Tabs are useful if you want to align several items in column-and-row format or space several words evenly across a wide column. By default, Publisher places tab stops at 0.5-inch intervals. Use the Tabs dialog box to alter those settings.

When not to use tabs.
You should never use the Tabs command to indent the first line of a paragraph. If you subsequently modify your design, you'll have to manually edit each paragraph. Use the Indents And Lists dialog box instead. It lets you modify indents globally.

Consider using the Table tool to format rows and columns. The Table tool, which can format text into rows and columns, is often easier to use than the Tabs command. Adding or deleting text from a table does not alter the row and column alignment. However, adding or deleting tabbed text can misalign text elements.

Identify tab markers.
Publisher always identifies the alignment associated with a tab marker.

Left aligned tab   Center aligned tab

Right aligned tab   Decimal aligned tab

Set and Delete Tabs in the Tabs Dialog Box

1 Click in any paragraph or highlight the paragraphs for which you want to set tabs.

2 Choose Tabs from the Format menu. The Tabs dialog box appears.

3 To add a tab stop, type the measurement of the distance between the left margin of the text frame and the alignment position of the tab, and then click the Set button. When you click the Set button, the new tab setting is included in the Tab Positions list box.

5 Select one of the four alignment options: Left, Center, Right, or Decimal.

6 Select a leader character (which fills the space between the point at which you press the Tab key and the tab stop).

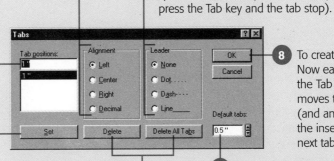

8 To create the tabs, click OK. Now each time you press the Tab key, Publisher moves the insertion point (and any text to the right of the insertion point) to the next tab stop.

7 Change the default tab setting for the current text frame by entering a value in the Default Tabs text box. For example, if you enter a value of *1* inch, Publisher places tab stops at 1-inch intervals.

4 To delete a tab stop, select the tab from the Tab Positions list box and click Delete. Click Delete All Tabs to remove all the tabs that have been set for the selected paragraphs.

Indents and Tabs Ruler

Every time you create or select a text object, a special ruler appears on the horizontal ruler. You can set or modify indent and tab positions by clicking and dragging icons that appear on this ruler.

Which is a better tab format for aligning numbers: Right or Decimal? Both the Right and the Decimal alignment options in the Tabs dialog box work well for numerical data, provided that all the values have the same number of decimal places, such as currency. If, however, you are attempting to align values that do not contain the same number of decimal places, choose Decimal alignment. Doing so creates true columns of numbers where single digits, tens, hundreds, and thousands are aligned from line to line in the text block.

Can I use the indents and tabs ruler to change the alignment of a tab stop? No, but you can use the indents and tabs ruler to access the Tabs dialog box quickly. Double-click the tab marker whose alignment you want to change. The Tabs dialog box, in which you can specify the alignment and a leader character, appears.

Set Indents on the Ruler

1 Click in a paragraph or highlight the paragraphs for which you want to adjust indents. The indents and tabs ruler appears.

2 Drag any of the triangles to a new position on the ruler.

The upper left triangle controls the First Line indent.

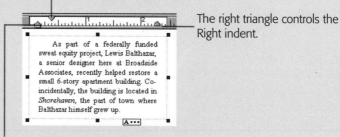

The right triangle controls the Right indent.

As part of a federally funded sweat equity project, Lewis Balthazar, a senior designer here at Broadside Associates, recently helped restore a small 6-story apartment building. Co-incidentally, the building is located in *Shorehaven,* the part of town where Balthazar himself grew up.

The lower left triangle controls the Left indent.

Set and Delete Tabs on the Ruler

1 Click in a paragraph or highlight the paragraphs for which you want to set tab stops.

2 Click the indents and tabs ruler where you want to place the tab stop. A tab marker, which looks like a bent line, appears on the ruler.

The default tab is left aligned and appears as a bent line.

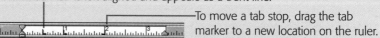

To move a tab stop, drag the tab marker to a new location on the ruler.

3 To remove a tab stop, drag the tab marker off the ruler.

Can I use a text style on one word in my document? You can't apply a text style to single words in a sentence or to particular characters within a text string. Using the Text Styles command always changes the entire paragraph.

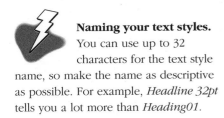

Naming your text styles. You can use up to 32 characters for the text style name, so make the name as descriptive as possible. For example, *Headline 32pt* tells you a lot more than *Heading01*.

Text Styles

When you want to apply the same formatting options to many paragraphs in your document, you can save time by creating a text style. A text style is a combination of formats that you name, save, and reuse. You can apply both character-level formats (such as font, point size, boldface, italics, and color) and paragraph-level formats (such as indents, alignment, line spacing, tabs, and bullets) with a single mouse click. In addition, text styles guarantee consistency throughout a long document.

Creating and Applying Text Styles

You can create text styles in one of two ways:

- By example. If you aren't sure how to format a particular paragraph, experiment with sample text. After you've created a good-looking paragraph, you can create a text style based on it.

- From scratch. If you know how to define the features of your paragraph, you can create a text style from scratch in the Text Style dialog box. You don't need to select a paragraph before you start.

Once you've created a text style, you can apply it to any of the paragraphs in your document.

Create a Text Style by Example

1. Format the paragraph using Publisher's standard tools.

2. Click inside the paragraph.

3. Click in the Style drop-down text box to highlight its contents. The Style drop-down list is located on the left end of the Format toolbar.

4. Type a new style name, and then press Enter. The Create Style By Example dialog box appears.

5. In the Create Style By Example dialog box, click OK to create the new text style.

Text Formats

Copy formatting from one object to another. Publisher gives you three ways to copy formatting attributes or text styles from one object to another:

- Format Painter. Select the text block whose style you want to copy. Click the Format Painter icon on the Standard toolbar, and then select the text you want to reformat. Alternatively, click a blank area in the text frame to reformat all the text in the frame.

- Right drag. Using the right mouse button, drag one text object over another text object. Then click the Apply Formatting Here command on the shortcut menu.

- Keyboard shortcuts. To copy formats, press Ctrl-Shift-C. To paste formats, press Ctrl-Shift-V.

Create a Text Style from Scratch

1 Choose Text Style on the Format menu. The Text Style dialog box appears.

2 In the Click To area, choose Create A New Style. The Create New Style dialog box appears.

3 In the Enter New Style Name text box, type a new name.

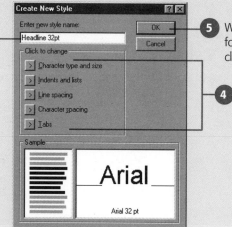

5 When you have changed the text formatting options to your liking, click OK to create the style.

4 Select one of these five options. Publisher presents you with the standard text and paragraph formatting dialog boxes.

6 Click Close in the Text Style dialog box.

Apply Text Styles

1 Click in a paragraph or highlight the paragraphs to which you want the style to apply.

2 Open the Style drop-down list box on the Format toolbar and select a style name.

Can I return a paragraph to the previously defined text style? Yes. After you select the paragraph and change its formatting, open the Style drop-down list box and click the name of the style you want to reapply. In the Change Or Apply Style dialog box that appears, select the Return The Selection To The Original Formatting Of The Style? option. Click OK.

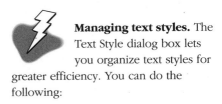

Managing text styles. The Text Style dialog box lets you organize text styles for greater efficiency. You can do the following:

@ Delete styles you no longer use.

@ Rename styles so that related styles are grouped together on the Style drop-down list box. Because Publisher arranges style names alphabetically, styles such as Table Text and Table Titles appear next to each other.

Modifying Existing Text Styles

Even after you've created a style and applied it to your text, you can still modify it. When you modify an existing text style, you make global formatting changes to all paragraphs associated with that style. You can modify an existing style by example or by using the Text Style dialog box.

Modify Existing Text Styles by Example

1 Highlight the paragraph whose style you want to change.

2 Change the formatting to your satisfaction.

3 Open the Style drop-down list box. Click the style that is currently assigned to the paragraph. The Change Or Apply Style dialog box appears.

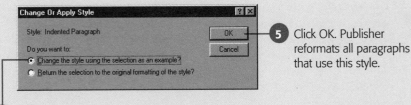

5 Click OK. Publisher reformats all paragraphs that use this style.

4 Click the first option to modify the style based on the currently selected paragraph.

Modify Existing Text Styles by Using the Text Style Dialog Box

1 Choose Text Style on the Format menu. The Text Style dialog box appears.

2 In the Choose A Style list box, select the name of the style you want to modify.

3 In the Click To area, select Change This Style. The Change Style Dialog box appears.

4 Use the option buttons—Character Type And Size, Indents And Lists, Line Spacing, Character Spacing, and Tabs—to access the standard text formatting dialog boxes.

5 When you have modified the text formatting options to your satisfaction, click OK.

6 Click Close in the Text Style dialog box to return to your document.

Text Formats

How does Publisher handle text styles when I insert a text file into a publication? If the text file you insert does not contain formatting information, Publisher assigns the Normal text style, which is defined as Times New Roman, 10 points, left-aligned. If the text file you insert does contain formatting information, and if Publisher can read the word processing file in its native format, Publisher tries to duplicate the formatting.

Import styles from a word processing file to reconcile duplicate text style names.

If you create text styles in a Publisher document, and subsequently insert a word processing file that includes duplicate text style names with different formatting attributes, you will produce a conflict. Publisher does not reconcile this conflict well, often producing text with the right style name but the wrong formatting attributes.

There is a solution. Before you insert the text itself, use the Import New Styles button to bring the style names from the word processing document into your Publisher document. If you explicitly import the style names, Publisher alerts you to the conflict and allows you to either keep the current definition of the text style or to accept the new definition from the word processing file.

Importing Styles from Other Documents

You can get more value from the styles you've created for one Publisher publication by using them in other Publisher documents. You can also import and use styles you've created in your word processing application if Publisher can read the word processing format in its native form.

Import a Text Style

1 Open the Format menu and choose Text Style.

2 In the Text Style dialog box, choose Import New Styles. The Import Styles dialog box appears.

3 Open the Files Of Type drop-down list box and select any text file type. The default is Publisher's format.

4 Use the Look In drop-down list box and the Files list box to locate the file.

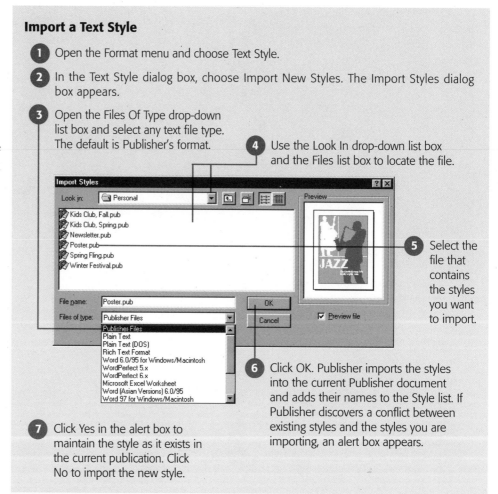

5 Select the file that contains the styles you want to import.

6 Click OK. Publisher imports the styles into the current Publisher document and adds their names to the Style list. If Publisher discovers a conflict between existing styles and the styles you are importing, an alert box appears.

7 Click Yes in the alert box to maintain the style as it exists in the current publication. Click No to import the new style.

WordArt Tool

With Microsoft Publisher's WordArt tool, you can enhance the appearance of text by creating special effects that are not available when you work with ordinary text objects. You can combine and control these effects to create a wide variety of display type designs, ranging from sophisticated logos to whimsical headlines. You can create WordArt objects using either the WordArt 3.2 tool found in Publisher's toolbar or the WordArt tool found in Microsoft Draw 98.

 Can I edit objects created with earlier versions of WordArt? Yes, you can transform WordArt 1.0 to WordArt 3.2. Select the WordArt object, on the Edit menu choose Convert from the Microsoft WordArt 3.2 Object command's cascading menu. WordArt 1.0 fonts will be converted to the closest matching TrueType fonts.

 For more information about changing the appearance of normal text, see Chapter 6. For more information about drawing a frame, see Chapter 1. Microsoft Draw is covered in Appendix A.

Entering Text into WordArt Frames

WordArt frames are similar—but not identical—to Publisher's normal text frames. One difference is that you must draw a WordArt frame and then use a special dialog box to enter text.

Enter Text into a WordArt Frame

1 Click the WordArt tool, shown in the following illustration, and draw a frame. The WordArt toolbar and dialog box appear.

How is entering text into a WordArt frame different from entering text into a normal text frame? When you work with a WordArt frame, you must enter your text manually in the special dialog box provided. Many of the automated functions associated with ordinary text simply are not available. A normal text frame can wrap a text block onto multiple lines or around another object. But in WordArt, you must manually break a multiple-line text block by pressing the Enter key, and text wrap is not an option.

You cannot insert text from a word processing file into a WordArt frame. You cannot spell check a WordArt object. And the normal commands found on the Edit menu to cut, copy, and paste text are unavailable. (Although the keyboard shortcuts for cut, copy, and paste still work.) Finally, you cannot mix different fonts within a WordArt frame. If, for example, you want to add a special character to the text, you will not have the option of choosing a different typeface in the Insert Symbol dialog box.

Enter Text into a WordArt Frame *(continued)*

2 Type your display copy here.

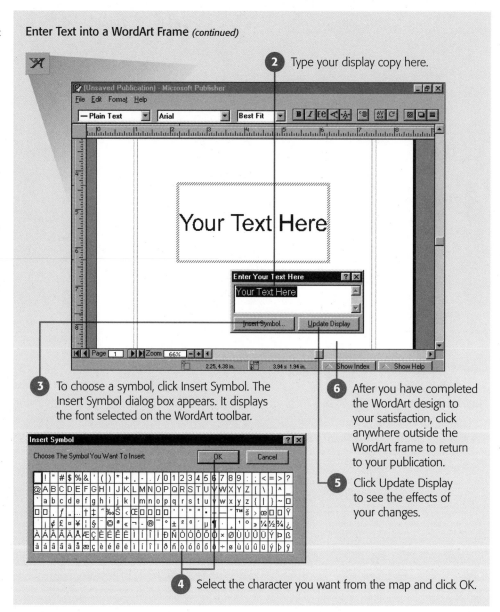

3 To choose a symbol, click Insert Symbol. The Insert Symbol dialog box appears. It displays the font selected on the WordArt toolbar.

6 After you have completed the WordArt design to your satisfaction, click anywhere outside the WordArt frame to return to your publication.

5 Click Update Display to see the effects of your changes.

4 Select the character you want from the map and click OK.

Why can't I see all the fonts installed on my system when I open the Font drop-down list box? WordArt uses only TrueType fonts, so only TrueType fonts appear in WordArt's Font drop-down list. Fixed-size fonts or Adobe Type 1 fonts cannot be accessed in WordArt.

Why does Publisher try to resize the WordArt frame when I specify a large point size for my text? If you choose a point size that is too large for the current dimensions of the WordArt frame, Publisher displays an alert box asking if you want to enlarge the WordArt frame. Click Yes to enlarge the frame. If you click No, you must either make the text smaller by choosing a smaller point size or resize the WordArt frame manually.

Choosing a Font and Point Size for WordArt

Publisher automatically installs numerous TrueType fonts on your computer system, any of which you can select. TrueType fonts that other software applications have installed on your computer are also available to you.

You can apply only one font and one size to all the text in each WordArt frame. If you need to use a second font or to mix types of different sizes, create a separate WordArt frame for the text. You can assign a specific point size to WordArt text, or you can use WordArt's powerful Best Fit option, which generates the best type size to fit your frame.

Select a Font and Size for WordArt Text

1 If the WordArt toolbar and dialog box are not active, double-click the WordArt object to invoke them.

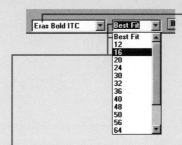

2 Open the Font drop-down list box from the toolbar and select a font name.

3 Specify a size for the text by using one of the following three procedures:

- Open the Font Size drop-down list box and select a numerical value from the list.

- Highlight the contents of the Font Size drop-down list box and type a size from 6 through 500 points in 1-point increments, and then press Enter.

- Select Best Fit. Now the WordArt frame functions like a picture frame. The text shrinks or grows to fit the frame when you resize the frame.

Shape and edit WordArt text to fit your design. To create successful WordArt designs, you must choose the most appropriate shape for your text—or edit your text so that it works with a particular shape. For example, to make a successful design for the button shown in the following illustration, you must enter the words out of order (*Kellerman, 1999, For Congress*) and then separate them with a hard return.

Some WordArt shapes don't work well with long phrases. In the next example, the Inflate shape distorts the letters of *Broadside Associates*. Shortening the phrase to a single word, or breaking it into two lines (shown here), avoids a cramped look.

Text Shaping Options

The single most powerful aspect of WordArt is its capability to manipulate the outlines of a font. The following illustrations demonstrate a few of the shapes you can create with WordArt.

Align text along wavy lines

Create arched or circular text

Squeeze and slant text

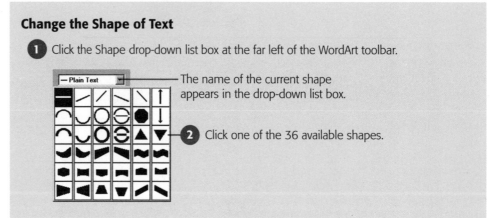

Change the Shape of Text

1. Click the Shape drop-down list box at the far left of the WordArt toolbar.

The name of the current shape appears in the drop-down list box.

2. Click one of the 36 available shapes.

Customizing the Text Shape with Special Effects

You can fine-tune any of the WordArt shapes by clicking the Special Effects button on the WordArt toolbar and changing the settings in the Special Effects dialog box. This dialog box presents you with different effects, which can include rotation, arc angle, and slider (or strength) values, depending on the shape you choose for your text.

How is the rotation effect in WordArt different from Publisher's object rotation feature? When you use the WordArt rotation effect, text is rotated *within* the frame. In addition, the WordArt rotation effect can simulate three-dimensional rotations for certain shapes, such as the Wave 1 shape shown here.

Publisher's object rotation feature, on the other hand, rotates an entire object—frame and all—and always rotates an object in two-dimensional space.

Twisted and Rotated

Change the Rotation and Angle of a Shape

1 Click the Special Effects button. If your WordArt follows a straight line or fills a shape, the following dialog box appears.

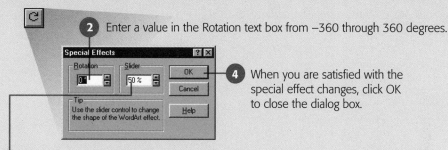

2 Enter a value in the Rotation text box from −360 through 360 degrees.

4 When you are satisfied with the special effect changes, click OK to close the dialog box.

3 Enter a value from 0 through 100 percent in the Slider text box. The slider effect decreases or increases the intensity of a shape effect. Changing the value will make the angles of individual letters more or less acute, or will flatten or exaggerate the arc of a curve.

Change the Rotation and Curve of Arced or Circular WordArt Text

1 Click the Special Effects button. If your WordArt text follows an arc or a circle, the following dialog box appears.

2 Enter a new value in the Arc Angle text box. Arc-shaped text can be modified to have a value from 0 through 180 degrees. Text in a circle can be modified to have a value from 0 through 360 degrees.

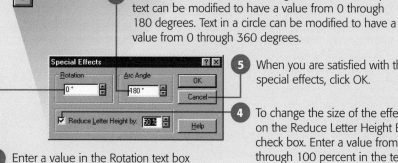

5 When you are satisfied with the special effects, click OK.

4 To change the size of the effect, turn on the Reduce Letter Height By check box. Enter a value from 0 through 100 percent in the text box.

3 Enter a value in the Rotation text box from −360 through 360 degrees.

WordArt effects can be toggled on and off. All the effects on the WordArt toolbar are applied to the WordArt object when the button is depressed. To remove the effect, simply click the button a second time.

Letterspacing (also known as character spacing) and the uses for tracking and kerning are explained in Chapter 6.

Formatting Options: Toolbar Button Effects

When the WordArt toolbar appears, you can change the overall appearance of your text by simply clicking the appropriate toolbar button. The effects can range from standard font styles that add emphasis to zany transformations, as illustrated in the following table.

Click this button...	To create this effect...	Sample text
B	Boldface text	**Broadside**
I	Italic text	*Broadside*
Ee	Uppercase and lowercase letters of the same height	Broadside
◁	Vertically stacked (top to bottom) text	B R O A D S I D E
A	Characters that stretch both vertically and horizontally to fill the boundaries of the WordArt frame	Broadside

Letterspacing and Alignment Controls

There are times when the success of a special effect depends entirely on small details such as letterspacing and alignment. Publisher gives you two controls to fine-tune them.

Tap the power of letter-spacing. Letterspacing is a powerful formatting feature. It can help you fit your text to a design. For example, it is especially crucial when you are wrapping text around a circle or arc. Increasing the letterspacing can prevent crashing letters. Decreasing the letterspacing can help you add artistic effects, such as overlapping letters.

Very Loose letterspacing

Very Tight letterspacing

What is the difference between the Stretch button and the Stretch Justify alignment option? The Stretch button stretches letters both horizontally and vertically to fill the boundaries of the WordArt frame. The Stretch Justify option stretches letters only horizontally. The following illustration gives a comparison.

BROADSIDE— Stretch

BROADSIDE— Stretch Justify

Modify Letterspacing

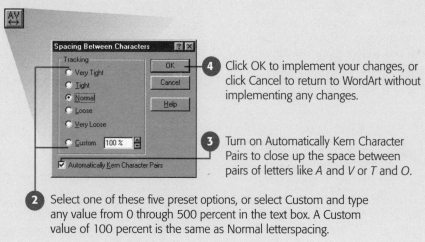

1 Click the Spacing Between Characters button. The Spacing Between Characters dialog box appears.

4 Click OK to implement your changes, or click Cancel to return to WordArt without implementing any changes.

3 Turn on Automatically Kern Character Pairs to close up the space between pairs of letters like *A* and *V* or *T* and *O*.

2 Select one of these five preset options, or select Custom and type any value from 0 through 500 percent in the text box. A Custom value of 100 percent is the same as Normal letterspacing.

Align Letters in a WordArt Frame

1 Click the Alignment button to open a drop-down list box of six options.

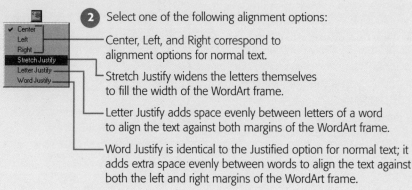

2 Select one of the following alignment options:

Center, Left, and Right correspond to alignment options for normal text.

Stretch Justify widens the letters themselves to fill the width of the WordArt frame.

Letter Justify adds space evenly between letters of a word to align the text against both margins of the WordArt frame.

Word Justify is identical to the Justified option for normal text; it adds extra space evenly between words to align the text against both the left and right margins of the WordArt frame.

Why can't I see a fill pattern? To see a fill pattern, you must choose different colors for the foreground and background. Although the terminology is identical, the foreground and background colors you choose in the Shading dialog box are not in any way related to the foreground and background pages in your document.

Fill a WordArt object with a custom color, tint, or shade. Normally you can fill a WordArt object with one of 35 standard colors. To fill a WordArt object with a customized color, tint, or shade, you must exit WordArt (by clicking outside the WordArt frame), select the WordArt frame, and then choose the Recolor Object command on the Format menu.

The WordArt Object will appear in the new color in the Publisher document on screen and at print time. However, if you double-click the WordArt object to edit it, the screen display will revert to the original (incorrect) color until you exit WordArt again.

Alternatively, you can use the WordArt tool found in Draw, which offers much more robust formatting features than Publisher's WordArt tool.

Color, Fill Pattern, Shadow, and Letter Outline Options

You can create dramatic and playful WordArt text designs using color, fill pattern, shadow, and letter outline options. You might find these WordArt options especially useful for short text displays, such as store signage.

You can assign colors and fill patterns to WordArt text.

You can alter the color and thickness of each letter's outline (border) without affecting its fill color.

You can apply three-dimensional shadows to all letters in the WordArt frame.

Shade WordArt Text by Choosing a Color and a Fill Pattern

1 Click the Shading button. The Shading dialog box appears.

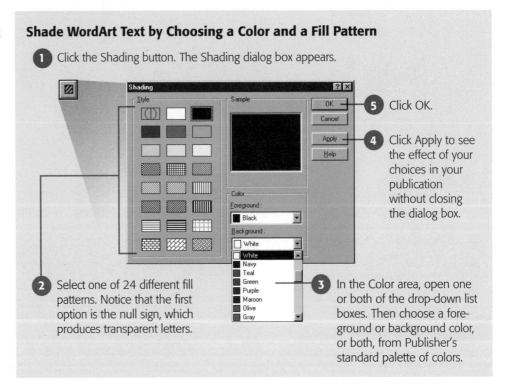

5 Click OK.

4 Click Apply to see the effect of your choices in your publication without closing the dialog box.

2 Select one of 24 different fill patterns. Notice that the first option is the null sign, which produces transparent letters.

3 In the Color area, open one or both of the drop-down list boxes. Then choose a foreground or background color, or both, from Publisher's standard palette of colors.

The Recolor Object command is explained in Chapter 10. For more information about tints and shades, see Chapter 15. To learn about the WordArt tool in Draw, see Appendix A.

Is there a difference between the WordArt shadow and outline effects and the same effects applied to ordinary text? The WordArt tool gives you more formatting options than Publisher's normal text tool. For example, Publisher's Font dialog box lets you apply a simple drop-shadow to the individual letters in a normal text frame. In contrast, the WordArt tool lets you choose from seven different shadow effects, including simulated three-dimensional shadows.

In the same way, you can format normal text with an outline and a clear (or null) fill. But only the WordArt tool lets you change the thickness and color of the letter's outline independently of its fill color and pattern.

Why does the shadow appear around the WordArt frame instead of the individual letters? You have selected the WordArt frame by single-clicking the object. Double-click to invoke WordArt where you can edit the text and apply shadows to individual letters.

Change the Letter Outlines

1 Click the Border button. The Border dialog box appears.

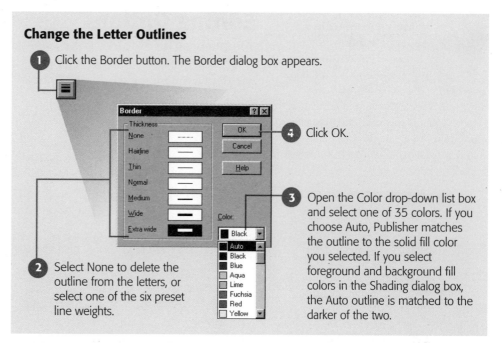

4 Click OK.

2 Select None to delete the outline from the letters, or select one of the six preset line weights.

3 Open the Color drop-down list box and select one of 35 colors. If you choose Auto, Publisher matches the outline to the solid fill color you selected. If you select foreground and background fill colors in the Shading dialog box, the Auto outline is matched to the darker of the two.

Create a Shadow

1 Click the Shadow button. The Shadow dialog box appears.

2 Choose a shadow option. The No Shadow option on the far left removes shadows from the WordArt text.

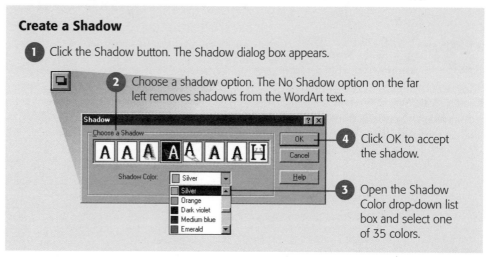

4 Click OK to accept the shadow.

3 Open the Shadow Color drop-down list box and select one of 35 colors.

Running WordArt in a separate window. If you choose Microsoft WordArt 3.2 Object from the Edit menu and then select Open, the WordArt functions appear in a separate window instead of on a toolbar, as shown in the following illustration. Which method you choose is purely a matter of preference and has no impact on performance.

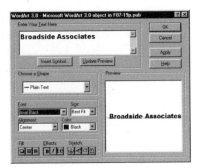

Additional formatting options for WordArt frames. Though they don't appear on the WordArt toolbar, you can use the Scale Object, Shadow, and Size and Position commands (found on the Format menu) to alter a WordArt frame.

Editing Options

You can open the WordArt toolbar and the Enter Your Text Here dialog box in a very direct manner; simply double-click an existing WordArt object. You can also use the Edit menu to access the WordArt functions.

Edit Text and Formatting

1 Select a WordArt frame.

2 Open the Edit menu and select Microsoft WordArt 3.2 Object.

3 Choose Edit on the cascading menu. The Enter Your Text Here dialog box and the WordArt toolbar appear. The toolbar displays the current formatting attributes for the selected object.

4 Type new text and/or choose new formatting options.

5 Click anywhere outside the WordArt frame to accept the changes and return to your publication.

Formatting WordArt Frames

Publisher treats the text within a WordArt frame differently than it treats the frame itself. To alter the appearance of the WordArt frame itself (as opposed to the text it contains), you must single-click the object. Standard frame formatting options then appear on the Format toolbar, as shown in the following illustration.

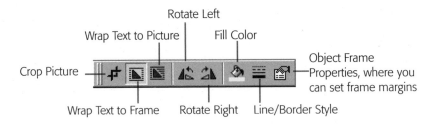

Table Tool

When you are dealing with lots of small, interrelated pieces of information, a table is often the best way to organize your text. You can change the size and shape of a table, and easily rearrange the information it contains. Altering the appearance of a table is as simple as assigning a different text format, creating borders, picking fill colors and effects, or adding a shadow. Tables are very flexible and can be used to create entire documents, such as a price sheet, résumé, or a business form. As a table of contents, index, schedule, or reply coupon, a table can also serve as a partial-page elements within a larger design.

Table Components: Rows, Columns, and Cells

A single table can contain as many as 128 rows, 128 columns, and thousands of individual cells. You can control the table structure with functions built into the table's borders and with commands on the Table menu. Whenever you select a table, Microsoft Publisher displays special row and column buttons in addition to the standard object selection handles. Use them to highlight portions of the table—or the entire table—efficiently.

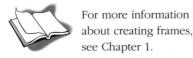

For more information about creating frames, see Chapter 1.

Create a Table

1 Click the Table tool and draw a table frame. The Create Table dialog box appears.

2 Enter a value from 1 through 128 in the Number Of Rows text box.

3 Enter a value from 1 through 128 in the Number Of Columns text box.

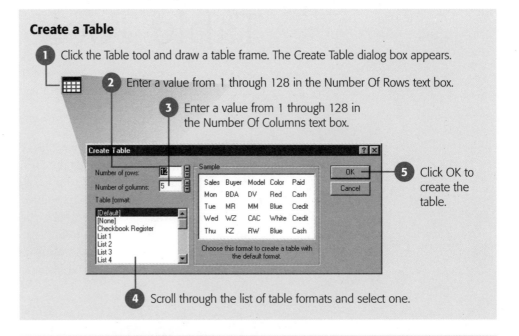

5 Click OK to create the table.

4 Scroll through the list of table formats and select one.

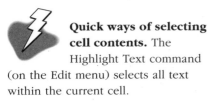

Quick ways of selecting cell contents. The Highlight Text command (on the Edit menu) selects all text within the current cell.

Select a Table, Rows, Columns, a Single Cell, or a Group of Adjacent Cells

1 Click anywhere within the table's boundaries to select it. The row and column buttons appear along the top and left side of the table.

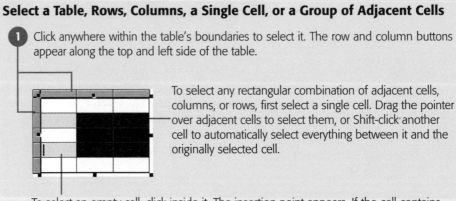

To select any rectangular combination of adjacent cells, columns, or rows, first select a single cell. Drag the pointer over adjacent cells to select them, or Shift-click another cell to automatically select everything between it and the originally selected cell.

To select an empty cell, click inside it. The insertion point appears. If the cell contains text, drag the I-beam pointer to select all or part of the contents of a cell.

How can I tell where one cell ends and another cell begins? A table normally displays gridlines showing the boundaries between the individual cells. The gridlines appear on screen to help you arrange elements, but they never print. If the gridlines don't appear on screen, choose Show Boundaries And Guides on the View menu. If you want to print lines between the columns and rows in a table, you must assign borders to the gridlines.

 For more information about Publisher's text editing features, see Chapter 5.

 Why does Publisher insert all my imported text into a single table cell? When you use the Text File command on the Insert menu to import text into a table, Publisher places the entire file into the current cell. In most cases, this isn't useful. If you want to preserve tabular material, don't use the Text File command; use the Clipboard as explained on pages 125 through 126.

Select a Table, Rows, Columns, a Single Cell, or a Group of Adjacent Cells *(continued)*

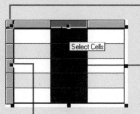

To select the contents of the entire table, click the table selector in the upper left corner of the frame.

To select an entire column in a table, position the pointer over the gray column selector at the top of the column. Click when the pointer changes to the Hand pointer.

Select Cells

To select an entire row in a table, position the pointer over the gray row selector directly to the left of the row. Click when the pointer changes to the Hand pointer.

Entering Text in a Table

When you first create a table, the upper left cell contains the insertion point, indicating that the cell is active. Text can be entered only in the active cell, but you can make any cell active by clicking it with the I-beam pointer. You can use any of the text editing commands, as if you were working in an ordinary text frame, to perform these tasks:

- Type normally.

- Import text from an external word processing file into the current cell.

- Cut, copy, and paste text via the Windows 95 Clipboard.

- Move and copy text from the current cell using the Drag-And-Drop feature.

- Fine-tune your copy with the Check Spelling, Auto Correct, Find, and Replace commands.

- You can also use special table commands to copy text into every cell in a selected range.

Table Tool

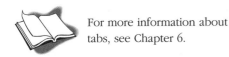

For more information about tabs, see Chapter 6.

Moving from Cell to Cell

Special key combinations help you navigate from cell to cell in a table, as explained in the following table:

How to Move Between and Within Table Cells	
To move...	**Press...**
To the next cell in a table	Tab
To the preceding cell	Shift-Tab
Forward one character (or to the next cell if there is no more text)	Right arrow key
Backward one character (or to the previous cell if there is no more text)	Left arrow key
Up one line or cell	Up arrow key
Down one line or cell	Down arrow key
To the next tab stop within a cell	Ctrl-Tab

When should I lock the table size? If the table *must* fit into a tight layout, turn off the Grow To Fit Text command to guarantee that the table won't interfere with other elements on the page. Be warned: unlike text frames, table cells do not alert you when the overflow area contains text. Therefore, you should try to lock a table's size only when you are satisfied with the content and formatting of your table. Otherwise, you could inadvertently print a publication that contains hidden table text in the overflow area.

For more information about table sizing, see pages 127 through 128.

Controlling How Text Behaves in Table Cells

Cells within a table automatically expand vertically to accommodate the text you type. To maintain alignment, Publisher increases the height (but not the width) of every cell in the current row.

To lock the table size and prevent Publisher from increasing row height, disable the Grow To Fit Text command (on the Table menu). Any text that doesn't fit into the current cell is placed in the invisible overflow area. To make text in the overflow area visible again, try these techniques:

@ Reduce the point size to fit more text into the current cell.

@ Edit the text to shorten your copy.

@ Make the cell larger by resizing the entire table, the column, or the row.

@ Unlock the table size by selecting the Grow To Fit Text command.

Inserting Identical Text in Cells

You can add the same piece of information to every cell in a selected range, which is useful when you need to repeat an identifying code or part number, as in catalogs or price sheets.

Repeat Text in a Range of Cells

Product	Contents	Item	Price
Lettuce, Apollo	2 gr.	#220-	$1.95
Lettuce, Bibb	2 gr.		$1.25
Lettuce, Brunia	3 gr.		$1.85
Lettuce, Oak Leaf	2 gr.		$1.75

1 Type the text you want to repeat in a cell.

2 Highlight the cell that contains the text, as well as the cells where you want to repeat the text.

3 Open the Table menu. Choose Fill Down to repeat the text in the selected area below the original cell, or choose Fill Right to repeat the text in the selected area to the right of the original cell.

Convert tabbed text into tables. Select a table before pasting tabbed text into a Publisher document. Each tabbed item will be pasted into a separate cell.

Why does the text I just imported into my table look so strange? When you import an external table or part of an external table, Publisher preserves its original formatting—which may be inconsistent with your existing table design. Use Publisher's text formatting features to reformat the inconsistent cells.

Importing a Table or Part of a Table from an External Source

Taking advantage of the Clipboard allows you to import a table or part of a table you've created in another application, such as Microsoft Excel, Microsoft Word, or Microsoft Works. You can either add the external table to an existing Publisher table, or you can create a completely new Publisher table from the external data. Publisher maintains the column and row structure by placing each individual table item in its own cell.

Import a Table or Part of a Table into an Existing Publisher Table

1 Open the application and then the file that contains the table you want to import.

2 Highlight the cells you want to copy.

Table Tool

Why did my original table data disappear when I pasted new data into the table? In all likelihood, you instructed Publisher to increase the size of the selection area in order to paste all the data on the Clipboard into the table. When you do so, Publisher imports data into as many adjacent cells as necessary to maintain the original row and column structure. Rather than inserting new cells, Publisher overwrites the contents of existing cells. To avoid losing important information by inadvertently pasting new data over old, be sure you've added the correct number of empty rows and columns to your table.

Import Excel worksheets. If you have installed a Microsoft product that shares the Excel Worksheet file filter, you can import a table in the Excel Worksheet format. You must have a text or table frame selected before you choose Text File from the Insert menu. Select Microsoft Excel Worksheet from the Files Of Type drop-down list box. In the Open Worksheet dialog box that appears, choose a specific worksheet within the file or a specific named range within a worksheet. When you click OK, Publisher creates a new table object that preserves the column and row structure of the original data.

Import a Table or Part of a Table into an Existing Publisher Table *(continued)*

3 Choose Copy on the Edit menu (or press Ctrl-C) to place the cells on the Clipboard.

4 Open the Publisher document that contains the table you want to edit.

5 Select the table. If you know how many cells the information on the Clipboard will occupy, highlight them. If not, select the first cell in which you want to insert information.

6 Choose Paste on the Edit menu (or press Ctrl-V) to add the data on the Clipboard to your Publisher table. If the data on the Clipboard is larger than the current selection, the following dialog box appears.

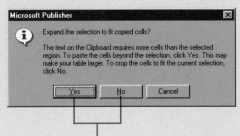

Click No to have Publisher truncate the data to fill only the highlighted cell or cells. Or click Yes to have Publisher increase the size of the selection area and paste all the data on the Clipboard into the table. If your table does not contain enough cells to hold the new data, Publisher adds sufficient rows or columns.

Create a New Publisher Table from an External Table

1 Open the application and then the file that contains the table you want to import.

2 Highlight the cells you want to copy.

3 Choose Copy on the Edit menu (or press Ctrl-C) to place the cells on the Clipboard.

4 Open your Publisher document.

5 Open the Edit menu and choose Paste or Paste Special. If you choose Paste, Publisher pastes the table into your publication as a new object and preserves the formatting of the original table. If you choose Paste Special, the following dialog box appears.

For more information about inserting text, see Chapter 5.

Can I use the Paste Special command to insert data from the Clipboard into an existing Publisher table? Yes. To insert data from the Clipboard into an existing table select the Paste option and then select either Table Cells With Cell Formatting or Table Cells Without Cell Formatting in the Paste Special dialog box.

Using the Paste Special command in this way is not recommended. It offers no benefits over the Paste command, and it requires several extra mouse clicks.

Can I create rows and columns of any size? You can easily increase the size of rows and columns in a table. The only limit is the size of your page. But columns cannot be smaller than 0.13 inch. And rows cannot be smaller than 0.24 inch or the point size of the text they contain.

Create a New Publisher Table from an External Table *(continued)*

6 Select Paste.

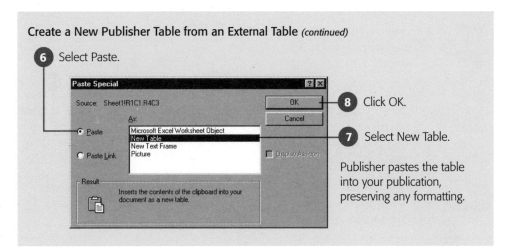

8 Click OK.

7 Select New Table.

Publisher pastes the table into your publication, preserving any formatting.

Resizing Tables and Table Components

Publisher offers you several different ways to change the size of a table. You can resize an entire table, resize individual rows and columns, and insert or delete rows and columns. You can even merge or divide cells to accommodate special information such as a table heading or minimum/maximum values.

When you resize an entire table, the dimensions of all the rows and columns are changed equally. To make specific changes to the height of a row or the width of a column, use the Adjust pointer.

Resize an Entire Table

1 Select the table you want to resize.

2 Position the pointer over one of the selection handles until the Resize pointer appears.

For more information about resizing objects in Publisher, see Chapter 3.

Resize an Entire Table *(continued)*

Product	Contents	Item	Price
Lettuce, Apollo	2 gr.	#220-01	$1.95
Lettuce, Bibb	2 gr.	#220-02	$1.25
Lettuce, Brunia	3 gr.	#220-03	$1.85
Lettuce, Oak Leaf	2 gr.	#220-04	$1.75

RESIZE

3 Drag the handle to a new location, either inside the table to decrease its size or outside the table to increase its size.

Change row or column size while maintaining the overall size of a table.

Using the Adjust pointer to resize rows and columns increases or decreases the size of the entire table. To resize a row or a column without changing the overall size of the table, hold down the Shift key as you drag the Adjust pointer. Notice that if you increase the size of a row or column, the adjacent row or column decreases by the same amount. If you decrease a row or column, the adjacent row or column increases by the same amount.

Resize Individual Rows and Columns

1 Select the table.

2 If you want to resize more than one row or column simultaneously, highlight the rows or columns by Shift-clicking the row or column selectors or by dragging the pointer across the row or column selectors.

3 Position the pointer on the gridline between two row or column selectors. The pointer changes to the Adjust pointer. Drag the Adjust pointer to a new position.

ADJUST

Product	Contents	Item	Price
Lettuce, Apollo	2 gr.	#220-01	$1.95
Lettuce, Bibb	2 gr.	#220-02	$1.25
Lettuce, Brunia	3 gr.	#220-03	$1.85
Lettuce, Oak Leaf	2 gr.	#220-04	$1.75

Notice that Publisher always shows you the new sizes of the rows or columns by displaying a dotted line. In this illustration, one column is being resized.

Insert Rows or Columns

1 Select the table and click a cell adjacent to where you want a new row or column to appear.

2 Open the Table menu and choose Insert Rows Or Columns. The Insert dialog box appears.

Insertion limits for table rows and columns. The number of rows and columns you can insert on a given page depends on the size of the cells in the row or column that contains the insertion point. The smaller the cells, the more rows or columns you can insert.

 Insert rows quickly. The fastest way to insert rows into a table is to press the Tab key when you reach the last cell in the table. Publisher adds a new row and also advances the insertion point.

 Why can't I use the Del or Backspace key to remove a table from my document? Tables are like a collection of miniature text frames, and like a text frame, the Del or Backspace key deletes text within a table cell, not the table itself. To remove a table from your document, select the table, and then select the Delete Object command on the Edit menu (or on the shortcut menu that appears when you right-click the table).

Insert Rows or Columns *(continued)*

3 Select Rows or Columns.

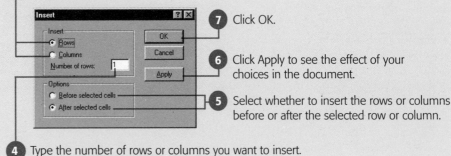

7 Click OK.

6 Click Apply to see the effect of your choices in the document.

5 Select whether to insert the rows or columns before or after the selected row or column.

4 Type the number of rows or columns you want to insert.

Delete Rows or Columns

1 Select the table.

2 Select the rows or columns you want to delete. Alternatively, select one or more cells in the rows or columns you want to delete.

3 Choose Delete Rows Or Delete Columns on the Table menu. The Delete dialog box appears.

4 Select Current Rows or Current Columns.

5 Click Apply to preview the effect in your document.

6 Click OK.

Can I merge cells vertically as well as horizontally? Yes, Publisher can merge two or more adjacent cells, regardless of whether the cells are arranged horizontally (in rows) or vertically (in columns).

Merge Cells in a Row

1 Select the table, and then select the cells you want to merge.

Ordering Information			
Product	**Contents**	**Item**	**Price**
Lettuce, Apollo	2 gr.	#220-01	$1.95
Lettuce, Bibb	2 gr.	#220-02	$1.25
Lettuce, Brunia	3 gr.		
Lettuce, Oak Leaf	2 gr.		

Ordering Information			
Product	**Contents**	**Item**	**Price**
Lettuce, Apollo	2 gr.	#220-01	$1.95
Lettuce, Bibb	2 gr.	#220-02	$1.25
Lettuce, Brunia	3 gr.	#220-03	$1.85
Lettuce, Oak Leaf	2 gr.	#220-04	$1.75

2 Open the Table menu and choose Merge Cells. One long horizontal cell is created.

Split a Merged Cell

1 Select the merged cell.

2 Open the Table menu and choose Split Cells. The merged cell is split according to the existing row and column structure.

Insert Cell Diagonals

1 Select a cell, a range of cells, a column, or a row where you want to insert diagonal divisions.

2 Choose Cell Diagonals on the Table menu.

Insert Cell Diagonals *(continued)*

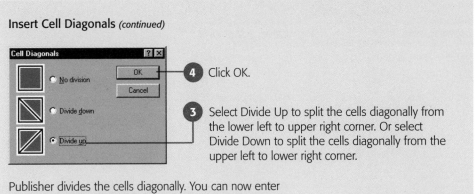

4 Click OK.

3 Select Divide Up to split the cells diagonally from the lower left to upper right corner. Or select Divide Down to split the cells diagonally from the upper left to lower right corner.

Publisher divides the cells diagonally. You can now enter discrete information into each half of the divided cells.

Remove Cell Diagonals

1 Select the cell, range of cells, column, or row where you want to remove diagonal divisions.

2 Choose Cell Diagonals on the Table menu.

3 In the Cell Diagonals dialog box, select No Division.

4 Click OK.

Formatting Tables and Table Components

You can change the appearance of a table by assigning formatting attributes. All of Publisher's formatting attributes can be applied to the entire table. Except for BorderArt and Shadow, all formatting attributes can also be applied to selected rows and columns or to individually selected cells. There are several ways to format the different table elements, as the following table describes.

Methods of Formatting Tables

Table Element	Formatting Method	Description
All table components	AutoFormat command on the Table menu	AutoFormat provides a collection of predefined table styles that include attributes such as borders; fill colors, tints, and shades; patterns; and text alignment. Except for the Default option, you cannot redefine the AutoFormat table styles. Nor can you create your own table formats and save them as AutoFormat options. But you can choose to apply only certain attributes contained in an AutoFormat table style.
Table text	Format toolbar, which is presented at the top of the work area when you select a table, and commands on the Format menu	Table text is identical to the text in regular text frames. You can apply both character-level and paragraph-level formats, as well as defined text styles. You can format text in the entire table or in selected rows, columns, or cells.
Cell margin (the amount of space between the text and the boundaries of each cell)	Table Cell Properties button on the Format toolbar, or the Table Cell Properties command on the Format menu	Allows you to specify left, right, top, and bottom margins.
Borders	Line/Border Style button on the Format toolbar, or Line/Border Style command on the Format menu	You can choose a predefined border or create a customized border for an entire table or for selected cells. You can add a decorative border to the perimeter of the entire table by selecting the BorderArt tab in the Border Style dialog box.
Shadow	Shadow command on the Format menu	You can add a shadow to the perimeter of the table.
The background of the entire table, rows, columns, range of selected cells, or an individual cell	Fill Color button on the Format toolbar, or Fill Color command on the Format menu	You can fill a table or any component with colors, tints, shades, patterns, and gradients. However, you can achieve the full transition from the Base Color to Color 1 in a gradient only when the gradient is applied to the entire table.

Select a Predefined Table Format

1 Select the table.

2 Choose Table Auto Format on the Table menu. The Auto Format dialog box appears.

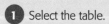

Why doesn't the typeface change when I use AutoFormat? AutoFormat changes font styles, such as boldface and italics, but does not change the typeface used in a table. You must change the typeface using the Format toolbar or the Font command on the Format menu.

For more information about templates, see Chapter 14.

Copy formatting from one table to another. You can quickly copy select formatting attributes to other tables by using the Format Painter on the standard toolbar. To copy fill color, border style, shadow, and table cell margins, select the table containing the formatting you want to duplicate. Click the Format Painter icon, and then highlight all the cells in the table to which you want to copy the formatting.

To copy text formats, highlight the text whose formatting you want to duplicate. Click the Format Painter icon, and then highlight all the cells in the table to which you want to copy the text formatting.

Select a Predefined Table Format *(continued)*

3 Select one of the 23 table formats.

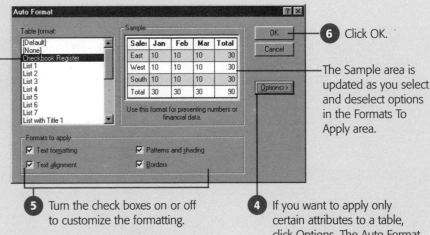

6 Click OK.

The Sample area is updated as you select and deselect options in the Formats To Apply area.

5 Turn the check boxes on or off to customize the formatting.

4 If you want to apply only certain attributes to a table, click Options. The Auto Format dialog box expands, revealing the Formats To Apply area.

Change Frame Attributes and Cell Margins for the Default Table Format

1 Select the Table tool, but don't create a table.

2 Select the new formatting attributes you want for the fill color, border style, shadow, and table cell margins.

3 Draw a new table frame.

4 Choose the Default table format in the Create Table dialog box that appears.

5 Click OK to create a table with the new default format.

6 Save the document to disk as a publication file or as a template. The new default settings will be applied whenever you create a table in this document or in documents based on it.

Quick Access to the Table Cell Properties dialog box.
You can open the Table Cell Properties dialog box by clicking the icon shown below on the Format toolbar.

Adjust Cell Margins

1 Select all or some of the cells in the table.

2 Choose Table Cell Properties on the Format menu. The Table Cell Properties dialog box appears.

3 Enter any value from 0 through 16 inches for the Left, Right, Top, and Bottom margins.

4 Click OK.

Add Predefined Borders to a Table, Row, Column, Range of Cells, or Individual Cell

1 Select the element that will have a border: the entire table, a row, a column, a range of cells, or an individual cell.

2 Click the Line/Border Style button on the Format toolbar, or click the Line/Border Style command on the Format menu.

3 Choose one of four predefined line weights: hairline, 1 point, 2 points, or 4 points, from the cascading menu. Publisher applies the border to the perimeter of the selected area.

Customize Borders of a Table, Row, Column, Range of Cells, or Individual Cell

1 Select the element whose border you want to customize: the entire table, a row, a column, a range of cells, or an individual cell.

See an accurate preview of the border style. The Select A Side preview area shows you only four cells. However, it is an accurate representation of the border style you have created because it can display the combination of line weights and colors that you have applied to the interior and perimeter lines of your table, as shown below.

Use BorderArt instead of line borders. Click the BorderArt tab in the Border Style dialog box to add one of more than 150 decorative borders to the perimeter of a table (but not to the interior gridlines within the table). Choose an appropriate BorderArt pattern for your table. For example, if you are using a table to create a reply coupon, select the Coupon Cutout Dashes (or Coupon Cutout Dots) to indicate that the form should be separated from the page before it is returned to you.

For more information about BorderArt, see Chapter 9.

Customize Borders of a Table, Row, Column, Range of Cells, or Individual Cell (continued)

2 Click the Line/Border Style button on the Format toolbar, or select the Line/Border Style command on the Format menu and choose More Styles from the cascading menu. The Border Style dialog box appears.

3 Select the Line Border tab.

4 Select the border options you want.

Select one of the predefined line weights, or enter any value from 0 through 127 points, in 0.25-point increments.

Publisher indicates which sides are selected by displaying triangles at either end of each selected line.

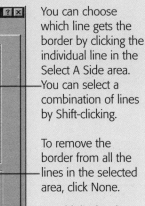

You can choose which line gets the border by clicking the individual line in the Select A Side area. You can select a combination of lines by Shift-clicking.

To remove the border from all the lines in the selected area, click None.

To add the border to the perimeter of the selected area, click Box.

Open the Color drop-down list box to select one of the available colors, tints, or shades.

To add the border to all the lines in the selected area— all four sides plus column and row divisions—click Grid.

5 Click Apply to preview the table with the border options you've selected. Click OK to implement your choices.

Table Tool

Add a Shadow to a Table

1 Select the table.

2 Select the Shadow command on the Format menu.

For more information about Publisher's color capabilities, see Chapter 15.

Fill a Table, Row, Column, Range of Cells, or Individual Cell with a Color or Fill Effect

1 Select the element you want to fill: the entire table, a row, a column, a range of consecutive cells, or an individual cell.

2 Click the Fill Color button on the Format toolbar, or choose the Fill Color command on the Format menu.

3 Choose one of the available colors, tints, shades, patterns, or gradient options.

Drawing Tools

You can draw a wide variety of shapes with Publisher's four drawing tools. These tools are not intended for complex illustrations, but you can create schematic drawings such as flow charts and symbols, or decorative elements such as backgrounds and borders quite effectively.

Lines, Boxes, Circles, and Custom Shapes

The drawing tools are located on the Objects toolbar. They are all easy to use: once a tool is activated, all you have to do is click and drag the Crossbar pointer in the workspace to create shapes.

For more information about creating objects, see Chapter 2.

You can increase the accuracy of your drawings by pressing special keys as you create shapes. The Shift key enables you to draw horizontal, vertical, and 45-degree lines and to draw perfect squares and circles. The Ctrl key allows you to draw an object from its center out. This method is especially useful when you want to draw multiple objects with a common center.

In what direction should I drag the pointer? When drawing a line, you can drag the pointer horizontally, vertically, or at any angle. For a two-dimensional shape, such as a circle or a rectangle, you must drag the pointer diagonally. However, given that restriction, you can drag in any direction. Typically you will drag from the upper left to the lower right. But if you are attempting to position an object as you draw it, you can drag from the lower right to the upper left, the upper right to the lower left, or the lower left to the upper right, as shown below.

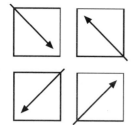

The arrow indicates the drag direction.

Draw a Shape

1 Select the Line, Oval, Rectangle, or Custom Shapes tool.

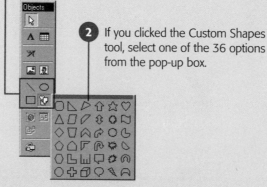

2 If you clicked the Custom Shapes tool, select one of the 36 options from the pop-up box.

3 Position the Crossbar pointer where you want the first corner of the object to begin.

4 Click and drag the pointer until you are satisfied with the size and shape of the object. Release the mouse button.

Create a Straight Line, Perfect Square, True Circle, or Proportional Shape Using the Shift Key

1 Select the drawing tool you want to use.

2 Hold down the Shift key.

3 Click and drag the Crossbar pointer to draw the object. Because you are holding down the Shift key, the tools perform in the following ways:

- The Line tool draws perfectly horizontal, vertical, or 45-degree diagonal lines.
- The Box tool draws perfect squares.
- The Oval tool draws perfect circles.
- The Custom Shapes tool draws the selected object with its original proportions.

4 Release the mouse button before you release the Shift key.

Other uses for the Shift and Ctrl keys. You can use the Shift and Ctrl keys alone or in combination when you create, re-size, or move text frames, picture frames, WordArt frames, and drawn shapes.

Use the Shift key to make any of the frames you draw of equal width and height, and use the Ctrl key to begin drawing any frame from its center. You can also use the Shift key to constrain the movement of an object to the horizontal or vertical axis. That is, if you want to realign an object in only one direction, you can move the object either up and down or from side to side. Finally, if you hold down the Ctrl key as you move an object, you will create a duplicate of the object, leaving the original object in its current location.

Center an Object Using the Ctrl Key

1 Click the tool you want to use.

2 Hold down the Ctrl key.

3 Position the Crossbar pointer where you want the object's center to be. Click and drag the pointer to draw the object.

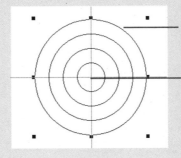

This series of perfectly round and concentric circles was drawn while holding down the Ctrl and Shift keys simultaneously.

Each circle was started from the same center (the coordinates where the guidelines intersect).

Changing the Shape of Drawn Objects

You can alter the shape of many of the objects created with the Custom Shapes tool.

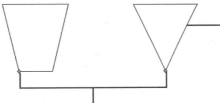

You can change the shape of arrows, create segments of a pie, and turn trapezoids into triangles (as shown here).

The Adjust handle, which looks like a gray diamond, appears at a vertex when you draw or select certain custom shapes.

Some objects contain two Adjust handles. Each
handle controls the object's shape in a different way.

If you manipulate the
right Adjust handle, you
can rotate the pie shape.

If you manipulate the left Adjust handle, you can change the size of the pie slice.

Can I create a free-form shape from a drawn shape? No. Unlike a drawing application, Publisher (a desktop publishing application) does not let you erase portions of drawn shapes to create free-form shapes. When you draw a rectangle, you can resize it or change it from a rectangle with unequal sides into a square, but you can't alter its boxlike nature. If you want to draw a free-form shape, you must use Microsoft Draw or another drawing application.

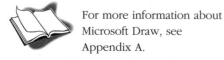

For more information about
Microsoft Draw, see
Appendix A.

Alter the Outline of a Shape

1 Position the pointer over the Adjust handle. The Adjust pointer appears.

2 Drag the Adjust handle to change the shape of the object.

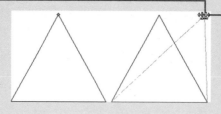

The arrows on the Adjust pointer tell you in which directions you can drag the handle to alter the shape. For example, you can change the angle in a triangle, but you can't turn the triangle into a square.

Combining Drawn Objects

To create more complex shapes, you can draw several simple objects and combine them by using the layout tools. For example, you can do the following:

@ Control how objects overlap by using Publisher's stacking order commands

@ Group separate objects together

@ Rotate and flip objects

@ Align multiple objects automatically using the Align Objects command on the Arrange menu

For more information about Publisher's layout tools, such as stacking, grouping, rotating, and aligning, see Chapter 3.

The international cancellation sign was created by grouping two objects (a line and a circle).

This simple airplane shape is composed of three shapes: an oval, a chevron, and a triangle. Notice how the shapes have been rotated to add a sense of movement to the plane.

 The benefits of formatting frames. By applying formatting directly to text, picture, table, or WordArt frames, you make the formats integral to the object, which in turn makes the combination easy to manage. When you move a text frame that has a BorderArt format, for example, the decorative border moves with the text automatically.

 Color and fill effects are discussed in Chapter 15.

Formatting Objects

You can dramatically change the appearance of objects by changing the formatting attributes. Publisher's formatting options fall into five general categories, each with a range of capabilities.

Borders and lines can range in width from 0.25 to 127 points.

Drop shadows can be added to any shape or frame to create a three-dimensional effect.

Fill options include solid colors, tints and shades of a color, repeating patterns, and gradients. The No Fill option makes objects transparent and reveals objects placed lower in the stacking order.

BorderArt designs come in over 150 patterns and range in width from 4 to 250 points.

Arrowheads of 10 different types can be added to a line.

Assign a heavier line weight to lightly colored or tinted lines. Thin lines that have been formatted with a light color or tint may not print well. Use a light color or tint only with a line thickness of 4 points or more.

For more information about color choices, see Chapter 15.

Formatting Lines

You can change the appearance of lines by specifying thickness and color. Formatting lines is very similar to formatting the borders of frames and drawn objects. However, you can also format a line by adding arrowheads to the right end, the left end, or both ends. Arrowheads are ideal whenever you want to point to a particular object or show direction in a flow chart.

Format Lines

1 Draw or select a line to format.

2 Click the Line/Border Style button on the Format toolbar or the Line/Border Style command on the Format menu. A flyout menu appears, containing four preformatted choices: Hairline (0.25 point), 1 point, 2 points, or 4 points.

3 Select one of these four options, or to access additional options, select More Styles from the flyout menu. The Line dialog box appears.

4 Select one of the six preset line weights or type a value from 0.25 through 127 points into the text box.

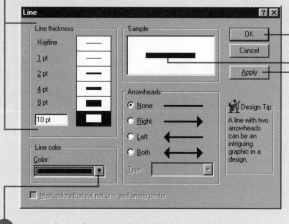

6 If you like the current effect, click OK.

Preview the current line settings in the Sample area, or preview the actual line within your publication by clicking the Apply button.

5 Open the Color drop-down list box and choose one of the available colors, tints, or shades.

Control the size of the arrowhead. The size of the arrowhead is determined by the thickness of the line. To increase the size of the arrowhead, make the line thicker.

Draw arrows with the Custom Shapes tool. You can create a wide variety of arrows by choosing one of the four arrow shapes in the Custom Shapes pop-up box. Unlike arrows created with the Line tool, these shapes include curves and can be modified using the Adjust handles.

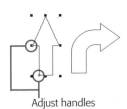

Adjust handles

Add a Default Arrowhead to a Line

1 Select the line you want to format.

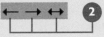

2 Click one of the three arrowhead buttons on the Format toolbar. The selected arrowhead appears on the line.

Access More Arrowhead Options

1 Select the line you want to format.

2 Click the Line/Border Style button on the Format toolbar or select the Line/Border Style command on the Format menu.

3 Choose More Styles from the flyout menu. The Line dialog box appears.

4 Select one of three options to specify the arrowhead's placement (Right, Left, or Both), or select None to remove arrowheads from a line.

6 To accept the current settings, click OK.

You can preview your choices in the Sample area, or click Apply to preview the arrowheads directly in your publication.

5 Choose one of the arrowhead types from the drop-down list box.

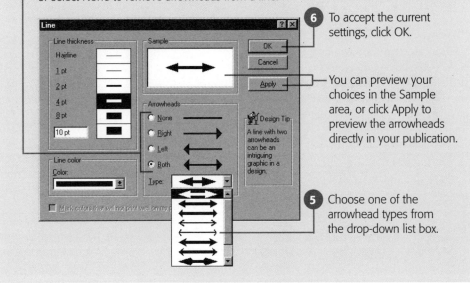

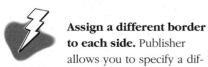

Assign a different border to each side. Publisher allows you to specify a different border for each side of a box, frame, cell, or range of cells. When you are working with a simple outline, such as a box or frame, you can change only the top, bottom, left, and right borders.

However, you can develop endless combinations of borders for a table object. The perimeter of this table is formatted differently from the interior cell division.

You can even subselect ranges of cells (or a single cell) within a table and format each side of that range with distinct top, bottom, left, and right borders. The table shown here is structurally identical to the previous table, but it appears to be structured differently because of the way in which the borders have been formatted. The gridline between the two lower rows is formatted with a border of None.

Borders and BorderArt

You can add borders to a wide range of elements within a Publisher document, including rectangles and text, table, picture, or WordArt frames. You can also create a border for an individual cell or range of cells in a table. You can even insert rules between columns of text in a text frame.

When you select a box, frame, or cells within a table, the BorderArt dialog box gives you the ability to create a custom border. When you select a drawn object that is not rectangular, such as a circle or a triangle, the border is applied to the irregular shape of the object.

If you want more than a simple border around an object, consider BorderArt, a collection of over 150 designs that includes geometric patterns, symbolic icons, and miniature illustrations. You can customize a BorderArt border by changing its size and color. You can even create your own BorderArt patterns based on clip art or other picture files.

Apply a Line Border to a Rectangle or Frame

1 Select the rectangle or frame you want to format.

2 Click the Line/Border Style button on the Format toolbar or select the Line/Border Style command on the Format menu.

3 Select one of the four preformatted line weights (Hairline, 1 point, 2 points, or 4 points), or choose More Styles to access additional options. The Border Style dialog box appears.

Does the frame size expand when I apply a border? Publisher draws the border inside the frame; the outside dimensions of the frame remain the same. This means that if you create a small text frame and then format it with a wide border, you might cover text within the text frame. To solve this problem, you can reduce the width of the border by entering a smaller value in the Choose A Thickness area or by enlarging the text frame.

Why can't I create interior rules in a text frame? You can create interior rules in a text frame only when the text frame contains multiple columns of text. Open the Text Frame Properties dialog box (found on the Format menu) and increase the number of text columns to two or more. When you return to the Border Style dialog box, the Select A Side area will contain an interior rule to separate text columns, as shown below.

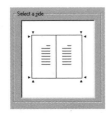

For more information about text frames, see Chapter 4.

Apply a Line Border to a Rectangle or Frame *(continued)*

4 If it's not already selected, choose the Line Border tab.

5 In the Select A Side area, choose the top, bottom, left, or right edge of the rectangle or frame. The currently selected side is indicated by two triangles pointing to it. You can choose any combination of sides by Shift-clicking, or you can click Box to place a border around the entire selection. In this example, one set of triangles points to the top of the frame.

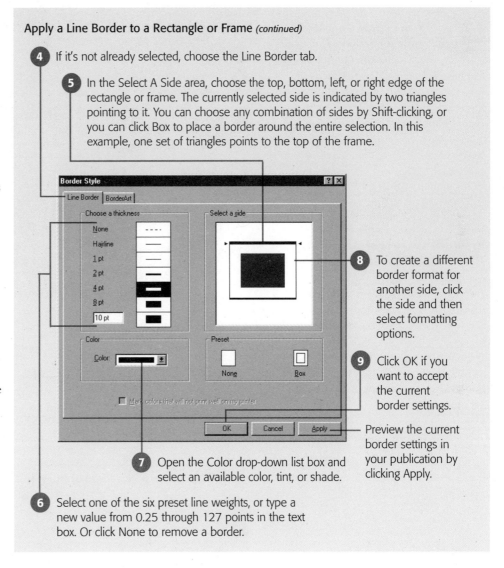

8 To create a different border format for another side, click the side and then select formatting options.

9 Click OK if you want to accept the current border settings.

Preview the current border settings in your publication by clicking Apply.

7 Open the Color drop-down list box and select an available color, tint, or shade.

6 Select one of the six preset line weights, or type a new value from 0.25 through 127 points in the text box. Or click None to remove a border.

Drawing Tools

Can I apply a border to only a portion of an oval or a custom shape? When you have selected an oval or irregular shape, the Border formatting selections apply to the entire object. You cannot apply different formats to individual sides of these objects. Notice that the Select A Side options are not available in the Border dialog box when you select a nonrectangular object.

Can I apply Border Art to an oval or custom shape, or to table cells? No. BorderArt can't follow the curved or irregular outlines of ovals and custom shapes. You can only apply standard line borders to ovals and custom shapes. You'll also find that you can't apply BorderArt to the interior cell divisions of a table. You can only apply BorderArt to the rectangular perimeter (or frame) of a table.

Apply a Line Border to an Oval or a Custom Shape

1 Select the oval or custom shape you want to format.

2 Click the Line/Border Style button on the Format toolbar or select the Line/Border Style command on the Format menu.

3 Select one of the four preformatted line weights (Hairline, 1 point, 2 points, or 4 points), or choose More Styles to access additional options from the Border dialog box. The Border dialog box appears.

4 Select one of the six preset line weights, or type a new value from 0.25 through 127 points in the text box.

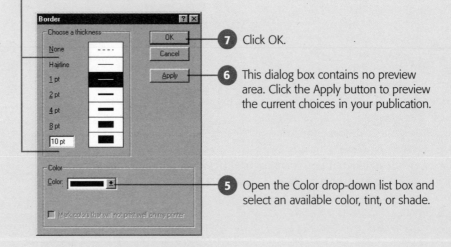

7 Click OK.

6 This dialog box contains no preview area. Click the Apply button to preview the current choices in your publication.

5 Open the Color drop-down list box and select an available color, tint, or shade.

Add BorderArt to a Frame or a Rectangle

1 Select the frame or rectangle to which you want to add BorderArt.

2 Click the Line/Border Style button on the Format toolbar or select the Line/Border Style command on the Format menu. Select More Styles from the flyout menu. The Border Style dialog box appears.

Add BorderArt to a Frame or a Rectangle *(continued)*

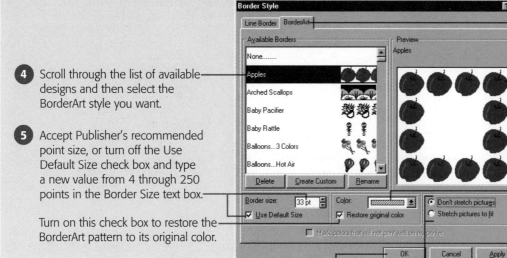

3 Select the BorderArt tab.

4 Scroll through the list of available designs and then select the BorderArt style you want.

You can view any border in the Preview area.

5 Accept Publisher's recommended point size, or turn off the Use Default Size check box and type a new value from 4 through 250 points in the Border Size text box.

Turn on this check box to restore the BorderArt pattern to its original color.

6 Open the Color drop-down list box and choose one of the available colors, tints, or shades to convert the BorderArt pattern into tints and shades of the chosen color.

8 Click OK.

7 Choose Don't Stretch Pictures to maintain the proportions of the images that form the border. Alternatively, choose Stretch Pictures To Fit to create a continuous BorderArt pattern in which some of the images may be distorted.

Create Custom BorderArt

1 Select the frame or rectangle to which you want to add BorderArt.

2 Click the Line/Border Style button on the Format toolbar or the Line/Border Style command on the Format menu and select More Styles on the flyout menu. The Border Style dialog box appears.

3 Select the BorderArt tab.

Drawing Tools

Manage BorderArt patterns. Whenever you select a BorderArt pattern in the Available Borders list box, two buttons become available. Click Delete to remove the currently selected BorderArt pattern from the list. Click Rename to change the name of the currently selected BorderArt pattern. Because BorderArt patterns appear in alphabetic order, you can use the Rename function to move a favorite BorderArt pattern from the bottom of the list to the top. Choose a new name that begins with the letter *A*. For example, you can rename Vine to A-Vine.

For more information about the Microsoft Clip Gallery and picture import functions, see Chapter 10.

Create Custom BorderArt *(continued)*

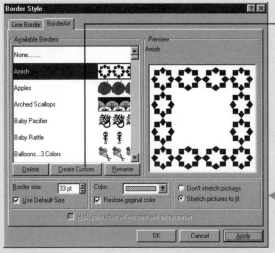

④ Click the Create Custom button. The Create Custom Border dialog box appears.

⑤ Turn on the Use Clip Gallery To Choose The Picture check box to choose from the images stored in the Microsoft Clip Gallery, or turn off this check box to be able to choose any picture file you have stored on disk.

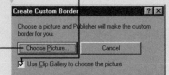

⑥ Click Choose Picture to use a picture file, in any graphics file format that Publisher supports, as a BorderArt pattern. If you turned on the Use Clip Gallery To Choose The Picture check box, the Microsoft Clip Gallery 4.0 dialog box appears; otherwise, the Insert Picture File dialog box appears.

⑦ In the Clip Gallery, locate the image you want to import and click Insert. In the Insert Picture File dialog box, locate the file you want to import and click OK. The Name Custom Border dialog box appears.

⑧ Replace the numerical designation used by the Microsoft Clip Gallery with a descriptive name.

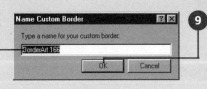

⑨ Click OK to add the custom border. Publisher adds the new BorderArt pattern to the Available Borders list box. The custom border can be applied to any frames or boxes you create in the future.

Create decorative lines and bullets using BorderArt.

You can use BorderArt to produce decorative lines and bullets. To make a decorative line, first select a box you've formatted with BorderArt. Then resize the box by pulling either the bottom selection handle up until it overlaps the top selection handle or by pulling the right selection handle left until it overlaps the left selection handle.

To create a decorative bullet, first select a box you've formatted with BorderArt. Then resize the box by drag-ging a corner selection handle until it overlaps the selection handle diagonally opposite.

When you design a BorderArt bullet, you basically collapse a box into a single corner. So it's a good idea to pick a design with a stand-alone pattern (such as a string of creatures) or a strong corner motif, such as the Cabin, Clock, or Eclipsing Square patterns shown here.

Removing Borders and BorderArt from Objects

Publisher offers several different ways to remove borders or BorderArt from an object, as explained in the following table. Your choices will vary depending on the type of object you're working with. For example, when working with frames and rectangles, you can choose to remove the entire border or only a portion of the border.

Remove Borders and BorderArt from an Object		
To remove…	**From…**	**Do This…**
The entire border or BorderArt pattern	A Frame, rectangle, oval, custom shape, cell, or range of cells	Select None from the Line/Border Style flyout menu (found on the Format toolbar or the Format menu). Publisher displays the object boundaries on screen (as a dotted line), but no border prints.
The entire border	A frame, rectangle, oval, custom shape, cell, or range of cells	In the Border Style dialog box (accessed by selecting More Styles on the Line/Border Style flyout menu), select the Line Border tab. In the Preset area, click None. Alternatively, make sure all sides of a rectangle, frame, cell, or group of cells are selected and click None in the Choose A Thickness area. Publisher displays the object boundaries on screen (as a dotted line), but no border prints.
A portion of a line border	A frame, rectangle, cell, or range of cells	In the Border Style dialog box (accessed by by selecting More Styles on the Line/Border Style flyout menu), select the Line Border tab. Select the side of the object from which you want to remove the border. Then click None in the Choose A Thickness area.
A BorderArt border	A rectangle or frame	In the Border Style dialog box (accessed by selecting More Styles on the Line/Border Style flyout menu), select the BorderArt tab. Select None from the Available Borders list box.

Create a color shadow.
You can create a color shadow instead of a gray shadow. Simply choose a color for the line border you have assigned to the object. When you subsequently assign a shadow to the object, it will appear in a tint of the border color.

This technique will even work with a BorderArt pattern, provided that you change the default colors associated with the pattern by choosing a new color from the palette within the BorderArt dialog box.

How can I apply shadows to individual letters? When you apply a shadow to a text frame, the shadow is applied to the entire frame. If you want to create a shadow effect for individual letters within a text frame, you have two options:

@ Highlight the text and use the Font dialog box (found on the Format menu) to choose the Shadow, Emboss, or Engrave effect. These effects all create gray shadows (or highlights) in predetermined locations.

@ Create a WordArt element. The Shadow effect in the WordArt module allows you to change the placement and color of the shadow.

Shadows

You can create the illusion of depth for frames, lines, and drawn objects by adding a drop shadow behind them.

Publisher mimics the outline of ovals and irregular shapes.

Box and frame shadows are rectangular.

> The Martin Krump Trio

The drop shadow falls behind and to the lower right of the frame or shape.

Regardless of the size of the frame or shape, the depth and placement of the shadow are always the same.

Add or Remove a Shadow

1 Select the frame, line, or drawn object.

2 Select Shadow on the Format menu.

3 Shadow is a toggle command. To remove a shadow, click the Shadow command again.

Picture and Clip Media Tools

Microsoft Publisher 98 can import a wide variety of computer-based media—not just pictures—into your documents. For example, you can incorporate sounds and motion clips into electronic documents you plan to publish on the World Wide Web. Pictures, however, remain the primary way to enhance both electronic and paper-based documents. The first step toward mastering Publisher's picture tools is learning to distinguish between different graphics types.

Categories of Graphics

Graphics file formats can be grouped into two overall categories: bitmapped (or raster) images and vector (or draw-type) images. Take a look at the following table, which compares the two file formats. As you can see, there are pros and cons to using each kind of image.

Comparison of Bitmapped and Vector Images		
Image Attribute	**Bitmapped Image**	**Vector Image**
How the image data is stored and interpreted by the computer	The image data is a collection of picture elements, or pixels. The information in the image file specifies the location, or map, of each pixel.	The image data is a series of drawing instructions.
Overall output quality	High, provided that the image contains the appropriate number of pixels (referred to as resolution) for your final output device.	Always high. An image always prints at the highest resolution of the output device.

Comparison of Bitmapped and Vector Images *(continued)*		
Image Attribute	**Bitmapped Image**	**Vector Image**
Enlargement capability	Poor. When enlarged in Publisher, the individual pixels of a bitmap picture create a jagged staircase pattern, known as aliasing. The lines of the image do not look smooth.	High. You can scale the image or change its proportions without reducing quality.
Color capability	Images contain a specific number of potential colors: 1 color (black-and-white), 16 colors, 256 colors or shades of gray, or 16.7 million colors.	All color information is stored as a series of instructions, which can generate black-and-white, gray-scale, or full-color (16.7 million) pictures.
Appropriate content	Scanned photographs and realistic illustrations.	Line drawings, illustrations, charts, and technical diagrams.
File size	Bitmapped images can require a great deal of storage space. As the resolution increases and as the number of potential colors increases, file size grows dramatically. For example, at the standard resolution used for the Internet (72 dots per inch), a color image measuring 640 by 480 pixels requires 900 KB of storage space. At the appropriate resolution for a color desktop printer (113 dots per inch), a full-color, full-page image requires nearly 3.5 MB of storage space.	Drawing indications and color information are stored as a series of instructions. This results in efficient file sizes that do not require a great deal of storage space.

The following images illustrate some of the differences between bitmapped and vector images.

The computer sees this circle as a series of black-and-white dots.   Enlarging a bitmapped image also enlarges the individual dots, which creates a jagged pattern (aliasing).

The computer sees this circle as a series of drawing instructions for radius, line thickness, and fill pattern.   You can enlarge or reduce a draw-type image without degrading quality.

To learn how to send a PostScript printer file to a printing service, see Chapter 17.

Why do EPS images appear as low-resolution pictures or with the name of the file instead of the actual picture?
Publisher cannot display an EPS file on screen. Instead, it shows you a low-resolution preview of the image to help you position the picture. If no preview is included, the EPS file appears as a simple box with an identifying filename and the name of the program that created the image.

The low-resolution screen display of an EPS image makes it unsuitable for Web publications. Furthermore, if you print a publication containing an EPS image on a non-PostScript printer, only the screen image will be printed. That means you will see either a low-resolution bitmap or a plain box in your printed document, as shown in the following illustration.

Title: CR
Creator:
CreationD

A Special Case: The Encapsulated PostScript Format

The Encapsulated PostScript (EPS) format is a graphics format that can contain both vector and bitmapped images. The information for both of these image types is stored in Adobe's PostScript printer language. In fact, EPS is a subset of the commands used to control a PostScript printer.

If you are planning a publication with numerous photographs and drawings, you should consider printing to a PostScript printer for the following reasons:

- PostScript is a robust printer language. PostScript commands can create very complex vector images efficiently.

- The same PostScript document file you send to your 600 dots-per-inch (dpi) PostScript laser printer will print at 1200 or 2400 dpi on the typesetting machines at your printing service. This means that you can print accurate proofs of your publication before you send them out to a commercial printer for professional-quality reproduction.

Importing Pictures

You can easily import many different types of pictures into your publications, giving you a lot of design flexibility. The following table lists the many graphics file formats Publisher can import. Pay attention to the Comments column for information about each format's performance in Publisher.

Types of Graphics Files Publisher Imports			
Format Name	**Image Type**	**Filename Extension**	**Comments**
Windows Bitmaps	Bitmapped	BMP	Best suited for black-and-white, 16-color, and 256-color images.
CorelDraw	Vector	CDR	Can include bitmapped data as well, but rarely does.

Why are file extensions so important? The three-letter extension following the period identifies the picture's file format. A picture called Picture.wmf, for example, is stored in the Windows Metafile format. Windows 95 does not display extensions by default. To display file extensions, open My Computer or Windows Explorer and select Options on the View menu. On the View tab, turn off the check box labeled Hide MS-DOS File Extensions For File Types That Are Registered.

You may already have access to additional graphics file formats. Publisher can take advantage of many graphics file filters that have been installed on your system by other Microsoft products. The exact choices that appear in the Insert Picture File dialog box will vary, but here are a few formats you may be able to access:

- Macintosh PICT (PCT)
- Enhanced Metafiles (EMF)
- Targa (TGA)
- Portable Network Graphics (PNG)
- AutoCAD Format 2-d (DXF)
- HP Graphics Language (HGL)

Types of Graphics Files Publisher Imports *(continued)*			
Format Name	**Image Type**	**Filename Extension**	**Comments**
Computer Graphics Metafile	Vector	CGM	Many third-party clip-art libraries are in this format.
Micrografx Designer/Draw	Vector	DRW	Can include bitmapped data as well, but rarely does.
Encapsulated PostScript	Bitmapped, vector	EPS	Can contain bitmapped and/or vector data. Must be printed to a PostScript device. EPS images are not suitable for Internet publications.
CompuServe Graphics Interchange Format	Bitmapped	GIF	Can contain a maximum of 256 colors. A popular graphics file format for the Internet. GIF files can contain multiple images that, when viewed sequentially, create animation effects.
Joint Photographic Experts Group	Bitmapped	JPG	The highly compressed format is ideal for high-resolution images, stored in what are called JPEG files. A popular graphics format for the Internet.
Kodak Photo CD	Bitmapped	PCD	Images stored at highest resolution can be too large for Publisher to save; lower resolutions take up less disk space and print faster.
PC Paintbrush	Bitmapped	PCX	Best suited for black-and-white, 16-color, and 256-color images.
Tagged Image File 5.0 Format	Bitmapped	TIF	TIFF compression options are ideal for high-resolution images.
Windows Metafile	Vector	WMF	Can include bitmapped data as well, but rarely does.
WordPerfect Graphics	Vector	WPG	Offers compatibility with WordPerfect.

It's best not to draw a picture frame when importing bitmapped images. Importing a picture without first drawing a picture frame is especially useful when working with bitmapped images. It guarantees that you will not inadvertently resize, and therefore degrade, the picture. If you want to resize a bitmap picture, use the cropping tool instead.

Draw multiple picture frames. Normally after you draw a picture frame, the crosshair pointer reverts to the arrow pointer. You can keep the crosshair pointer active and continue to draw picture frames by Ctrl-clicking the Picture tool. After you've drawn a series of picture frames, select another tool on the toolbar to return to normal selection mode.

Drag-And-Drop pictures. If your draw or paint application supports Microsoft Windows 95 Drag-And-Drop functions, you can simply move a picture from its window into a Publisher document. You can also drag a picture file from Microsoft Windows Explorer directly into a Publisher document.

Picture Import Methods

Before you import a picture into your publication, decide whether you need to draw a picture frame. If you import a picture at its original size, don't draw a picture frame first. Publisher will create a picture frame to fit the image.

Alternatively, you can create a picture frame prior to importing an image. This method works best if you want to fit a picture into a predetermined layout.

In either case, Publisher always maintains the picture's original aspect ratio—the proportional relationship between the width and height of the image.

Import a Picture into Your Publication

1 To size the imported image to fit into a predetermined layout, choose the Picture tool (shown here) and draw a picture frame, or select an existing picture frame. To import a picture in its original size, begin this procedure with step 2.

2 Open the Insert menu and choose Picture File. From the cascading menu, select From File. The Insert Picture File dialog box appears.

3 Open the Files Of Type drop-down list box and choose the format of the file you want to import. All the files of your chosen format appear in the main list box.

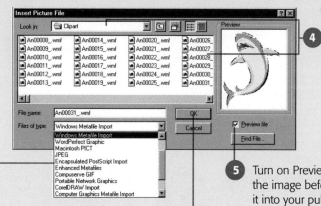

4 Locate and select the picture file you want by using the Look In drop-down list box and the files list box. If you have difficulty locating the file, click Find File to search for it.

5 Turn on Preview File to view the image before you import it into your publication.

6 Click OK.

What if I created my picture in an application that doesn't support a standard format? If you want to import a picture created in a Windows 95–based application that does not support any of the formats listed in the table on pages 153 through 154, copy the picture to the Clipboard and paste it into the publication instead of using the Picture File command on the Insert menu. The Clipboard converts files to a standard file format that all Windows 95–based applications can use.

 For more information about using the Windows 95 Clipboard, see Chapter 3. The Find File command is described in Chapter 2. For more information about aspect ratio and proportionally resizing an object, see page 171.

 Shortcut for quickly accessing the Insert Picture File dialog box. You can access the Insert Picture File dialog box quickly by double-clicking a picture frame. If the image you double-click contains a picture from the Microsoft Clip Gallery, the Microsoft Clip Gallery 4.0 dialog box appears.

Imported Picture Display Options

You might notice performance degradation as the number of pictures in a publication increases. It takes a fair amount of processing power to update the display of graphics. You can speed Publisher's performance by reducing the quality of the picture display.

Control the Display of Pictures

1 Choose Picture Display on the View menu. The Picture Display dialog box appears.

2 Select an option. The choice you make in this dialog box affects the display of pictures on screen, but the pictures will still print at the highest quality.

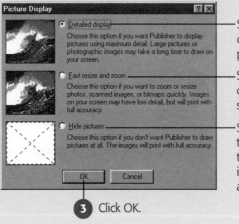

Selecting Detailed Display might slow down Publisher's performance if the publication contains complex graphics.

Selecting Fast Resize And Zoom displays low-resolution images but speeds performance.

Selecting Hide Pictures gives Publisher the largest performance boost, but all the pictures in your document (including WordArt and OLE objects) appear as crossed-out frames.

3 Click OK.

Printing hidden pictures.
If you choose to hide the pictures on your screen to speed performance, and then print the document, Publisher asks if you want to print the pictures or suppress them. Click Yes to print the pictures; click No to print the document with blank spaces where the pictures should be. Publisher prints a dotted outline to indicate where a hidden picture would normally appear on the page. Suppressing pictures can greatly decrease the time required to print a proof of your publication.

Share the Clip Gallery with other Microsoft applications. Many other Microsoft products, such as Word and Excel, can take advantage of the Clip Gallery. To access the Clip Gallery from another MS Office application, select Picture on the Insert menu. From the cascading menu, choose Clip Art.

Alternatively, if your application supports OLE, choose Object on the Insert menu. In the Object Type list box, select Microsoft Clip Gallery. Then use the Clip Gallery as you normally would within Publisher.

The Clip Gallery

The CD-ROM version of Publisher includes over 10,000 clip-art images, 500 photographs, and 300 animated GIF files. You can store and manage these files—and other media files stored on your system—using the Microsoft Clip Gallery, as long as the file formats are ones Publisher recognizes. You can use the Clip Gallery to organize vector pictures, bitmapped images, digital sound files, and motion clips. Specifically, you can do the following:

@ Assign a descriptive phrase to a media file

@ Search for a picture or clip file based on criteria such as file type or keywords

@ Insert a picture or clip file into a Publisher document

@ Group media files by category

Importing a File from the Clip Gallery

During installation, Publisher copies over 670 media files, including vector images, bitmapped photos, and sound files, to your hard disk. In addition, Publisher installs thumbnail sketches (miniature previews) of all the clip art contained on CD-ROM on your hard disk. This means you can search and preview the entire clip-art collection of images, even if you don't have the compact disc in the CD drive. To actually insert artwork stored on the CD into your publication, however, you must have the compact disc in the CD drive.

In many cases, you can find the image, sound, or motion clip you want by searching through the thumbnail sketches that appear in the preview window. By default, the files are organized into general categories, such as People at Work, Sports & Leisure, and Nature. You can also search for a specific file in the Clip Gallery by clicking the Find button, which opens the Find Clips dialog box. This command is especially useful if you are sorting through the thousands of images that ship with Publisher, or if you have amassed a large collection of your own images, sounds, and motion clips.

Available sound and motion clip formats. Publisher can import any digital sound or motion clip format supported by the Windows 95 Media Player. If you have the proper hardware and the necessary software drivers installed on your computer system, you should be able to import files in the following multimedia formats:

- WAV sound files
- MIDI sound files
- RMI sound files
- AVI video files
- GIF animation files

Boost the power of the Find Clips dialog box. The Find Clips dialog box works in conjunction with keywords. You'll get much better search results if you assign descriptive information to a file when you import it into the Clip Gallery.

For more information about OLE, see Chapter 11.

Import a File from the Clip Gallery

1 If you want Publisher to size the clip-art image to fit into a predetermined layout, choose the Clip Art Gallery tool and draw a picture frame. If you want to import a clip-art image at its original size, open the Insert menu, select Picture, and choose Clip Art from the flyout menu. The Microsoft Clip Gallery 4.0 dialog box appears.

2 Select the Clip Art tab to import vector images; click the Images tab to import bitmapped images; click the Sounds tab to import sound files; or click the Motion Clips tab to import animation and video files.

5 Click Insert.

Click here to view the currently selected thumbnail sketch at an enlarged size.

3 Choose one of the categories in the Categories list box, or select (All Categories) to see all the available files.

4 Use the scroll bar to move through the thumbnail previews and select the file you want to import.

The Clip Gallery always reports the number of files in the category.

Search for a Clip File Using the Find Button

1 From the Microsoft Clip Gallery 4.0 dialog box, click the Find button. The Find Clips dialog box appears.

Refine the search criteria.
You can help the Clip Gallery find the exact instance of the word or phrase for which you are searching. In the Find Clips dialog box, click Find Whole Words Only to find the keyword where it appears only as a whole word and ignore where it is part of another, longer word. For example, if you search for the whole word *ice*, Publisher will not find keywords such as *office* or *dice*.

Preview multimedia files.
When you select the Sounds or Motion Clips tab in the Clip Gallery, Publisher displays an icon or the first frame of an animation. Unlike a thumbnail of a picture, this symbolic preview may not provide enough identifying information. Instead of relying on a filename, use the Play button to listen to the sound file or view the motion clip. It's a good way to guarantee that you've selected the right clip.

Search for a Clip File Using the Find Button *(continued)*

2 If you've assigned descriptions to your clip files and want to find all the files that match a specific keyword, type a keyword or phrase into the Match These Keywords text box.

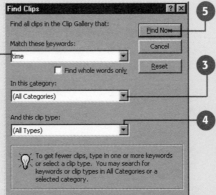

5 Click Find Now to begin the search. Publisher returns to the Microsoft Clip Gallery 4.0 dialog box.

3 To narrow the search, open the In This Category drop-down list and select a subset of the Clip Art Gallery.

4 To locate a specific file type, open the And This Clip Type drop-down list box and choose a file format. If you leave (All Types) selected, the Clip Gallery will search for vector images, bitmapped images, sounds, and motion clips that match the search criteria.

A new temporary category, which contains the results of the search, appears in the Categories list box.

When Publisher returns to the Clip Gallery, you will see thumbnail sketches for only those files that match your search criteria.

6 If you selected All Types, you can click the appropriate tab to see the vector images, bitmapped images, sounds, or motion clip files that match your search criteria.

For more information about the World Wide Web and Web pages, see Chapter 12.

What's the difference between the Find button in the Clip Gallery and the Find File command on Publisher's File menu? The Find button in the Clip Gallery searches for only graphics, sound, and motion clip files, and it looks through only the files that have been added as thumbnail sketches. In addition, in the Clip Gallery you can search for files based on keywords you assign when you add a file to the Gallery. In contrast, the Find File command searches for document files that Publisher can open and searches any disk you specify.

Building a Library of Clips

You can add vector images, bitmapped pictures, sounds, or motion clips to the Clip Gallery at any time. Publisher makes it easy for you to add files from a variety of sources, including your local hard disk, removable disks, and networked drives. Microsoft maintains a special version of Clip Gallery, called Clip Gallery Live on the World Wide Web. If you have an Internet provider, such as the Microsoft Network, and browsing software, such as Microsoft Internet Explorer, you can download additional clips from Clip Gallery Live.

Add a File to the Clip Gallery

1 Choose Clip Art from the Picture flyout menu (found on the Insert menu). The Microsoft Clip Gallery 4.0 dialog box appears.

2 Click the Import Clips button. The Add Clips To Gallery dialog box appears, which allows you to search local and networked drives for clip files.

3 Open the Files Of Type drop-down list box and choose either a specific file format or a general category, such as Clip Art, Images, Sounds, or Motion Clips, to see all the files available for import.

4 Use the Look In drop-down list box and the files list box to locate and select the file or files you want to add to the Clip Gallery.

5 Click Open. The Clip Properties dialog box appears.

Add more than one file to the Clip Gallery at a time.

If you purchase a Microsoft Clip Gallery package, you can install all the clip files along with keywords, categories, and previews in one step. In the Import Clips dialog box, open the Files Of Type drop-down list box and select Clip Gallery Packages.

Even if you are not installing a Microsoft Clip Gallery package, you can still add multiple files. In the files list box, Shift-click to select a group of contiguous filenames, or Ctrl-click to select nonadjacent filenames. The Clip Properties dialog box offers additional options. You can add all clips to the selected categories in one step, and you can click the Skip This Clip button to bypass the current file and proceed to the next file you selected.

Why doesn't a thumbnail sketch of my new file appear in the preview area? If you've added a number of files to the Clip Gallery, Publisher may not have updated the screen display. Close and then reopen the Clip Gallery. Your thumbnail sketches should appear in the preview area.

In some cases, however, Publisher cannot create a preview from a file. For sound clips, Publisher substitutes an icon for the clip preview. Publisher is also unable to display an EPS file on screen unless it has a TIFF header.

Add a File to the Clip Gallery *(continued)*

6 Enter descriptive phrases in the Keywords text box.

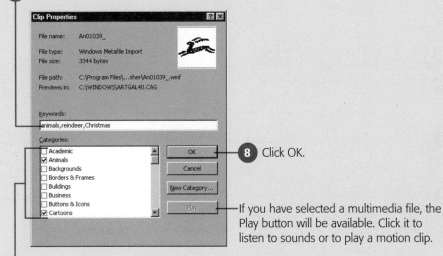

8 Click OK.

If you have selected a multimedia file, the Play button will be available. Click it to listen to sounds or to play a motion clip.

7 Select one or more of the categories in the Categories list box, or click the New Category button and enter a new category name in the dialog box that appears.

Use Clip Gallery Live on the World Wide Web

1 Make the connection to your Internet provider. The connection must be active before you attempt to connect to Clip Gallery Live.

2 In Publisher, select Clip Art from the Picture flyout menu (found on the Insert menu). The Microsoft Clip Gallery 4.0 dialog box appears.

3 Click the Clips From Web button, shown on the following page. Publisher will load your Web browser application and locate the Clip Gallery Live 1.2 Web page. (You will get an error message if Publisher doesn't recognize your Web browser. If this happens, use a different Web browser.)

Use Clip Gallery Live on the World Wide Web *(continued)*

4 If this is the first time you are using Clip Gallery Live, read the licensing agreement and click the Accept button.

Clip Gallery Live Reports the number of files that are in a given category or that match your search criteria.

5 Click one of the four icons representing the clip types: Clip Art, Pictures, Sounds, or Videos.

6 Click Browse to view clips by category, or click Search to select clips on the basis of keyword descriptions.

7 If you clicked Browse, open the drop-down list box and choose a category. If you clicked Search, type in a keyword or multiple keywords separated by commas.

8 Click Go.

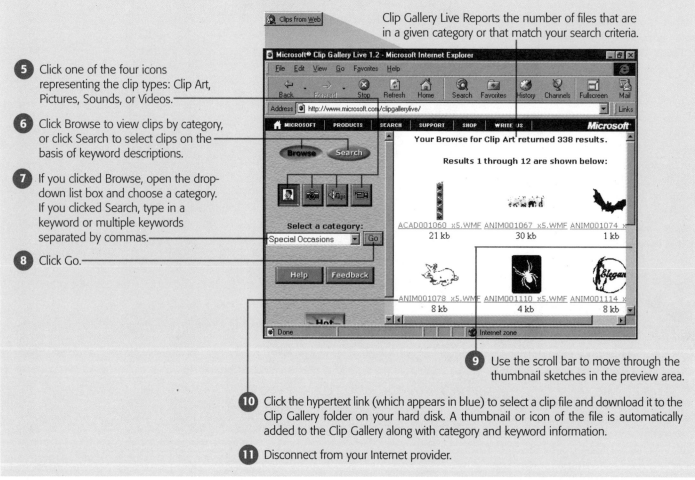

9 Use the scroll bar to move through the thumbnail sketches in the preview area.

10 Click the hypertext link (which appears in blue) to select a clip file and download it to the Clip Gallery folder on your hard disk. A thumbnail or icon of the file is automatically added to the Clip Gallery along with category and keyword information.

11 Disconnect from your Internet provider.

Where are the files I've downloaded from Clip Gallery Live stored? By default, files downloaded from Clip Gallery Live are stored at the following location on your hard disk: Program Files/Common Files/Microsoft Shared/ArtGallery/Downloaded Clips. You, of course, can use Windows Explorer to move the files to another folder. However, if you leave the files in this directory, they will be accessible to other Microsoft applications.

Delete unwanted Clip Gallery images. Publisher automatically copies hundreds of clip-art images to your hard disk during installation. You can conserve disk space by deleting from your hard disk those clip-art images you don't use.

Can I delete clip files from my disk from within the Clip Gallery? No. You must delete a file by using Windows Explorer or by dragging a file icon to the Windows 95 Recycle Bin. Be sure to update the Clip Gallery after you delete files from your disk.

Maintaining the Clip Gallery

Whenever you add a vector image, bitmapped image, sound, or motion clip to the Clip Gallery, a new thumbnail sketch is added to the already extensive collection of thumbnail sketches Publisher creates during installation. The Clip Gallery continues to show you the same thumbnail sketch even when you have moved, modified, or deleted the actual file from your disk. In addition, you'll find the Clip Gallery to be more useful if you create your own categories and assign your own keywords to your file.

You can reorganize the Clip Gallery in three ways:

@ By updating the thumbnail sketches to match the current contents of your local hard disk, removable disks, and networked drives.

@ By renaming or deleting existing categories, or by creating entirely new categories.

@ By assigning a file to a different category or to additional categories, or by changing the descriptive search phrase associated with the file.

Update the Contents of the Clip Gallery

1 Select Clip Art from the Picture flyout menu (found on the Insert menu). The Microsoft Clip Gallery 4.0 appears.

2 Click the Clip Art, Images, Sounds, or Motion Clips tab to update the corresponding file types.

Delete an individual thumbnail. If you know which files have been deleted from your hard disk, you can avoid the (rather lengthy) automatic update process and delete an individual thumbnail from the Clip Gallery. Open the Clip Gallery and right-click the thumbnail you want to remove. Select Delete Clip from the shortcut menu.

Update the Contents of the Clip Gallery *(continued)*

3 Right-click any thumbnail sketch to update all the clip previews.

4 Select Update Clip Previews to reconcile all the thumbnail sketches with the contents of your disks. The Update dialog box appears.

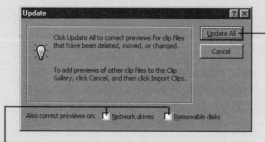

6 Click Update All to start the update process. If Publisher finds a thumbnail sketch for which it cannot find a corresponding file, it displays a second Update dialog box.

5 Turn on Network Drives to have Publisher update remote drives on a network. Turn on Removable Disks to update the contents of removable media, such as floppy disks and Zip disks.

Update the Contents of the Clip Gallery *(continued)*

The full path and filename are displayed.

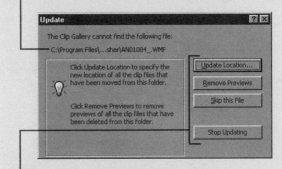

7 Click one of the four buttons:

@ Update Location to allow you to browse for the file and re-establish a link between the thumbnail sketch and the file.

@ Remove Previews to remove all thumbnail sketches without corresponding files from the Clip Gallery.

@ Skip This File to take no action and move on to the next thumbnail sketch for which there is no corresponding file.

@ Stop Updating to take no action and immediately return to the Clip Gallery.

Reorganize Categories Within the Clip Gallery

1 Select Clip Art from the Picture flyout menu (found on the Insert menu). The Microsoft Clip Gallery 4.0 dialog box appears.

2 Click the Clip Art, Images, Sounds, or Motion Clips tab to edit categories associated with the corresponding file types.

3 Click the Edit Categories button. The Edit Category List dialog box appears.

Use categories to create a personal clip collection.
The existing categories in the Clip Gallery are based on the content of an image. You can, however, create categories based on your favorite images, frequently used files, or a particular project. For example, you can create a category called Company Logos that allows you to quickly access all the variations of your company logo stored on your hard disk.

Reorganize Categories Within the Clip Gallery *(continued)*

4 Select a category from the categories list box.

5 Create, delete, and rename categories as necessary.

6 When you have finished reorganizing categories, click Close to return to the Clip Gallery, and then click Close in the Clip Gallery to return to your publication.

Click Delete Category, and then click Yes or No in the confirmation dialog box that appears.

Click New Category to open the New Category dialog box where you can add new organizational groups to the existing list.

Click Rename Category to open the Rename Category dialog box where you can type a new name for the selected category.

Change the Information for an Individual Clip File

1 Select Clip Art from the Picture flyout menu (found on the Insert menu). The Microsoft Clip Gallery 4.0 dialog box appears.

2 Click the Clip Art, Images, Sounds, or Motion Clips tab to modify the information associated with the corresponding file types.

3 Select the thumbnail sketch for which you want to modify information.

4 Click the Clip Properties button, or right-click the thumbnail sketch and select Clip Properties from the shortcut menu. The Clip Properties dialog box appears.

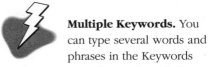 **Multiple Keywords.** You can type several words and phrases in the Keywords text box. Separate the words and phrases with single commas and no spaces. If you search for the file in the future, you can use any of the keywords or phrases to locate it.

Change the Information for an Individual Clip File *(continued)*

A thumbnail sketch appears along with the filename, format type, and file size.

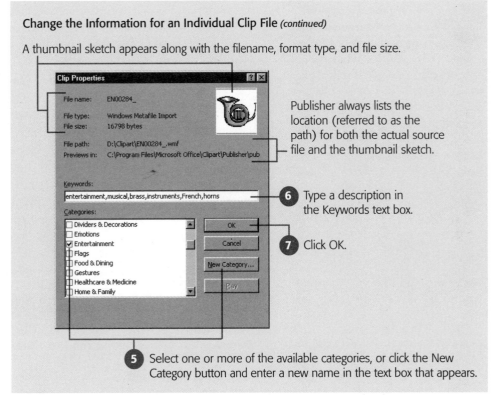

Publisher always lists the location (referred to as the path) for both the actual source file and the thumbnail sketch.

6 Type a description in the Keywords text box.

7 Click OK.

5 Select one or more of the available categories, or click the New Category button and enter a new name in the text box that appears.

 For more information about bitmapped picture formats, see pages 151 through 152.

Image Acquisition Functions in Publisher

Publisher supports the TWAIN32 image acquisition interface. If your hardware uses a TWAIN32 driver, you can directly access a scanner or digital camera from within your Publisher document. Scanners and digital cameras produce bitmapped images. To a large extent, the quality of a bitmapped image is determined by its resolution, so it is important for you to understand how digital cameras and scanners address the issue of picture resolution.

Digital cameras produce pictures at predetermined resolutions that are typically identified by the total number of pixels in the picture (size is expressed as

Computing gray-scale and color photograph resolution for printed output. The tonal variation in a gray-scale or color photograph is printed using a cluster of dots called a halftone cell. Halftone resolution is measured in lines per inch (lpi). Ask your service bureau for the proper lpi setting. Then scan your photographs at a dpi value of 1.5 times the lpi value. Note the following scanning recommendations:

- For 52 lpi, scan at 80 dpi.

- For 75 lpi, scan at 113 dpi.

- For 90 lpi, scan at 135 dpi.

- For 120 lpi, scan at 180 dpi.

- For 133 lpi, scan at 200 dpi.

the number of horizontal pixels multiplied by the number of vertical pixels). For example, consumer-oriented digital cameras generate pictures at 320 by 240 pixels or 640 by 480 pixels. These resolutions are suitable for screen display (when publishing on the Internet) and for comparatively low-resolution output devices, such as black-and-white or color desktop printers.

In comparison, desktop scanners generate images at the size and resolution you choose. As a result, resolution is specified as the number of dots—or pixels—per inch (dpi) and can range from 300 to 1200 dpi. When creating an image with a scanner, you will want to produce the smallest possible file size without degrading image quality. To accomplish this, you should scan a picture with the colors and resolution required by the final output device. For example, you should not create a full-color scanned image if you are printing to a black-and-white device. Nor should you scan a picture at 300 dpi if you intend to display it on a monitor with a resolution of 72 dpi. Unfortunately, there are no hard and fast rules concerning scanning parameters. The following table lists the most efficient resolutions for standard output devices.

Appropriate Resolutions for Standard Output Devices			
Hardware Device	Resolution	Black-and-White Drawing	Gray-Scale or Color Photograph
Laser printer	300 dpi	300 dpi	80 dpi
Laser printer	600 dpi	600 dpi	113 dpi
Inkjet printer	720 dpi	720 dpi	135 dpi
High-resolution desktop printer or printing service imagesetter	1200 dpi	800 dpi	180 dpi
Printing service, imagesetter	2400 dpi	800 dpi	200 dpi
Monitor	72 dpi	Not applicable; for best results, scan black-and-white drawings as gray-scale artwork.	72 dpi

Why doesn't the From Scanner Or Camera command appear on the Insert Picture cascading menu? If the From Scanner Or Camera command does not appear or if your scanner does not appear in the Sources list box, your scanner might not support the TWAIN32 interface. If that is the case, you must create the scanned photograph outside Publisher, save it in a file, and then use the Picture command on the Insert menu to incorporate it into your publication.

What does the Out Of Memory error message mean? Standard bitmapped file formats, such as TIFF and JPEG, use compression routines to shrink the size of a scanned image and save disk space. When Publisher incorporates a TWAIN picture (or inserts any bitmapped images), it converts the picture to an uncompressed format. This uncompressed form might require more memory than your computer has available. Rescan the image at a lower resolution or with fewer colors.

Acquiring a Picture While Working in Your Publication

Before you can create a scanned image, you must establish a link between Publisher and the image acquisition hardware. Unless you are switching from one device to another, you should perform this operation only once.

Link Publisher to Your Digital Camera or Scanner

1 Choose Picture on the Insert menu. On the cascading menu, select From Scanner Or Camera.

2 On the next cascading menu, choose Select Source. The Select Source dialog box appears.

3 In the Sources list box, choose the device (either a scanner or a digital camera) you want to use.

Acquire a Scanned Image

1 If you want Publisher to size the image to fit into a predetermined layout, choose the Picture tool and draw a frame, or select an existing picture frame. If you want Publisher to automatically create a frame for the scanned image, begin this procedure with step 2.

2 Choose From Scanner Or Camera from the Picture flyout menu (found on the Insert menu).

3 Select Acquire Image on the next cascading menu. The scanner control window appears.

Why do I have different options in the control panel for my TWAIN32 device? Although the TWAIN32 interface is an industry standard, the actual options you see will vary depending on your particular hardware and software setup. Manufacturers use different terminology to describe identical functions. So while one manufacturer employs a scaling function to size images, another requires you to specify explicit values for width and height.

More fundamentally, the TWAIN interface was designed to handle all sorts of input devices, including scanners, video frame grabbers, and digital cameras. The options that appear (or don't appear) in the control panel reflect the capabilities of the device. For example, the interface for a digital camera (shown below) will provide commands for viewing and downloading photos you previously snapped. You won't find commands to change the size or resolution of an image, because digital cameras produce pictures at a predetermined resolution.

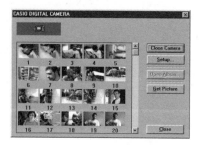

Acquire a Scanned Image *(continued)*

④ Click Preview (or the corresponding button for your scanner) to see a low-resolution version of the image.

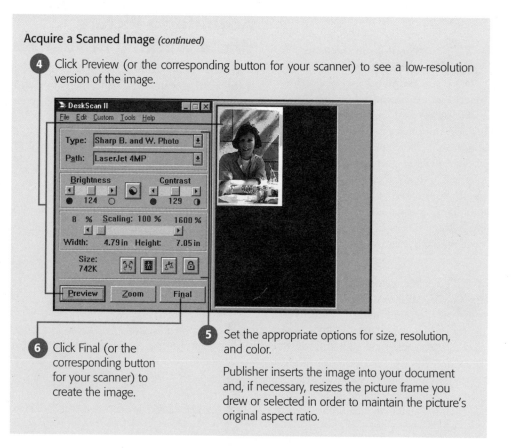

⑥ Click Final (or the corresponding button for your scanner) to create the image.

⑤ Set the appropriate options for size, resolution, and color.

Publisher inserts the image into your document and, if necessary, resizes the picture frame you drew or selected in order to maintain the picture's original aspect ratio.

Modifying the Size and Appearance of Your Image

Whether you use commercial clip art, create original drawings, or scan personal photographs, you can use Publisher's tools to modify the pictures in a publication. The standard layout tools allow you to change a picture's size, position, or rotation. In addition, specialized picture editing tools let you emphasize a portion of a graphic, integrate images with text, and alter the colors of imported artwork.

For more information about aspect ratio and resizing objects, see Chapter 3.

How does the Scale Picture command differ from the Size And Position command? The Scale Picture command allows you to resize an image or Clip Gallery object by specifying a percentage of the picture's original size. You can easily maintain the correct aspect ratio by entering identical values in the width and height text boxes. The Size And Position dialog box requires you to enter explicit values for the picture's width and height. This approach makes it all too easy to size a picture disproportionately—distorting the aspect ratio.

Can I use the Scale Object command to resize WordArt objects? Yes. Because WordArt is inserted into a publication as an OLE object, you can use the Scale Object command to alter its size. However, you cannot revert to the WordArt object's previous size by using the Original Size check box in the Scale Object dialog box.

Scaling a Picture

The Scale Picture Or Scale Object command gives you precise controls that enable you to easily maintain the aspect ratio (the original proportions) of the picture.

Resize an Image Using Scale Picture Or Scale Object

1. Select the picture or Clip Gallery object you want to resize.

2. If you are working with an imported image, choose Scale Picture on the Format menu. If you are working with a Clip Gallery image, choose Scale Object on the Format menu. The Scale Picture Or Scale Object dialog box appears.

3. To maintain the picture's aspect ratio, enter equal percentage values for the height and width.

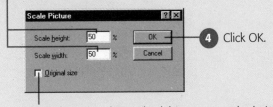

4. Click OK.

Select the Original Size check box to return the height and width to 100 percent.

Featuring a Section of Your Image

You can hide portions of a picture by using Publisher's Crop Picture tool. Think of the picture frame as a window with a window shade. Using the Crop Picture tool is like pulling down the window shade. Although the view doesn't change, you can see more of the landscape (or the picture) when the window shade is up and less when it is down. Cropping is not the same as resizing, which enlarges or shrinks the entire picture.

Crop all sides or opposite sides of your picture equally. To crop all four sides of a picture equally, hold down the Ctrl key as you drag a corner selection handle. To crop opposite sides of a picture equally, hold down Ctrl as you drag any selection handle except a corner handle.

Cropping letters and words. The Crop Picture tool can also be used with WordArt frames. You can create special effects, abstract patterns, or logos by trimming portions of the letters in a WordArt frame.

Crop a Picture

1 Select the picture or Clip Gallery object you want to crop.

2 Click the Crop Picture button on the Format toolbar. Alternatively, choose Crop Picture or Crop Object on the Format menu.

3 Place the pointer over any selection handle so that it changes into the Crop pointer.

4 Using the Crop pointer, drag a selection handle inward until only the portion of the picture you want visible is displayed. Repeat this step with as many selection handles as necessary to achieve the effect you want.

5 If you want to restore the cropped portions of the picture, use the Crop pointer to drag a selection handle outward until all of the original picture appears in the frame.

6 When you have finished trimming a picture, deactivate the Crop Picture tool by clicking the Crop Picture button on the Format toolbar again, or by selecting the Crop Picture or Crop Object command on the Format menu again.

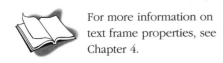

For more information on text frame properties, see Chapter 4.

Text Wrapping

One of the best ways to show the relationship between the various elements in a design is to wrap the text around other objects. You can wrap text around frames regardless of whether the frame contains a picture, WordArt, text, a table, or an OLE object. For text wrap to work properly, two conditions must be met, as shown in the following illustration.

Occasionally we discover an exceptional wine at an exceptional price. Such is the case with Chateau La Coste, a Bordeaux-style red wine from France. With an excellent balance of fresh ripe cherries and soft tannins, this ruby wine is ready to drink right now. But, this full-bodied mix of Cabernet Sauvignon, Merlot, and Grenache grapes can also be cellared for the next three to five years and will only improve with age.

The text frame must be formatted with the Wrap Text Around Objects attribute (found in the Text Frame Properties dialog box).

The text frame must be positioned at the bottom of the stack. The object the text wraps around (such as the picture shown here) must lie on top of the text object.

By default, Publisher wraps text around the rectangular frame of an object. But if you are working with a picture or WordArt object, you can sometimes create a more interesting and tighter text wrap by flowing the text around the outline of the actual image rather than the rectangular frame.

Wrap Text Around a Frame

1 Select the text frame containing the text you want to wrap around a picture or WordArt frame.

2 In the Text Frame Properties dialog box, confirm that Wrap Text Around Objects is selected.

3 Select the picture or WordArt frame you want to flow text around and click the Bring To Front button on the Standard toolbar.

Turn off text wrap. You can create interesting design effects by turning off text wrap. To have an object (such as the picture shown below) print on top of text, select the text frame and turn off Wrap Text Around Objects in the Text Frame Properties dialog box. This technique works well for headlines or logos.

To have text print over another object, select the text frame and bring it to the front of the stack. In order for this technique to work, the text frame must be transparent (so you can see the object beneath it), and the text itself must contrast with the background object (so that the copy remains legible).

Wrap Text Around a Frame *(continued)*

The Crop Picture button appears on the Format toolbar, when the Wrap Text To Frame button is selected.

4 If it is not already selected, click the Wrap Text To Frame button on the Format toolbar.

Occasionally we discover an exceptional wine at an exceptional price. Such is the case with Chateau La Coste, a Bordeaux-style red wine from France. With an excellent balance of fresh ripe cherries and soft tannins, this ruby wine is ready to drink right now. But, this full-bodied mix of Cabernet Sauvignon, Merlot, and Grenache grapes can also be cellared for the next three to five years and will only improve with age.

—The text wraps around the frame.

Wrap Text Around the Outline of a Picture or WordArt Design

1 Select the text frame containing the text you want to wrap around a picture or WordArt frame.

2 In the Text Frame Properties dialog box, confirm that Wrap Text Around Objects is selected.

3 Select the picture or WordArt frame you want to flow text around and click the Bring To Front button on the Standard toolbar.

The Edit Irregular Wrap button appears on the Format toolbar when the Wrap Text To Picture button is selected.

 **4** Select the Wrap Text To Picture button on the Format toolbar.

Wrapping text around drawn objects. You can wrap text around closed geometric or irregular shapes that you create with Publisher's drawing tools. If you want to wrap text around a drawn object, you must deal with these inherent restrictions:

@ Text will not wrap around a transparent drawn shape. You must fill the shape with a color, tint, shade, pattern, or gradient to wrap text.

@ You can't control the shape of the irregular wrap around a drawn object. The wrap always follows the outline of the drawn shape very closely. A star shape, for example, will create a zig-zag wrap.

@ You can't wrap text around a line or an arrow created with the Line tool. If you want to wrap text around an arrow, create the arrow using the Custom Shapes tool.

Wrap Text Around the Outline of a Picture or WordArt Design (continued)

Occasionally we discover an exceptional wine at an exceptional price. Such is the case with Chateau La Coste, a Bordeaux-style red wine from France. With an excellent balance of fresh ripe cherries and soft tannins, this ruby wine is ready to drink right now. But, this full-bodied mix of Cabernet Sauvignon, Merlot, and Grenache grapes can also be cellared for the next three to five years and will only improve with age.

—Publisher wraps text around the image outline.

5 If you want to change back to the default setting and wrap text around the picture frame, click the Wrap Text To Frame button.

Fine-Tuning the Text Wrap

When you wrap text around a picture or a WordArt design, Publisher maintains a nonprinting boundary between the image or frame and the text. You can change that boundary to wrap text more tightly around the image. You can even create a special boundary shape (such as a triangle or a free-form shape) that the text will flow around.

You can modify the irregular text wrapping boundary by moving the existing Adjust handles or by adding or deleting Adjust handles. Adding handles allows you to follow the outline of an image more precisely. Deleting handles simplifies the boundary and makes individual handles easier to grab.

Access text wrapping options through the Picture Frame Properties or the Object Frame Properties dialog box. You can also access text wrapping options by choosing Object Frame Properties on the Format menu:

@ Select Entire Frame to wrap text around the rectangular picture or WordArt frame.

@ Select Picture Only to wrap text around the outline of the image.

Control how text wraps around an image. The distance between text and the picture or WordArt design it wraps around is affected by the following elements:

@ The text wrapping boundary, which you can reshape using the Edit Irregular Wrap tool.

@ The picture frame margins, which are controlled by the Object Properties dialog box or the Picture Crop tool.

@ The margins you set in the text frame, which are controlled by the Text Frame Properties dialog box.

Adjust an Irregular Text Wrapping Boundary

1 Select the image you want to fine-tune and click the Wrap Text To Picture button on the Format toolbar.

2 Click the Edit Irregular Wrap button on the Format toolbar or choose Edit Irregular Wrap on the Format menu.

3 Position the pointer over one of the Adjust handles that appear along the dotted boundary line. The pointer changes to the Adjust pointer.

The Adjust handles are located at the vertices of the text wrapping boundary. As the shape of the boundary line becomes more complex or irregular, the number of Adjust handles increases.

4 Drag the Adjust handle to change the shape of the boundary around the image.

5 Release the mouse button. Publisher rewraps the text around the newly formed boundary.

Add and Delete Adjust Handles in an Irregular Text Wrapping Boundary

1 Select the picture or WordArt design whose frame you want to adjust. Click the Wrap Text To Picture button on the Format toolbar.

2 Click the Edit Irregular Wrap button.

Why can't I find individual text boxes for the left, right, top, and bottom margins in the Object Frame Properties dialog box? You have created an irregular text wrap boundary for the selected picture or WordArt element. To adjust the margin for the entire perimeter of the image, enter a value from 0 through 16 inches in the Outside text box. This will insert a uniform amount of space outside the image but within the text wrap boundary.

Add and Delete Adjust Handles in an Irregular Text Wrapping Boundary *(continued)*

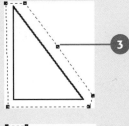

3 To add an Adjust handle, position the pointer along the text wrapping boundary where you want a new handle. Hold down the Ctrl key to turn the pointer into the Add pointer, and then click the left mouse button.

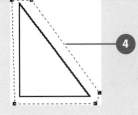

4 To delete an Adjust handle, position the Adjust pointer over a handle you don't need. Hold down the Ctrl key to turn the pointer into the Delete pointer and then click the left mouse button.

 For more information about adding graphic accents such as borders, BorderArt, or shadows to a picture frame, see Chapter 9.

Adjusting Picture Frame Margins

You can create white space between a picture and the frame surrounding it to add a decorative touch to a picture or to add breathing room between a picture and an elaborate border.

The picture becomes smaller if you increase the margins.

The picture becomes larger if you decrease the margins.

The margin (and background) can be filled with a color, tint, shade, pattern, or gradient.

Create margins with the Crop Picture tool. To create a picture frame margin using the Crop Picture tool, select a handle and pull the picture frame out until all of the image is revealed. As you continue to pull the frame, Publisher adds white space between the image and the frame, generating a custom margin. When you use the Crop Picture tool (instead of the Picture Frame Properties dialog box) to increase the margins, you increase the size of the picture frame without affecting the size or aspect ratio of the picture itself.

 For more information about WordArt, see Chapter 7. For more information about color choices in Publisher, see Chapter 15.

 Why can't I change the color of an Encapsulated PostScript picture? Publisher merely passes an Encapsulated PostScript (EPS) file to a Post-Script printer. As a result, Publisher can't access the actual picture data. Therefore, you can't recolor an EPS picture. To change the colors in an EPS file, use a drawing program that can edit EPS images, such as CorelDraw, Adobe Illustrator, or Macromedia Freehand.

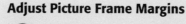 **Adjust Picture Frame Margins**

(1) Select the picture or WordArt frame.

(2) Choose Object Frame Properties. The Object Frame Properties dialog box appears.

(3) Enter values from 0 through 16 inches in the Left, Right, Top, and Bottom text boxes.

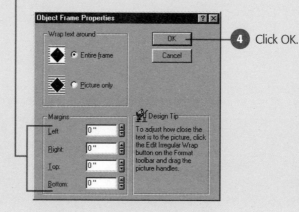

(4) Click OK.

Color Options for Imported Pictures and WordArt

With a single command, Publisher allows you to change all the colors in an imported picture. You might want to adjust a color scheme for artistic reasons, or for technical reasons regarding the capability of your output device. For example, you can recolor a multi-colored picture to shades of gray if you are planning to output your publication to a black-and-white printer. You can also circumvent the 35-color limit of the WordArt module by using the Recolor command to fill a WordArt object with a custom color, tint, or shade.

Can I change the color of individual elements in a picture? No, the Recolor Object command changes all the elements contained in a picture to shades or tints of a single color. To recolor individual elements in a picture, you must use a graphics application. Use a drawing program (such as Microsoft Draw) to change the colors of a vector picture. Use a paint program (such as Microsoft Paint) to change the colors of a bitmapped picture.

Use Draw to alter the appearance of bitmapped pictures. Though Draw is primarily a vector illustration program, you can use it to adjust the quality of bitmapped pictures. The controls provided by Draw are limited but useful. You can change the brightness and contrast of an image or make a selected color transparent. Four different display modes let you view a bitmap with its original colors, using gray-scale equivalents, in high-contrast black-and-white, or as a faint watermark.

For more information about Draw, see Appendix A.

The Recolor Object command works identically for vector and bitmapped pictures, but it has different effects, described here, depending on the number of colors contained in the original picture.

@ If your original picture contains multiple colors, the Recolor Picture command replaces the different colors with varying tints of the new color you choose.

@ If your original picture contains shades of gray, Publisher assigns a different tint of the new color you choose to each shade of gray.

@ If your original picture is black-and-white, Publisher substitutes the new color for all black areas. White areas remain unchanged.

Recolor a Picture

1 Select the picture or Wordart element you want to recolor.

2 Choose Recolor Object on the Format menu. The Recolor Object dialog box appears.

3 Open the Color drop-down menu and choose an available color, tint, or shade.

Confirm the effects of your choices in the Preview area.

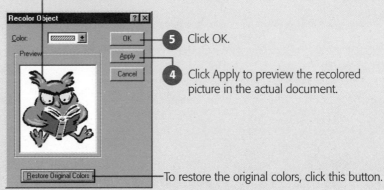

5 Click OK.

4 Click Apply to preview the recolored picture in the actual document.

To restore the original colors, click this button.

Working with OLE

Y ou can easily establish connections (known as links) between Microsoft Publisher files and files created and stored in other applications by using a process called Object Linking and Embedding (OLE). The OLE process allows you to embed objects from other applications into your Publisher documents. You can also embed only portions of a file as an OLE object. For example, you might need only the summary information from a very large spreadsheet.

The two functions of OLE—linking and embedding—are related but exhibit important differences, which are described in the following table.

Functions of OLE		
	Linking Files	**Embedding Files**
Process description	You connect an OLE frame in Publisher to a file (or portion of a file) created with an external application. The file is stored on your hard disk or a network drive.	You store a copy of a file (or portion of a file) in an OLE frame in Publisher. Or you create an object while working in Publisher by using another application.
Access	After you establish the link, both the originating application and Publisher have complete access to the file on disk.	Because the object is stored internally in Publisher, only Publisher has access to the object.
Advantages	You can use the same file in more than one publication. You can access files created or revised by other people on a network. Other people on a network can access and update the external files linked to your publication.	You can easily create and edit objects in Publisher because you have direct access to all the source application's functions. No one other than you can access the OLE object embedded in your Publisher document.
Object behavior	You determine whether the links in a publication will be updated automatically or manually on a case-by-case basis. Double-clicking a linked object starts the source application.	Double-clicking an embedded object starts the source application.

When can I take advantage of OLE? You can take advantage of OLE only if the other Windows 95–based applications on your computer support it. To see a list of OLE-compliant programs, open the Insert menu and choose Object. In the Insert Object dialog box, scroll through the Object Type list to see all the source programs currently installed on your system.

 Switch between Open Editing and In-Place Editing. You can make changes to an OLE object using Open Editing (in a separate window) instead of the default In-Place Editing (which is integrated into Publisher's window). Select the OLE object. On the Edit menu, select the command that identifies the application you used to create the object (such as Microsoft WordArt 3.2 Object). On the cascading menu, choose the Open command.

Creating an OLE Object

You have two options when you create an OLE object: you can draw a frame yourself, or you can let Publisher size the object for you.

If you create an OLE object without first drawing a frame, Publisher creates a frame to fit the object. This method maintains the original size and aspect ratio—the proportional relationship between the width and height of the image—and minimizes the distortion of OLE objects. This is Publisher's preferred method.

Alternatively, you can draw a frame before you create an OLE object. You should draw a frame only if you want to fit an OLE object into a predetermined layout. Publisher attempts to maintain the proportions of the OLE object, but some distortion can occur within very small frames. After the OLE object has been created, you can use Publisher's tools to modify the size of the object.

The current version of the OLE specification supports two editing modes, depending on the source application. When you create a new OLE object, the source application appears on screen in one of the following ways:

@ An application or utility using the Open Editing mode appears in a separate window. Microsoft Clip Gallery, which is discussed in Chapter 10, is a good example of an application that uses Open Editing.

@ An application or utility using In-Place Editing becomes part of the Publisher work area. Toolbars, menus, and dialog boxes appear for you to use. WordArt, discussed in Chapter 7, is a good example of a utility that uses In-Place Editing.

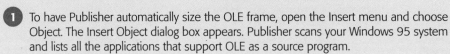

Create a New OLE Object While Working in Publisher

1 To have Publisher automatically size the OLE frame, open the Insert menu and choose Object. The Insert Object dialog box appears. Publisher scans your Windows 95 system and lists all the applications that support OLE as a source program.

Picture frames can contain OLE objects. If you want Publisher to size and proportion the OLE object to fit into a predetermined layout, click the Picture tool and draw a frame. With the picture frame selected, choose Object from the Insert menu. In the Insert Object dialog box, choose an Object type and proceed normally to create or embed an OLE object.

Why do certain OLE object types generate an error message when I attempt to insert them into a document? The OLE specification continues to evolve. A superset of OLE—called either ActiveX objects or Collaborative Data Objects (CDO)—unfortunately is not supported by Publisher. ActiveX and CDO objects (such as the Microsoft Direct Animation Control) are recognized by Windows as OLE objects, but they cannot be inserted into a Publisher document.

Create a New OLE Object While Working in Publisher *(continued)*

2 Choose the type of object you want to incorporate into the publication.

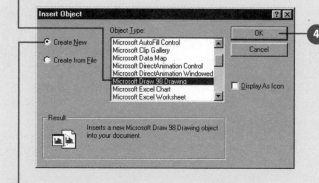

4 Click OK. The source utility or application appears.

3 Select Create New.

5 In the source application, create the object you want to embed.

6 Do one of the following:

@ If you are working within Publisher's window, click anywhere outside the OLE object to accept your changes and return to the Publisher document.

@ If you are working in a separate window, open the source application's File menu and select Exit And Return. A dialog box will appear that asks whether you want to update your publication. Click Yes to embed the object.

Link or Embed an Externally Stored File As an OLE Object

1 To have Publisher automatically size the OLE frame, open the Insert menu and choose Object. The Insert Object dialog box appears. Publisher scans your Windows 95 system and lists all the applications that support OLE as a source program.

Display information as an icon. The Display As Icon check box appears in both the Insert Object and Paste Special dialog boxes. This option is useful when you want easy access to information from another file but don't want the information to appear in your publication. Instead of viewing the contents of a file, you can use this option to insert an icon into your document. You can activate the source program and display the file by double-clicking the icon.

For more information about the Windows 95 Clipboard, see Chapter 3.

Link or Embed an Externally Stored File As an OLE Object *(continued)*

2 To use a file that exists on disk, select Create From File.

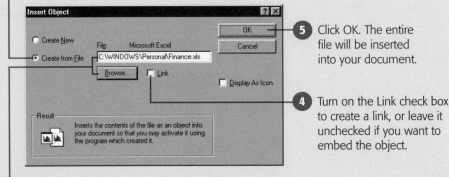

5 Click OK. The entire file will be inserted into your document.

4 Turn on the Link check box to create a link, or leave it unchecked if you want to embed the object.

3 Specify the location and name of the file. Alternatively, click Browse to search through the drives and folders on your system; then click Insert to return to the Insert Object dialog box.

Link or Embed Portions of a File As an OLE Object

1 Open a source program that supports OLE, such as Microsoft Word or Microsoft Excel.

2 In the source application, create or open the file you want to link. If you create a file, be sure to save it as a file on disk before you continue.

3 In the source application, select the portion of the file you want.

4 Open the Edit menu and select Copy to place the selection on the Windows 95 Clipboard.

5 Switch to Publisher.

6 Open Publisher's Edit menu and choose Paste Special. The Paste Special dialog box appears.

Why can't I access the Paste Link option in the Paste Special dialog box?

Not all Windows 95–based applications support OLE in the same way. If the Paste Link option is grayed out, you cannot create a link between Publisher and the source application.

Publisher treats OLE objects like pictures. You can alter the appearance of OLE objects by using Publisher's picture editing tools.

- You can increase or decrease the size of OLE objects by dragging a selection handle or by entering sizing percentages into the Scale Object dialog box (accessed from the Format menu).

- The Recolor Object command (found on the Format menu) applies varying tints of a chosen color to an OLE object.

- The Crop Picture tool lets you hide or reveal portions of an OLE object by resizing the frame without resizing the information it contains.

Link or Embed Portions of a File As an OLE Object *(continued)*

7 To embed the object, choose Paste. To link the object, choose Paste Link.

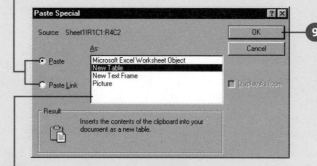

9 Click OK to return to your Publisher document.

8 In the As list box, choose the appropriate format for the object. The choices in the As list box vary depending on the type of data stored on the Clipboard. For example, if you've placed an Excel worksheet on the Clipboard, you can choose among Microsoft Excel Worksheet Object, New Table (which creates a Publisher table), New Text Frame, or Picture.

Determining How OLE Links Behave

After you create an OLE link, you can choose whether the correspondence between the OLE object in your publication and the external file with which it is associated will be updated automatically or manually.

Select Link Options for a Particular File

1 Open the Edit menu and select Links. The Links dialog box appears.

2 Select the linked object you want to update from the file list.

Clicking versus double-clicking. A single click selects an OLE object, allowing you to then move it or edit it with Publisher's picture tools. A double click starts the source program, allowing you to change the content and internal formatting of the object.

 Does clicking the Close button in the Links dialog box cancel the changes I've made? No. The Close command only returns you to your document. The functions of the Links dialog box take effect immediately when you click on an option or a button. If you want to cancel the modifications you've made, you must change the options back to the previous settings.

Select Link Options for a Particular File *(continued)*

3 Tell Publisher how often to update the link from the external file:

@ Click Automatic if you want Publisher to check the status of the external file each time you open your document. If the external file has been changed, Publisher will update the contents of the OLE frame with the latest version of the source file.

@ Click Manual if you want to control the frequency of the updates. Manual updates occur whenever you click the Update Now button, activate the source application by double-clicking the OLE object, or print the publication containing the OLE object.

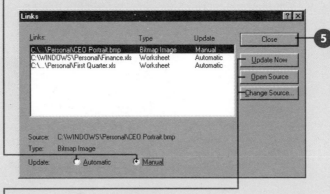

5 When you've finished modifying links and updating files, click the Close button.

4 Take one or more of the following actions:

@ Click Update Now to import the latest version of the file.

@ Click Open Source to start the source application and display the contents of the OLE object.

@ Click Change Source to choose a new source file or to reestablish a link with a source file that is in a new location. In the Change Source dialog box that appears, locate and select the new file, and then click OK.

Creating Documents for the World Wide Web

How do I find an Internet Service Provider?
You'll find that most well known online services, including the Microsoft Network, America Online, and CompuServe, offer Internet access. Major phone companies are providing national service; look into AT&T World Net, Sprint, or MCI One. Another option is to look up a local Internet Service Provider in your hometown yellow pages.

Procuring a Web browser.
Your Internet Service Provider (ISP) should supply you with a suite of Internet applications, including a browser program. Once you have access to the Internet, you can download a browser directly from a vendor's Web site. This guarantees that you'll have the most current version of a browser program, which is essential if you want to access the hottest features of the Web, such as Dynamic HTML, online animation or video, frame-based Web designs, and Java applets.

Microsoft Publisher can generate electronic documents. In contrast to regular desktop publishing documents, which are typically printed on paper, the following is true of electronic documents:

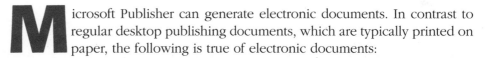

@ Web pages are intended to be read directly from the computer screen.

@ Web pages can include multimedia objects, so you can listen to sound files and view animations or digital videos.

@ Hyperlinks, in the form of hypertext or picture hot spots, allow you to move, or "surf," to other pages in an electronic publication, to other Web sites, or to other externally stored files regardless of their physical location.

@ Web documents can contain electronic forms that allow you to enter text, make selections from drop-down lists, or click check boxes.

@ Web documents allow readers to respond to authors, either by sending an email message (via a hyperlink) or by submitting a completed electronic form.

@ Electronic documents in the Hypertext Markup Language (HTML) format are easy to distribute via disk, network, or the Internet.

Load Microsoft Internet Explorer from CD. If you purchased the CD-ROM version of Publisher, you can install Microsoft's Web browser. On the CD, open the folder titled Msie (Microsoft Internet Explorer), and then double-click the Ie4setup.exe file. Follow the on-screen instructions to install the program.

What do those abbreviations and acronyms for communications hardware and software mean? Computer lingo can be confusing. Here are definitions of a few key terms you'll encounter when you hook up your computer to the Internet:

@ The device that sends and receives data over the phone lines does so by MOdulating and DEModulating a signal—hence the name modem.

@ Modem speed is always measured in bits per second (bps). The speeds are typically noted in units of thousands (indicated by the letter *K*), so a 28.8 K modem operates at 28,800 bits per second.

@ ISDN is an abbreviation for Integrated Services Digital Network.

@ TI is the designation used by Bell Systems to identify a digital carrier line.

Gaining Access to the Web: Internet Service Providers and Web Browsers

In order to take full advantage of Publisher's electronic document tools, you should have access to the Internet. You can think of the Internet as a global network (actually a collection of networks) that enables computers of all sorts—PCs, Macintoshes, and UNIX boxes—to communicate and exchange data. The Internet provides easy access to the World Wide Web (also referred to as WWW, or simply the Web).

Before you can fully access the Web, you must have a properly configured modem, an Internet Service Provider (ISP), and appropriate Internet applications, such as email and a Web browser. The following diagram illustrates the relationship between these various elements.

A high-speed modem physically connects your computer to a phone line. If you are using regular analog telephone lines, your modem speed should be 28,800 bits per second (bps) or, better yet, 56,000 bps. Though it's more expensive, digital access via an Integrated Services Digital Network (ISDN), or T1 connection, provides much better performance.

Applications allow you to perform specific tasks on the Internet. Here a Web browser application—Microsoft Internet Explorer—allows you to read documents online.

An ISP, such as the Microsoft Network (MSN), supplies communication software that connects you (via the phone line) to the Internet. You must then run separate applications to perform tasks on the Internet.

Design for the capabilities of browser software.

When you design an HTML document, try to keep the capabilities of browsers in mind. It is possible for an HTML document to contain formatting instructions that a browser application can't display. For example, older browsers cannot display tables properly. If you're designing a document for an internal network (called an intranet), or if you will supply browser software to your readers, you can take advantage of the superior functions offered by the browser program your readers will use. If, on the other hand, you're publishing your document on the Web and you have no control over which browser your readers will use, you have two choices:

@ You can design for the lowest common denominator of browser software, eliminating sophisticated design elements such as Dynamic HTML elements, frames, and tables.

@ You can put an alert at the top of your Web page advising readers that the document is best viewed with a particular browser.

Design Considerations: Publisher's HTML Tools

When you generate an electronic document, it must be converted from Publisher's native format (PUB) to the Hypertext Markup Language (HTML), which is the standard document format used on the Web. HTML was developed to facilitate speedy transmission of documents over standard phone lines. To make HTML as efficient as possible, its designers limited the layout and formatting options available. An HTML document is therefore much more restricted in appearance than a normal Publisher document.

Whenever you create a Web page, Publisher modifies the layout options. New commands and buttons appear on the toolbars or menus, and dialog boxes present you with only those choices that are appropriate for Web publishing. The following discussion is not meant to replace the detailed explanations of Publisher's design and layout tools covered in Chapters 1 through 11. Instead, it highlights the modified functions and new tools that are specific to Web design.

Beginning Work on a Web Publication

Just as with a normal Publisher document, a Web publication requires that you start a new publication and set up the page size, the background, and layout guides.

Starting a Web Publication from Scratch

You should choose the Web Page layout to begin a Web publication. Doing so signals Publisher to make the special Web publishing tools available to you.

Begin a New Web Publication

1 Access the Catalog dialog box, either by opening Publisher or by choosing New on the File menu.

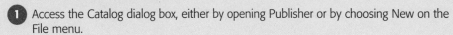

Use Publisher's automated design tools to create an electronic publication. If you click the Publications By Wizard tab in the Catalog dialog box, you can choose from 39 different Web site designs that are appropriate for a business, a community group, or home use. The Wizard generates a multiple page document complete with hyperlinks. You can also insert individual Web elements, such as a masthead or navigation bar, from Publisher's Design Gallery.

Web publications created with a Wizard or with elements from the Design Gallery are especially easy to change, because many objects are synchronized. When you change one instance of a synchronized object, all instances are updated automatically.

For more information about Wizards and the Design Gallery, see Chapter 14.

Begin a New Web Publication *(continued)*

2 Select the Blank Publications tab.

3 Select the Web Page layout.

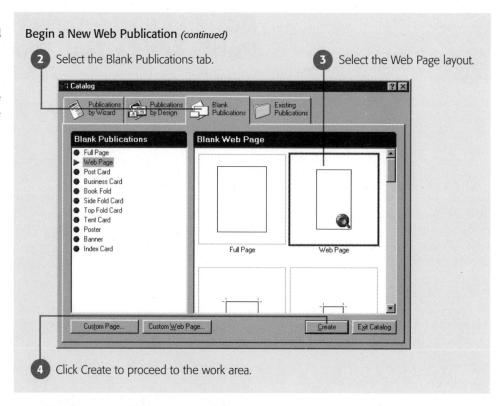

4 Click Create to proceed to the work area.

Setting Up a Web Page

Although HTML documents are referred to as having pages, they are meant to be read on screen. So when you access the Page Setup dialog box, Publisher gives you width options that correspond to standard VGA and SVGA screen resolutions.

Choose a page size that matches the screen resolution used by your readers. SVGA resolution is becoming more common, but there are still many users who own older VGA monitors. When choosing the page width of your Web publication, remember that your readers may not have the same high-resolution monitor that you do. For example, if you choose the Wide (or SVGA) option, readers with a VGA monitor will be forced to scroll horizontally as well as vertically to read the entire page.

For more information about Publisher's standard Page Setup dialog box, see Chapter 2.

Set Up a Web Page

1 Choose Page Setup on the File menu or click the Custom Web Page button on the Blank Publications tab in the Catalog dialog box. The Web Page Setup dialog box appears.

2 Choose one of these three options.

@ Select Standard for a screen width that corresponds to the VGA resolution of 640 by 480 pixels.

@ Select Wide for a screen width that corresponds to the SVGA resolution of 800 by 600 pixels.

@ Select Custom to set the specific width and height of your Web page.

When you choose the Standard or Wide page formats, the width is predetermined and cannot be changed. If you want to specify a different width, choose the Custom option.

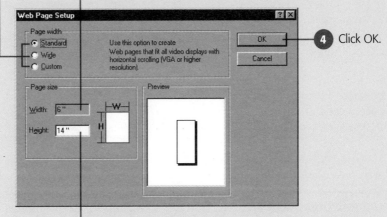

4 Click OK.

3 Enter a value from 0.25 through 240 inches in the Height text box. The page you create can be longer than a typical screen because Web browsers allow users to scroll down to view more information.

What is the difference between the Color and Background Scheme command and Publisher's standard background page? The Color And Background Scheme command lets you choose a color or a texture to display on all the pages in your Web publication. It's like choosing to print on colored paper: your selection affects the appearance of the final publication.

Publisher's Standard Background page functions identically in a Web publication or a paper-based publication. Place any elements you want to repeat—such as your company logo, a running head, or a page number—on the background, and Publisher automatically repeats them on every page of the document.

 For more information about Publisher's Standard Background, see Chapter 2.

 Why doesn't the Background And Text Colors command appear on the Format menu? This command appears on the Format menu only when you are working on a Web page. Open an existing Web document or create a new one to have the command appear on the Format menu.

Choosing a Web Page Background

You can choose to add a color, a texture, or both to the background of a Web Page layout. You can choose from 210 preformatted backgrounds, or you can create your own.

Choose a Color or Texture for a Web Page Background

1 Select Color And Background Scheme on the Format menu. The Color And Background Scheme dialog box appears.

2 Select either the Standard or Custom tab. The options for background color and texture are identical on both tabs.

3 In the Background area, open the Solid Color drop-down list and choose one of the available colors, tints, or shades.

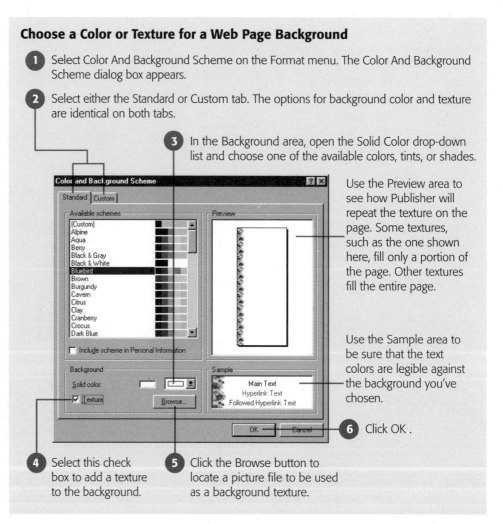

Use the Preview area to see how Publisher will repeat the texture on the page. Some textures, such as the one shown here, fill only a portion of the page. Other textures fill the entire page.

Use the Sample area to be sure that the text colors are legible against the background you've chosen.

6 Click OK .

4 Select this check box to add a texture to the background.

5 Click the Browse button to locate a picture file to be used as a background texture.

Create an efficient custom background texture. Don't use a large bitmapped graphic as the background texture for your Web document. A picture with large dimensions, high resolution, and many colors takes a long time to download—and will keep your readers waiting for your Web page to appear. Instead, use a small picture. You should strive for a file of 20 KB or less. For example, the following picture of patterned marble measures only 1 by 1 and occupies only 9 KB of disk space. Make sure the picture is "in repeat," which means that the top, bottom, left, and right edges form a seamless match when multiple copies of the image are tiled to fill the screen. When a reader accesses your Web page, only the small original picture is transmitted. The Web browser repeats the image to form a continuous pattern.

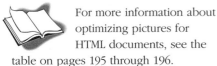For more information about optimizing pictures for HTML documents, see the table on pages 195 through 196.

Setting Up Layout Guides

Publisher's layout guides function normally within a Web publication and can help you design your Web page. Layout guides allow you to divide the screen into columns and rows, as shown in the following illustrations. You should use the column and row guides to be sure that text and picture frames do not overlap. Since HTML does not support overlapping objects, Publisher automatically converts overlapping objects (even text objects) into a graphic region.

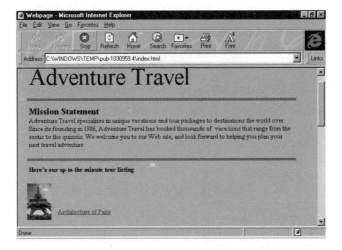

Typical Web pages rely on a simple linear layout, in which text and pictures align along the left margin. This Web page can be viewed by a large number of browser applications, including older programs.

Divide the page into rows to create a standard (linear) Web page design.

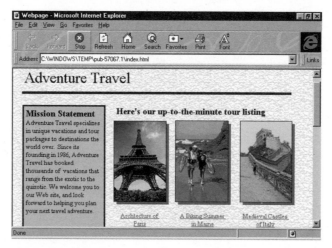

More sophisticated Web designs rely on frames to separate the screen into separate regions. To view this page properly, the browser application must be able to display frames.

Use custom column and row guides to separate a Web page into regions.

Can I import other graphics file formats into a Web publication? Yes. You can import pictures into your Web publication in any format Publisher supports. When you generate the HTML document, however, Publisher automatically converts the image to a GIF file.

For more information about graphics file formats, see Chapter 10.

Managing Art in a Web Document

To create efficient Web documents, you must understand how both HTML and Publisher handle pictures, sounds, and motion clips.

In-Line GIF Graphics

In-line graphics are an integral part of a Web page. They appear within the browser window and are embedded in the text flow. Currently, graphical Web browsers restrict in-line graphics to two bitmapped file formats: the GIF (CompuServe Graphics Interchange Format) and JPEG (Joint Photographic Experts Group) formats. However, Publisher converts all imported graphics to the GIF format by taking a "snapshot" of your Web pages as they are displayed on your screen.

The GIF format offers cross-platform compatibility (meaning that it can be viewed on PCs, Macintoshes, and UNIX machines) and sophisticated compression schemes. This last point is very important because bitmapped pictures can grow quite large. Your goal will be to produce the smallest, most efficient graphics files without sacrificing image quality. The following table summarizes various optimization techniques you can use when creating GIF images.

Optimizing GIF Images for Web Publications		
Feature	**Description**	**Optimization Technique**
Dimensions	The size at which a picture will appear on screen. Measure your graphics in pixels because monitors are measured in pixels. For example, a picture measuring 200 by 200 pixels will fill nearly 1/7 of a 640-by-480 monitor.	Create pictures that measure between 80 and 150 pixels (vertically and horizontally). Images that will be used as button icons should be even smaller—as small as 30 by 30 pixels.
Resolution	Resolution is defined as the number of dots that occur in a particular unit of measurement. Most scanning utilities measure the number of dots per inch (dpi).	It is preferable to size a picture using the actual dimensions measured in pixels (see "Dimensions" above). If your scanning utility requires you to enter a resolution, scan at 72 dpi, which is the resolution of most monitors. Because images in a Web document are always displayed at a 1:1 ratio with the screen resolution, scanning a picture at a higher resolution will not make the image appear more detailed; it will simply make it larger.
Colors	A bitmapped graphic contains a specific number of colors. The color capability of a bitmapped file is measured by bit depth. A 4-bit file contains 16 colors, an 8-bit file contains 256 colors, and a 24-bit file contains potentially 16.7 million colors.	Use a graphics program to reduce the number of colors in a bitmapped picture. Use a full-featured graphics utility or image editing program that allows you to specify the bit depth, palette, and dither pattern. Reduce a picture to 256 colors or less, as the GIF format supports a maximum of 256 colors.
Compression	The GIF format uses a sophisticated compression routine that can dramatically reduce file size. GIF uses LZW compression, named after the two individuals who invented it (Lempel-Zir and Welch). LZW compression does not discard any picture data and typically delivers modest compression ratios of 2:1. (A compressed file is approximately half the size of an uncompressed file.)	In your graphics utility or image editing program, save the image using the GIF format. The LZW compression scheme is automatically applied.

Creating Web Documents

Feature	Description	Optimization Technique
Interlacing	This encoding method keeps track of the odd-numbered and even-numbered scan lines in a picture. When the image is downloaded, all the odd-numbered scan lines are transmitted first. The result, from the user's point of view, is that the full image, though blurry, appears on screen in half the time it would take the full image to appear. The image will come into focus as the second half of the image data (the even-numbered scan lines) are downloaded to complete the picture. Note that interlacing increases the *apparent* transmission speed of the image, not the actual speed.	To take advantage of interlacing, your graphics utility or image editing program must be able to export interlaced GIF files.
Transparency	When displayed, one or more colors within a picture appear to be transparent. This technique is especially useful if you want to create silhouettes, the effect where the irregular outline of a picture appears against the background of an HTML page. Instead of filling the picture with the same color or pattern as the background page, you designate the fill color as transparent. Publisher allows you to use transparent GIFs as background textures; the solid background color you've chosen will show through the transparent areas of the background GIF file.	To take advantage of transparency, your graphics utility or image editing program must be able to designate a chosen color as transparent and also export version 89a of the GIF format.
Animation	A single GIF file can contain a series of images. When viewed sequentially, these images flow together to create the illusion of movement.	When viewed in a Web browser, a GIF file plays continuously. You should create an animation loop where the movement or gesture in the last image flows seamlessly into the movement or gesture in the first image.

Why doesn't Publisher recognize certain features of my GIF file, like transparency and animation? You have pasted the GIF file into your document from the Microsoft Windows 95 Clipboard. The Clipboard doesn't recognize, and won't preserve, transparent color information or multi-image GIF files. Delete the problematic GIF file. Insert a new copy of the file into your document by using the Insert Picture command or by dragging the file from Windows Explorer into Publisher.

For more information about hyperlinks, see pages 209 through 214. For more information about inserting an HTML code fragment, see page 224.

Why can't I see pictures or WordArt elements when I view a Publisher-generated Web page with my browser? Many browsers allow you to turn off the display of graphics in order to speed up performance. If you (or your readers) have turned off the display of graphics, all pictures and any text that has been converted to a graphic region will not appear on screen. To view these elements, turn on the display of graphics.

Using JPEG Images in a Web Publication

All graphical Web browsers can display JPEG images. Like GIF files, JPEG images can be viewed on any computer platform. Progressive JPEG images, like interlaced GIF files, appear to download more quickly as they fade in on the reader's screen. The JPEG format, however, has the following advantages over the GIF format:

@ JPEG files can contain 16.7 million colors, which delivers a higher-quality photographic image.

@ JPEG files employ a lossy-compression scheme, which achieves very high compression ratios by discarding redundant data. A 30:1 compression ratio (where a compressed file is 1/30 the size of the original uncompressed file) is not uncommon.

Unfortunately, if you use Publisher's normal Insert Picture command to place a JPEG file in a Web document, Publisher automatically converts it to a GIF image when it generates the HTML code. You can still display JPEG images from within your publication, using one of these two methods:

@ Create a hyperlink from the in-line GIF file to an external JPEG picture file. When your reader clicks the hyperlink, the reader's Web browser will retrieve and display the external JPEG file as a separate page.

@ Insert an HTML code fragment. When you view the file in Publisher, the HTML code fragment will be displayed as a simple text command. When you view the publication using a Web browser, however, the actual JPEG image will be displayed at the location of the frame containing the HTML code fragment.

Graphic Regions

When you insert or create an object in a Web publication that is not supported by the HTML specification, Publisher converts the object to a picture, called a graphic region. Within an HTML document, graphic regions behave just like any other bitmapped picture. For example, they can increase download times substantially.

The advantages and disadvantages of graphic regions. Graphic regions have important functions: they preserve your layout. Overlapping objects, for example, will appear on screen exactly as you created them, even though HTML does not support overlapping objects. However, graphic regions do have a drawback: they can increase download times substantially.

Use graphic regions to incorporate unusual fonts in your Web documents. You can use an unusual font in your Web page for special text elements, such as headlines. But you must convert the font into a picture—or graphic region—to be sure that the typeface will be displayed properly by your reader's browser application. The easiest way to convert text to a picture is to create it using WordArt.

Architecture of Paris
A full week's worth of walking tours take you to every corner of Paris. With the help of an informed tour guide, you'll see well known landmarks, like the Eiffel Tower, from a new perspective.

If you overlap frames, Publisher alerts you that it will create a graphic region by outlining the objects with a flashing red box. It does this only once—at the moment two objects overlap. The flashing red box delineates the size of the graphic region, which is equal in size to a rectangle large enough to encompass all the objects. (For a single object, the graphic region is equal to the size of the object's frame.)

Within a Web document, Publisher creates a graphic region whenever you take one of the following actions:

@ Overlap frames. This applies if you position a picture frame over a text frame, in order to create a text wrap, or if you overlap two text frames.

@ Create a WordArt object.

@ Rotate a text frame.

@ Add BorderArt to a text frame.

@ Fill a text frame with a pattern or gradient.

Managing Multimedia Objects in a Web Page

By using Publisher's Clip Gallery, you can easily insert multimedia objects, such as sounds, digital videos, and GIF animations, into a Web document. Publisher allows you to import any multimedia format supported by the Microsoft Windows 95 Media Player. For example, you can import sound files in the WAV format and videos in the AVI format, because the drivers for these standard formats were automatically loaded when you installed the media player as part of Windows 95. Other file formats, such as the MIDI and RMI formats for sound, require that you specifically install drivers.

When imported into a document, multimedia files appear to be static images. Sound files are represented by an icon. Clicking the icon while running a Web browser plays the recording. Motion clips are represented by the first frame of the movie or animation.

Why can't I play a sound file or view a motion clip that I've placed in a Publisher document? You cannot play sounds or motion clips within Publisher. The images (or icons) representing multimedia files are used for position only. To hear a sound file or view a motion clip, you must preview the Web site using your browser application. Alternatively, you can preview sounds and motion clips by using the Play button in Microsoft Clip Gallery 4.0.

 For more information about Microsoft Clip Gallery 4.0, see Chapter 10.

 What is the difference between Collaborative Data Objects, a plug-in, and MIME? These three specifications allow Web browsers to display file formats not directly supported by HTML and to play multimedia files. The older MIME specification allows the browser to open a window and run a separate helper application in order to play the multimedia file. For example, the Windows 95 Media Player functions as a MIME helper app when it plays videos in a separate window. Browser applications that support Microsoft Collaborative Data Objects (also known as ActiveX Controls) and Netscape's plug-in specification can display files and access multimedia objects within the main browser window.

 A WAV file is identified by a picture of a speaker.

 GIF animations play continuously when viewed in a Web browser.

 East_01.mid
The icon for a MIDI file always includes the filename.

 Kyack.avi
Digital video files are always identified with a filename. Clicking the image while running a Web browser plays the movie.

Users who want to play the multimedia files in your Web document must have the proper hardware and software on *their* systems, including:

- A sound card to play sound files and the soundtrack associated with video files.
- A color monitor to display videos.
- The Windows 95 Media Player and appropriate sound and video drivers.
- A browser application that can display animated GIF files.
- A browser application that supports Microsoft Collaborative Data Objects (or ActiveX Controls), the Netscape plug-in specification, or MIME (Multipurpose Internet Mail Extension) helper applications.

Choosing a Background Sound for the Pages in Your Web Site

You can choose to play a background file whenever someone accesses a page in your Web site. You can choose a brief sound to add a musical flourish when the page first appears on screen. Or you can also choose to loop the sound file to play it a specified number of times or continuously while the page is displayed.

Creating Web Documents

For more information about the Web Properties dialog box, see pages 229 through 230.

Loop appropriate sounds.
A sound loop refers to a traditional analog technique that physically joins the beginning and end of a piece of audio tape—creating a never-ending loop that plays continuously. Publisher can play a digital sound file a specified number of times or continuously. However, only you can choose an appropriate piece of music. Choose a soundtrack in which the last note of the composition flows seamlessly into the first note.

For more information about HTML code fragments, see pages 223 through 224.

Background sounds differ from the sound files you insert into your publication.

@ You associate a sound file with a specific page in your publication using the Web Properties dialog box. The sound file never appears as an object in the layout.

@ The sound file plays as soon as the page is opened in a Web browser. It plays according to the parameters you have chosen in the Web Properties dialog box.

@ Your reader has no control over the sound file. The only way to stop the music is to go to another page.

Specify a Background Sound File for Your Web Site

1 Move to the page in your Web publication where you want to play a background sound.

2 Select Web Properties on the File menu.

3 Click the Page tab.

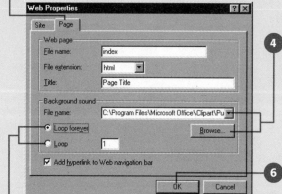

4 Enter the filename and location of the sound file you want to play. Alternatively, you can open the drop-down list box to access a list of recently used sound files, or click the Browse button to find the file using the Files And Folders list box.

6 Click OK.

5 Click Loop Forever to play the sound continuously, or click Loop and then enter a value between 1 and 99 in the text box to play the sound a specified number of times.

Inserting Dynamic HTML Elements into a Web Page

The latest modification to the HTML specification, called Dynamic HTML (DHTML), makes your Web pages come to life. DHTML can generate special effects, such as pop-up boxes, scrolling text and graphics, buttons that change appearance when the mouse passes over them, and objects that can appear, disappear, or move around the screen.

Publisher does not offer any tools to directly create DHTML effects. However, you can bypass this limitation by copying DHTML code from a source application (a programming tool or authoring program) and pasting it into Publisher's HTML Code Fragment Properties dialog box.

If you include DHTML elements in your Web pages, you must be aware that only the most current versions of browser software, specifically Microsoft Internet Explorer 4.0 and Netscape Communicator, can display DHTML documents. Furthermore, Internet Explorer 4.0 and Netscape Communicator implement DHTML differently. DHTML code written for one of these browsers won't run properly with the other. For a simple solution to this conflict, instruct your readers to use a specific browser when they access your Web site. Alternatively, you can find a DHTML authoring tool that generates the proper code for both browsers and provides an HTML routine to determine which browser the reader is using and which version of the DHTML code to display.

Managing Text Elements in a Web Publication

Text is the most important element in a Web document. It conveys most, if not all, of the information in your publication. Equally significant, text downloads much more quickly than a picture. Your goal as a Web publisher is twofold:

@ To produce a text design that fits within the limitations of the HTML specification

@ To avoid converting true text objects into graphic regions, which, as pictures, download much more slowly

Why does the text in my HTML document take a long time to download?

You may simply be experiencing the transmission delays that normally occur when there is a lot of traffic on the World Wide Web. However, your document may contain graphic regions rather than true text. Open the original PUB file and check for any conditions that may have forced Publisher to convert true text into a graphic region.

For more information about graphic regions, see pages 197 through 198.

The HTML specification does not offer absolute control over the appearance of text. It primarily defines the relationship between text elements. Think of this structure as a big outline where you define the relative importance of text, for example, headings versus body copy. You can request specific text formatting attributes, such as font and point size, but the reader's browser program may not be able to fulfill those requests and may make undesirable substitutions.

In addition, many standard text formatting attributes, such as line spacing and tabs, are simply not supported by HTML. When Publisher converts the PUB document to an HTML document, most of your formatting will be lost. The following comparison illustrates this process.

Unusual font choices, such as Eras Bold ITC, might look correct in your Publisher document, but they will be replaced with a standard font, such as Times New Roman, if your readers do not have the same fonts installed on their computer systems.

Because HTML supports only single-spaced text, the additional line spacing in the Publisher document doesn't appear in the final Web document.

The following table summarizes formatting attributes that may prove to be troublesome when the PUB document is converted to HTML, or when a reader accesses the document using a Web browser.

Text and Text Frame Formatting Guidelines for Web Publications			
Text Attribute	**In a Publisher Document**	**In an HTML Document**	**Recommended Text Formats**
Font	You can format text with any font installed on your system.	Publisher will insert a request for the font into the HTML document, but if your reader does not have the same font installed, a standard font will be substituted.	Format text in a Web document with the following standard fonts: Arial, Arial Black, Comic Sans MS, Courier New, Goergia, Impact, Symbol, Times New Roman, Trebuchet MS, Verdana, and Wingdings. You can enhance these typefaces with font styles, such as regular, italic, bold, and bold italic.
Point size	Publisher can format text from 0.5 through 999.5 points in 0.5-point increments.	HTML supports only seven font size designations. The actual point size at which type will appear on screen is determined by the reader's browser application.	Format text ranging from 10 through 30 points Reserve the 10-point size body copy.
Line spacing	Publisher allows you to set line spacing from 0.25 through 124 spaces in quarter-space increments (or from 3 through 1488 points in 0.5-point increments).	HTML documents are displayed with single line spacing. All line-spacing attributes within the Publisher document are ignored.	Set all copy using single line spacing.
Indents	Publisher allows you to create indents for the left side, right side, and first line of a paragraph.	HTML does not allow indents. Any indents within the Publisher document will be ignored.	Distinguish the beginning of a paragraph with an extra line space. As an alternative to indents, increase the text frame margins.
Bulleted and numbered lists	Publisher can automatically create bulleted and numbered lists.	HTML supports both bulleted and numbered lists. Many of the advanced formatting options within Publisher (such as the ability to specify the style of bullet or change the indent) will be ignored when the publication is converted to HTML.	Create simple bulleted and numbered lists.

Text Attribute	In a Publisher Document	In an HTML Document	Recommended Text Formats
Alignment	Publisher gives you four alignment options: left, right, center, and justified.	HTML supports left, right, and center alignment only.	For maximum legibility, keep most of your text left aligned. Reserve the center alignment option for headlines and short lists.
Tabs	Publisher allows you to set four kinds of tab stops: left, right, center, and decimal.	HTML does not recognize tabs of any kind. When you insert a tab, Publisher converts it to a space.	Avoid tabs.
Hyphenation	Publisher offers both automatic and optional hyphenation.	HTML does not support automatic or optional hyphenation.	Turn off automatic hyphenation and refrain from using optional hyphens. However, you can manually insert the hyphen character or a non-breaking hyphen.
Character spacing	Publisher allows you to modify the spacing for an entire paragraph (called tracking) or for selected characters (called kerning).	HTML does not support tracking or kerning. All adjustments you make in the Publisher document will be ignored.	Do not apply tracking or kerning to text in a Web document.
Underlining	Publisher allows you to choose among 17 underlining effects.	HTML displays only a single solid underline. Publisher's other underlining styles will be converted to a single solid underline.	In Web documents, underlining is often used to signal hypertext links. You should therefore avoid underlining other types of text elements because it can confuse your readers.
Text color	You can choose colors to identify normal text, hyperlink text, and followed hyperlinks. Publisher also lets you assign any color, tint, or shade to selected text.	The color you assign to text will be maintained in the HTML document.	Because readers may view your Web document on a 16- or 256-color monitor, you should choose solid text colors that contrast contrast with the background color. Do not confuse readers by choosing the same or similar colors for normal text and hypertext links.
Table text	Publisher can produce true tables that are arranged like a spreadsheet, in rows and columns.	The current version of HTML does accept tables. However, some older browsers don't display tables properly.	Include tables in your Web publications if you are certain your readers will be using a full-featured browser that can display tables.

Text Attribute	In a Publisher Document	In an HTML Document	Recommended Text Formats
Multiple columns	In a standard publication, you can create up to 63 columns in a text frame. In a Web publication, however, this option is unavailable.	HTML does not support multiple columns.	If you want to create multiple text columns, draw individual text frames and link them to accommodate text flow.
Object fill	Publisher lets you fill a text frame with any color, tint, shade, pattern, or gradient.	When the PUB document is converted to HTML, all text frames containing a pattern or gradient will be converted to a graphic region. In addition, older browsers may not be able to display solid fill colors in a text frame.	Avoid filling text frames with patterns and gradients. Use colors, tints, and shades in a text frame with discretion. Readers viewing your Web page with an older browser or on a 16-color monitor may see a different (dithered) color or no color at all. The text itself, however, will display normally.
Borders and BorderArt	Publisher allows you to assign either a line border or BorderArt to a text frame.	Older browsers may not be able to display line borders. Because BorderArt is not recognized by HTML, text frames with BorderArt are converted to graphic regions.	Avoid using BorderArt on text frames. Use line borders with discretion. If a reader views your Web site with an older browser, the line border might not be displayed. The text itself, however, will display normally.
Shadow	Publisher can create a drop shadow for a text frame.	Older browsers may not be able to display shadows on text frames.	Use shadows on text frames with discretion. If a reader views your Web site with an older browser, the shadow might not be displayed. The ext itself, however, will display normally.
Rotation	Publisher can rotate a text frame in 1-degree increments.	HTML does not support rotated text. The rotated text frame will be converted to a graphic region.	Avoid rotated text.

Using Color to Differentiate Normal Text from Hypertext

Web documents often use different colors to distinguish normal text from hyperlink text that triggers and event when it is clicked. A third color is used to show readers that they have already explored (or followed) the links associated with a hypertext element. You control the color of Main Text, Hyperlink Text, and Followed Hyperlinks using the Color And Background Scheme dialog box.

For more information about choosing colors, see Chapter 15.

Why doesn't the text in my document change color when I choose a new color and background scheme?

In all likelihood, you have applied a non-scheme color to a particular word or phrase in your document. Highlight the text and use the Font Color button on the Format toolbar, or the Font command on the Format menu, to change the color of the text to the appropriate scheme color.

Choose Standard or Custom Colors for Normal and Hyperlink Text

1 Click Color And Background Scheme on the Format menu. The Color And Background Scheme dialog box appears.

2 Click the Standard tab and select one of the predefined color schemes. Publisher automatically chooses the best colors for the Main Text, Hyperlink Text, and Followed Hyperlink Text elements. Alternatively, click the Custom tab to choose your own colors.

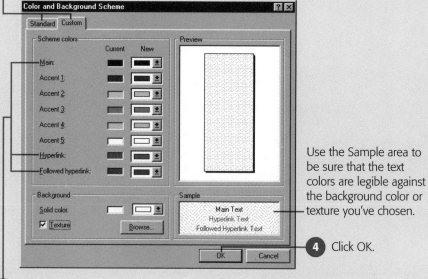

Use the Sample area to be sure that the text colors are legible against the background color or texture you've chosen.

4 Click OK.

3 Open the color drop-down lists for the Main Text, Hyperlink Text, and Followed Hyperlink Text elements; choose an available color, tint, or shade.

Special considerations for multilingual documents.

Only newer browsers that support the HTML 4.0 (or later) specification will be able to properly display multilingual documents. If you are creating a multilingual document, select the HTML 4.0+ Browsers option (found on the Site tab of the Web Properties dialog box). You must also identify the language for each paragraph in a multilingual document by highlighting the text and by choosing a language in the Set Language dialog box (found on the Language cascading menu on the Tools menu).

Choosing a Language for Your Web Site

When you publish documents on the World Wide Web, you have the potential to reach many non-English-speaking readers. You can publish your Web site in a language other than your system's default language. You can even create a multilingual document that contains text in more than one language. For the text to appear on screen correctly, you must choose a character set, and you must identify that character set for the reader's browser program.

Choose a Language for Your Web Site

1 Click Web Properties on the File menu. The Web Properties dialog box appears.

2 Click the Site tab.

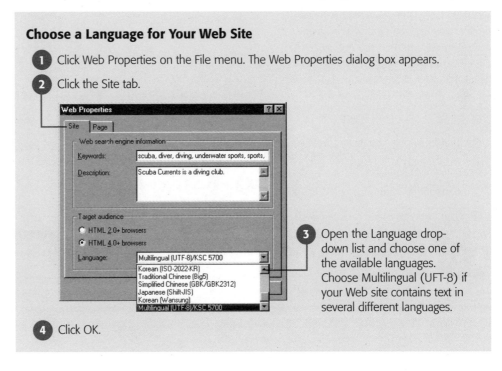

3 Open the Language drop-down list and choose one of the available languages. Choose Multilingual (UFT-8) if your Web site contains text in several different languages.

4 Click OK.

Creating Web Documents

Why isn't the language I need available in the Language drop-down box?

To create documents in different languages, you must install Multilanguage support for the Windows 95 operating system. The Windows Setup tab (in the Add/Remove Programs window of the Control Panel) lets you install support for Greek, Cyrillic, and Central European alphabets. In addition, the Publisher CD contains the following languages. To install them, double-click the associated filename in the LANGPACK folder:

- Japanese, IIELPKJA.EXE
- Pan-European, IELPKPE.EXE
- Korean, IELPKKO.EXE
- Simplified Chinese, IELPKZHC.EXE
- Traditional Chinese, IELPKZHT.EXE

Is the Design Checker available only when I convert a standard print publication to a Web publication? No, the Design Checker is always available. It is accessed from the Tools menu.

For more information about the Design Checker, see Chapter 3. For more information about publishing a Web site, see pages 230 through 231.

Converting a Print Publication to a Web Publication

Publisher can create a Web document from a standard publication that has been designed for printed output. Although the Create Web Site From Current Publication command is convenient, this function should be used with caution. Many design elements commonly used in print publications (such as overlapping objects, WordArt elements, and rotated text) are not supported by HTML. If you convert a print publication to a Web publication without a careful examination of the layout and an intelligent redesign, you will produce inefficient Web documents. Luckily, Publisher's Design Checker can alert you to potential problems.

Create a Web Publication from an Existing Publisher Document

1 Open the publication file you want to convert to a Web document.

2 Choose Create Web Site From Current Publication on the File menu. Publisher will display an alert box prompting you to save the file. Click Yes.

3 Publisher then displays an alert box asking if you want to run the Design Checker.

4 Click Yes to activate the Design Checker to discover problems specific to Web pages.

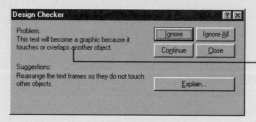

The Design Checker looks for objects that will be converted to graphic regions.

Publication Wizards easily convert documents between print and screen versions. If you use a Publication Wizard to create a print document, such as a newsletter or a brochure, use the Wizard again to convert the publication to a Web site. The command is listed in the Wizard window. Because Wizards keep track of the Smart Objects in a publication, the conversion is more intelligent and less likely to generate an inefficient Web site. For example, the Wizard can automatically generate hyperlinks, and it won't overlap objects. You can even use a Publication Wizard to convert a Web site to a paper-based publication. The Wizard allows you to create either a newsletter or a brochure from the Web site.

To learn more about Wizards and Smart Objects, see Chapter 14.

Create a Web Publication from an Existing Publisher Document *(continued)*

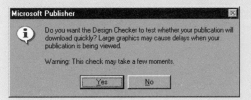

The Design Checker can also discover large graphics that will increase the time it takes to download your Web publication.

5 When you've finished running the Design Checker and making any necessary changes, save the publication file with a new name.

6 When you're ready to create an HTML document, use the Save As HTML or Publish To Web command found on the File menu.

Creating and Managing Hyperlinks in a Web Document

You've probably heard the Internet described as the Information Highway. In keeping with the road map metaphor, hyperlinks are the road signs that point to specific addresses on the World Wide Web. A Web address is called a URL, or Uniform Resource Locator. Hyperlinks can be associated with text, in which case they're called hypertext links. Hyperlinks associated with graphics objects, such as imported pictures and drawn shapes, are called picture hot spots. The following diagram illustrates how a hyperlink works.

Creating Web Documents

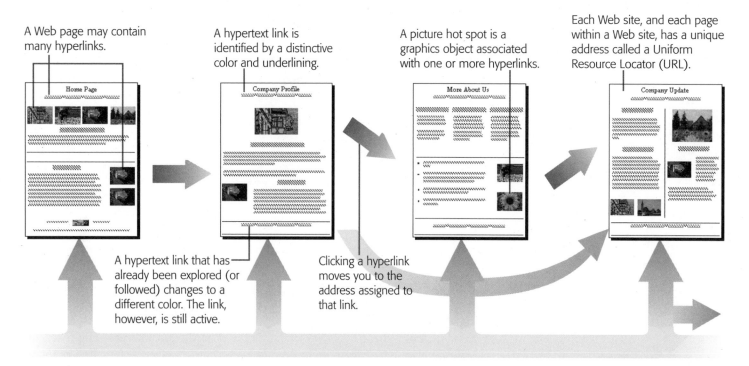

A Web page may contain many hyperlinks.

A hypertext link is identified by a distinctive color and underlining.

A picture hot spot is a graphics object associated with one or more hyperlinks.

Each Web site, and each page within a Web site, has a unique address called a Uniform Resource Locator (URL).

A hypertext link that has already been explored (or followed) changes to a different color. The link, however, is still active.

Clicking a hyperlink moves you to the address assigned to that link.

Hyperlinks are not linear: they can move you forward in a document, backward in a document, or to a completely different location on the Web.

Creating Hyperlinks

A hyperlink can be assigned to a text phrase, a picture, a shape, or a picture hot spot. The Picture Hot Spot tool is especially useful when you want to add more than one hyperlink to a graphics object.

Creating a hyperlink is a two-part process. You first assign a hyperlink to a selected text phrase, picture, shape, or picture hot spot. You must then choose the type of the hyperlink. Publisher can create four types of hyperlinks, as explained in the following table.

Types of Hyperlinks

Create this hyperlink...	To perform this action...	Based on this information...
To another page in your Web site	This is an exploring hyperlink. It will move the reader to another page in the current Web publication.	You must specify a relative or absolute page number. Relative pages (first page, previous page, and next page) are useful for generic controls such as page turn icons that appear on every page of a document. Absolute page numbers are useful when you're cross-referencing specific information or creating an index.
To another document already on the Web	This is an exploring hyperlink. It will move the reader to another address anywhere on the Web.	You must specify a Web address, or URL.
To an Internet email address	This is a response hyperlink. When clicked, it allows the reader to send a message to the specified address.	You must enter a valid Internet email address. If you enter your own email address, your readers can contact you or your company easily.
To a file on a Web server	This hyperlink downloads a file from your Web server (which can be your local hard disk) to the reader's hard disk.	Type the full path, including the drive designation, the folders, and the filename with its extension. If you don't know the full path, click the Browse button (in the Hyperlink dialog box) to search for the file. When you select the file and click Open, Publisher will enter the correct path information in the text box.

Fast access to the Hyperlink dialog box. You can activate the Hyperlink dialog box quickly in one of two ways:

@ Click the Hyperlink button on the Standard toolbar.

@ Right-click the object to which you want to assign a hyperlink. On the shortcut menu, choose the Hyperlink command.

Create a Hyperlink

1 Highlight text, or select a picture or a drawn shape.

2 Choose Hyperlink on the Insert menu. The Hyperlink dialog box appears.

Creating Web Documents

Entering Internet addresses correctly. If you want the hyperlinks in your Web pages to function properly, you must enter the URL correctly. Look closely at the following sample URL and note what each part of the address signifies.

Identifies the Hypertext Transfer Protocol, the method used on the Web to locate files.

Identifies the World Wide Web.

`http://www.microsoft.com`

Identifies the domain, or host, name.

Identifies the organization type. Abbreviations include *com* (commercial), *edu* (education), *gov* (government), *mil* (military), and *org* (organization).

Why is the Picture Hot Spot tool grayed out? Publisher makes the Picture Hot Spot tool available when you're working on a Web publication—and only then. If the Picture Hot Spot tool appears grayed out, you're probably designing a standard print publication. You need to open an existing Web publication, choose the Web Site or Web Page layout in the Startup dialog box, or convert the current publication to a Web site.

Create a Hyperlink *(continued)*

3 Choose the type of hyperlink you want to associate with the selected object.

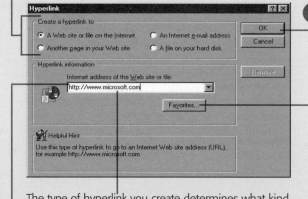

5 Click OK. If your selected object is a text phrase, Publisher changes the color and underlines the selected text. If your selected object is a picture or a shape, Publisher creates the hyperlink but does not change the appearance of the selected object.

The type of hyperlink you create determines what kind of information you must enter in the Hyperlink Information text box. For example, if you create a hyperlink to a document on the Web, you must enter an Internet address. If you create a hyperlink to a file on your hard disk, you must enter the path to locate that file.

Click here to select an address from a list of the Web sites you visited most recently.

4 Enter the appropriate information in the Hyperlink Information area. In this case, you must enter an Internet address.

Create a Picture Hot Spot

1 Select the Picture Hot Spot tool (shown here) from the toolbar. The pointer changes to the Crossbar pointer.

2 Position the Crossbar over the picture where you want to add a hot spot.

Why do I have trouble selecting hot spot objects?

By default, the Picture Hot Spot tool creates transparent, borderless rectangles. Like all other objects in a Publisher document, hot spots have object boundaries (which disappear when you generate an HTML document). Object boundaries are light gray dotted lines, which can be difficult to see on screen, especially when the hot spot is stacked on top of a picture. You can, however, temporarily format a hot spot object with attributes such as a line border or a fill color to make it easy to see and select.

You can also group a hot spot with a picture. When you select, move, or resize the picture, the hot spot will also be selected, moved, or resized.

Create a Picture Hot Spot *(continued)*

3 While holding down the mouse button, drag the mouse diagonally to create a transparent rectangle. You may create a rectangle that completely surrounds the underlying picture, or you may create a rectangle that surrounds only a portion of the underlying picture.

4 When the shape and size of the hot spot are to your liking, release the mouse button. The Hyperlink dialog box appears.

5 Choose the type of hyperlink you want to assign to the selected picture.

6 Enter the appropriate information in the Hyperlink Information area.

7 Click OK to create the hyperlink.

Editing Hyperlinks

You can change the characteristics of a hyperlink, including its type, file location, and URL. The ability to edit the URL associated with a hyperlink is especially important because the World Wide Web is constantly in flux. New Web sites are created, existing Web sites are altered or abandoned, and files are moved. As a Web publisher, you have an obligation to your readers to keep the URLs up to date. You can also delete a hyperlink from your document.

Change the Type or Destination of a Hyperlink

1 Select a picture hot spot or a text, picture, or drawn shape hyperlinked object.

2 Select Hyperlink on the Insert menu, or right-click the object and choose Hyperlink from the shortcut menu. The Hyperlink dialog box appears.

3 Make the appropriate changes by choosing a new hyperlink type or by entering new information in the Hyperlink Information area.

4 Click OK.

ScreenTips identify hyperlinks. When you position the pointer over an existing hyperlink, a ScreenTip will appear. The tip will identify the type of hyperlink by displaying the associated page reference, URL, email address, or filename, as shown in the following illustration.

> A Biking Summer
> in Maine
> Hyperlink to Next Page

Remove a Hyperlink

1 Select a picture hot spot or a text, picture, or drawn shape hyperlinked object.

2 Choose Hyperlink on the Insert menu, or right-click the object and choose Hyperlink from the shortcut menu. The Hyperlink dialog box appears.

3 Click the Remove button to delete the hyperlink associated with the currently selected object. The appearance of a picture hot spot, text, picture, or drawn shape will remain unchanged in the publication when the hyperlink is removed. Text color will revert to the Main Text color, and the underline will disappear when the hyperlink is removed.

4 If necessary, use Publisher's standard tools to delete the picture hot spot, text, or drawn shape.

Creating and Formatting Forms in a Web Document

Web pages can contain electronic forms. Electronic forms appear in Publisher as static objects. When viewed in a Web browser, the forms are interactive and can be filled out by the reader. You compose an electronic form by creating and combining six different form control objects that in turn determine the type of information a reader can enter. When you design a form, you must choose the appropriate form control object for the type of information you want to gather, as described in the following table.

Types and Uses of Form Control Objects		
Use this form control...	**To have the reader...**	**For this kind of information...**
Single-line text box	Type a short text phrase.	A name or address.
Multiline text box	Type longer text blocks.	A product evaluation or customer comment.
Check box	Turn a single item on or off. Or select multiple items from a list where more than one choice might apply.	The answer to a Yes-or-No question. A list of products a customer might want to purchase.

Use this form control...	To have the reader...	For this kind of information...
Option button	Select a single item from a group of related, but mutually exclusive, items.	An answer to a multiple choice question or a choice on a rating scale.
List box	Make a single selection or multiple selections from a scrollable list box or drop-down list box.	A listing of state names in an address form, or a listing of colors in a catalog.
Command button	Click a button to execute a command.	Submit the information or reset the form.

For more information about drawing frames, see Chapter 2.

Can I paste form controls from a Web page created with another application into Publisher? No. Publisher does not share a common form control format with other programs. You cannot paste form control objects from another program, such as an HTML authoring program like Microsoft FrontPage, into Publisher.

Create a Form Control

1 Select the Form Control tool on the Objects toolbar (shown below).

2 From the cascading menu, select the type of form control you would like to insert. The pointer changes to the Crosshair pointer.

3 To create a command button, center the Crosshair pointer where you want the button to appear and click the mouse. To create all other form control objects, drag the Crosshair pointer to draw a frame.

4 Repeat steps 1 through 3 for each control you want to add to the form.

Create logical groups within a form. You can make your forms almost self-explanatory by dividing a form into logical groups. All the items in a group should have a similar function. For example, the option buttons to choose a credit card and the text boxes to enter a credit card number and expiration date should be clustered together. In addition, a heading, such as "Payment Method," should clearly identify the requested information.

Entering Form Control Item Labels

Item labels are the text phrases that appear next to each object in the electronic form. Keep these labels clear and concise. Remember that self-explanatory labels help your readers to complete the form quickly and correctly.

Check boxes and option buttons contain item label text frames. Highlight the default text and type new text. You can change the appearance of the item label by using Publisher's standard text formatting tools.

You can choose or type an item label for a command button in the Command Button Properties dialog box. You cannot change the font, point size, or alignment of this label.

You can enter item labels in list boxes and type default text for text boxes (not shown) using the associated Properties dialog box. You cannot change the font, point size, or alignment of this text.

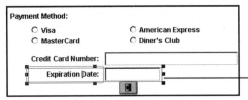

You can draw standard text frames to create labels for form control objects. Though you can group a text frame with a form control object, you must not overlap the two frames.

Setting Form Control Properties

To have your electronic form function properly and return information to you in a usable format, you must set properties for each form control object in your document. With the exception of the object's appearance, these properties remain hidden from your reader. They work behind the scenes to help you process and evaluate the reader's responses. The properties you can set vary from object to object but fall into five main categories, as detailed in the following table.

Form Control Properties

Property Type	Availability	Description
Default appearance	All form control objects	Can include the default state (selected or unselected) of an item, an item label, or sample text that can be replaced by the reader.
Function	Command button, list box, single-line or multiline text box	Can associate a specific action with a button, allow or disallow multiple list box selections, or make a text box mandatory.
Data processing label	Single-line text box, multiline text box, check box, option button, list box	An internal label (hidden from the reader) that will identify the data when it is returned to you. For example, "Payment Method" could be used to identify a reader's credit card choice.
Data processing value	Single-line text box, multiline text box, check box, option button, list box	The actual data returned to you. In most cases, the value should match the item label. For example, if a reader chooses Visa as the payment method, the value for the option button should be "Visa."
Data retrieval method and Information	Command button	The manner and file format in which the completed form is delivered to you.

Fast access to form controls Properties dialog boxes. You can right-click on any form control object to open a shortcut menu. On the shortcut menu, select the command to open the associated form control Properties dialog box. Alternatively, you can double-click a form control object (not its label) to immediately open the associated Properties dialog box.

Set Properties of a Single-Line or Multiline Text Box

1. Select the single-line text box or a multiline text box you want to modify.

2. Choose the Single-Line Text Box Properties or Multiline Text Box Properties command on the Format menu.

Creating Web Documents

Why can't I enter a value for a single-line or multi-line text box? Publisher assumes that the value of a single-line or multiline text box is the text typed by the reader. For example, the value of a First Name text field is the reader's given name.

Set Properties of a Single-Line or Multiline Text Box *(continued)*

3 Type default text, such as "Enter Your Text Here." The text you type will appear in the form but will be replaced when the reader enters new information.

4 Enter a value from 0 through 255 to limit the number of characters that can be typed into a single-line text box. This option is not available for a multiline text box.

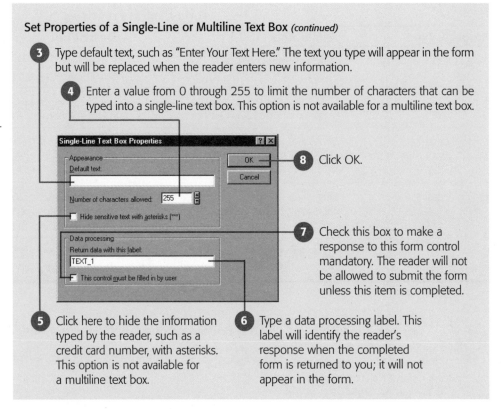

8 Click OK.

7 Check this box to make a response to this form control mandatory. The reader will not be allowed to submit the form unless this item is completed.

5 Click here to hide the information typed by the reader, such as a credit card number, with asterisks. This option is not available for a multiline text box.

6 Type a data processing label. This label will identify the reader's response when the completed form is returned to you; it will not appear in the form.

Set Properties of a Check Box

1 Select the check box you want to modify and choose the Check Box Properties command on the Format menu.

Why can I select more than one option button in a list when I view the form in my Web browser? You have not assigned all the option buttons in the list to the same group (designated by the data processing label). Return to your Publisher document, select each option button in the list, and choose the same data processing label in the Option Button Properties dialog box (found on the Format menu). When you next view the form in your Web browser, the option button choices will be mutually exclusive.

Set Properties of a Check Box *(continued)*

2 Choose the default appearance of the check box—selected or not selected.

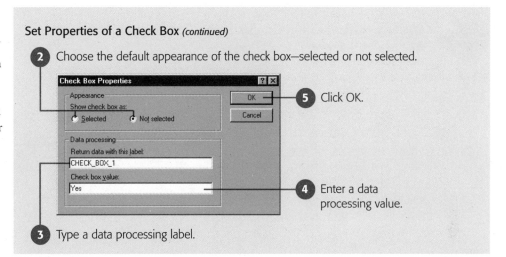

5 Click OK.

4 Enter a data processing value.

3 Type a data processing label.

Set Properties of an Option Button

1 Select the option button you want to modify and choose the Option Button Properties command on the Format menu.

2 Choose the default appearance of the option button—selected or not selected.

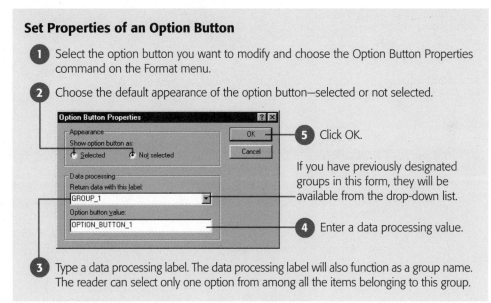

5 Click OK.

If you have previously designated groups in this form, they will be available from the drop-down list.

4 Enter a data processing value.

3 Type a data processing label. The data processing label will also function as a group name. The reader can select only one option from among all the items belonging to this group.

Are there cases where the data processing value should not match the item label? There are valid reasons to have the data processing value differ from the item label. Here are two possible scenarios:

- In your form you ask a Yes-or-No question. For example, if the item label reads "Click Here to Receive Our Catalog," the data processing value should be "Yes" (and the data processing label should be "Send Catalog").

- In your form you present a list of English-language choices to the reader, but you want to associate those items with internal code numbers. For example, your reader chooses five music CDs based on album or artist name from a list. In the Properties dialog box for each item, you enter the recording company's catalog number to facilitate your purchase order process.

Set Properties of a List Box

1 Select the list box you want to modify and choose the List Box Properties command on the Format menu.

2 Type a data processing label to identify the list box.

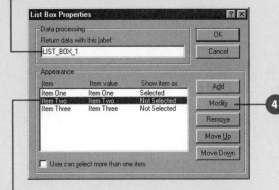

4 Click the Modify button. The Add/Modify List Box Item dialog box appears.

3 Select one of the default items.

5 Type a new label for the item. This label will appear in the form.

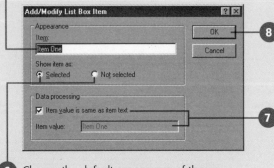

8 Click OK to return to the List Box Properties dialog box.

7 Click here to have the value match the item label, or de-select this check box and type a new value in the text box.

6 Choose the default appearance of the list item button—selected or not selected.

Create a scrollable list box or a drop-down list box. To create a scrollable list box, draw the frame large enough to display two or more item labels. Publisher will automatically add a vertical scroll bar. To create a drop-down list box, draw a small frame that displays only one item label. Publisher will automatically add a drop-down arrow button. These controls will not be functional within your Publisher document but will operate when viewed in a Web browser.

Drop-down list

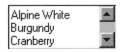

Scrollable list box

Set Properties of List Box *(continued)*

Click to add a new item to the list. The Add/Modify List Box Item dialog box appears.

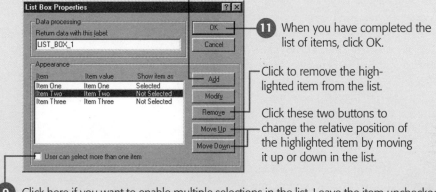

11 When you have completed the list of items, click OK.

Click to remove the highlighted item from the list.

Click these two buttons to change the relative position of the highlighted item by moving it up or down in the list.

9 Click here if you want to enable multiple selections in the list. Leave the item unchecked if you want the reader to select only one item from the list.

10 If necessary, modify, add, or remove other items in the list box.

Set Properties of a Command Button

1 Select the command button you want to modify and choose the Command Button Properties command on the Format menu.

Why can't I resize a command button? The size of a command button is determined by the length of its label. When you create a command button, the frame is just large enough to contain the default label (either Reset or Submit). You cannot change the size of a command button by dragging a resize handle, but you can change the size by typing a new, longer label in the Command Button Properties dialog box.

If I opt to save form data on my Web server, which file format should I choose? Choose a file format based on the method and program you will use to evaluate the reader's responses. For example, if you intend to read the completed form, choose HTML to view the file in your Web browser or Formatted Text to view the file in your word processing program. If you plan to import the completed form into a database, spreadsheet, or forms processing program, choose the Comma Delimited or Tab Delimited Text format. Delimited text uses a designated character (in this case, either a comma or a tab) to separate the data from each form control object. When you import delimited text into the appropriate program, the data from each form control object will be treated as a separate field.

Set Properties of a Command Button *(continued)*

2 Choose the actual command that will be executed when the reader clicks this button. Submit returns the completed form to you. Reset clears all the reader's data and redisplays the default values.

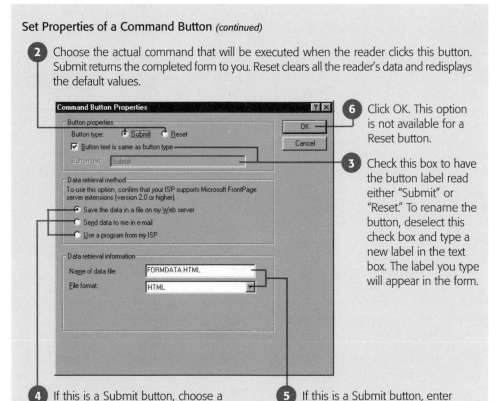

6 Click OK. This option is not available for a Reset button.

3 Check this box to have the button label read either "Submit" or "Reset." To rename the button, deselect this check box and type a new label in the text box. The label you type will appear in the form.

4 If this is a Submit button, choose a data retrieval method. This option is not available for a Reset button.

5 If this is a Submit button, enter a filename and choose a file format. This option is not available for a Reset button.

Retrieving the Completed Form

To retrieve a completed form, you must match Publisher's capabilities with the services offered by your ISP (or supported by your Web server software). The information you'll need, and the decisions you should make, are summarized in the following table.

Retrieval Options in the Command Button Properties Dialog Box		
If your Web server or ISP...	**Choose this data retrieval method...**	**In the Data Retrieval Information area, enter...**
Supports Microsoft FrontPage Server Extensions 2.0 or later	Save The Data In A File On My Web Server	A filename. You must also specify the file format. Publisher can save the data as HTML, Formatted Text, Comma Delimited Text, or Tab Delimited Text.
Supports Microsoft FrontPage 98 Server Extensions 3.0 or later	Send Data To Me in Email	Your email address. You can also specify the subject of the message.
Does not support Microsoft FrontPage Server Extensions	Use A Program From My ISP	The URL of the ISP's transfer program. You must also contact your ISP to determine if you should use the Get or Post transfer method and if you must insert identifying or handling information (in hidden fields) into the file.

 Are there other effects I can create by inserting HTML code fragments? If you are a proficient HTML programmer, you can create any number of effects by inserting HTML code fragments. Here's a brief list:

- Insert alternative text that displays if your reader has chosen not to view images in his or her browser.

- Create an anchor to identify a particular location on a page, and then insert a hypertext link that jumps to the anchor point (instead of the top of the page).

- Create blinking text (though Microsoft Internet Explorer does not recognize the BLINK tag).

- Insert DHTML code to hide, reveal, and animate elements on your Web page.

Inserting an HTML Code Fragment

When you save or publish a Web document, Publisher automatically generates HTML code. There are certain HTML formats and functions that Publisher does not have the capability to generate. For example, Publisher cannot insert a JPEG image as an in-line graphic.

The HTML Code Fragment tool gives you the power to circumvent Publisher's limitations by typing or pasting HTML code into a special dialog box. The following illustration shows you how an HTML code fragment appears in the Publisher document.

In a Publisher document, the HTML code fragment appears as simple text in a frame.

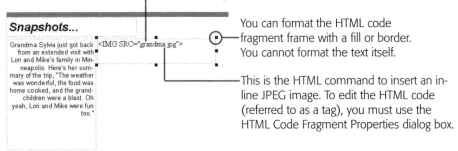

You can format the HTML code fragment frame with a fill or border. You cannot format the text itself.

This is the HTML command to insert an in-line JPEG image. To edit the HTML code (referred to as a tag), you must use the HTML Code Fragment Properties dialog box.

Creating Web Documents

For more information about Dynamic HTML, see page 201.

Why do I get an error message when I view a Web site containing an HTML code fragment in my browser?

Many HTML commands include a URL that refers to an externally stored file. You must include both the correct name of the file *and* its location (or URL) in the HTML Code Fragment Properties dialog box.

HTML supports two kinds of URLs. Absolute URLs show the entire address on the World Wide Web, such as www.mysite.com/publish/images/grandma.jpg. Relative URLs show only a portion of the address, where the location of the file is dependent on the folder of the current Web page. For example, if you have created a folder to hold your images within the folder that holds your Web site, you would type */images/grandma.jpg*. Relative URLs use standard DOS commands: a slash (/) moves you to the next lower folder; two periods (..) move you to the next higher folder. Ask your ISP if you should use absolute or relative URLs when publishing your Web site.

Snapshots...

Grandma Sylvia just got back from an extended visit with Lori and Mike's family in Minneapolis. Here's her summary of the trip, "The weather was wonderful, the food was home cooked, and the grandchildren were a blast. Oh yeah, Lori and Mike were fun too."

When viewed in a Web browser, the actual image will appear at the location of the HTML code fragment frame.

Insert an HTML Code Fragment

1 Click the HTML Code Fragment tool on the Objects toolbar and draw a frame where you want the HTML object to appear. The HTML Code Fragment Properties dialog box appears.

2 Type or paste the HTML code. Publisher does not check the code for accuracy, so be sure the spelling and syntax are correct.

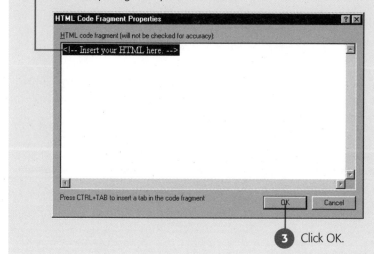

3 Click OK.

One-click previews. You can use the Standard toolbar to create a preview of your Web site. Simply click the Preview Web Site button shown here.

Press Ctrl-Shift-B to preview a Web site.

Turn on the Preview Troubleshooter. By default, the Preview Troubleshooter will not appear on screen after you've previewed a Web site. You can, however, instruct Publisher to show the Preview Troubleshooter whenever you preview a Web site. Choose Options on the Tools menu. Click the General tab and select the Preview Web Site With Preview Troubleshooter check box.

Previewing a Web Publication

Before you actually publish your Web site on the Internet, you should preview the document on your own system. A preview will reveal any formatting changes Publisher makes to accommodate the limitations of the HTML specification. A preview allows you to test all the functions you've built into your Web document. For example, you can play sound and video files. You can also follow the hyperlinks to their destinations. Ideally you should preview the document on a variety of computers to determine if the document looks the same when it is viewed:

- On different platforms, such as a PC and a Mac.

- Using different browsers, such as Microsoft Internet Explorer and Netscape Communicator, or different versions of the same browser, such as Microsoft Internet Explorer 4.0 versus 3.0.

- At different resolutions. Compare a standard VGA screen to a high-resolution SVGA screen.

- With different numbers of screen colors, such as a 16-color display versus a 256-color or full-color display.

Preview a Web Site

1 Open the Web document you want to preview.

2 Select Preview Web Site on the File menu. If your publication contains more than one page, Publisher displays the Web Site Preview dialog box.

3 Click Web Site to preview all the pages in the publication, or click Current Page to preview only one page of the document.

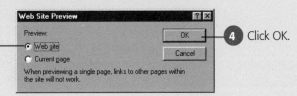

4 Click OK.

Test your Web site. When you preview your Web site, take the time to carefully explore the document. Use this checklist to be sure that you've examined the document thoroughly:

- @ Has any of the text changed in appearance?

- @ Do GIF animations play continuously?

- @ When clicked, does each multimedia object play properly?

- @ When clicked, does each hyperlink to another page in your Web site move you to the proper page?

- @ When clicked, does each hyperlink that contains a URL move you to the appropriate Web site?

- @ When clicked, do email hyperlinks activate an email application and insert your Internet address?

- @ When clicked, does each hyperlink that allows readers to download a file find the correct file on your hard disk?

- @ Can you select Check Boxes, Option Buttons, and list items in a form?

- @ Can you enter text in a single-line or multiline text box in a form?

- @ When clicked, do the Reset and Submit command buttons perform the correct action?

Preview a Web Site *(continued)*

5 Publisher displays a progress dialog box while it converts the PUB file to HTML. Publisher then activates your browser application.

6 Using the functions of your Web browser, explore the HTML document. If you are previewing the entire Web site, you can move from page to page. If you have chosen to preview a single page, hyperlinks to other pages within the site will not work.

7 When you have finished exploring the Web document, exit from the Web browser. Publisher will reappear on screen. If you've chosen to use the Preview Troubleshooter, it will appear on screen.

Use the scroll bar to review a list of possible problems.

The Preview Troubleshooter appears in Publisher's standard help window.

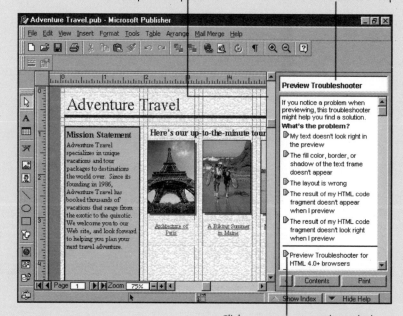

Click arrows to move through the various Preview Troubleshooter screens.

What is the difference between previewing a Web site and publishing a Web site? When you preview your Web site, you are viewing the document using a Web browser, but all the files reside on your local hard disk. When you publish your Web site, you transfer the document and all related files to a Web server. Anyone with access to the World Wide Web can open and read your publication.

Why would I want to publish my Web document to a folder on my local hard disk? If you discover that you can't use the Web Publishing Wizard to post your Web site directly to the World Wide Web, publish your Web site to a folder instead. Then follow the instructions or use the software supplied by your Internet Service Provider to send (or upload) your Web site to the Internet.

Generating a Web Site

To produce the finished version of a Web publication, Publisher performs the following operations:

- Converts your document to HTML. The first page of the document, or the home page, is normally saved as Index.html. Subsequent pages are normally saved as Page2.html, Page3.html, and so on.

- Exports all pictures and graphic regions as GIF files. Each image is stored in a separate GIF file identified by a number. As an example, a Web site containing two pictures and one graphic region would contain Img0.gif, Img1.gif, and Img2.gif.

- Copies any hyperlinked or externally stored files to the local folder or to the World Wide Web. Files that fall into this category include sound and video files and any files the reader can download using a hyperlink.

You have two choices for the final destination of your Web publication: you can publish it locally to a folder on your hard disk or network, or you can publish it to the World Wide Web.

Saving an HTML File to a Local Folder or Intranet

Saving a Web site to your local hard disk is the simplest option, but it doesn't give other people access to the publication. Saving a Web site to a folder on a network gives other people within your company access to the publication. If you want to publish your Web site to a folder on a network, speak to the network administrator to be sure that the following conditions are true:

- An intranet—an internal network including a Web server—is active.

- You have the appropriate write privileges to save your Web publication on the server.

Creating Web Documents

Use separate folders for each Web site. Publisher alerts you if you attempt to save a Web site to a folder that already contains a Web site. If you proceed, Publisher will overwrite existing files and destroy the Web site that already resides there. You should use separate folders for each Web site you create. However, you can use this system to update an existing Web site with new information.

 Does the Web Publishing Wizard support other file transfer protocols? Yes, the Web Publishing Wizard can transfer files using FTP, HTTP Post, or the Microsoft Content Replication System (CRS). Contact your ISP to learn their preferred protocol.

Save a Web Site As an HTML Document

1 Choose Save As HTML on the File menu. The Save As HTML dialog box appears.

2 Select a folder on your local hard disk or network where you want to publish the Web site.

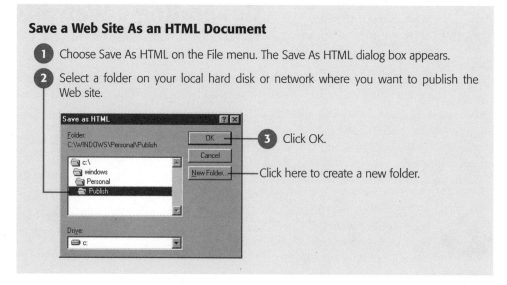

3 Click OK.

Click here to create a new folder.

Publishing to the World Wide Web

Publishing to the Web can be quite a complicated process. Publisher makes it easy to set key global parameters for your Web site, such as file naming conventions and compatibility levels for different versions of the HTML specification. Microsoft further simplifies the operation by providing a Web Publishing Wizard that prompts you for the necessary information, connects to the Internet, and copies the entire Web site to the designated folder.

Before you attempt to publish your Web site, contact your ISP to be sure that you have both the capability and the necessary information to copy your files to the Web server. In particular, you should be sure that the following conditions are true:

@ Your ISP supplies space on its server (its computer) where you can store your Web site. Usually 1 or 2 MB are made available to you. This service might be part of the basic subscription cost, or it might require an additional fee.

Do I have to change the file extension for each page in my Web site? No. Whenever you choose a filename extension for one page in your publication, the change is automatically copied to all the pages.

@ You have direct access to an Internet server and are not accessing the Internet through a proxy server or network gateway.

@ You have the correct URL of your Web site on the ISP's server.

@ You know your ISP's file naming convention. For example, DOS-based servers require filenames to have a three-letter (HTM) file extension; they do not support a four-letter (HTML) file extension.

@ You know if your ISP allows you to use the standard file transfer protocol (FTP), as well as the name of the FTP server (also known as the FTP host address).

@ You know the name of the subfolder (also known as the default or remote directory) where you will copy your files.

Change Properties for an Individual Page in a Web Site

1. Move to the page in your publication whose properties you want to change.

2. Choose Web Properties on the File menu. The Web Properties dialog box appears.

3. Click the Page tab.

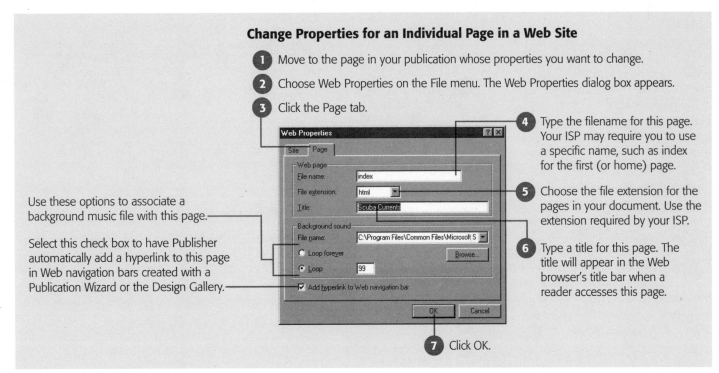

4. Type the filename for this page. Your ISP may require you to use a specific name, such as index for the first (or home) page.

5. Choose the file extension for the pages in your document. Use the extension required by your ISP.

6. Type a title for this page. The title will appear in the Web browser's title bar when a reader accesses this page.

Use these options to associate a background music file with this page.

Select this check box to have Publisher automatically add a hyperlink to this page in Web navigation bars created with a Publication Wizard or the Design Gallery.

7. Click OK.

For more information about Web site language options, see pages 207 through 208.

How will the keywords and description I enter in the Web Properties dialog box be used? Search engines—Web utilities that help people find Web sites—will use this information to catalog and describe your Web site. An Internet user looks for topics of interest by typing search criteria into a search engine, such as Yahoo!, Lycos, or InfoSeek. If one of your keywords matches the search, your Web site (and URL) will be listed as a good source of information. Search engines routinely scan the Web to find and index new Web sites. They will automatically register your Web site when they access it. However, you can increase your visibility on the Web by registering your site with as many search engines as possible. Contact your ISP for more information.

Why does Publisher display an alert box when I attempt to publish my Web site? You don't have the Web Publishing Wizard installed on your system. To install the Wizard, click Yes.

Change Properties for the Entire Web Site

1 Choose Web Properties on the File menu. The Web Properties dialog box appears.

2 Click the Site tab.

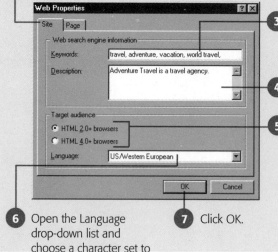

3 Type short phrases to identify the content of your Web site. Separate each phrase with a comma.

4 Type a general description of your Web site.

5 Select an HTML-compatibility option. Choose HTML 2.0+ Browsers if you want to ensure compatibility with a broad range of programs, including older browsers. Choose HTML 4.0+ Browsers if you are sure that your audience will be using the latest versions of a full-featured browser and you want to take advantage of new HTML functions, such as DHTML.

6 Open the Language drop-down list and choose a character set to use when displaying the text in your Web site.

7 Click OK.

Publish a Web Site to the World Wide Web

1 Begin an online session by connecting to your ISP.

2 Open the Web document you want to publish to the Web.

3 On the File menu, choose Publish To Web. Publisher displays a progress box while it converts the publication to HTML. The Web Publishing Wizard dialog box appears.

4 In the Web Publishing Wizard dialog box, click Next to start the Wizard.

5 In the following dialog box, enter a descriptive name for your Web site. Then click Next.

How can I access the Web Publishing Wizard? You can access the Web Publishing Wizard in one of three ways:

- On the Publisher File menu, choose the Publish To Web command.

- On the Windows 95 Start menu, choose Microsoft Web Publishing and then Web Publishing Wizard.

- In Windows Explorer, right-click a single filename, a group of files, or an entire folder to display the Shortcut menu. Select the Send To command and choose the Web Publishing Wizard from the cascading menu.

Once I have published my Web site, can I update it with new information? You must return to the original PUB file to update your Web page. The PUB file contains standard desktop publishing objects, which can be edited. Make your changes using Publisher's standard tools, and then generate a new HTML file using the Publish to Web or Save As HTML command.

Publish a Web Site to the World Wide Web *(continued)*

6 Enter the URL of your Web site.

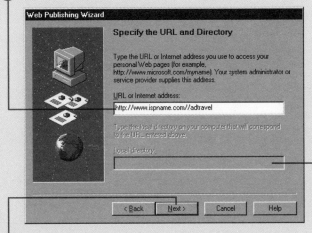

If you have accessed the Web Publishing Wizard by right-clicking a selected file or folder in Windows Explorer, the Local Directory text box will be available. You can create an association between the designated folder on your local hard disk and the Web server URL. Subsequently, whenever you publish a file from this folder, it will be saved to the same URL.

7 Click Next to proceed with publishing your document. The subsequent dialog boxes will differ depending on the file transfer protocol you've chosen. For example, if you chose FTP, you will be prompted for the FTP host address and your default directory.

8 After the Wizard has uploaded the files, end your online session.

Working with Mailing Lists

Direct mail remains a great business tool because postal delivery is still one of the most cost-effective ways to get your message out to your customers. Microsoft Publisher 98's mail merge feature puts powerful direct mail tools at your fingertips. You can easily manage the standard tasks associated with mail merge, such as automatically addressing envelopes and inserting a subscriber's address in a newsletter.

Publisher's mail merge tools are extremely flexible. They let you create, modify, filter, and sort address lists directly within Publisher. You can even link a publication to an address list created in another program, such as Microsoft Word or Microsoft Access.

Mail Merge Fundamentals: Address Lists and Field Codes

Publisher's mail merge functions require you to create an address list and to insert field codes into your publication. The following illustration diagrams the relationship between these two key components and provides an overview of the mail merge process.

Personalize your mailings. Don't limit Publisher's mail merge tools to the address information on envelopes and labels. Use them to personalize any printed Publisher document. That sweepstakes offer that starts with the line, "You, Tom Smith, may have just won a million dollars!" is an example of a personalized document. No one is suggesting that you start your own sweepstakes, but you can use mail merge to customize a wide variety of documents including sale announcements and promotional brochures.

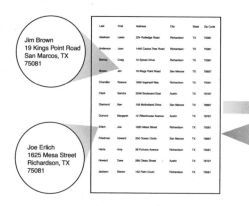

You must connect the Publisher document to the address list.

<<First>> <<Last>>
<<Address>>
<<City>>, <<State>> <<ZIP>>

Jim Brown
19 Kings Point Road
San Marcos, TX 75081

Joe Erlich
1625 Mesa Street
Richardson, TX 75081

The address list contains names, addresses, and other information you want to insert in your document. You can create an address list in Publisher or an external application.

A field code inserted into the document does not contain specific information but instead points to a category heading (or field) within the address list, such as a first name or a zip code. A field code is always surrounded by double brackets (<< >>).

The merged document can be previewed on screen or printed. In both cases, the field code is replaced with specific information, such as a name or address.

 Can I use Publisher's mail merge feature with electronic Web documents?

No. Publisher's mail merge feature works with printed publications only.

Creating and Modifying an Address List in Publisher

An address list is simply a database of information. The data will typically be contact information, such as a name, an address, a telephone number, and perhaps an email address. You can create and modify an address list using database functions built into Publisher.

Organize data into discrete fields. When designing your address list, break the information into discrete units so that each category is a separate field. For example, split city and state information into different fields. You can then search, sort, and filter the information in the address list with much more accuracy.

 Use the same address list for multiple publications. When you create an address list using Publisher's mail merge functions, you are prompted to save the file to disk. Doing so allows you to attach any number of publication files to the address list. This means you can create one central address list and then use it over and over for a wide range of projects.

Create an Address List in Publisher

1 Choose Create Publisher Address List on the Mail Merge menu. The New Address List dialog box appears.

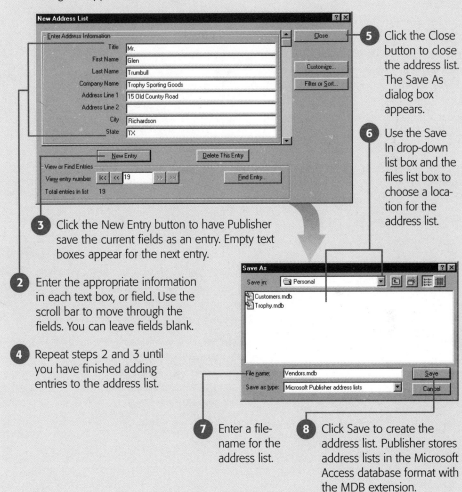

5 Click the Close button to close the address list. The Save As dialog box appears.

6 Use the Save In drop-down list box and the files list box to choose a location for the address list.

3 Click the New Entry button to have Publisher save the current fields as an entry. Empty text boxes appear for the next entry.

2 Enter the appropriate information in each text box, or field. Use the scroll bar to move through the fields. You can leave fields blank.

4 Repeat steps 2 and 3 until you have finished adding entries to the address list.

7 Enter a filename for the address list.

8 Click Save to create the address list. Publisher stores address lists in the Microsoft Access database format with the MDB extension.

Can I work simultaneously on an address list and the Publisher document to which it is attached? If you have created your address list within Publisher, you can modify the list at any time. There is no need to close the current publication in order to access the address list connected to the publication. Simply choose Edit Publisher Address List on the Mail Merge menu. If, however, you are using an address list created with another program, you must close the publication file before you attempt to edit the address list connected to it.

Edit Entries in a Publisher Address List

1 Choose Edit Publisher Address List on the Mail Merge menu. The Open Address List dialog box appears.

2 Locate and select the address list you want to modify. Click Open to display the address list dialog box.

3 Locate the entry you want to change.

4 Edit or insert information.

5 Click here to save your changes and close the address list.

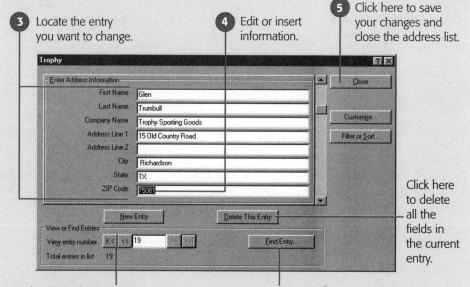

Click here to delete all the fields in the current entry.

Use the forward or backward arrow to move to the adjacent entry, or type an entry number in the text box and then press Enter. Use the double arrows to move to the first or last entry in the address list.

Click here to search for an entry using a text phrase. In the Find Entry dialog box that appears, type up to 25 characters. Publisher ignores the capitalization of the search phrase, but spelling must be exact. You can search all fields or specify a particular field, such as Company Name.

Manage existing fields in an address list. You can easily reorganize the fields in an address list or remove fields you no longer use. By clicking the clearly labeled buttons in the Customize Address List dialog box, you can accomplish several tasks:

- ℮ Delete unwanted fields

- ℮ Rename a field

- ℮ Move a selected field up one position in the list box

- ℮ Move a selected field down one position in the list box

 Use Publisher's address list for nonaddress informa-tion. Publisher's address list functions just like a traditional database. By adding and modifying fields, you can customize the address list for any kind of information. You could, for example, add a field to identify large corporate customers in order to offer them special volume pricing. Or you might want to keep a list of your customers' birthdays, to offer them a personal discount one day a year.

Add a New Field to a Publisher Address List

1 On the Mail Merge menu, choose Create Publisher Address List or Edit Publisher Address List (to customize an existing address list).

2 If you are customizing an existing address list, the Open Address List dialog box appears. Select the file containing the address list you want to customize, and then click Open.

3 In the address list dialog box, click the Customize button. The Customize Address List dialog box appears.

4 Click a field to select it.

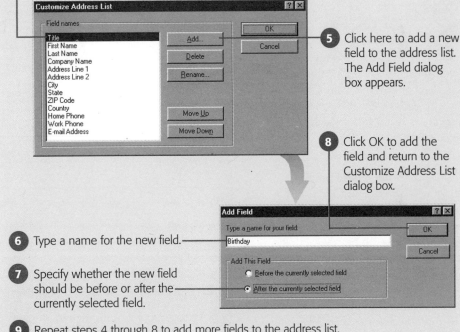

5 Click here to add a new field to the address list. The Add Field dialog box appears.

8 Click OK to add the field and return to the Customize Address List dialog box.

6 Type a name for the new field.

7 Specify whether the new field should be before or after the currently selected field.

9 Repeat steps 4 through 8 to add more fields to the address list.

10 Click OK to save your changes.

Can I still use my program as an external data source if Publisher does not list my database or spreadsheet program in the Open Data Source dialog box? Publisher accepts external data sources if they are in a standard file format. Generate your address list in a standard file format, such as XLS or DBF.

Can I use a text file as an external data source? Yes, you can use a text file as an external data source if the information is organized properly. You must be sure to separate each field with a special character, known as a delimiter, such as a comma or a tab.

What will happen if I open a new data source for my publication? If you have not inserted any field codes in the publication, you can proceed with the mail merge normally. However, if you have inserted field codes and they refer to fields that do not exist in the new data source, Publisher will not be able to retrieve information for those field codes. Publisher identifies these fields codes by changing the text to read <<Missing mail merge field>>.

Connecting a Publication to an Address List or Other Data Source

Before you can use an address list with a Publisher document, you must associate the document with the data source that contains the list. Only one data source can be associated with a publication at any given time. However, you can replace a data source with a new data source at any time. Publisher can access address list data stored in many different formats, as the following table summarizes.

Address List File Formats	
File Extension	**Program**
DBF	dBASE III, dBASE IV, dBASE 5
MDB	Microsoft Access
XLS	Microsoft Excel
DBF	Microsoft FoxPro
MDB	Microsoft Publisher address list
DOC	Microsoft Word tables or mail merge documents
WDB	Microsoft Works Database
TXT, CSV, TAB, ASC	Text files

Connect a Publication to a Data Source

1 Choose Open Data Source on the Mail Merge menu. The Open Data Source dialog box appears.

2 Choose Merge Information From A File I Already Have. A second Open Data Source dialog box appears.

Create and connect to an address list in one operation. If you choose Create An Address List In Publisher in the first Open Data Source dialog box, Publisher will display the New Address List dialog box. When you've finished entering your information, Publisher will ask if you want to merge the information from this address list into the current publication. Click Yes to connect the current publication to the address list.

Why can't I connect my publication to an external data source? There are two possible reasons that you cannot connect to an external data source:

@ The data source file may be open. Return to the application in which you created the data source and close the file.

@ You may have saved the data source in an incompatible file format. Return to the application in which you created the data source and save it in a compatible file format, such as DBF.

Connect a Publication to a Data Source *(continued)*

4 Use the Look In drop-down list box and the files list box to locate and select the data source.

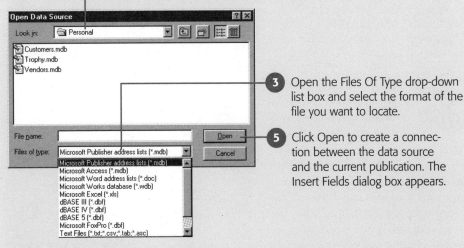

3 Open the Files Of Type drop-down list box and select the format of the file you want to locate.

5 Click Open to create a connection between the data source and the current publication. The Insert Fields dialog box appears.

6 You can insert a field code, or you can click Close to return to your document. Even if you click Close without inserting any field codes, the connection between the current publication and the data source remains active, allowing you to insert field codes later in the work session.

Choose a New Data Source

1 On the Mail Merge menu, choose Open Data Source. Publisher asks you if you want to replace the currently selected data source with a new data source.

2 Click Yes to access the Open Data Source dialog box and choose a new data source. Click No to continue using the currently selected data source.

Why is the Insert Field command grayed out? You cannot insert a field code until you connect your publication to a data source. Use the Open Data Source command to associate the current publication with a data source. The Insert Field command will now be available.

Why does the Insert Fields dialog box remain on screen after I click the Insert button? The Insert Fields dialog box remains on screen to let you add more than one field code to a publication easily. Instead of closing, the dialog box simply becomes inactive. While the Insert Fields dialog box is inactive, you can add text or punctuation to your publication without affecting the field code. Click the Insert Fields dialog box to once again make it active.

Inserting Field Codes into a Publication

A field code is a generic placeholder in your publication. It tells Publisher where to insert information from the address list. In the working view of your publication, field codes are identified by double brackets and display the name of the field to which they refer.

Insert Field Codes in a Publication

1 Select a text frame in the publication and move the text insertion point where you want the first field code to appear.

2 Choose Insert Field on the Mail Merge menu. The Insert Fields dialog box appears.

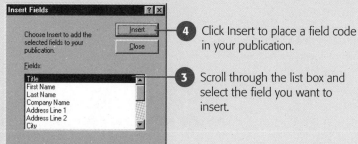

4 Click Insert to place a field code in your publication.

3 Scroll through the list box and select the field you want to insert.

5 To insert additional field codes, repeat steps 3 and 4.

6 Click Close to exit the Insert Fields dialog box and return to your publication.

7 In your publication, single-click the field code to select it. The entire field code will be highlighted.

8 Use Publisher's normal text tools to apply character formatting. You can also cut, copy, or paste the field code.

Why can't I change the text in the field code? It doesn't matter if you are viewing a field code or previewing an entry in a merged publication, you cannot change the text using Publisher's standard text editing tools. Remember that the field code points to the address list. The field code text exactly matches the field name in your address list or data source. And the entry you see when you merge or preview a publication matches the content of that field.

You must return to the Publisher address list or the external data source to change either the name of the field or the content of the field.

Why isn't Show Merge Results available on the Mail Merge menu? The Show Merge Results command is available only after you've connected your publication to a data source, inserted at least one field code, and issued the Merge command.

Merging and Previewing a Publication with an Address List or Data Source

Before you can print a mail merge document, you must substitute the address list entries for the field code placeholders. The Merge command accomplishes this task and shows you an on-screen preview of the results. Once you've merged an address list with a publication, you can choose to view the merge results (or the field codes) at any time.

Merge and Preview a Publication with an Address List

1 Choose Merge on the Mail Merge menu. Publisher replaces the field codes with the first entry from your address list. The results appear in the document window, and the Preview Data dialog box appears.

2 Use the forward and backward arrows to move through the entries, or type an entry number in the text box and press Enter.

3 When you've finished previewing the merged document, click Close to return to your publication. The address list entries are replaced by the field code designations.

Publisher displays the total number of entries in the address list.

Toggle the Display of Merge Results and Field Codes

1 Open the Mail Merge menu.

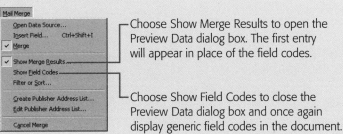

Choose Show Merge Results to open the Preview Data dialog box. The first entry will appear in place of the field codes.

Choose Show Field Codes to close the Preview Data dialog box and once again display generic field codes in the document.

Sorting and Filtering Information in an Address List

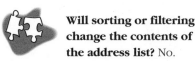

Will sorting or filtering change the contents of the address list? No. Sorting does not actually change any of the entries in the address list; it merely changes the order in which entries appear on screen and print. Likewise, when a filter is applied to an address list, entries are not deleted. Entries that do not meet the selection criteria are skipped when the address list is merged with the publication.

Publisher provides two powerful tools to help you manage address lists: sorting and filtering. Sorting allows you to change the order of entries in the address list, which normally appear in the order you type them. For example, you might sort entries alphabetically by last name to locate an item more easily. And you can comply with bulk mailing regulations by sorting and then printing all zip codes sequentially.

Filters allow you to use only a portion of a larger address list. Filters can be thought of as selection criteria. Only the entries that meet the selection criteria will be displayed or printed. One common filtering technique targets specific geographic areas by selecting entries from a particular city, state, or zip code. You can also create specialized filters. For example, you can filter a mailing by the age or income of the recipient, provided that you have created the appropriate fields in the address list.

You can apply up to three different sorting and filtering criteria to an address list. Furthermore, you can specify sorting rules and filters in two different locations—with two different results.

@ The address list dialog box lets you sort and filter entries. The results are visible only within the dialog box and do not affect the merge operation.

@ The Mail Merge menu lets you sort and filter an address list. The results are visible in your document when you preview the merge on screen or print the merged publication.

Change the Order of Entries

1 To change the order in which entries are previewed and printed, choose Filter Or Sort on the Mail Merge menu. To change the order in which entries appear within the Publisher address list dialog box, click the Filter Or Sort button in the address list dialog box itself. The Filtering And Sorting dialog box appears.

2 Select the Sort tab.

3 Open the drop-down list box and choose a field to sort by.

4 Select Ascending to sort entries from A through Z or from 0 through 9. Select Descending to sort entries from Z through A or from 9 through 0.

5 To apply additional sorting criteria, repeat steps 3 and 4 for one or two more fields.

Filtering and Sorting

Filter (choose which entries to print or view) | Sort (change the order of entries)

Sort by this field:
First Name — ○ Ascending / ○ Descending

Then by this field:
Last Name — ○ Ascending / ○ Descending

Then by this field:
City — ○ Ascending / ○ Descending

You can sort any of these fields in ascending order (A to Z or zero to 9) or descending order (Z to A or 9 to zero).

Remove Sort

OK   Cancel

6 Click OK.

Click here to remove the sort order. After removing the sorting criteria, Publisher will arrange the entries in the order they were originally entered.

Why can't I view or print all the entries in my data source? In all likelihood, you have applied a filter to the data source. You must remove the filter before Publisher can display, preview, or print all the entries in the address list.

Apply a Filter to an Address List

1 To merge only selected entries from an address list with a publication, choose Filter Or Sort on the Mail Merge menu. To locate and display specific entries within the Publisher address list dialog box, click the Filter Or Sort button in the address list dialog box itself. The Filtering And Sorting dialog box appears.

What is the difference between the And and Or choices in the Filtering And Sorting dialog box? If you choose the And operator, entries must meet both criteria to be merged with the document or displayed in the address list dialog box. If you choose the Or operator, entries can meet either criteria (but not necessarily both) to be merged with the document or displayed in the address list dialog box. For example, if you create a filter in which the City field is equal to Paris *and* the State field is equal to TX, Publisher will find entries for Paris, Texas. But if you create a filter in which the City field is equal to Paris *or* the State field is equal to TX, Publisher will find entries for Paris, Texas; for all cities in Texas; and for Paris, France.

Why does Publisher tell me that no entries match my filter criteria when I know there are matching entries? You've probably misspelled the phrase in the Compare To text box. Publisher ignores capitalization but requires you to spell the phrase in the text box exactly as you have spelled it in your data source. If you type "Tx" (an incorrectly capitalized abbreviation for Texas), Publisher will find entries listed as TX in the data source. However, a filter will not work if you search for entries in the city of "Ausin," when your data source contains entries for the city of Austin.

Apply a Filter to an Address List *(continued)*

2 Select the Filter tab.

3 Open the drop-down list box and choose a field that will be part of the filter criteria.

4 Choose one of the four comparison phrases: Is Equal To, Is Not Equal To, Is Less Than, or Is Greater Than.

5 Type a text phrase or a number to be compared to the contents of the Field box.

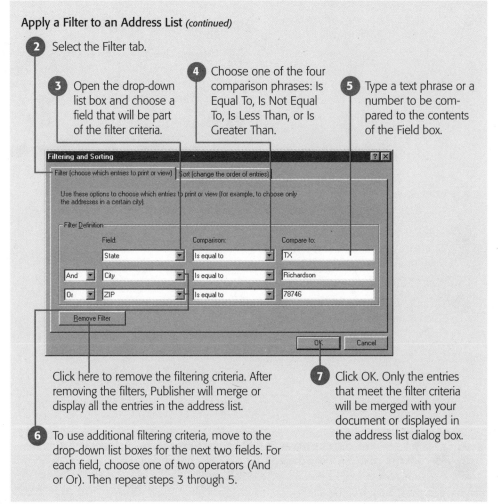

Click here to remove the filtering criteria. After removing the filters, Publisher will merge or display all the entries in the address list.

6 To use additional filtering criteria, move to the drop-down list boxes for the next two fields. For each field, choose one of two operators (And or Or). Then repeat steps 3 through 5.

7 Click OK. Only the entries that meet the filter criteria will be merged with your document or displayed in the address list dialog box.

Use filters to proofread entries in an address list.
You can check on the accuracy of the information in an address list by creating filters that search for potential problems. For example, if you want to find incomplete mailing addresses, create a filter where the ZIP Code field is equal to an empty Compare To field.

For more information about printing mail merge documents, see Chapter 16.

Printing Considerations for Mail Merge Documents

When you output a mail merge document, the normal Print command is replaced by the Print Merge command. Publisher's Print Merge command helps you generate mail merge documents more efficiently by offering specialized functions, that allow you to do the following:

@ Print a test to be sure that the mail merge is working properly.

@ Specify a range of entries (rather than a page range) for printing.

@ Specify where on a sheet of labels Publisher should begin printing. If you've already used two rows of labels, for example, you can begin printing at the third row.

14

Wizards, Design Gallery, and Custom Templates

Microsoft Publisher offers powerful tools, in the form of Wizards and the Design Gallery, that quite literally automate the design process. Wizards are interactive programs that ask you for project information and then create a layout based on your answers. The Design Gallery contains a wide variety of fully formatted objects that can add a professional touch to your documents at the click of a button.

Publisher 98 introduces two new technologies, Smart Objects and synchronization, both of which make it easy to change a publication. Publications created with a Wizard and Design Gallery elements contain Smart Objects. Unlike standard text and picture frames, Smart Objects remain linked to a Wizard. Modifying a Smart Object is as simple as asking the Wizard for help. Synchronization links similar objects within the current publication to each other. Making a change to one synchronized object automatically updates the other synched elements.

Once you've created a document, either with a Wizard or from scratch, you can reuse it easily by saving it as a template. Custom templates allow you to build new publications on the solid foundation of an existing design.

What kinds of publications can I create with a Wizard?
When you click the Publications By Wizard tab in the Catalog dialog box, you have a choice of the following publication types:

- 6 advertisements
- 14 award certificates
- 40 banners
- 53 brochures
- 19 business cards
- 102 business forms
- 16 calendars
- 19 envelopes
- 58 flyers
- 10 gift certificates
- 81 greeting cards
- 54 invitation cards
- 49 labels
- 19 letterheads
- 12 menus
- 28 newsletters
- 4 origami designs
- 4 paper airplanes
- 85 postcards
- 3 programs
- 26 signs
- 39 Web sites
- 23 With Compliments cards

Creating a Publication with a Wizard

You first encounter Publisher's Wizards when you begin a new document, where options in the Catalog dialog box allow you to start a Wizard in order to create an entire document. However, at any time while working within Publisher, you can access the Wizard you used to create the publication in order to modify the layout. If you've assigned new formats to elements within the publication, deleted elements, or added elements, you can use the Wizard to restore the original layout.

Microsoft Publisher 98 ships with Wizards to create hundreds of different documents. To help you locate a specific Wizard more quickly, Publisher organizes the Wizards in two different ways:

- Publications By Wizard groups the same type of publication together. As an example, Newsletters constitute one grouping.

- Publications By Design groups the same design styles together. As an example, the Arcs group (under the Master Sets heading) includes a newsletter, a flyer, a brochure, and a Web site that all share the same look.

The publications created with a Wizard vary dramatically in both content and complexity. This variety is reflected in the questions that the Wizard poses as you move through the creation process. For example, the Newsletter Wizard asks you how many columns of text you want on each page. This question would be inappropriate for a calendar. Instead, the Calendar Wizard asks whether you want to create a monthly or yearly calendar.

Create a New Publication with a Wizard

1 Access the Catalog dialog box by starting Publisher or by choosing New on the File menu.

2 Select either the Publications By Wizard tab or the Publications by Design tab.

3 Scroll through the publication types (represented by detailed icons), and decide which one you want to use.

An outline-style list of all available Wizards appears at left.

A circle indicates that there are no subcategories in a group.

A blue triangle indicates that there are subcategories in a group. Click the triangle to show or hide the subcategories.

A red arrow indicates the currently selected category.

Use subcategories to quickly find a particular document. For example, designs that use special papers from Paper Direct (shown here) or Avery are clearly identified.

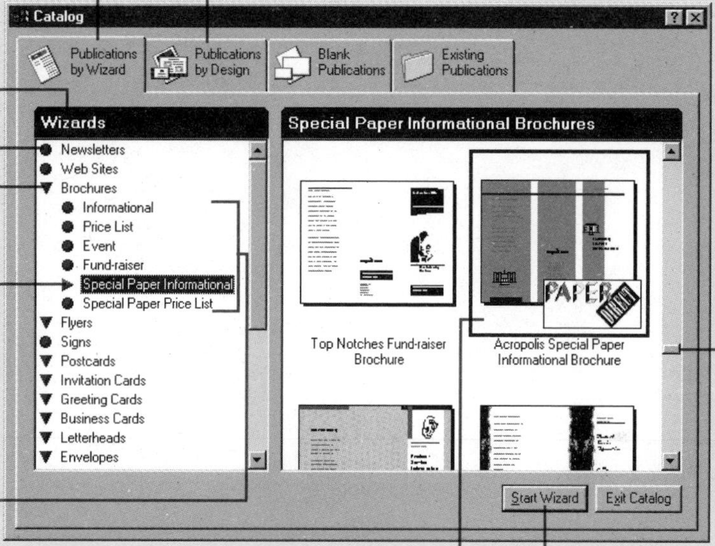

Catalog

Publications by Wizard | Publications by Design | Blank Publications | Existing Publications

Wizards
- Newsletters
- Web Sites
- ▼ Brochures
  - Informational
  - Price List
  - Event
  - Fund-raiser
  - Special Paper Informational
  - Special Paper Price List
- ▼ Flyers
- Signs
- Postcards
- ▼ Invitation Cards
- ▼ Greeting Cards
- ▼ Business Cards
- ▼ Letterheads
- ▼ Envelopes

Special Paper Informational Brochures

Top Notches Fund-raiser Brochure

Acropolis Special Paper Informational Brochure

Start Wizard | Exit Catalog

Publisher displays the document in the workspace and displays the Wizard in a special window along the left edge of the screen.

4 Double-click the icon, or single-click the icon and then click Start Wizard.

Wizards

Choose the printer before you start the Wizard. Wizards assume that you will use the default printer already designated in the Windows 95 Control Panel. If you create a publication using a Wizard and then change printers in the Print Setup dialog box (accessed from the File menu), your publication might not print correctly. If you want to change to a different printer, be sure to do so before you start the Wizard.

For more information about how to change the default printer, see Chapter 16.

Create a New Publication with a Wizard *(continued)*

5 Make a choice (or enter text) in response to the Wizard's question.

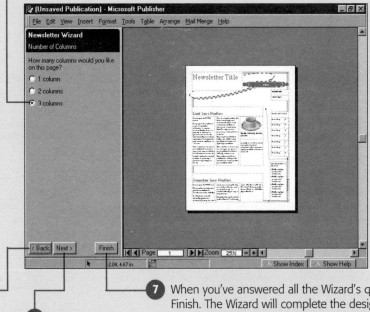

Click here to return to the previous question in order to review or change your answer.

6 Click here to proceed to the Wizard's next question.

7 When you've answered all the Wizard's questions, click Finish. The Wizard will complete the design and remain on screen. You can close the Wizard to work on your own, or use the Wizard to change the layout.

When should I choose the Publications By Design tab in the Catalog dialog box? You should choose the Publications By Design option when you want to create a number of documents with a single design theme. For example, you can create a consistent company identity by using the same design motif for your correspondence (letterhead, business card, and envelope), your company newsletter, and your promotional publications (such as a flyer or brochure). When you select a Master Set group on the Publications By Design tab, you will find 27 coordinated publications.

You should also use Publications By Design when you want to find all the necessary publications for a one-time event, like a conference or a fundraiser. For example, the Fund-raiser Sets category contains similar designs for an invitation, a brochure, and a Web site.

Modify a Publication Created with a Wizard

1 If the Wizard isn't displayed, click the Show Wizard button, located at the lower left corner of the work area. The Wizard will appear in a separate window at the left side of the screen.

2 Select the aspect of the layout you want to change.

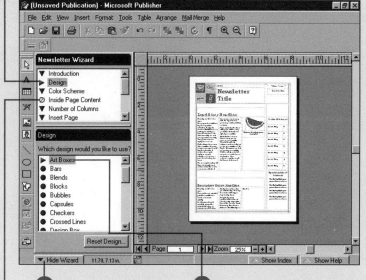

5 When you're satisfied with your modifications, click Hide Wizard.

A cancellation sign indicates that this layout option is not available for the currently displayed page or the current publication type.

3 Answer the Wizard's question by choosing a new option, typing new information, or executing a command.

4 If you want to change other aspects of the layout, repeat steps 2 and 3.

Wizards

Why isn't the Show Wizard button available? You're working in a publication you created from scratch by using the Blank Publications option in the Catalog dialog box. The Show Wizard button is available only within a publication you've created by using a Wizard.

Can I modify individual elements within a publication I've created with a Wizard? Yes. You must first determine if the element you want to modify is a standard text or picture frame or if it is a Smart Object. You can use Publisher's standard formatting tools to modify text and picture frames and to insert text and pictures into a Smart Object. You must, however, use a Wizard to modify the appearance of a Smart Object.

Why isn't the Reset Design button available? The Reset Design button is available only when you've selected the Design item in the Wizard window.

Remove Modifications to a Publication Created with a Wizard

1 If the Wizard isn't displayed, click the Show Wizard button, located at the lower left corner of the work area. The Wizard will appear in separate window at the left side of the screen.

2 In the Wizard window, select the Design option.

3 Click the Reset Design button, shown below. The Reset Design dialog box appears.

4 Choose some or all of the options in the dialog box.

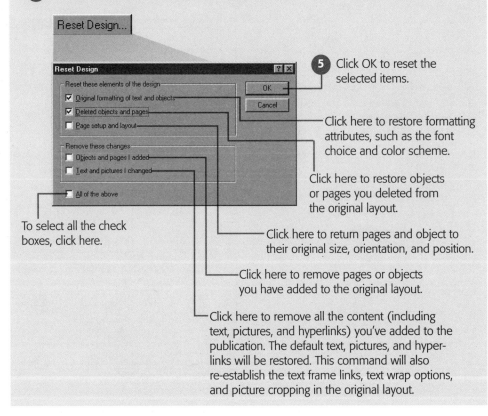

5 Click OK to reset the selected items.

Click here to restore formatting attributes, such as the font choice and color scheme.

Click here to restore objects or pages you deleted from the original layout.

To select all the check boxes, click here.

Click here to return pages and object to their original size, orientation, and position.

Click here to remove pages or objects you have added to the original layout.

Click here to remove all the content (including text, pictures, and hyperlinks) you've added to the publication. The default text, pictures, and hyperlinks will be restored. This command will also re-establish the text frame links, text wrap options, and picture cropping in the original layout.

For more information about Smart Objects, see pages 259 through 260.

What kinds of elements can I insert from the Design Gallery? Your choices in the Design Gallery, which are listed below, change depending on whether you are working with a print publication or a Web site.

- 6 advertisements
- 36 attention getters
- 3 barbell accents
- 3 box accents
- 14 calendars
- 3 checkerboard accents
- 3 coupons
- 24 dot accents
- 10 logos
- 1 phone tear off
- 8 picture captions
- 28 print or 39 Web mastheads
- 28 print or 9 Web pull quotes
- 10 print or 3 Web reply forms
- 28 print or 9 Web sidebars
- 28 tables of contents or 39 Web navigation bars

Using the Design Gallery

Think of the elements in Publisher's Design Gallery as the building blocks of a publication. You can create an entire layout by selecting and combining multiple elements from the Design Gallery. Or you can use one or two elements to enhance a publication you design from scratch. Publisher's Design Gallery contains hundreds of fully formatted elements, and all of them are composed of Smart Objects. To help you locate a specific element more quickly, Publisher organizes the Design Gallery in two different ways:

- Objects By Category groups the same type of publication together. As an example, Calendars constitute one grouping.

- Objects By Design groups the same design styles together. As an example, the Capsules group includes a masthead, a calendar, a pull quote, and a sidebar that all share the same look.

You can customize the Design Gallery by adding your own creations to it. Elements you add to the Design Gallery are composed of standard objects, including drawn shapes, text, picture, and table frames. Unlike Smart Objects, custom Design Gallery elements do not have special functions attached to them, nor can they be modified with a Wizard.

Insert a Design Gallery Object in a Publication

1 Click the Design Gallery tool, shown on the following page, or choose Design Gallery Object on the Insert menu. The Design Gallery dialog box appears.

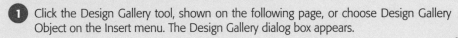

Wizards

Use design motifs consistently throughout a publication. Each element in the Design Gallery is clearly identified by a name that includes a reference to a design motif, such as Arcs or Marble. Using elements with the same design motif guarantees that objects "match," or complement, one another throughout your publication.

Why do I get an error message saying the Wizard files are not installed when I try to insert a Design Gallery object? All the Design Gallery objects that ship with Publisher are created and edited with Wizards. When you installed Publisher, you did not choose to install Publisher's Wizards. Run Setup again and install Publisher's Wizards to access the Design Gallery.

Insert a Design Gallery Object in a Publication *(continued)*

2 Select either the Objects By Category tab or the Objects By Design tab. If you've previously added custom objects to the Design Gallery, you can access them by clicking the Your Objects tab.

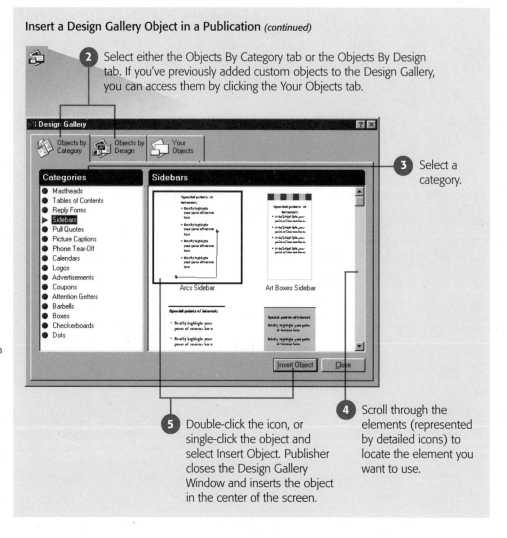

3 Select a category.

4 Scroll through the elements (represented by detailed icons) to locate the element you want to use.

5 Double-click the icon, or single-click the object and select Insert Object. Publisher closes the Design Gallery Window and inserts the object in the center of the screen.

Can I add more than one object at a time to the Design Gallery? Yes, you can perform a multiple selection and add several objects to the Design Gallery simultaneously. However, the multiple selection is not added to the Design Gallery as a series of individual objects; instead, it is added to the Design Gallery as a single grouped object.

Customizing the Design Gallery

You can customize the Design Gallery by adding elements you've created to it. When you add an object or a group to the Design Gallery, Publisher saves it with the current publication only. You can use it over and over again in the current publication. But if you want to have access to the same custom object in more than one publication, you must either copy the object from document to document using the Clipboard or import the object from the publication where it is saved.

You can identify the objects you add to the Design Gallery with names, organize them into categories, and delete them when they're no longer needed.

Add a Custom Object to the Design Gallery

1 Select the object you want to add to the Design Gallery.

2 Choose Add Selection To Design Gallery on the Insert menu. Alternatively, click the Design Gallery tool, select the Your Objects tab, click the Options button, and then select Add Selection to Design Gallery. The Add Object dialog box appears.

3 Type an object name.

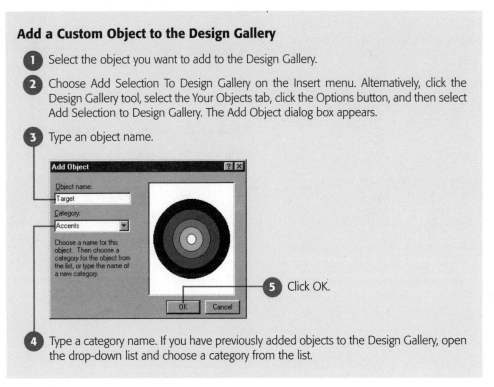

5 Click OK.

4 Type a category name. If you have previously added objects to the Design Gallery, open the drop-down list and choose a category from the list.

Why can't I see the custom Design Gallery objects for the current publication in the Design Gallery dialog box? You've used the Browse button to view custom Design Gallery objects saved with other publications. If you want to see the custom Design Gallery objects saved with the current publication, click the Options button and choose View Gallery For Current Publication from the cascading menu.

Import Design Gallery Objects from Other Publications

1 Open the publication to which you want to add custom Design Gallery objects.

2 Click the Design Gallery tool on the Objects toolbar, or choose Design Gallery Object on the Insert menu. The Design Gallery dialog box appears.

3 Click the Options button (located at the lower left corner of the Design Gallery dialog box), and then choose Browse on the menu. The Other Designs dialog box appears.

4 Locate the file containing the custom objects you want to copy.

5 Highlight the filename. Use the Preview area to confirm that you've selected the correct file.

6 Click OK. All the custom objects, along with their names and category designations, will be copied to the Design Gallery associated with the current publication.

Rename, Delete, or Create Categories in the Design Gallery

1 Open the publication that contains the category you want to modify.

2 Click the Design Gallery tool on the Objects toolbar, or choose Design Gallery Object on the Insert menu. The Design Gallery dialog box appears.

3 Click the Your Objects tab.

4 Click the Options button and choose Edit Categories from the cascading menu.

Use the shortcut menu to modify the Design Gallery. You can delete, rename, and create categories directly from the Design Gallery dialog box. In the Categories list box, right-click the category you want to modify. On the shortcut menu that appears, choose the appropriate command.

Rename, Delete, or Create Categories in the Design Gallery *(continued)*

5 If you want to delete or rename a category, select it.

6 Do one of the following:

@ Click here to rename the selected category. In the Rename Category dialog box that appears, type a new name and a new description. Click OK to rename the category.

@ Click here to delete the selected category. In the confirmation dialog box that appears, click Yes to delete the category.

@ Click here to create a new category. In the Create New Category dialog box that appears, type a name and a description. Click OK to create the category.

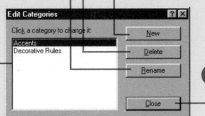

7 Click Close in the Edit Categories dialog box, and then click Close in the Design Gallery dialog box to return to your publication.

8 Save the publication to make the changes permanent.

Delete or Rename Objects in the Design Gallery

1 Open the publication that contains the Design Gallery object you want to delete or rename.

2 Click the Design Gallery tool on the Objects toolbar, or choose Design Gallery Object on the Insert menu. The Design Gallery dialog box appears.

Press the Delete key (without clicking the right mouse button) to remove a custom object from the Design Gallery. In the confirmation dialog box that appears, click Yes.

Delete or Rename Objects in the Design Gallery *(continued)*

3 Click the Your Objects tab.

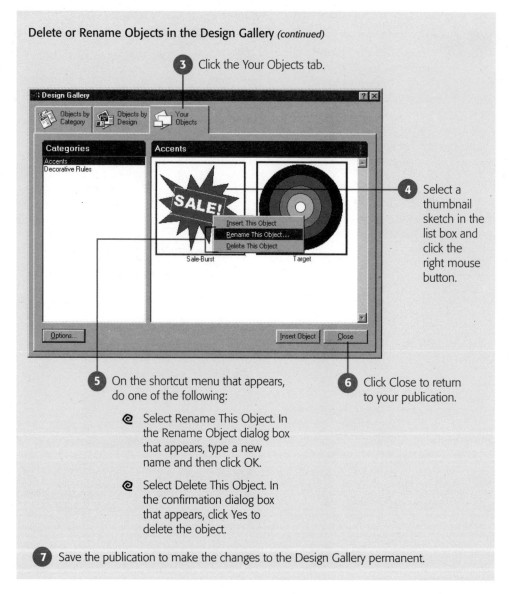

4 Select a thumbnail sketch in the list box and click the right mouse button.

5 On the shortcut menu that appears, do one of the following:

- Select Rename This Object. In the Rename Object dialog box that appears, type a new name and then click OK.

- Select Delete This Object. In the confirmation dialog box that appears, click Yes to delete the object.

6 Click Close to return to your publication.

7 Save the publication to make the changes to the Design Gallery permanent.

Can I resize, move, rotate, or change the layering and alignment of individual elements within a Smart Object? No. You can use Publisher's standard tools to change the position, rotation, layering, or alignment of a Smart Object, but the changes will be applied to the entire Smart Object. For example, if you use the Send To Back command, the entire Smart Object will be sent to the bottom of the stack. Within the Smart Object itself, the layering of the individual elements will remain unchanged.

Convert a Smart Object to standard text and picture frames. If you want to alter the relative size, position, rotation, layering, or alignment of the objects within a Smart Object, you can convert the Smart Object to standard text and picture frames. Select the Smart Object and choose Ungroup from the Arrange menu. Publisher will display an alert box warning you that the Wizard will no longer be able to change the design of the Smart Object. Click Yes to proceed with the conversion.

Editing Smart Objects

Many of the publications you create using a Wizard contain Smart Objects. In addition, almost all the elements in Publisher's Design Gallery are Smart Objects. On the simplest level, a Smart Object is a group of text, table, and picture frames. To add your own content, you can subselect an individual frame within the Smart Object and type text or insert a picture. You can also subselect individual elements and change the object's formatting attributes using Publisher's standard tools. For example, you can change the font used in a text frame or recolor a picture.

Smart Objects, however, are not ordinary groups. As shown in the following illustration, Smart Objects do not display a group button; instead, they display a Wizard button, which you can click to open the associated Wizard and change the design of the Smart Object.

You can subselect individual objects within a group, such as the picture shown here.

Standard groups are identified by the Group button.

You can subselect individual objects within a Smart Object.

Smart Objects are identified by the Wizard button. Click the button to open the associated Wizard.

Wizards

Use the Format Painter to copy attributes from Smart Objects to standard text and picture frames. If you've already inserted a Smart Object into your document, you can use the Format Painter to copy its attributes to other objects in the document. Using the Format Painter allows you to choose which formats to copy. For example, you can select a drawn object in order to copy its fill color and border to another object. Here's how: subselect the individual element within the Smart Object whose formats you want to copy. Click the Format Painter tool on the Standard toolbar. Position the Paintbrush pointer over the object you want to reformat. Click the object.

Use a Wizard to Modify a Smart Object

1 Select the Smart Object you want to change.

2 Click the Wizard button, found along the lower right edge of the Smart Object. The Wizard dialog box appears.

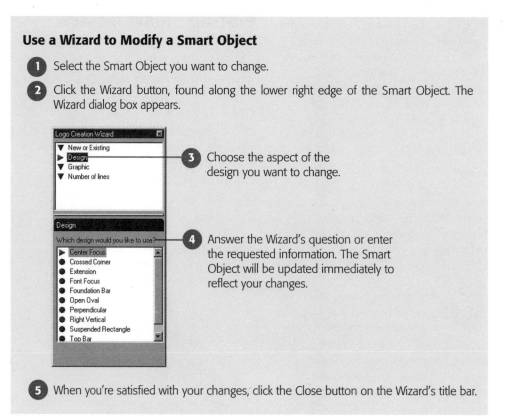

3 Choose the aspect of the design you want to change.

4 Answer the Wizard's question or enter the requested information. The Smart Object will be updated immediately to reflect your changes.

5 When you're satisfied with your changes, click the Close button on the Wizard's title bar.

Understanding Synchronization

Certain elements should be consistent throughout a document. For example, your logo, which will appear several times within a promotional brochure or company newsletter, should be identical each time it recurs. Publisher makes it easier to maintain consistency by synchronizing certain kinds of objects. Synchronized objects are linked to one another within the current publication. If you change one instance of a synchronized object, the change ripples through to all the other linked instances. To use the previous example, if you change the font

Synchronize colors using a color scheme. Publisher lets you manage the colors in your document by using a color scheme (a defined set of colors). Any object in a document (not just a synchronized object) that has been formatted with a color from a color scheme will be automatically updated when you change the scheme.

For more information about Publisher's color schemes, see Chapter 15. For more information about personal information components, see Chapter 5.

of a logo, Publisher automatically changes all the copies of the logo to match your font choice (provided you created the logo with a Wizard).

Synchronization is always under your control. You can turn synchronization on or off for a group of synchronized objects within the current publication. You cannot synchronize objects across different publications. Nor can you choose to update only a single object within a group.

In some cases, Publisher updates the content of an object but not the formatting, or the formatting but not the content. Though it may seem confusing at first, there is an inherent logic to this approach. For example, Publisher always updates the content of a personal information component, because your name, address, and phone number shouldn't vary from page to page. But because Publisher does not update the formatting of a personal information component, you can change the font on an individual basis to match the surrounding text. The following table summarizes the types of objects Publisher can synchronize and the ways in which Publisher implements synchronization.

A Summary of Synchronized Elements			
If you created...	**Using...**	**Publisher synchronizes...**	**In these locations...**
Logo	The Personal Information command on the Insert menu	The content of text and picture frames, and all formatting attributes	All copies of the logo on all the pages in the current publication.
Personal information component	A Wizard, or the Personal Information command on the Insert menu	The content of the text frame, but not the formatting attributes of the text	On all the pages in the current document where the personal information component appears.
A multipage, yearly calendar	A Wizard	The formatting attributes of the names of the months, days of the week, and dates	On all pages in the current document.

Wizards

If you created...	Using...	Publisher synchronizes...	In these locations...
Phone tear-offs	A Wizard or the Design Gallery	The content of the text frames, as well as the formatting attributes	Subsequent instances of the Phone tear-off within the Smart Object. Publisher will not update other copies of the Phone tear-off within the publication.
A running header and footer in a newsletter	A Wizard	The content of the text frames but not the formatting attributes	All copies of the header and footer on all pages within the current document.
Web navigation bars	A Wizard or the Design Gallery	The content of the text and picture frames but not the formatting attributes	All copies of the navigation bar on all pages in the current Web site.
Graphic accents (barbells, boxes, checkerboards, or dots)	A Wizard or the Design Gallery	The formatting attributes	Subsequent instances of the drawn shape within the Smart Object. For example, if you change the color of one dot, all other dots in the selected object will change. However, Publisher will not update other copies of the graphic accent within the publication.

Automatically update hyperlinks in a Web site navigation bar. The navigation bar in a Web site is an electronic table of contents; it contains hyperlinks that move a reader from page to page. You can have Publisher keep track of the pages in your Web site and automatically add (or remove) entries in the navigation bar when you add or remove pages. Move to the page you want to add to the navigation bar. Choose Web Properties on the File menu. In the Web Properties dialog box, click the Page tab. Click Add Hyperlink To Web Navigation Bar, and then click OK.

Edit a Synchronized Element

1 Select the synchronized element you want to change.

2 Do any of the following:

    @ Enter new text in a text frame.

    @ Insert a new image in a picture frame.

    @ Change the formatting attributes.

3 Deselect the object. Publisher will apply the changes you've made to all instances of the synchronized object.

Why can't I find the Undo Synchronization command on the Edit menu? You're attempting to turn off synchronization for a personal information component. The command reads "Undo Propagate Personal Information." Though the language is different, the effect is identical to the Undo Synchronize command.

 Why haven't my changes been synchronized with other similar elements in my publication? There are several reasons why Publisher may not be synchronizing your changes:

@ You may not have deselected the object you edited. Publisher doesn't know that you've finished editing an object until you deselect it.

@ You're working with an object that can't be synchronized. If you draw a text, picture, or table frame using the standard tools on the Objects toolbar, Publisher cannot synchronize the frame.

@ You've turned off synchronization.

Turn Off Synchronization

1 Select a synchronized object.

2 Change the object's text content, picture content, or formatting attributes, and then de-select the object. Publisher will update all synchronized objects.

3 Choose Undo Synchronize on the Edit menu. Publisher will change all the synchronized objects back to their previous state. These elements will remain unsynchronized until you once again activate synchronization.

Note that other object types, which are synchronized, will continue to be updated automatically whenever you make a change. For example, when you turn off synchronization for a Web Navigation Bar, it doesn't affect synchronization for any personal information components that may be in your document.

Turn On Synchronization

1 In the Options dialog box (on the Tools menu), click the Editing And User Assistance tab.

2 Click the button labeled Click To Reset Wizard Synchronizing.

3 Click OK. The next time you modify a synchronized object, Publisher will apply the change to all other instances of that element.

Modifying Wizard Publications and Smart Objects

Using a Wizard or a Smart Object can jump-start your design process. However, you will probably need to modify the layout by using Publisher's standard text, table, picture, and WordArt tools. Before you start importing text and pictures, take a few moments to analyze—and optimize—the publication.

Learn by example. Taking apart a group of objects created with a Wizard or the Design Gallery can teach you quite a lot about design, such as how to combine text, table, and picture elements. After you've dismantled the design, you can simply discard it because it can be re-created easily.

For information about page setup and layout guides, see Chapters 2 and 3.

Align guides to objects. You'll find it easier to align guides with existing frames if you turn off Snap To Ruler Marks and Snap To Guides but turn on Snap To Objects.

Layout Issues

Publisher's Wizards don't generate an underlying structure for a document. They don't set up layout guides, and they don't place repeating elements on the background. You can make the publications easier to modify if you take these steps:

@ Confirm which publication layout, paper size, and orientation have been selected in the Page Setup dialog box. For example, if the Normal layout option has been selected, the actual page size of the publication will vary, depending on the size of the paper installed in your printer.

@ Create layout guides or ruler guides based on the Wizard's design. If you subsequently decide to rearrange the elements in the layout, you'll be able to move and align them with precision.

@ Select objects, such as page numbers or headers and footer, and choose the Send To Background command on the Arrange menu.

Object Attributes

Identifying an element properly can help you edit it more efficiently. Click each object in the layout and note the following:

@ Check whether it is a Smart Object or a standard text, table, picture, WordArt, or drawn object. For example, if you identify a logo design as a Smart Object, you know you can change the design by using a Wizard.

@ Determine whether a particular design element is composed of one object with complex formatting or of multiple objects. It is much easier to edit a single text frame with attributes for a border, object color, and shadow than it is to edit a group consisting of a text frame, a tinted rectangle, and several lines.

Preserve text formatting in Wizard publications and Design Gallery objects. Before you type or import copy, select the text in the publication or object and use the Create Style By Example dialog box to save (and reuse) the text formatting attributes.

For more information about creating a text style by example, see Chapter 6.

Type Styles

Wizards and Design Gallery objects do not contain defined type styles; instead, they contain preformatted text frames. Preformatted text frames behave in the following ways:

- If you type your copy, Publisher preserves the formatting attributes of the Wizard or Design Gallery object.

- If you import copy and your word processing file contains type styles, Publisher attempts to replace the formatting attributes of the Wizard or Design Gallery objects with the imported type formatting attributes.

Fonts

Publisher's Wizards and the Design Gallery use standard TrueType fonts that ship with either Windows 95 or Publisher. You should change the selected font if any of these statements are true:

- The font does not complement other text objects in your document.

- The font does not appeal to you aesthetically.

- You've deleted fonts from your system, and the Wizard or Design Gallery object uses a font that is no longer installed on your computer.

- You are creating a Web site that should not contain unusual fonts.

Text Frames

When you import text into a preformatted document, it flows through all the connected text frames. To control the text flow process, you should take these steps:

- Locate all the connected text frames in the publication by clicking the Frame Jump buttons that appear at the upper left or lower right corner of a selected text frame.

- Disconnect the text frames before you import the text. Then reconnect the frames as needed to handle text overflow.

Object Organization

Elements inserted from the Design Gallery are always Smart Objects. Publications created with a Wizard can contain Smart Objects or groups.

- ⊚ You can resize and reposition all the elements in a group or a Smart Object simultaneously without ungrouping them.

- ⊚ If you want to change the size, position, rotation, or stacking order of an individual element within a group or Smart Object, you must first ungroup the objects.

- ⊚ You can change the content and formatting of an individual element within a group or Smart Object without ungrouping it. Simply click on the individual object to subselect it.

 Why can't I find a Templates tab in the Startup dialog box or a Templates subfolder on my hard disk? Publisher no longer lists templates on a separate tab in the Catalog. Instead, you access templates by clicking the Templates button on the Existing Publications tab in the Catalog. If you're installing Publisher for the first time, no templates exist. Publisher will automatically create a Templates folder the first time you save a publication as a template.

Templates

A template is like a standard Publisher document, with one important difference: when you open a template file, Publisher makes a copy of the template for your use and leaves the original template file undisturbed.

Publisher's template feature is a powerful tool that allows you to save your own custom designs for reuse. For example, you could save a customized letterhead as a template. Then, whenever you write a letter, you can start with a clean document (equivalent to a fresh piece of stationery) that already contains your logo, your company address, and predefined type styles for the body of the letter.

You can also use Publisher's template feature to modify the working environment. Before you save a template, change the settings (called the defaults) for many of Publisher's tools, including the layout guides, default unit of measurement, and frame attributes for text, picture, table, and drawn objects. For example, you could create a flowchart template where lines are automatically created with arrowheads, and the layout guides have been set up as a 0.25-inch drawing grid.

Where should I store my template? When Publisher saves a document as a template, it always stores the file in a predetermined location: the Publications folder found in the Microsoft Office Templates folder.

Save a Publication As a Template

1 Choose Save As on the File menu. The Save As dialog box appears.

2 Type a meaningful name for the document that doesn't duplicate the name of an existing template. For example, Letterhead could identify your company stationery. (Don't type a file extension; the extension .pub will be added automatically.)

3 Turn on the Template check box at the bottom of the dialog box.

4 Click Save. Now when you look through the list of available templates, your letterhead template appears in the list in alphabetical order.

Create a Document Based on a Template

1 Click New on the File menu.

2 In the Catalog, click the Existing Publications tab, and then click the Templates button. The Open Template dialog box appears.

3 Publisher will display a list of templates. Select the template you want to use as a basis for the current publication.

4 Click Open. Publisher opens a copy of the template as an Unsaved Publication.

Change Publisher's Default Settings

1 Open a new, blank publication.

2 Change any of the following settings:

@ Page Setup, including paper size and orientation, and the publication layout

@ Layout guides for page margins and column/row division

@ Ruler guides

Wizards

Can I modify Publisher's working environment without saving a template?

Yes. You can change the defaults for many of Publisher's tools in a standard document. However, the changes you make will be in effect for the current work session or for the current document. The next time you open Publisher or start a new publication, the application reverts to the original "factory settings."

Change Publisher's Default Settings *(continued)*

- The default unit of measurement on the General tab in the Options dialog box (found on the Tools menu)

- Text frame properties, including fill color, line and border style, shadow, text frame margins, and text columns

- Picture frame properties, including fill color, line and border style, shadow, and picture frame margins

- Table frame properties, including fill color, line and border style, shadow, and table cell margins

- Drawn shapes properties, including fill color, line and border style, and shadow

3 Save the document as a template.

4 Close the publication. The new settings will be used for all the publications you create based on the template.

Color and Fill Effects

Dithering is a process in which small dots (or screen pixels) of two or more colors are juxtaposed to create the optical illusion of a new color. For example, blue and yellow dots produce the illusion of green. When you try to view a file containing a wide variety of colors on a 256-color or 16-color monitor, the computer's operating system (either a Mac or a PC) attempts to simulate the correct color by dithering the image. Dithering is also a common printing technique, referred to as halftoning (for a regular dither pattern) or mezzotinting (for an irregular dither pattern). Dithering can make images look grainy, render text at small point sizes difficult to read, and degrade the appearance of thin lines or borders.

You can add visual interest to a page and draw the reader's attention to important information by adding color to your publications. However, you should choose colors carefully, making sure that the color combinations meet these standards:

- Are pleasing and don't produce jarring juxtapositions. Bright red type against a bright green background, for example, will appear to vibrate.

- Provide sufficient contrast between the text and the background color. Black text against a dark blue background is unreadable.

- Look good when printed. Colors that appear on your screen as bright, pure hues may look washed out, very dark, or muddy when printed on paper.

- Look good when viewed on the World Wide Web. Colors that appear on your PC's 256-color (or full-color) screen as bright, pure hues may look totally different or exhibit dithering when viewed by your reader on a Macintosh computer or 16-color computer screen.

Microsoft Publisher's color functions, including the Color Scheme and Image Color Matching (ICM) system, can help you choose colors that are aesthetically pleasing and that look good on screen or in print. In addition, fill effects, such as tints, shades, patterns, or gradients, can help you add variety to a design without adding more colors.

Add visual interest to monochromatic documents. Even if you don't own a color printer, you can add visual interest to your designs by using black, white, and shades of gray in combination. For example, you can place white text against a black background or fill a text frame with a gray tint. The rules of good design apply equally to color *and* monochromatic documents. For example, if you place a gray background behind black text, you must make the tint light enough to keep the text legible.

Do older Publisher files contain a color scheme? An older publication file created with an earlier version of Publisher does not contain a color scheme. When you open this type of document, Publisher 98 analyzes the colors used in the design and automatically creates a custom color scheme.

Access the Color Scheme dialog box from the Format toolbar. To do so, select a frame or a drawn object, click the Object Fill button (shown below), and select More Scheme Colors from the drop-down menu.

Color Schemes

When you start a new publication, Publisher uses a default color scheme (named Bluebird). However, you can choose a different color scheme from the list of 62 predefined color schemes that ship with Publisher. At any given time, you can have only one color scheme associated with each publication.

Publisher's color schemes contain five colors that work well together. When you format an object using a color in a color scheme, Publisher keeps track of the color slot number and the name of the scheme, as shown in the following illustration. When you change color schemes, Publisher automatically changes the colors of all the objects in your publication that use scheme colors.

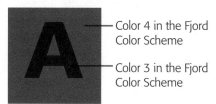 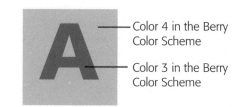

Color 4 in the Fjord Color Scheme

Color 3 in the Fjord Color Scheme

Color 4 in the Berry Color Scheme

Color 3 in the Berry Color Scheme

When you choose a new color scheme, Publisher recolors the objects in your publication that use scheme colors. It substitutes the color in slot 3 from the current color scheme for the color in slot 3 from the previous color scheme.

When you begin a new publication, or as you are working on a publication, you can choose to work with a standard color scheme or create a custom color scheme.

Choose a Standard Color Scheme

1 Start a new publication, or open an existing publication.

2 If you are working with a Web document, choose Color And Background Scheme on the Format menu. If you are working with a print document, choose Color Scheme on the Format menu. The Color And Background Scheme dialog box (not shown) or the Color Scheme dialog box appears.

Why can't I find the Color Scheme command on the Format menu? The Color Scheme command is only available when you are working on a full-color print document (the Color And Background Scheme command is available if you are working on a Web document). If, however, you have created a black-and-white or spot-color document for a printing service, the Color Scheme command will not appear on the Format menu.

For more information about preparing documents for a printing service, see Chapter 17.

For more information about the Color And Background Scheme dialog box, see Chapter 12.

Choose a Standard Color Scheme *(continued)*

3 Click the Standard tab.

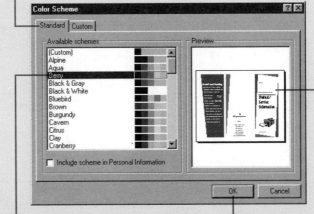

The Preview area displays the actual objects on the current page of your document as they will appear with the selected color scheme.

4 Scroll through the list of predefined color schemes and select one.

5 Click OK. Publisher recolors all the objects in your publication that use scheme colors.

Create a Custom Color Scheme

1 Start a new publication, or open an existing publication.

2 If you are working with a Web document, choose Color And Background Scheme on the Format menu. If you are working with a print document, choose Color Scheme on the Format menu. The Color And Background Scheme dialog box (not shown) or the Color Scheme dialog box appears.

Color and Fill Effects

How do color schemes work with Wizard publications and Design Gallery objects? When you use a Wizard to create a publication, the Wizard will ask you to choose a color scheme. You can, however, change the color scheme at any time.

When you insert an object from the Design Gallery, the object uses the colors in the current scheme. You can change the colors in the Design Gallery object by choosing a new color scheme, or you can subselect individual elements within the Design Gallery and choose a new color.

For more information about Wizards and Design Gallery objects, see Chapter 14.

Reuse a custom color scheme in another publication. Normally, when you create a custom color scheme, Publisher saves the information with the current publication only. The custom color scheme is not available to other documents.

You can reuse a custom color scheme in another publication by associating it with a personal information set. When you subsequently select that personal information set in a new document, Publisher makes the custom color scheme available.

Create a Custom Color Scheme *(continued)*

3 Click the Custom tab.

The Preview area displays the actual objects on the current page of your document as they will appear with the custom color scheme.

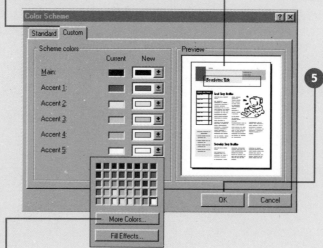

5 Click OK. Publisher lists the color scheme you've created, with the name Custom, in the Standard Color Scheme list box. Publisher recolors all the objects in your document that use scheme colors.

4 In the New area, open the drop-down list for the color you want to define. Choose one of the available colors, tints, or shades.

Associate a Color Scheme with a Personal Information Set

1 Choose Personal Information on the Insert menu.

2 Choose Select from the cascading menu. On the second cascading menu, choose one of the four personal information sets: Primary Business, Secondary Business, Other Organization, or Home/Family.

3 Select Color Scheme (or Color And Background Scheme if you are working in a Web publication) on the Format menu.

For more information about personal information components, see Chapter 5.

Associate a Color Scheme with a Personal Information Set *(continued)*

4 Choose one of the standard color schemes on the Standard tab, or click the Custom tab and create a custom color scheme.

5 On the Standard tab, click the box labeled Include Scheme In Personal Information.

6 Click OK.

Publisher will use this color scheme whenever you associate a publication with the personal information set you chose in step 2.

Choosing Colors for Fills, Lines, Borders, and Text

For more information about preparing documents for a printing service, see Chapter 17.

To a large extent, the color choices available to you and the colors that Publisher uses to display imported pictures are dependent on the printing process you chose when you set up your document, as explained in the following table.

Color Availability in a Publisher Document		
If you set up...	**Available colors include...**	**Publisher displays imported pictures using...**
A black-and-white document for a printing service	Black, white, and shades of gray shades of gray.	Only black, white, and shades of gray.
A spot-color document for a printing service	Black, white, and the spot color (or colors) you have chosen. Each Publisher document can contain a maximum of two spot colors.	Black, white, and shades of gray. However, you can recolor imported artwork using the spot colors in the document.
A full-color document for a printing service, a locally printed document, or a Web document	Color scheme colors, and the full range of computer generated colors.	The colors contained in the original picture.

Color and Fill Effects

What is a nonscheme color? A nonscheme color is any color that is not contained in the current color scheme. Colors you pick from the basic and custom palettes are nonscheme colors. When you choose a new color scheme, nonscheme colors are not automatically updated with the new colors.

 Access colors from the Format menu. You can assign colors, especially scheme colors, to a selected object quickly by using the buttons found on the Format toolbar. The buttons available to you will differ depending on the type of object you have selected, but they include the ones below:

Fill Color button   Font Color button

Line/Border Style button

You can fill the interior of a frame or drawn object with color, apply color to the border of a frame or drawn object, change the color of a line, change the color of text, and even recolor imported pictures. In a full-color document, Publisher provides a multitiered palette system that includes color-scheme colors, the most recently used nonscheme colors, a basic palette of standard computer colors, and a custom palette where you can mix your own colors using specific red, green, and blue (RGB) values or the hue, saturation, and luminescence (HSL) system. You can display the drop-down color menu from different locations within Publisher, as explained in the following table.

How to Access Publisher's Color Palette	
To change the color of...	**Access the Color menu by...**
The interior, or fill, of a frame or drawn object	Selecting the object you want to fill with a new color. Select the Fill Color command on the Format menu.
A line or the border, or BorderArt, of a frame or drawn object	Selecting a line or the object containing the border or BorderArt pattern you want to recolor. Choose Line/Border Style on the Format menu. Click the More Styles command on the cascading menu.
Text	Highlighting the text you want to recolor. Select the Font command on the Format menu. Click the Color drop-down list in the Font dialog box.
An imported picture, WordArt design, or OLE object	Selecting the object you want to recolor. Select Recolor Object on the Format menu. Click the Color drop-down list in the Recolor Object dialog box.
A drop cap	Placing the text insertion point in the paragraph containing the drop cap you want to recolor. Select Drop Cap on the Format menu. Click the Custom Drop Cap tab and click the Color drop-down list.

For more information about tints, shades, patterns, and gradients, see pages 278 through 281.

Why didn't objects in my publication change color when I chose a new color scheme? If objects in your publication don't change color when you choose a new color scheme, they're not formatted with a scheme color. You can choose the Color Scheme command on the Format menu, and when Publisher displays an alert box asking if you want to change nonscheme colors to the closest matching color in the new color scheme, click Yes. When you choose a new color scheme, Publisher will pick a scheme color for all the objects in your publication that currently use nonscheme colors. Though Publisher does its best to choose appropriate colors, the results may not be what you expect.

If you want more control, you must select each object that uses nonscheme colors, and choose a color from the current color scheme.

Choose a Color from the Current Color Scheme

1 Select the object to which you want to apply a color, and access the color palette.

The No Fill option makes an object transparent.

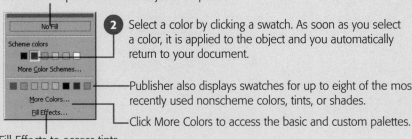

2 Select a color by clicking a swatch. As soon as you select a color, it is applied to the object and you automatically return to your document.

Publisher also displays swatches for up to eight of the most recently used nonscheme colors, tints, or shades.

Click More Colors to access the basic and custom palettes.

Click Fill Effects to access tints, shades, patterns, and gradients.

Choose a Nonscheme Color from the Basic Palette

1 Select the object to which you want to apply a color, and access the color palette.

2 In the color palette, click the More Colors button. The Colors dialog box appears.

Access the basic colors from the drop-down color dialog box. If you routinely use colors from the basic palette, click Show Basic Colors In Color Palette. This will display all the basic colors on the Fill Color and Font Color drop-down menu, making it unnecessary to open the Colors dialog box.

Why can't I activate the option to mark colors that will not print well on my printer? This option is offered only for color printers, and even then it is available only if the printer supports the Image Color Matching (ICM) system. To have this option fully functional, you must also turn on the Improve Screen And Printer Color Matching check box in the Options dialog box (available from the Tools menu) and choose the appropriate Image Color Matching options in the printer's Properties dialog box.

For more information about the Windows 95 Image Color Matching system, see pages 282 through 284.

Choose a Nonscheme Color from the Basic Palette *(continued)*

3 Select the Basic Colors option.

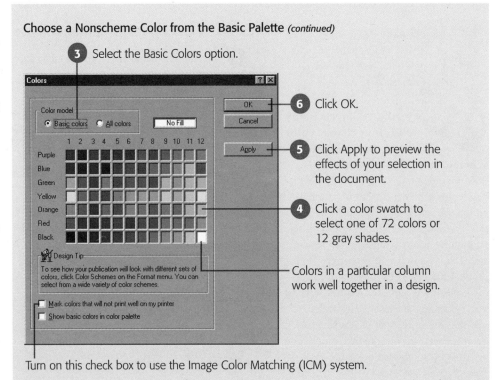

6 Click OK.

5 Click Apply to preview the effects of your selection in the document.

4 Click a color swatch to select one of 72 colors or 12 gray shades.

Colors in a particular column work well together in a design.

Turn on this check box to use the Image Color Matching (ICM) system.

Specify a Custom Color in the Colors Dialog Box

1 Select the object to which you want to apply a color, and access the color drop-down menu.

2 Click the More Colors button. The Colors dialog box appears.

Specify a Custom Color in the Colors Dialog Box *(continued)*

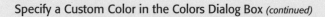

3 Select the All Colors option to display the custom palette. You can access any of 16.7 million colors in the custom palette.

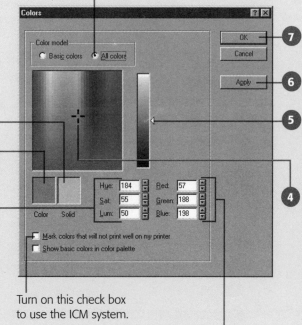

7 Click OK to accept the new color.

6 Click Apply to preview the effects of your selection in the document.

5 Move this arrow to pick the luminescence, or lightness, of the color. The luminescence is a value on a black-to-white scale.

4 Click in this box to place the crossbar at your chosen hue and saturation. Move the crossbar left and right to pick a hue. Move the crossbar up and down to pick a saturation (also called intensity). Colors are at full intensity at the top of the box and are grayer toward the bottom of the box.

Whenever it is impossible to apply a dithered color to an object, Publisher uses this solid color instead. Solid colors are typically applied to pattern fills and the outlines of letters.

Publisher previews the color you choose as accurately as possible. Pixels will be dithered to create the color if necessary.

Instead of picking colors visually, enter a value from 0 through 359 in the hue text box. In the saturation text box, enter a value from 0 (pure gray) through 100 (full saturation). In the luminescence text box, enter a value from 0 (black) through 100 (white).

Turn on this check box to use the ICM system.

Instead of picking colors visually, enter a value from 0 (no color) through 255 (maximum color) in each of the Red, Green, and Blue text boxes. As you increase the intensity of the color, you also make the color lighter. Entering a value of 255 in each of the three text boxes, for example, produces pure white.

Color and Fill Effects

Why can't I choose a color from the basic palette or create a custom color? You are not working in a full-color document. If you are working in a black-and-white document, Publisher limits your choices to black, white, and 14 tints of gray. If you are working in a spot color document, Publisher limits your choices to 16 percentages of black, Spot Color 1, and Spot Color 2, as shown in the following illustration.

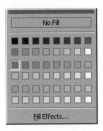

 How does color or a fill pattern appear in a picture frame? When you fill a picture frame, the pattern or color will appear only if the picture you import into the frame has a clear background. Most of the vector clip art pictures in the Clip Gallery have a clear background, but scanned or bitmapped pictures have opaque backgrounds that will obscure any shading within the picture frame.

Fill Effects

In addition to filling an object with a solid color, Publisher lets you create special effects, including tints, shades, patterns, and gradients.

Publisher can mix a selected color with white to create tints or black to create shades.

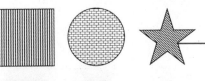

Publisher provides 18 fill patterns. You can also make an object transparent so that filled objects placed farther back in the stacking order show through.

A gradient fill creates a transition from one color to another. Publisher provides 44 gradient fills.

Choose a Tint or a Shade

1 Select the frame or drawn shape you want to fill.

2 Choose Fill Color on the Format menu, or click the Fill Color button on the Format menu.

3 Select Fill Effects on the cascading menu. The Fill Effects dialog box appears.

Why aren't darker shades of my chosen color available? If you've chosen to print your publication to a commercial service using spot colors, Publisher restricts your choices to tints only. In order to access tints *and* shades, you must change your print options using the Prepare File for Printing Service command (found on the File menu).

For more information about preparing a file for a printing service, see Chapter 17.

Add a tint or a shade to a custom color scheme. When you create a custom color scheme, you can fill a color slot with a tint or a shade. In the Color Scheme dialog box, click the Custom tab. Open the color palette by clicking the New drop-down arrow and select Fill Effects. The tint or shade you specify will appear as part of the custom color scheme.

Choose a Tint or a Shade (continued)

4 Select the Tints/Shades option.

5 Open the Base Color drop-down list box and select one of the available colors.

6 Scroll through the tint and shade options. Either click one of the 10 predefined tints to create a lighter version of the current color, or click one of the 10 predefined shades to create a darker version of the current color.

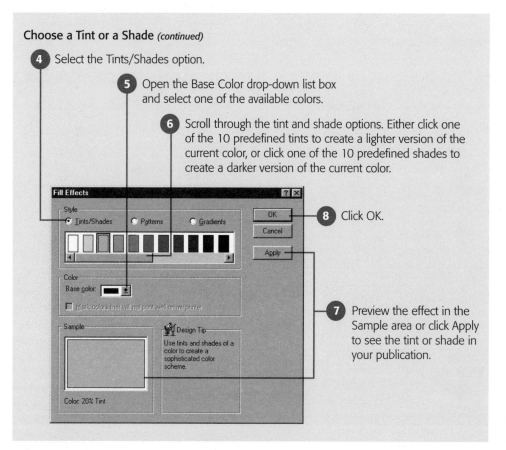

8 Click OK.

7 Preview the effect in the Sample area or click Apply to see the tint or shade in your publication.

Choose a Pattern

1 Select the frame or drawn shape that you want to fill with a pattern.

2 Choose Fill Color on the Format menu, or click the Fill Color button on the Format menu.

3 Select Fill Effects on the cascading menu. The Fill Effects dialog box appears.

Color and Fill Effects

Choose a Pattern *(continued)*

The very first box contains a circle with a vertical line through it to indicate that it is the transparent, or clear, option. Objects or frames formatted with the Clear pattern allow objects farther back in the stacking order to show through.

4 Select the Patterns option.

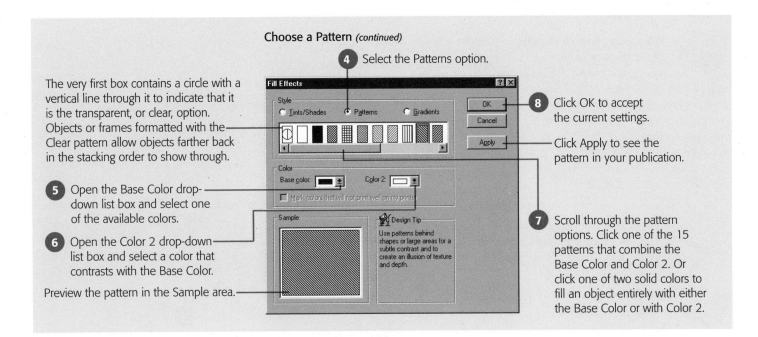

8 Click OK to accept the current settings.

Click Apply to see the pattern in your publication.

5 Open the Base Color drop-down list box and select one of the available colors.

6 Open the Color 2 drop-down list box and select a color that contrasts with the Base Color.

Preview the pattern in the Sample area.

7 Scroll through the pattern options. Click one of the 15 patterns that combine the Base Color and Color 2. Or click one of two solid colors to fill an object entirely with either the Base Color or with Color 2.

Why doesn't the fill pattern get bigger when I increase the size of an object? Because Publisher's patterns aren't pictures, they can't be resized. Publisher's patterns are a type of formatting attribute—like a color or a tint. You wouldn't expect an object to change its color if you enlarged it. In the same way, no matter how large or small an object may become, the pattern that fills it will remain the same size.

Choose a Gradient

1 Select the object you want to fill.

2 Choose Fill Color on the Format menu, or click the Fill Color button on the Format toolbar.

3 Select Fill Effects from the cascading menu. The Fill Effects dialog box appears.

4 Select the Gradients option.

To make an opaque object transparent, or to make a transparent object opaque, select it and press Ctrl-T.

 Remove tints, shades, patterns, and gradients.
If you want to remove a special fill from an object, select the object and then select either a new color or the Clear option from the color palette.

If you want to change the color of an object *without* removing the special fill, pick a new color from within the Fill Effects dialog box.

Choose a Gradient (*continued*)

⑤ Open the Base Color drop-down list box and select one of the available colors.

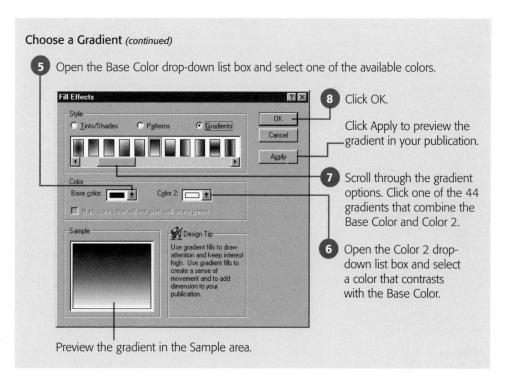

⑧ Click OK.

Click Apply to preview the gradient in your publication.

⑦ Scroll through the gradient options. Click one of the 44 gradients that combine the Base Color and Color 2.

⑥ Open the Color 2 drop-down list box and select a color that contrasts with the Base Color.

Preview the gradient in the Sample area.

On-Screen Color and Printer Color Compatibility

The colors you see and choose on screen might not be the colors that appear in the final printout. Computer monitors and color printers use different—and not entirely compatible—color systems. The colors you see on your computer monitor are created by using the RGB color model. However, images produced by a color printer rely on the CMYK color model. Translating RGB values to CMYK values can result in color shifts. The following table compares treatment of color by monitors and printers.

See accurate colors on screen. The number of colors you see on your computer monitor will vary depending on the video mode you are using. The standard VGA resolution, for example, can produce only 16 colors. Any other colors are *simulated* with a process known as dithering. Dithered colors are not accurate. If your document contains only flat color (meaning solid colors, tints, and shades), a 256-color video mode should be sufficient. But for the most accurate view of the colors in your document (and especially in imported pictures), your monitor and video card should be capable of displaying the full 16.7 million colors. This video mode is often referred to as True Color, or 24-bit color.

Why don't I have the same Image Color Matching options available for my printer? The exact structure of the printer Properties dialog box will change depending on your particular printer. For example, some color printers can't perform color matching calculations, and will only offer an option to perform image color matching on the host computer. Use the instructions given in the adjacent section as a guideline.

Comparison of Color Technologies		
Characteristic	**Computer Monitor**	**Color Printer**
Color primaries	Red, green, and blue (RGB) pixels.	Cyan, magenta, yellow, and black (CMYK, where K stands for black ink).
Color properties	Pixels emit light.	Inks reflect light.
Color mixing	Is additive. Colors get lighter as you increase intensity. Full intensity of all three primaries is white.	Is subtractive. Colors get darker as you increase intensity. Full intensity of all four colors is black.
Number of available colors	The RGB color system can produce a wide color spectrum of up to 16.7 million colors. The RGB color system can simulate CMYK printing.	Color printers vary dramatically in resolution and subsequently in the number of colors they can produce. Color printers can produce only a small subset of the RGB spectrum.

Image Color Matching

Windows 95 provides a color matching mechanism called Image Color Matching (ICM). You don't need to understand exactly how ICM works in order to use it, but an overview of its functionality is useful. The ICM engine reads special files called ICC (International Color Consortium) device profiles. These profiles contain information about how a particular device, such as a monitor or printer, defines colors. The ICM engine then translates from one device profile to another. ICM allows you to see an accurate screen preview of the final printed colors and alerts you to colors that will not print well on the chosen output device.

Publisher can take advantage of ICM only if all of the following are true:

@ You have properly identified your monitor in the Display Properties dialog box. (Double-click the Display icon in the Control Panel.)

@ Your printer supports ICM, and you have turned on the feature in the printer Properties dialog box.

@ You have turned on ICM in Publisher.

Turn On the ICM Feature in the Printer Properties Dialog Box

1 On the Windows 95 Start menu, choose Settings. On the cascading menu, choose the Printers folder.

2 In the Printers folder, right-click the icon for your color printer, and then choose Properties on the shortcut menu.

3 In the printer Properties dialog box, select the Graphics tab.

4 Select the Use Image Color Matching option.

5 Click the Choose Image Color Matching Method button. The Image Color Matching dialog box appears.

6 Select a color matching method. Be aware that color matching on the host (where the computer that sends the document to the printer) can slow down system performance.

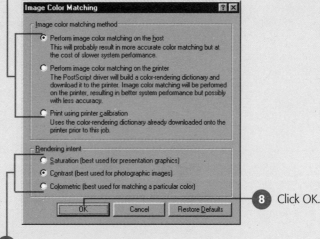

8 Click OK.

7 Choose a rendering model.

- Saturation is best for solid-colored pictures (such as charts and diagrams).

- Contrast works best for photographic images.

- Colormetric requires the printer to have the exact color of ink you require.

Color and Fill Effects

Have the printer perform color matching calculations. You can increase your system's speed by using the printer's processor, rather than your computer's processor, to perform the calculations for color matching. This technique will work only if you have a PostScript Level 2 or Level 3 color printer, which can use a color dictionary to map screen colors to printer colors. To take advantage of this feature, choose Perform Image Color Matching On The Printer to download a color dictionary to the printer with each job, or choose Print Using Printer Calibration to use a color dictionary that has already been downloaded to the printer. Though this method of color matching will free up your system resources, it may result in less accurate color matching.

Which colors will print well? The best way to tell which colors will print well is to compare the colors on screen to paper output. To help you do this, Publisher provides a color sampler document that contains all 50 standard color schemes and the colors in the basic palette. To print it, open Publisher's Help system. Search for the phrase ICM. Click the topic, Color Matching, read through the information, and follow the on-screen directions to print the Color Sampler document.

Turn On ICM in Publisher

1 Open the Tools menu and choose Options. The Options dialog box appears.

2 Select the General tab.

3 Turn on the Improve Screen And Printer Color Matching check box.

4 Click OK. If the current printer does not have an ICC profile, or if the printer has not been configured to use ICM, an alert box will appear. You must first configure ICM in the printer Properties dialog box. Then return to step 1.

5 Select an object.

6 Choose Fill Color on the Format menu. The Colors dialog box appears.

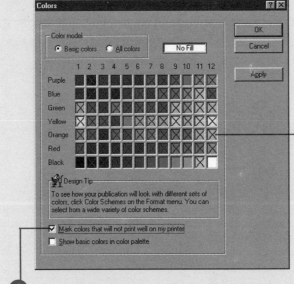

Publisher puts an X through those color swatches that will not reproduce well on your printer.

7 Turn on the Mark Colors That Will Not Print Well On My Printer check box.

Use a Wizard to create designs for special papers. You can use a Wizard to create a design that works perfectly with a preprinted specialty paper. When you begin a new publication, click the Publications By Design tab in the Catalog. Choose the category called Special Papers. The icons will clearly display each special paper design and will identify the special paper by name and with the Paper Direct logo, as shown in the following illustration.

Acropolis Special Paper
Informational Brochure

Why don't the special paper designs print along with the rest of my publication? The Special Paper designs are screen previews only; Publisher does not print them. If you want these designs to appear in your publications, you need to buy the papers from Paper Direct at 1-800-272-7377.

Why is the Special Paper command on the View menu grayed out? Your publication is set up for a printing service. The Special Paper command is available only if you are printing to a local printer (a desktop printer connected to your computer).

Printing on Colored Paper

Even if you own a black-and-white printer, you can easily add color to your publications by printing on colored paper. Papers that are laser compatible and inkjet compatible come in a wide variety of colors. Many specialty papers are available in multicolor designs. If you design your document to be printed on one of these papers, you might find it helpful to see a screen preview of it. Publisher provides screen previews of over 40 popular papers for letterheads, brochures, postcards, and business cards. The papers are all available from Paper Direct, a paper manufacturer.

Turn the Display of Special Papers On and Off

1 Choose Special Paper on the View menu. The Special Paper dialog box appears.

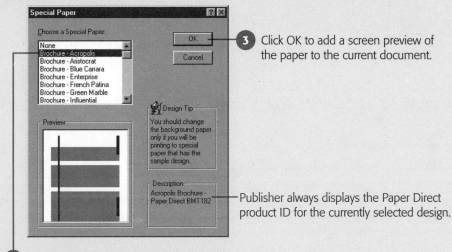

3 Click OK to add a screen preview of the paper to the current document.

Publisher always displays the Paper Direct product ID for the currently selected design.

2 Highlight the paper you want to use, or select None to deactivate the display of special paper.

Color and Fill Effects

Printing Your Publication

You can improve overall printing speeds and enhance the final appearance of your publication by taking control of the printing process. Using the printer Properties dialog box, accessed from either the Windows 95 Control Panel or from within Publisher, you can configure the actual printer hardware. In addition, Microsoft Publisher's Print dialog box allows you to produce a wide range of projects right on the desktop—including folded cards, multipage books, oversized banners and posters, undersized business cards and labels, and mail merge documents.

Changing Printer Properties

The Windows 95 Control Panel and Publisher's Print Setup command offer options for changing printer characteristics.

Choosing a Default Printer

When you begin a new publication, Publisher assumes that you want to use the printer designated as the default printer in the Windows 95 Control Panel. You can select the printer you would like to use as the default.

Wizards and the default printer. Wizards make decisions about page size, orientation, and font availability depending on the capabilities of the default printer. Make sure you choose the correct printer as the default printer *before* you create a publication using a Wizard.

Select the Default Printer

1 On the Windows 95 Start menu, choose Settings. On the cascading menu, choose Printers.

Is the Set As Default command found only on the shortcut menu? No. In the Printers folder, you can select the icon that represents the printer you want to use as the default. Then choose the Set As Default command on the File menu.

 For a complete description of Control Panel, refer to the Windows 95 online help system.

 Is there any difference between accessing the printer Properties dialog box from the Windows 95 Printers folder and accessing it from within Publisher? Yes, there is an important difference. If you use the Properties button in Publisher's Print or Print Setup dialog box to access the printer Properties dialog box, the changes you make will apply only to the current document. If you use the Windows 95 Printers folder to access the printer Properties dialog box, the changes you make will apply to the printer for all applications and all print jobs.

Select the Default Printer *(continued)*

2 In the Printers folder, right-click the icon that represents the printer you want as your default. The shortcut menu appears.

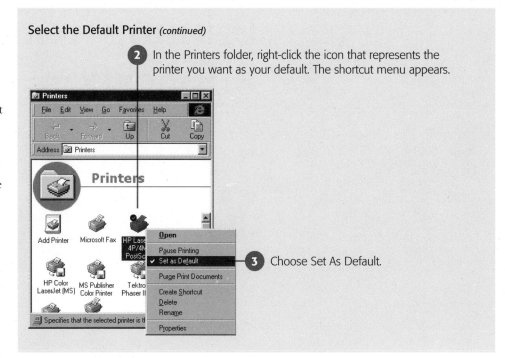

3 Choose Set As Default.

Choosing Printer and Paper Options

By using Publisher's Print Setup dialog box, you can choose a new printer and specify unique paper options for each document you create in Publisher.

Select the Printer and Paper Options Within Publisher

1 Choose Print Setup on the File menu. The Print Setup dialog box appears.

2 Select the options you want.

When to use the Manual Feed paper option. Specify Manual Feed if you want to feed envelopes, small cards, or heavier stocks through your printer. Feeding small or thick paper by hand can help you avoid paper jams.

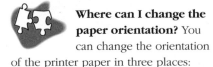

Where can I change the paper orientation? You can change the orientation of the printer paper in three places:

@ The printer Properties dialog box, accessed from the Printers folder, sets the default orientation for the printer.

@ The Print Setup dialog box, accessed from the File menu, sets the orientation for the current document. The orientation you choose in the Print Setup dialog box is automatically reflected in the Page Setup dialog box and is saved along with the Publication.

@ The Page Setup dialog box, accessed from the File menu, sets the orientation for the current document. The orientation you choose in the Page Setup dialog box is automatically reflected in the Print Setup dialog box and is saved along with the publication.

Select the Printer and Paper Options Within Publisher *(continued)*

Open the Size drop-down list box to choose one of the standard paper sizes.

Open this drop-down list box to choose a printer from the list of currently installed printers.

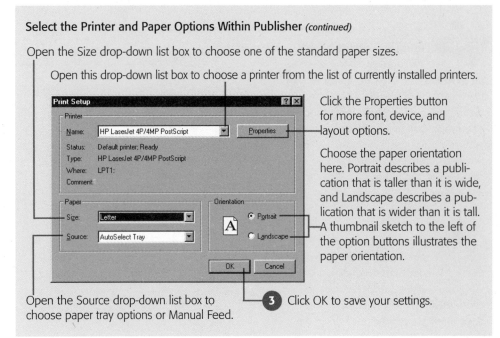

Click the Properties button for more font, device, and layout options.

Choose the paper orientation here. Portrait describes a publication that is taller than it is wide, and Landscape describes a publication that is wider than it is tall. A thumbnail sketch to the left of the option buttons illustrates the paper orientation.

Open the Source drop-down list box to choose paper tray options or Manual Feed.

3 Click OK to save your settings.

Customizing the Paper Size

You can give your designs an aesthetic boost by using special paper stock, such as note paper, folded cards, and postcards. Many stationery stores, office supply stores, and mail order companies carry specialty papers that will work with a desktop laser printer. To print on these nonstandard papers, you must define a custom paper size in the Properties dialog box.

Select an Atypical Paper Size for Your Document

1 Choose Print or Print Setup on the File menu.

2 In the Print or Print Setup dialog box, click the Properties button. The printer Properties dialog box appears.

Why isn't the Custom button available in the Properties dialog box for my printer? The Custom button is available only for printers that accommodate custom paper sizes. Your printer does not support custom paper sizes. To produce publications of unusual size, you must print your document to a full-size sheet of paper and then trim the excess paper.

 Why can't I select a custom paper size from the Size drop-down list in Publisher's Print Setup dialog box? If you attempt to select a custom-sized paper directly from the drop-down list of paper sizes available in the Print Setup dialog box, Publisher doesn't recognize the paper size and defaults your selection to a different size. Therefore, you should always choose a custom paper size in the Properties dialog box, accessed by clicking the Properties button in the Print Setup dialog box.

Select an Atypical Paper Size for Your Document *(continued)*

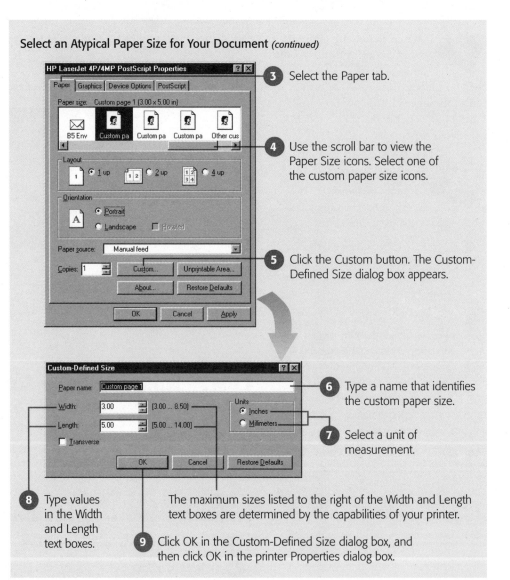

3 Select the Paper tab.

4 Use the scroll bar to view the Paper Size icons. Select one of the custom paper size icons.

5 Click the Custom button. The Custom-Defined Size dialog box appears.

6 Type a name that identifies the custom paper size.

7 Select a unit of measurement.

8 Type values in the Width and Length text boxes.

The maximum sizes listed to the right of the Width and Length text boxes are determined by the capabilities of your printer.

9 Click OK in the Custom-Defined Size dialog box, and then click OK in the printer Properties dialog box.

How can I determine nonprinting margins on an older printer? Older printers typically do not supply Windows 95 with information about nonprinting margins. You can still determine the size of the nonprinting margins empirically by creating a new publication. In the Print Setup dialog box, select the printer and the largest paper size your printer can accommodate. In the Page Setup dialog box, choose the Normal option (indicating that the page size matches the paper size). Using the Box tool, draw a rectangle that covers the entire page. With the rectangle selected, choose Fill Color on the Format toolbar, and then choose a color or gray tint in the drop-down list that appears. Don't choose the Clear or White options. Print the page. The unshaded areas around the edge constitute the nonprinting margins.

Accommodating Nonprinting Margins

Most printers are alike in one important way: they reserve a portion of the page for gripping the paper and feeding it through the printing mechanism. This portion of the page cannot contain any printed images or text. Whenever you plan a publication, be sure you set page margins that are at least as wide as your printer's nonprinting margins.

Determine the Standard Nonprinting Margins for Your Printer

1 Choose Print or Print Setup on the File menu.

2 In the Print or Print Setup dialog box, click the Properties button. The printer Properties dialog box appears.

3 Select the Paper tab.

4 Click the Unprintable Area button. The Unprintable Area dialog box appears.

5 Select a unit of measurement.

6 Click the Restore Defaults button.

7 Click OK.

How is resolution measured? Printer resolution is measured in dots per inch (dpi). Halftone resolution is measured in lines per inch (lpi), also known as screen frequency.

Adjusting the Print Quality of Documents

Many printers allow you to change resolution settings. Lowering the resolution results in faster printing time—a useful feature if you need to print your document many times, as when you are experimenting with a design or proofreading text. Depending on the capabilities of your printer, you might also have access to a resolution setting, called halftoning, which affects the appearance of scanned pictures.

Why can't I change the resolution or halftone settings for my printer?

Different printers have different hardware capabilities. Some printers, for example, do not allow you to specify a dpi value for the resolution but instead ask you to choose between draft and quality printing. Other printers have a fixed resolution, such as 300 dpi.

The variation between printers is even more dramatic where halftoning functions are concerned. Laser printers and PostScript printers offer the widest range of functions. If you are working with an inkjet printer, especially a color inkjet, you may find that you can adjust the printed quality of imported pictures by changing the dithering setting, as shown below.

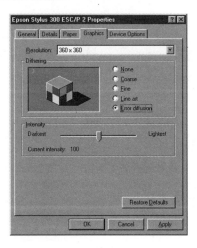

Specify the Resolution Settings

1 Choose Print or Print Setup on the File menu.

2 In the Print or Print Setup dialog box, click the Properties button. The printer Properties dialog box appears.

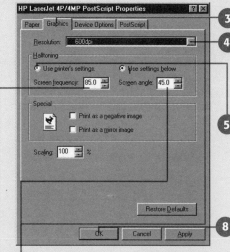

3 Select the Graphics tab.

4 Open the Resolution drop-down list box and choose the appropriate resolution or quality setting. Choose lower dpi values for faster printing; choose higher dpi values for quality output.

5 Use the printer's default halftoning settings or your own specifications. The default, or "factory," settings are designed to provide the best combination of picture resolution with a wide range of gray tones.

8 Click OK.

7 If you are specifying your own halftoning settings, enter a value in the Screen Angle text box. The default setting of 45 degrees minimizes the regular dot pattern in the halftone screen, producing smooth tonal transitions in photographic images.

6 If you are specifying your own halftoning settings, enter a value in the Screen Frequency text box. Higher values increase the apparent resolution of a picture but decrease the number of gray tones. Lower values decrease the resolution of scanned pictures but increase the number of gray tones.

How to bypass the Print dialog box. To bypass the Print dialog box, click the Print button, shown here, on the Standard toolbar.

 You can access the Print dialog box by pressing Ctrl-P.

 Drag-and-drop printing. You can print a document by dragging an icon representing a Publisher file and dropping it on top of the icon for your printer. Windows 95 will open Publisher in order to print the file.

Printing a Document Using Default Settings

Print a Document with the Default Settings

1 Choose Print on the File menu. The Print dialog box appears.

2 Click OK.

Overriding Defaults: Controlling the Current Print Job

In some cases, the default options won't suit your needs. The Print dialog box allows you to control the printing process in a number of ways.

Choose Printer Options for the Current Print Job

1 Select Print on the File menu. The Print dialog box appears.

2 Change the settings as appropriate.

Choose Printer Options for the Current Print Job *(continued)*

Open the drop-down list box to select a different printer that is installed on your system.

Click here to access the printer Properties dialog box.

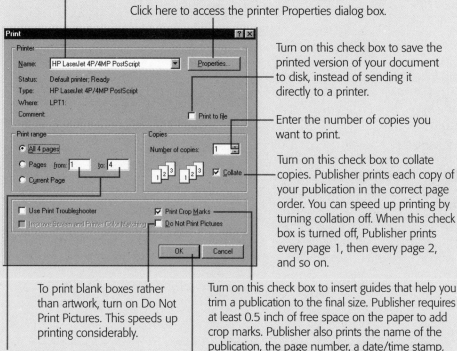

Turn on this check box to save the printed version of your document to disk, instead of sending it directly to a printer.

Enter the number of copies you want to print.

Turn on this check box to collate copies. Publisher prints each copy of your publication in the correct page order. You can speed up printing by turning collation off. When this check box is turned off, Publisher prints every page 1, then every page 2, and so on.

To print blank boxes rather than artwork, turn on Do Not Print Pictures. This speeds up printing considerably.

If you decide to print a section of a larger publication or a single page, enter the starting and ending page numbers in the From and To text boxes, respectively.

Turn on this check box to insert guides that help you trim a publication to the final size. Publisher requires at least 0.5 inch of free space on the paper to add crop marks. Publisher also prints the name of the publication, the page number, a date/time stamp, and (in the case of spot-color separations) registration marks along the edge of the paper.

3 Click OK to begin printing.

Select printer spooling options. Windows 95 provides configuration options for spooling that affect the speed and quality of the print job. The choices you make in the Spool Settings dialog box (located on the Details tab of the printer Properties dialog box) can spool a job more quickly, reduce the amount of free disk space required for the spooling operation, or increase compatibility with your printer.

For more information about spooling options, see the Windows 95 online help system.

Canceling, Pausing, or Reordering the Print Job

When you print a publication, Publisher spools your document to the print queue (the lineup of print jobs) instead of sending it directly to the printer. Spooling lets you continue to work while your document prints. The file is spooled to the print queue at high speed, and as soon as the entire file is in the print queue, you can resume work. Even after you send a document to the print queue, you can cancel printing, pause printing, or rearrange the order in which files will print.

Interrupt Printing

1 Issue the Print command by clicking OK in the Print dialog box. The Printing dialog box appears.

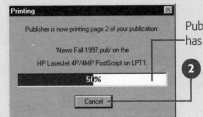

Publisher tells you how much of the file has been spooled to the print queue.

2 Click the Cancel button. Publisher stops sending information to the print queue. However, any pages that have already been sent to the printer and stored in its memory will print.

Control the Print Queue

1 Double-click the printer icon that appears on the taskbar during printing. (Or double-click the printer icon in the Printers folder.) The print queue window appears.

2 Select a file from the print queue.

The print queue window lists files in the order in which they will print. To change the order, select a file and drag it to a new position in the list.

3 Select Pause Printing or Cancel Printing on the Document menu.

Why aren't the tiling options available in the Print dialog box? Tiling is available only when you use the Special Size option in the Page Setup dialog box *and* the printer's paper size is smaller than the document's page size.

Print only a single tile of your poster or banner. You don't have to reprint an entire banner or poster to check a section of your design—to correct a spelling mistake, for example. Instead, select Print One Tile From Ruler Origin in the Poster and Banner Printing Options dialog box. (Because Publisher treats the entire poster or banner as a single-page document, you can't use the Print Range area in the Print dialog box.) Before you use this option, however, you must change the zero points of both the horizontal and the vertical rulers in your publication so that they align with the upper left corner of the tile you want to print.

For more information about the Page Setup command, see Chapter 2. For more information about changing the position of a ruler's zero point, see Chapter 3.

Printing Atypically Sized Publications

It doesn't matter to Publisher how big or small your publication might be. An oversized banner or a poster is still considered to be a single page. If the paper size happens to be smaller than the document page size, Publisher prints the publication page across several sheets of paper in a process known as tiling. If the paper size happens to be larger than the document page size, Publisher lets you print either a single copy or multiple copies on a single sheet of paper.

Print a Poster or a Banner

1 Choose the Page Setup command on the File menu and confirm that the Special Size layout option for a poster or banner is selected.

2 Select the Print command on the File menu. The Print dialog box appears.

3 Click the Tile Printing Options button. The Poster And Banner Printing Options dialog box appears.

4 Select Print Entire Page.

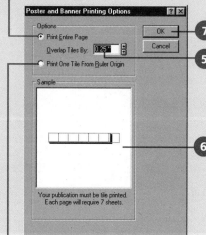

7 Click OK to return to the Print dialog box.

5 Enter a value from 0 through 6.25 inches in the Overlap Tiles By text box. By default, Publisher overlaps the image by 0.25 inch to avoid any white gaps between sections of the poster or the banner.

6 Preview the layout of the poster or the banner in the Sample area.

Select this option to print a single section, or tile, of the poster or the banner.

Why isn't the Page Options button available in the Print dialog box?
Page options that allow you to print more than one copy of a publication on a single sheet of paper are available only when you use the Special Size or Label option in the Page Setup dialog box *and* the printer's paper size is large enough to accommodate more than one copy of the document's page size.

The trouble with 0-value margins. Although Publisher allows you to enter a value of 0 in the Side Margin and Top Margin text boxes, you would rarely want to do so. Setting these margins at 0 places a portion of the page into the printer's nonprinting margin. When you print the publication, part of your design might be cut off.

For more information about nonprinting margins, see page 291.

Print a Small Publication

1 Choose the Page Setup command on the File menu and confirm that the Special Size layout option for a small publication, such as a business card, is selected.

2 Select the Print command on the File menu. The Print dialog box appears.

3 Click the Page Options button. The Page Options dialog box appears.

4 Specify how you want the document to be printed on the page.

Select this option to print one copy of the publication centered on the paper.

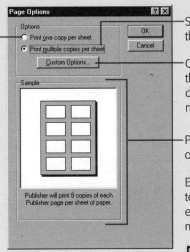

Publisher will print 8 copies of each Publisher page per sheet of paper.

Select this option to print multiple copies of the publication on a single sheet of paper.

Click the Custom Options button to display the Custom Options - Small Publications dialog box and modify the default arrangement of copies on the paper.

Publisher always shows (and lists) the number of copies that will fit on a single sheet of paper.

Enter new values in the margin and gap text boxes. The minimum value you can enter is 0. The maximum value is determined by the paper size and the page size.

Turn on this check box to have Publisher automatically calculate the spacing between copies.

5 Click OK in the Custom Options - Small Publications dialog box. Then click OK in the Page Options dialog box.

Why are the pages for my folded document printed upside down or out of order? When Publisher prints the pages for a folded publication, they may appear to be upside down or out of order. Don't worry. This odd-looking arrangement, called the imposition, ensures that the pages will appear in the correct order when you fold the paper to create the final document.

Why does Publisher insert blank pages when I print my book? The book layout works only when the number of pages in your document is a multiple of 4 (4, 8, 12, and so on). If the number of pages is not a multiple of 4, you will have "blanks" at the end. If you want to insert blank pages in specific locations, use the Page command on the Insert menu.

Printing Folded Publications

Publisher can print documents that are ready to be folded into a card or book. If you are printing a card, Publisher prints all the pages on one sheet of paper. To complete a card, you simply fold it in half (for a tent card) or in quarters (for a top- or side-fold card). A multipage book, however, requires you to bind the pages together.

Print a Card or a Book

1 Choose the Page Setup command on the File menu and confirm that the Special Fold layout is selected.

2 Select the Print command on the File menu. The Print dialog box appears.

3 In the Print Range area, select an appropriate option:

- Click All Pages to have Publisher create an imposition for the entire document. Publisher automatically prints two pages on each sheet of paper for a book or tent card, or four pages on each sheet of paper for a side- or top-fold card.

- Click Pages and enter page numbers in the From and To text boxes to print a section of the book. This option is available only when you are printing a multipage book.

- Click Current Page to print a single selected page of the document.

4 Click OK.

5 If you are printing only a portion of a book, a confirmation dialog box appears. Click Yes to print the selected pages as a separate booklet. Publisher recalculates the imposition for the selected pages so that the first page in the range becomes a right-hand page. Click No to print the selected pages as part of the entire book. Publisher preserves the imposition for the entire book by printing the selected pages along with the appropriate facing page in each spread.

Arranging the Pages of a Book by Hand

Most laser printers print on only one side of the paper, but you can still create a book using Publisher, your laser printer, and a copy machine. Look at the following illustration of an eight-page book, which will help you understand how a

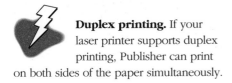

Duplex printing. If your laser printer supports duplex printing, Publisher can print on both sides of the paper simultaneously.

Why can't I find the Print Merge command on the File menu? If the Print Merge command is not available, it means that you haven't properly set up the publication for mail merge. Connect the publication to a data source and insert at least one field code in the publication. The Print Merge command should now be available.

For more information about mail merge functions, see Chapter 13.

book or magazine is constructed. You need to perform two basic operations when assembling a book:

@ Use a copy machine to make double-sided pages.

@ Bind the book by folding, assembling, and stapling the pages.

When Publisher prints the pages in a book, it starts from the outside and works toward the center two facing pages, also called the center spread. When you assemble your book, you must also work your way toward the center.

Then copy the sheet containing pages 6 and 3 onto the back of the sheet containing pages 4 and 5.

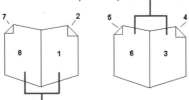

The first page of your book must be a right-hand page, and the last must be a left-hand page.

For an eight-page publication, copy the sheet containing pages 8 and 1 onto the back of the sheet containing pages 2 and 7.

Printing Mail Merge Documents

When you print a mail merge document, Publisher prints the results of the Merge operation, meaning that each copy of the publication contains a different entry from the address list. The Print Merge command offers specialized options that can help you test whether the mail merge is working properly. In addition, several of Publisher's standard print options have new significance when you're printing a mail merge publication.

Print a Merged Document

 Choose Print Merge on the File menu. The Print Merge dialog box appears.

Page layout options for mail merge labels. In the Page Setup dialog box (available from the File menu), Publisher offers over 80 page layouts for Avery labels—the standard brand for sheets of multiple labels. Each layout choice is identified by an Avery product number. Even if you're working with labels from another manufacturer, you can still print labels efficiently. Create a special size publication, where the page size equals the size of one label. In the Print dialog box, click the Page Options button to open the Page Options dialog box, where you can adjust the placement of labels on the page.

For more information on customizing Page Options, see "Print a Small Publication" on page 297.

Are there special options to print envelopes in the Print dialog box? No, the Print dialog box does not contain any special commands to print envelopes. Instead, you must coordinate the settings you have chosen in the Options dialog box (found on the Tools menu), the Page Setup dialog box (found on the File menu), and the Print Setup dialog box (found on the File menu).

Print a Merged Document *(continued)*

2 Select All Entries to print all the entries in your data source, or enter a range of entries to be printed. These print options reflect any filter or sort criteria you applied to the data source.

Open this drop-down list box to specify where on a sheet of labels Publisher should begin printing. For example, if you've already used two rows of labels from a sheet of labels, you can begin printing at row 3. If you're not printing labels, this option will be unavailable.

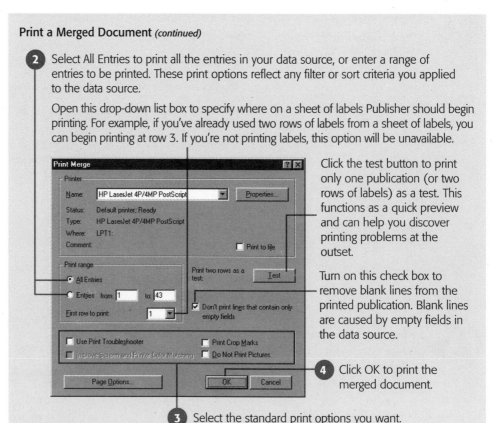

Click the test button to print only one publication (or two rows of labels) as a test. This functions as a quick preview and can help you discover printing problems at the outset.

Turn on this check box to remove blank lines from the printed publication. Blank lines are caused by empty fields in the data source.

4 Click OK to print the merged document.

3 Select the standard print options you want.

Printing Envelopes

Printers differ in their capability to generate envelopes. Some printers support envelopes as a standard paper size; others require custom settings. Publisher offers special configuration options that can help you output envelopes correctly on your particular printer.

Why doesn't Publisher output envelopes correctly on my printer? The answer depends on the settings you chose on the Printing tab in the Options dialog box.

@ If you chose Automatically Use Envelope Paper Sizes, you must select one of the envelope publication layouts in the Page Setup dialog box (found on the File menu).

@ If you chose Print Envelopes To This Printer Using These Settings, you must be sure that the Orientation and Placement options you've selected on the Printing tab in the Options dialog box match those required by your printer. You must also be sure to specify a paper size that is equal to the size of your envelope in the Print Setup dialog box.

Choose Envelope Printing Options

1 Choose the Options command on the Tools menu.

2 Click the Printing tab.

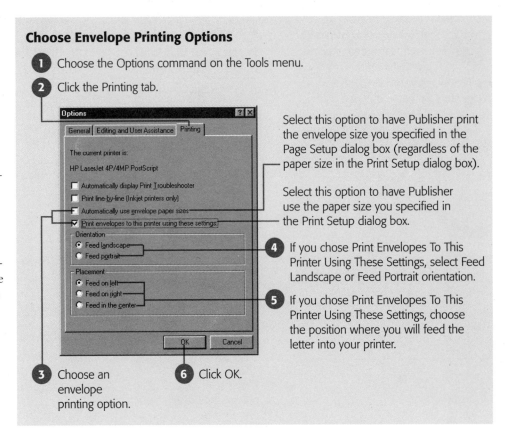

Select this option to have Publisher print the envelope size you specified in the Page Setup dialog box (regardless of the paper size in the Print Setup dialog box).

Select this option to have Publisher use the paper size you specified in the Print Setup dialog box.

4 If you chose Print Envelopes To This Printer Using These Settings, select Feed Landscape or Feed Portrait orientation.

5 If you chose Print Envelopes To This Printer Using These Settings, choose the position where you will feed the letter into your printer.

3 Choose an envelope printing option.

6 Click OK.

Printing Color Documents

Publisher can print black-and-white, full-color, and spot-color documents to any Windows 95–compatible printer. When you print a black-and-white or full-color document to a local printer, you'll see standard options in the Print dialog box. When you print a spot-color document, however, the Print dialog box will offer you additional commands that allow you to print proofs on a desktop printer.

The actual colors of your final printed publication will vary depending on the capabilities of the printer, as explained in the following table.

Print on colored paper.
Even if you own a black-and-white printer, you can easily add color to your publications by printing on colored paper. Laser-compatible and inkjet–compatible papers come in a wide variety of colors. Many specialty papers are available in multi-color designs.

For more information about specialty papers, see Chapter 15.

Color Output Results		
If you print this kind of color document...	**To this kind of printer...**	**Publisher...**
A full-color document. The colors can be created in Publisher or imported as part of a picture file or an OLE object.	A black-and-white printer	Converts all the colors in the publication, imported artwork, or OLE objects to black, white, and shades of gray.
A full-color document. The colors can be created in Publisher or imported as part of a picture file or an OLE object.	A color printer	Prints all the colors in the document, imported artwork, and OLE objects. The actual quality of the color varies from printer to printer.
A spot-color document. The maximum number of colors in a document is three: black, Spot Color 1, and Spot Color 2.	A black-and white printer	Prints a proof. In a composite proof, the spots colors and any tints of the spot colors are converted to black, white, and shades of gray. In a separated proof, black, Spot Color 1, and Spot Color 2 are printed on different sheets of paper.
A spot color document. The maximum number of colors in a document is three: black, Spot Color 1, and Spot Color 2.	A color printer	Prints a proof of the publication, where the spot colors and any tints of the spot colors are converted to full color (CMYK values). The simulated color may not match the spot color you specify at the commercial printer.

Can Publisher generate color separations? Yes and no. Publisher can generate spot-color separations but has no built-in capabilities to generate full-color separations. You can, however, send a full-color document to a printing service for mass reproduction.

For more information about color separations and printing services, see Chapter 17.

Why don't the spot colors look the same on screen and in the printed proof?

When you set up a spot-color document, Publisher lets you choose a color from a palette of 35 hues. Publisher represents the spot color on screen using RGB values. When you print the spot-color publication to a color desktop printer, Publisher simulates the spot color using CMYK values. It is very difficult to match RGB screen colors with CMYK printer colors.

Neither the screen colors nor the full-color printout are an accurate indication of the spot color. You should use the proofs only to judge the position of the elements in relation to one another.

You must specify the exact color you want to print (using a system such as the Pantone Matching System) when you send the publication to a commercial printing service for final output.

Printing Spot-Color Proofs

Desktop printers either print in black-and-white or in full color. To produce final output of a spot-color publication, you'll have to use a commercial printing service. You can, however, print a proof of a spot-color document on your desktop printer. You can print two kinds of proofs, described in the following illustration:

A composite proof prints black, Spot Color 1, and Spot Color 2 on a single sheet of paper. This proof allows you to check how elements on the page register with one another. Notice that Publisher converts colors to shades of gray on a composite black-and-white printout.

A separated proof prints black, Spot Color 1, and Spot Color 2 on different sheets of paper. This proof shows the structure of the separation—including surprinting and knockouts. Notice that Publisher prints the true tint percentage of each color. A 100 percent tint of a light yellow, for example, prints as solid black.

Print a Proof of Your Spot-Color Document

1 Choose Prepare File For Printing Service on the File menu. In the Set Up Publication dialog box confirm that you're printing a spot-color document.

2 Select the Print Proof command on the File menu. The Print Proof dialog box appears.

Print a Proof of Your Spot-Color Document *(continued)*

3 In the Print Range area, select All or Current Page. Notice that you can't print a specified number of pages.

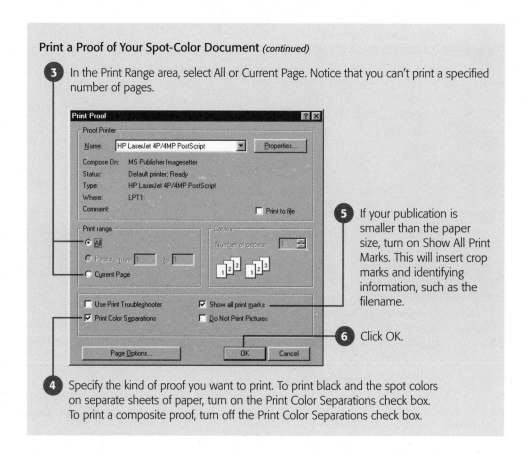

5 If your publication is smaller than the paper size, turn on Show All Print Marks. This will insert crop marks and identifying information, such as the filename.

6 Click OK.

4 Specify the kind of proof you want to print. To print black and the spot colors on separate sheets of paper, turn on the Print Color Separations check box. To print a composite proof, turn off the Print Color Separations check box.

Common Printing Problems and Solutions

Publisher is a WYSIWYG (What You See Is What You Get) desktop publishing program, which means that the screen preview attempts to show you how the final printed page will appear. In some situations the printed output will not match the screen preview. The following table summarizes some of the most common problems you will encounter and offers possible solutions.

How can I be sure I'm choosing a TrueType font?
You can recognize different font types by the icons that appear in the font drop-down list (found on the Format Toolbar or in the Font dialog box). The Double-T icon indicates a TrueType font.

Use printer-resident fonts to reduce printer memory requirements for long, text-intensive publications. A printer typically has a small selection of scalable fonts built into its ROM (Read Only Memory). Unlike software-based fonts (which must be downloaded to the printer's memory), hardware-based fonts don't use up any additional printer memory. If you are receiving memory error messages when you attempt to print a lengthy, text-based document, try substituting printer-resident fonts for fonts (such as TrueType fonts) that must be downloaded to the printer. You can usually identify a printer-resident font in the Font drop-down list because it is preceded by a printer icon.

Printing Problems and Solutions

If you're having this problem…	Because of these circumstances…	Try this solution…
Rotated or white text isn't printing.	You're printing special text, such as text that has been rotated for a card layout, to an inkjet printer (or an older dot matrix printer).	Optimize printing for an inkjet printer by selecting Print Line-By-Line (Inkjet Printers Only) on the Printing tab in the Options dialog box (found on the Tools menu). Alternatively, you can convert all the problematic text to WordArt. WordArt is sent to the printer as a picture—not as text.
The printed font looks different than the font on screen.	You're using a printer-based font that Publisher can't accurately preview on screen.	Use TrueType fonts, which Publisher can preview on screen. Or, if you're using PostScript fonts, install a type manager utility such as Adobe Type Manager, which generates accurate screen previews.
The printer generates a memory error message or prints only half the page.	You're printing a document that contains many pages, large or numerous pictures, or a wide variety of fonts.	Reduce the memory required for the current document by printing only one page (or a small range of pages) in a multipage document, reducing the resolution of imported pictures, or reducing the number of fonts used in the publication. Alternatively, you can install more memory in your printer.

For information about picture resolution, see Chapter 10. For more information about Image Color Matching, see Chapter 15.

Special effects influence printer performance.

Certain types of objects or formatting attributes can increase the size of the file sent to the printer, require more printer memory, and increase printing times. If you are having problems printing your document, search the publication for OLE objects, such as Microsoft Draw 98 pictures or WordArt effects. Printing pages that contain these objects separately can, in many cases, solve the output problems. You should also look for large drawn shapes or frames that are formatted with pattern fills. Simply changing a pattern fill to a solid color, tint, or shade can dramatically improve the printer's performance.

Printing Problems and Solutions (continued)

If you're having this problem...	Because of these circumstances...	Try this solution...
The printed colors don't match the colors on screen.	You're printing computer colors specified with RGB values to a CMYK printer.	Turn on Image Color Matching (ICM) in the printer Properties dialog box and within Publisher to mark those colors that will not print well on your printer.
The color of lines, borders, and text does not match the color you chose.	You've formatted a thin line, a thin rule, or small text with a dithered color. At print time, Publisher may substitute a solid color, or your printer may print the object in black or shades of gray.	Within the publication, choose a new color for the object. Use the All Colors options in the Colors dialog box to compare the color you've chosen to the solid color that may be used at print time.
Text and pictures aren't properly positioned on the page or are cut off at the edge of the paper.	You've ignored the non-printing margins required by your printer. Or you're printing on a paper size that differs from the paper size you specified in the printer Properties dialog box.	Create page margins (using the Layout Guides dialog box found on the Arrange menu) that are larger than the non-printing margins of your printer. Confirm that the paper size you've specified in the Print Setup or printer Properties dialog box matches the size of the paper you've actually inserted into your printer.
Gradient fills print as a series of stripes or bands.	You're printing on a low-resolution printer that can't produce a sufficient number of shades to create a gradual tonal transition.	Minimize banding by turning on error diffusion or dithering, found on the Graphics tab in the printer Properties dialog box. Not all printers support this feature.

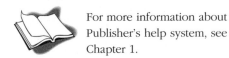

The Print Troubleshooter

The Print Troubleshooter is part of Publisher's online help system. It pinpoints the cause of many common printing problems and suggests solutions to them. You can access the Print Troubleshooter in one of three different ways:

- Click Use Print Troubleshooter in the Print dialog box (found on the File menu).

- Click Automatically Display Print Troubleshooter on the Printing tab in the Options dialog box (found on the Tools menu).

- Choose Print Troubleshooter from the Help menu.

The Print Troubleshooter appears in Publisher's standard help window.

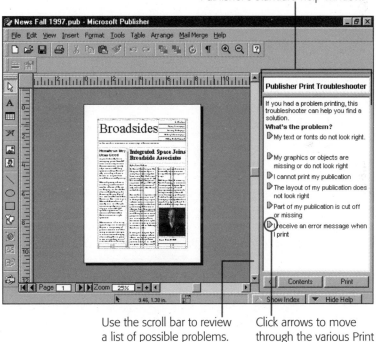

Use the scroll bar to review a list of possible problems.

Click arrows to move through the various Print Troubleshooter screens.

Printing Your Publication

17

Working with a Commercial Printing Service

How can I find a printing service that offers full-color digital output?

You may be able to find a local graphics service bureau that offers digital printing by looking up desktop publishing services in the yellow pages. You can also take advantage of an online printing service, called Printovation, that allows you to place an order and transfer your output file by modem. You can contact Printovation at 1-800-386-7127 or download software from their Web site at http://www.printovation.com.

Microsoft Publisher provides a special feature to help you send your publication to a commercial printing service for high-resolution or full-color output. Commercial printing services are incredibly varied. Traditional printers (as well as high-end service bureaus) generate either film or press plates from your electronic file. The printer subsequently uses these plates on an offset printing press to mass produce your publication. But a new breed of copy shops and digital graphic service bureaus can generate multiple copies of your publication directly from an electronic file. In fact, a small but growing number of companies can mass produce full-color documents directly from a PostScript printer file. The output from this new digital printing service looks like a traditionally printed document, but the cost is much lower.

Depending on your design and your budget, Publisher can generate full-color, spot-color, and black-and-white documents for a commercial printing service. Obviously, full-color output is the most expensive option. Spot color is a good alternative, because it allows you to add one (or two) accent colors to a design at a relatively low cost. And the black-and-white option almost guarantees that your publication will be inexpensive to produce, because it restricts your color choices to black, white, and shades of gray. This limitation prevents you from including color objects in your publication, which can cause time-consuming and costly printing problems at output time.

The following table can help you decide which commercial printing service you should use for your project.

Description of Output from Commercial Printing Services			
This document type...	**At a final resolution of...**	**Is suitable for...**	**Is not suitable for...**
Black-and-white	600 dpi through 2540 dpi	A copy shop, digital graphics service bureau, or offset printer.	
Full-color	300 dpi through 600 dpi	A copy shop or a digital graphics service bureau.	An offset printer. Publisher cannot create separate files for the cyan, magenta, yellow, and black printing plates required by an offset printer.
Spot-color	1200 dpi through 2540 dpi	An offset printer. Publisher produces separations for the black, Spot Color 1, and Spot Color 2 printing plates.	A copy shop or a digital graphics service bureau cannot combine the color separated plates into a final image. Each color will print in black-and-white on a separate sheet of paper.

Preparing Your Document for a Printing Service

If you want to use a commercial printing service, set up the document—including choosing colors—*before* you design your publication to guarantee that what you see on your screen will match what appears in the final printout. A series of three dialog boxes helps you to prepare your publication properly.

Prepare Your Document for a Printing Service

1 Choose Prepare File For Printing Service on the File menu.

2 On the cascading menu, choose Set Up Publication. The first Setup Publication dialog box appears.

What should I do if the color I want to use doesn't appear in the Spot Color drop-down list? Choose the closest match from the 35 available colors. Think of these colors as placeholders. They provide a screen preview that only approximates the final printed color. You will pick the ink color that will actually be used on press from a swatch book provided by your commercial printer. The printing industry uses the Pantone Matching System (PMS) to pick spot colors.

 Knockouts versus overprinting. A knockout occurs when a black object prints against a white background, even if "holes" must be cut into (or knocked out of) the spot color. Turning off Overprint Black Objects creates a knockout. Knockouts are prone to misregistration on press; ugly white gaps can appear when the black printing plate and the spot color printing plate are misaligned. For this reason, most printers prefer to have black objects and black text at small point sizes overprint other colors. You should seek the advice of your printing service before you turn off Overprint Black Objects.

Prepare Your Document for a Printing Service *(continued)*

3 Choose one of the three color options: black-and-white, full-color, or spot-color printing.

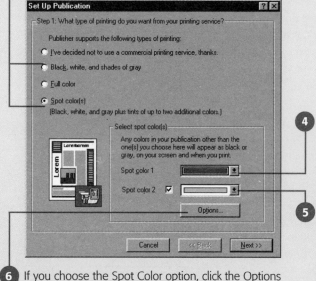

4 If you choose the Spot Color option, open the drop-down list for Spot Color 1 and choose one of 35 colors.

5 If you want to add another spot color to your publication, turn on the check box to activate Spot Color 2. Then open the drop-down box and choose one of 35 colors.

6 If you choose the Spot Color option, click the Options button. The Spot Color Options dialog box appears.

7 Choose the options you want.

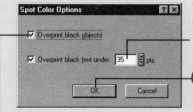

Turn on this check box to print black text on top of all other colors only if the text is smaller than the specified point size. Enter a value from 0 through 999.9 points.

8 Click OK to return to the Set Up Publication dialog box. Then click Next to proceed to the second dialog box.

Turn on this check box to print black objects on top of other colors.

Commercial Printing

Publisher's outside printer drivers. When you install Publisher, two generic printers are added to your system: MS Publisher Color Printer and MS Publisher Imagesetter. These are generic PostScript drivers that prepare a document properly for medium resolution full-color output or high-resolution output, respectively.

How do I choose a different printer driver? In the second Set Up Publication dialog box, you can click the button provided to access a modified Print Setup dialog box where you can choose a specific printer. You can also change the printer after you've set up the publication for a printing service. Select the Change Printer Settings command (from the Prepare File For Printing Service cascading menu) and choose a new printer.

Your choices are always limited to the printers you have installed on your system. You can install a new printer driver by double-clicking the Add A Printer icon in the Windows 95 Printers folder. When the Add Printer Wizard appears follow the on-screen instructions.

Prepare Your Document for a Printing Service *(continued)*

9 In the second Set Up Publication dialog box, select either Publisher's generic outside printer driver or choose a specific driver that has been recommended or supplied by the printing service.

10 Click Next. The third Set Up Publication dialog box appears.

11 Indicate the printing options you want.

Turn on this check box to have Publisher choose a special paper size, called Extra, which is large enough to accommodate printer marks.

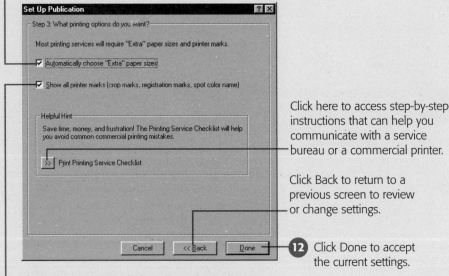

Click here to access step-by-step instructions that can help you communicate with a service bureau or a commercial printer.

Click Back to return to a previous screen to review or change settings.

12 Click Done to accept the current settings.

Turn on this check box to include crop marks, registration marks, and identifying information such as the color name, page range, publication name, and date/time stamp.

What is the Printing Service Checklist? The Printing Service Checklist is basically a script. If you follow the script, you'll be able to describe your project using terminology the service bureau or printer will understand. The checklist also prompts you to discuss basic printing and production issues that will affect the project's cost, and allows you to get an accurate quote from the commercial printing service. You can't read the Printing Service Checklist on screen. You must click the button provided in the Set Up Publication dialog box and print a copy to paper.

Print another copy of the Printing Service Checklist. Once you've set up your publication for a printing service, you can use a straightforward menu command to print a copy of the Printing Service Checklist. Choose Prepare File For Printing Service on the File menu. On the cascading menu, select Print Publication Information. On the second cascading menu, choose Printing Service Checklist. One copy of the checklist is sent directly to your printer. To print multiple copies, repeat these steps.

Return the Publication to Local Printing Mode

1 Choose Prepare File For Printing Service on the File menu, and then choose Set Up Publication on the cascading menu. The first Setup Publication dialog box appears.

2 Click the first option, I've Decided Not To Use A Commercial Printing Service.

3 Click Done.

Sending a Publication to a Printing Service

Once you've set up a document for a printing service, you have the following output options, available from the File menu:

@ You can create a PostScript printer file.

@ You can use the Save As command to create a copy of the Publisher file.

There are advantages and disadvantages to each method, and your choice might be limited by the capabilities of the printing service you have chosen.

Sending a PostScript File to a Printing Service

When you set up your document for a printing service, Publisher chooses a generic PostScript printer driver for the current document. PostScript files are compatible with high-resolution, professional-quality output devices found at copy shops, service bureaus, and commercial printers. Because PostScript output is not device-specific, the same PostScript file can print on any PostScript printer.

When you create a PostScript print file, you are translating Publisher's native file format into a format that contains all the information needed to print the file, including all the font information and all the commands necessary to operate the printer. Publisher assumes that the printer is not connected to your computer and, therefore, always stores the print file on disk.

Use the Design Checker to create efficient PostScript files. If you are generating a PostScript printer file, every object in the publication—including empty frames and hidden objects—will be included in the output file. Use the Design Checker to find and eliminate these objects. The result will be a smaller, cleaner PostScript file that is less prone to printing errors.

Create a PostScript Print File

1 Choose Prepare File For Printing Service on the File menu.

2 On the cascading menu, choose Create File In Postscript. The Create PostScript file dialog box appears.

3 Select the appropriate options.

Specify whether Publisher should print all pages or the current page.

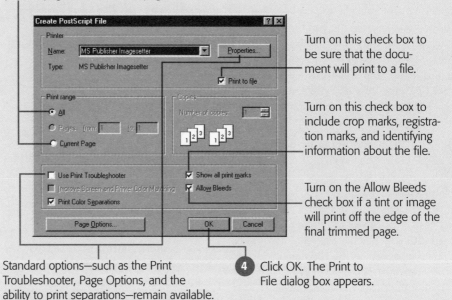

Turn on this check box to be sure that the document will print to a file.

Turn on this check box to include crop marks, registration marks, and identifying information about the file.

Turn on the Allow Bleeds check box if a tint or image will print off the edge of the final trimmed page.

Standard options—such as the Print Troubleshooter, Page Options, and the ability to print separations—remain available.

4 Click OK. The Print to File dialog box appears.

5 In the File Name text box, type an output filename that clearly identifies the publication, including an extension that identifies the file as a printer-ready document (for example, .prn for printer or .ps for PostScript).

6 In the Folders list box, choose an appropriate location on your hard disk for the printer file.

Transporting large files to a printing service. A 3.5-inch floppy disk can hold 1.44 MB of information. If the printer file is too large to fit on a floppy disk, you can transport the file using one of the following methods:

- Use a third-party compression utility, such as Pkzip or WinZip, to reduce the size of the file. The printing service must have the same version of the utility to decompress the file.

- Use high-capacity removable media, provided that both you and your printing service have access to the same type of Syquest, Bernoulli, Zip, or Jaz drive.

- If your computer is equipped with a modem and Internet access, ask if the printing service accepts files via standard telecommunications software or their Web site.

- Use a backup utility (such as the Norton Utilities or Windows 95 Backup) to copy the file to several disks. The printing service must have the same utility in order to restore the file.

Can I generate an EPS file if I am using Windows NT? No. The Windows NT PostScript printer driver does not support EPS output.

Create a PostScript Print File *(continued)*

7 Click OK.

8 After Publisher has created the file, it will ask if you want to print a final proof and a Publication InfoSheet. Click Yes to print these documents.

9 When the file has been successfully printed to your hard disk, use Windows Explorer to transfer the output file to a floppy disk (or other removable media), which you will take to the printing service.

Creating an Encapsulated PostScript File

Some printing services, especially Mac-based printing services, prefer to receive files in the Encapsulated PostScript (EPS) format. You can easily produce EPS files from your publications by changing a configuration option in the PostScript printer driver. However, there are two important restrictions that apply to EPS files. EPS files cannot contain color separations or multiple pages.

Configure the PostScript Printer Driver for EPS Output

1 Choose Prepare File For Printing Service on the File menu.

2 On the cascading menu, choose Change Printer Settings. The Change Printer Settings dialog box appears, and the PostScript printer appears in the Name list box.

3 Click the Properties button. The Properties dialog box appears.

4 Click the PostScript tab.

5 Open the PostScript Output Format drop-down list and choose Encapsulated PostScript (EPS).

6 Click OK to return to the Change Printer Settings dialog box. Click OK.

Use a printer that is not connected to your computer. You can print any publication on any printer that is not physically connected to your computer. For example, you might want to create a publication at home but print it at the office where you have a high-resolution or color printer.

In Publisher's normal Print dialog box, make sure the off-site printer is selected as the output device, and be sure to click the Print To File check box. After you've saved the output file to your hard disk, transfer it to the hard disk of the computer that is attached to the printer you want to use.

On the Windows 95 Start menu, select Programs, then select MS-DOS Prompt. At the MS-DOS prompt, type the following command to send the file to the printer:

```
copy filename.prn lpt1: /b
```

Replace *filename*.prn with the actual name of your output file. Be sure to type the correct parallel port information for the printer you are using. For example, the printer might be attached to LPT2. The /b ensures that the entire file will be printed, even if it contains more than one page.

For more information about printer ports and the MS-DOS prompt, see the Windows 95 online help system.

Sending a Publisher Document to a Printing Service

You can send the original Publisher document to a printing service, but only if the printing service uses the current version of Publisher. Confirm that the printing service has a copy of Microsoft Publisher 98.

Sending a Publisher document to a printing service offers one major advantage over sending a PostScript file: if the commercial printer encounters a problem, it can open the file and fix it. The major disadvantage is that Publisher documents are "live" in the sense that they can contain links to other objects or services on your computer system. Discrepancies between your computer system and the printing service's computer system can create printing problems. The most common problems relate to the use of fonts and OLE objects.

Font Issues

A Publisher document doesn't actually contain fonts; it contains instructions that refer to fonts installed on your system. If the printing service does not have the fonts you are using in your design, its output device will likely substitute different fonts at print time. When you use a standard Windows 95 font such as Arial or Times New Roman, the substitution might be nearly impossible to detect. When you use a decorative or unusual font, however, the substituted font may not be acceptable. Be sure that the printing service has the fonts you are using in your design.

Should I use TrueType fonts or PostScript fonts?

Many printing services have an established collection of PostScript fonts. If you plan to produce a very lengthy document or a significant number of publications, you should consider purchasing PostScript fonts that duplicate at least a portion of the printing service's font library.

If you plan to take advantage of the free TrueType fonts that ship with Publisher, be sure to alert the printing service to that fact *before* you send your files for output. Ideally, the printing service will confirm that they have the same TrueType fonts available. Even if the printing service does not have the appropriate TrueType fonts installed, they can configure the Windows PostScript printer driver to send TrueType fonts to the printer as outlines (which are vector graphics) rather than as a font request. This may increase the size of the output file and the time needed to print the publication.

For more information about OLE objects, see Chapter 11.

OLE Object Issues

OLE objects in your Publisher document point to other applications installed on your computer system. The printing service must have the same source programs installed on its computer system in order to make any last-minute content changes to the OLE objects before printing. If the source program is not available, the printing service will be able to display the OLE object on screen and print it but will not be able to make changes to the OLE object.

Preparing a Publication InfoSheet

You should send an information sheet to the printing service along with the PostScript or publication file. Publisher can automatically generate a Publication InfoSheet that details the number of pages in the document, the colors contained in the publication, the fonts used, and any special effects (such as WordArt). The printing service can use the Publication InfoSheet to troubleshoot common problems. You can print the Publication InfoSheet on paper using your local printer or save it as a printer output file.

Print an Information Sheet

1 Open the document you want to send to the printing service. (The document must be open for Publisher to generate an information sheet.)

2 Select Prepare File For Printing Service on the File menu. On the cascading menu, select Print Publication Information.

3 On the second cascading menu, select Publication InfoSheet. Publisher prints the Publication InfoSheet to the default local printer.

4 Include the printed Publication InfoSheet in the package you send to the printing service.

Print proofs locally. When you set up a document for a printing service, Publisher maintains two different printers for each publication. The PostScript printer that you specify in the Set Up Publication dialog box is used to generate the final output for the printing service. However, your local printer, which may or may not be a PostScript printer, is maintained to print proofs of black-and-white, full-color, and spot-color documents. You should always include a paper proof of your publication when you send a project to a printing service.

 For more information about Publisher's standard print commands, and to learn how to print proofs of spot-color documents, see Chapter 16.

Save a Publication InfoSheet As a Printer Output File

1 Click the Windows 95 Start button, select Settings, and click Printers on the cascading menu.

2 Using the right mouse button, click MS Publisher Imagesetter, and choose Set As Default from the shortcut menu.

3 In Publisher, open the publication you'll be sending to the printing service.

4 Select Prepare File For Printing on the File menu. On the cascading menu, select Print Publication Information.

5 On the second cascading menu, select Publication InfoSheet. Because the MS Publisher Imagesetter printer is configured to save file to disk, Publisher opens the Print To File dialog box.

6 Type a filename in the File Name text box.

7 Use the Folder box to open the folder where you want to store the Publication InfoSheet.

8 Click OK.

9 Return to the printer panel by clicking the Windows 95 Start button, Settings, and Printers on each of the cascading menus.

10 Right-click your local printer, and select Set As Default from the shortcut menu.

11 Transfer the electronic version of the Publication InfoSheet to the printing service along with your project on a disk or by modem.

PART 2

Design Projects

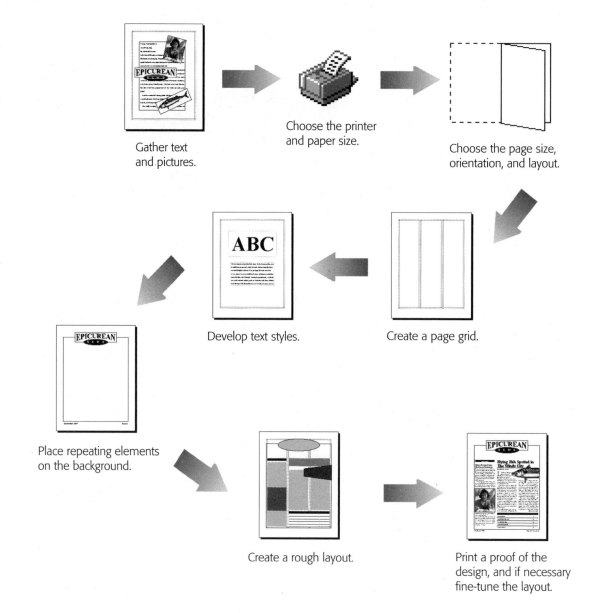

Gather text and pictures.

Choose the printer and paper size.

Choose the page size, orientation, and layout.

Create a page grid.

Develop text styles.

Place repeating elements on the background.

Create a rough layout.

Print a proof of the design, and if necessary fine-tune the layout.

An Overview of the Design Process

There is no denying that the design process begins with inspiration. But there are certain concrete tasks—shown in the diagram on the previous page—that are common to all design projects. This chapter provides essential background information to help you tackle each of these tasks.

As you develop your own layouts, you'll discover that the design process is iterative. The only way to achieve the right combination of words, pictures, and graphics elements is to experiment with variations of a layout.

Planning a Publication

Every publication should have a specific purpose. The purpose can be modest or ambitious. You may merely want to print a throw-away banner to welcome your son home from college. Or you may need to produce a full-color brochure that explains your company's products to potential customers. Once you've defined the goal of your publication, you will be able to gather appropriate pictures and write meaningful text. You'll also be able to answer other questions about your project regarding the design strategy and production budget. For example, you won't want to spend a lot of money on a banner that will only be displayed for a few hours.

The following table lists the essential questions you must consider and also provides the answers for three (very different) sample projects. As you examine them, try to see the relationship between the purpose of the project and the production or design decisions.

Where can I find step-by-step instructions to help me recreate the design projects? If you want step-by-step instructions to help you use Publisher's tools and dialog boxes, you must refer to the appropriate chapters in Part 1, "Publisher 98 Fundamentals." The chapters in Part 2, "Design Projects," focus on design theory and practice and contain only general instructions concerning Publisher's tools.

Sample Projects			
Question	**Sale Flyer**	**Company Brochure**	**Web Site**
What is the purpose of this publication?	To alert customers about an upcoming sale and encourage them to visit the store	To provide information about company products and services	To deliver up-to-the-minute product information and elicit customer feedback
Who is the intended audience?	Local customers	Potential corporate clients	Existing and potential customers
What is the life span of this publication?	2 weeks	1 year	3 months
How will you deliver the publication?	Store handout, direct mail	Personal sales calls, mail	On the World Wide Web
How will you print the publication?	Desktop laser printer	Commercial printing service	Not applicable
What is an appropriate document size?	One standard letter-sized page	Eight-page booklet measuring 7 by 10 inches	Standard VGA screen
What type of paper will you use?	Laser-compatible paper	High-quality paper	Not applicable
What type of artwork will you include?	Black-and-white clip art	Spot-color artwork	Full-color bitmapped images
What is the budget?	Inexpensive	Expensive	Moderate

For more information about selecting a printer and choosing printer options, see Chapter 16.

Choosing a Printer

The printer you choose sets limits on many of the design choices you can make. Your choice of printer determines:

@ Available paper sizes. Microsoft Publisher uses the current paper size when determining the imposition of pages for specially sized and folded publications. For example, if you intend to print an 8.5-by-11-inch booklet, you must be sure that the printer can handle paper that measures at least 11-by-17 inches.

@ Resident fonts. Printers have a collection of fonts built into read-only memory (ROM), but the fonts vary from model to model. If you use printer resident fonts in a design, and then switch to a different printer, the fonts you have chosen may not be available on the new printer.

Use TrueType or PostScript software fonts. Instead of using printer resident fonts, use TrueType or Type 1 fonts. TrueType fonts stored on your computer system will be available regardless of the printer you select. If your printer does not directly support TrueType, the Windows 95 printer driver can send the fonts as vector outlines. PostScript fonts can also be stored on your computer system and downloaded to a PostScript printer at output time. You can print PostScript fonts to a non-PostScript printer, but only if you have installed a font utility, such as Adobe Type Manager, that converts the PostScript information into a format your printer can understand.

 For more information about setting up pages, see Chapter 2. For more information about Web documents, see Chapter 12.

Document color. If you are printing to a local printer, Publisher gives you access to the full spectrum of computer-generated colors. Preparing your document for a printing service, however, restricts the number of colors to match the capabilities of your chosen output device. As an example, setting up a document for a high-resolution black-and-white printer limits your color choices to black, white, and shades of gray.

Choosing Page Size and Orientation

The page layout you choose will to a large extent determine the number of pages in the document, the amount of paper needed to print it, and the amount of time spent trimming and folding it.

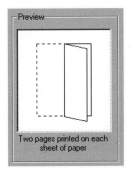

Two pages printed on each sheet of paper

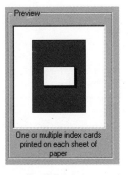

One or multiple index cards printed on each sheet of paper

The Book Fold layout requires that the total number of pages in a publication be a multiple of 4. A printing service may require multiples of 8 or 16 pages.

Small publications require extra production time (or money) to trim excess paper. This is especially time consuming if you are trimming paper manually.

The Web Page layout is best viewed on an SVGA (or higher) monitor. Readers with VGA screens will have to scroll through the page horizontally as well as vertically.

Overview of Design

Standardize your project to save time and money. The more standardized your publication, the cheaper it will be to produce. Try to design your publication to fit on standard-size paper and—if necessary—in a standard-size envelope.

Even when you vary the size of the publication, make sure you are adhering to the requirements of printing and mailing equipment. Consult your printer to find a document size that avoids paper waste, unnecessary handling, and extra trimming (all of which increase the cost of the job). Confirm that your publication size (meaning the envelope size, not just the page size) meets postal requirements for automated handling. Finally, if you are mailing your publication, be aware that oversized pages and heavy paper can dramatically increase the cost of postage.

Create combination grids. You can develop a flexible grid to accommodate pictures and text frames of various sizes. In general, the grid or guides should be based on the smallest common denominator of the various elements in your layout. For example, if your publication contains pictures measuring 1/3 or 1/2 of a page's width, use a six-column grid; 1/6 is the smallest common denominator of 1/2 and 1/3. A six-column grid lets you size elements at a number of different column measures: 1/6, 1/3, 1/2, or 2/3 of the page width.

Setting Up a Grid

The key to a well-designed publication is an underlying structure, called a grid, that helps you size, position, and align elements consistently. Form usually follows function, so before you set up the grid, think about the number and the type of elements you will add to your document.

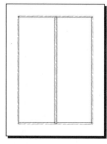

A one-column, wide-column, or two-column format accommodates long text lines and is suitable for books and technical reports.

Custom column widths accommodate differently sized elements, such as ID numbers, photographs, and product descriptions in a catalog. Consistent row height allows readers to find information quickly.

Newsletters that incorporate pictures of varying sizes and shapes require a more flexible grid composed of several columns of the same width.

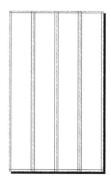

In a Web publication, grids can prevent you from overlapping objects—a condition that causes Publisher to create graphic regions.

Save type designs as text styles. Once you've developed a type design, save it as a defined text style. This allows you to use the style repeatedly, which saves you time and ensures consistency throughout a document.

For more information about text styles, see Chapter 6.

A font's x-height influences the legibility and length of a story. When you need type that's highly legible at small point sizes, select a typeface with a large x-height. When you need to fit a large amount of text into a few pages, select a typeface with a shorter x-height.

Choosing Type

The power of your message depends in large part on the fonts you choose. Once you understand the basic characteristics and categories of type, you can choose fonts with confidence and combine fonts to add visual interest to your documents.

Font Categories

Fonts are divided into three categories, as explained in the following illustration:

Goudy Old Style

Serif fonts employ small lines or curves (called serifs) at the ends of each stroke of a character.

Century Gothic

Sans-serif fonts are fonts without serifs. Note the straighter lines.

Lucida Handwriting

Script fonts resemble cursive handwriting.

Font Structure

Serif, sans-serif, and script fonts all share a similar structure. The following illustrations identify the various parts of a letter and help you select an appropriate font for your designs.

Ascenders and descenders are the portions of a lowercase letter that rise above or drop below the main body (x-height) of the letter.

A font's x-height is the proportional height of the lowercase letter x in that font. The letter x is the standard because it has no ascenders or descenders. A font with a large x-height has lowercase letters almost as tall as the capital letters (as shown here). A font with a small x-height has lowercase letters that are much shorter in relation to the capital letters.

Display type suffers most from font substitution.

There are several circumstances in which a font you specify might be replaced with a different font. This unintentional substitution can happen when you send a PUB file to a service bureau for output, or when a reader opens a Web document. In both cases, if the requested font is not installed on the other computer system, a standard font will be used instead. Although such a substitution might not be detectable for standard body copy fonts, it is quite noticeable for display typefaces. Use one of these techniques to avoid font substitution:

- Use only standard fonts such as Times New Roman or Arial in your designs.

- Contact your commercial printing service to be sure they have the fonts you need installed.

- Use WordArt (which will be generated as a graphic region) to employ unusual display fonts in a Web publication.

Weight refers to the thickness of the strokes that form the characters themselves. A font's weight is often designated by words such as light, heavy, bold, and ultra bold.

Gill Sans Ultra Bold Condensed

The width of a font is referred to as either condensed or expanded. The letters in a condensed font are narrower, so you can fit more text on a line. The letters in an expanded font are wide and widely spaced. You can usually tell whether a font is condensed or expanded by its name.

Lucida Sans Typewriter

Leading (pronounced "ledding") refers to the distance from the baseline of one line of text to the baseline of the next line of text. Leading is typically measured in points.

Letterspace refers to the white space between letters.

The Difference Between Display Type and Body Copy

When you create your text designs, separate text elements into categories according to their purpose, as either display type or body copy.

Display type refers to text that organizes or decorates a publication. Headlines, subheads, fancy first letters, jump heads, pull quotes, and logos are all examples of display type.

Body copy or *body text* refers to the running text of a story. Body copy is most often organized into sequential paragraphs; it can flow from column to column and from page to page.

Publisher offers a wide variety of body copy fonts. Publisher ships with a number of fonts that are particularly well suited for use as body copy. Though most of the fonts listed here are serif fonts, a few sans-serif fonts provide enough stroke variation to make reading them a pleasure. As you look at the following samples, take note of the variations among fonts. It is especially dramatic when you consider that all the fonts are technically the same size— 11 points.

Baskerville Old Face

Book Antiqua

Calisto MT

Century Schoolbook

Eras Medium ITC

Footlight MT Light

Garamond

Lucida Bright

Lucida Sans

Maiandra GD

Perpetua

When you choose a font for display type, think about the personality it projects. Fonts can be formal or casual; they can project an aggressive corporate image or an avant-garde attitude. Sans-serif fonts are widely used for display type because their simple outlines are suited to bold messages. However, at large point sizes (30 points or more), serif fonts work equally well in headlines.

Cooper Black

Cooper Black adds weight to your words—quite literally—with very heavy strokes.

Eras Medium ITC

Eras Medium ITC gives your text an ultramodern look.

COPPERPLATE GOTHIC LIGHT

Copperplate Gothic Light looks like a traditional engraver's typeface and adds a formal note to a design.

Snap ITC

Snap ITC exaggerates and distorts letterforms for a playful effect.

When you choose a font for body copy, consider legibility first. Documents with hard-to-read type can lower comprehension. Because readers score higher on comprehension tests in which the text is set in serif fonts, designers frequently use serif fonts for body copy. You don't need to completely avoid sans-serif fonts for body copy, but you should use them with discretion. Restrict your use of sans-serif type to short or moderately short text blocks, such as captions, catalog entries, or pull quotes (a quotation from the main text, often set in a larger point size or otherwise emphasized).

Let's face it. Chicago is famous for stockyards not fisheries. But times are changing. People are eating fish instead of red meat. Seafood is an important part of a heart-healthy diet, because it is low in cholesterol and fat.

The decorative flourishes, or serifs, at the ends of a font's vertical and horizontal lines help readers group words together. The thin and thick strokes vary more than the strokes of sans-serif fonts. This visual variety among letters can prevent fatigue when someone is reading a long text passage.

Let's face it. Chicago is famous for stockyards not fisheries. But times are changing. People are eating fish instead of red meat. Seafood is an important part of a heart-healthy diet, because it is low in cholesterol and fat.

More modern sans-serif fonts vary the letter thickness to make the text more legible.

Can I combine two serif fonts or two sans-serif fonts in a type design?

In general, unless you have a lot of typography experience, you should never combine different serif fonts or different sans-serif fonts in a single publication. Your goal when combining different fonts is to create contrast and variety. Two serif fonts (or two sans-serif fonts) do not provide enough contrast; instead, they are just different enough to distract the reader.

Font Combinations

Most designers create visual interest in a publication by choosing fonts that have contrasting yet complementary letterforms. There are no hard and fast rules where type design is concerned, but here are a few basic guidelines:

- Use no more than two font families in a document. (A font family is the set of fonts depicting different styles of a single typeface. For example, Arial, Arial Black, and Arial Narrow are all contained within the same font family.)

- Use different styles within a font family—regular, bold, italic, and bold italic—for variety and emphasis.

- Combine a serif and a sans-serif typeface for contrast.

- Look for variations of the font you're using. For example, some fonts are available in condensed or expanded widths, or in heavier or lighter weights.

For more information about the background, see Chapter 2.

Creating Background Elements

Consistency is an important part of any design. You can create visual consistency by including many of the following organizational elements on the background of your design, which repeats them on every page in your publication.

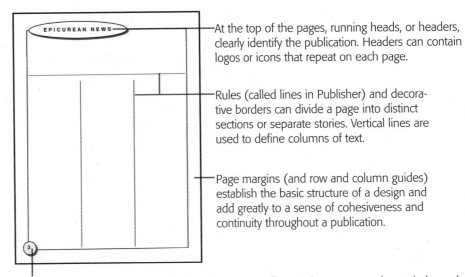

At the top of the pages, running heads, or headers, clearly identify the publication. Headers can contain logos or icons that repeat on each page.

Rules (called lines in Publisher) and decorative borders can divide a page into distinct sections or separate stories. Vertical lines are used to define columns of text.

Page margins (and row and column guides) establish the basic structure of a design and add greatly to a sense of cohesiveness and continuity throughout a publication.

At the bottom of pages, running feet, or footers, usually contain a page number to help readers locate information easily. Footers can also provide volume, chapter, or date information.

Take advantage of Publisher's automated checks. Publisher offers several automated functions that can help you spot potential problems in a document. The Design Checker locates common oversights such as empty text frames, text hidden in the overflow area, and covered objects. The Check Spelling function looks for words and capitalizations it doesn't recognize.

For more information about the Design Checker, see Chapter 3. For more information about Publisher's spell check functions, see Chapter 5.

Positioning Text and Pictures

You can move, resize, and—most important—edit text and pictures to create an integrated layout. When arranging a layout, forget that text frames are full of words and that picture frames contain images. You'll find it easier to begin your design by using colored and shaded drawn objects and frames before you import actual text and pictures. This preliminary design, called a mock-up (shown on the following page, left), helps you determine approximately how much text you'll need, as well as the size, shape, and position of artwork.

Overview of Design

Identify visual problems with text. Editors and designers use the following terms to identify situations that disrupt the appearance and flow of text:

- Widows consist of a single word, a portion of a word, or a few short words left on a line by themselves at the end of a paragraph.

- Orphans are created when the last line of a preceding paragraph prints alone at the top of a page or column of text.

- Rivers are excessive space between words in a justified paragraph, creating a distracting pattern of white space.

- Ladders are formed when there are too many consecutive hyphens (three or more) in a block of hyphenated text.

Normally, these problems are corrected by changing the text or the text formatting.

Think of text frames as gray or patterned boxes.

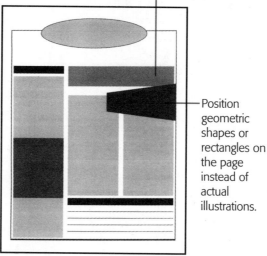

Position geometric shapes or rectangles on the page instead of actual illustrations.

The shapes and differing gray densities create a pattern for your eyes to follow.

Notice how the text and pictures follow the same overall pattern as the mock-up.

Fine-Tuning the Layout

Even when a layout is "mostly right," text and pictures often need minor adjustments. The following checklist can help you fine-tune your documents.

Edit the Text

In most cases, you will edit the text in your publications for sense—meaning that you'll change the copy to make sentences more understandable and to correct grammar and spelling errors. However, you should also edit text to improve the appearance of the publication. Be prepared to add, delete, or modify words for these reasons:

For more information about Publisher's text editing tools, see Chapter 5. For more information about Publisher's text formatting functions, see Chapter 6.

Avoid narrow columns. As you can see in the following illustration, narrow text columns cause all sorts of typesetting problems. Narrow columns contain only a few words on each line. This forces Publisher to make much larger spacing adjustments to each word. In contrast, wider text columns contain more words on each line. This gives Publisher the opportunity to make smaller—and less noticeable—adjustments to each word.

Excessive hyphenation

River of white space

Let's face it. Chicago is famous for stock-yards not fisheries. But times are changing. People are eating fish instead of red meat. Seafood is an impor-tant part of a heart-healthy diet, because it is low in cholesterol and fat.

Loose character spacing

- Change the length of a story to fit the layout. This process, known as copyfitting, shouldn't require you to substantially rewrite the story. But you may have to cut or add several lines of text.

- Eliminate widows and orphans by cutting text to lose lines or by adding text to lengthen sentences.

- Search for typewriter-style characters and replace them with typographic characters for a professional appearance.

- Add texture and visual contrast with display type such as captions, sub-heads, pull quotes, or drop caps. Many display text elements, such as pull quotes and Continued notices, should be added only after a layout has been roughed out.

Modify Text Formatting

On a practical level, you can expand a story to fill a layout or fit a long story into a tight layout by tweaking text formats. On an aesthetic level, you can use these same tools to increase the legibility of the text, to improve line breaks, and to change the density of text on the page.

- Alter the point size and line spacing of body copy by a fractional value. A decrease or increase of 0.1 point will not be noticeable to your reader but can significantly contract or expand a story.

- Change the hyphenation zone. Increasing this value eliminates consecutive hyphens (or ladders) but can lengthen a story. Decreasing it eliminates rivers by tightening up loose lines, creates more hyphens, and shortens a story.

- Adjust the tracking values. Tighter tracking fits more words on each line. Looser tracking can help to fill out a story that is short by a few lines. Looser tracking can also increase the legibility of sans-serif fonts, highly condensed fonts, or small point sizes.

- Avoid awkward white spaces that can occur at large point sizes by decreasing the line spacing and kerning the letters in a headline.

Highlight Important Information

As a designer, you can direct the reader's attention to the important information in your publication by using any of the following techniques:

- @ Use a design device, such as a drop cap or a rule, to signal the beginning of an article or a section of a long story.

- @ Place a separate but related story into a text box, called a sidebar. Fill the text box with a color or a gray tint.

- @ Assign color to text elements based on their function. For example, you could print all the subheads in a long article in a contrasting color to help your reader skim the story. Functional color choices are especially important in a Web publication, where colors are used to flag hyperlinks.

Edit Imported Artwork

You can probably find suitable artwork for your project in Publisher's Clip Art Gallery, which contains over 10,000 clip-art images, 500 photographs, and 300 animated GIF files. Whether you use Publisher's art or artwork from another source, you will often have to adjust it in order to make it work with your layout. Here are a few suggestions:

- @ Crop pictures instead of resizing them. Cropping a picture can save space, hide part of an unnecessary background in the picture, or create drama by showing only the essential part of an image.

- @ Recolor images to create artistic effects. Using a very light color to tint artwork can create an interesting background (called a watermark) for text.

- @ Combine pictures to create your own, more complex illustrations. This technique works well when you can find pictures executed in the same style. In addition, the individual pictures should have transparent backgrounds so they can be overlapped to create what looks like a single illustration.

- @ Use Microsoft Draw to change the content of a clip-art image. Draw allows you to edit the actual content of a vector image by recoloring individual elements, altering the shape of an object, or creating a mirror image of a picture.

Think metaphorically (and creatively) when choosing clip art. Try not to be too literal when you search for the "perfect" clip-art image. Clip-art pictures can be used as illustrations, but they can also evoke a mood or convey a concept. A picture of a handshake, for example, communicates the idea of cooperation more clearly than a literal image of two people working together at a desk.

A literal image of cooperation   A symbolic image of cooperation

For more information about Publisher's picture tools and Clip Gallery, see Chapter 10. For more information about Draw, see Appendix A.

The
Martin Krump
Trio

**Friday, July 24th and
Saturday, July 25th
At 10 p.m.**

**City Lights Café
449 Harrison Street
Cincinnati, Ohio**

**Call for Reservations
513-555-2222**

JAZZ

The Martin Krump Trio
At City Lights Café
Saturday and Sunday
July 24th and 25th

Postcard Announcement

A postcard announcement contains only a few essential pieces of text, such as the name (or purpose) of the event, the location, and the date and time. It provides an opportunity to build the design around a strong central image, such as the picture of the jazz band used in this project.

Preparing the Publication

Microsoft Publisher's unique page layout options make it easy to create small documents such as this postcard.

Postal regulations influence design decisions.

To mail your postcard announcements without incurring postal surcharges, you must meet the U.S. Postal Service requirements for automated handling. These regulations determine the size of the postcard (which must be between 3.5-by-5 inches and 4.25-by-6 inches) and the type of paper used for printing (a heavy card stock with a thickness—or caliper—between .007 and .0095 inch). For more information and a template to check the size of your postcards, contact your local post office.

Set Up the Page

1 Create a new document, with a special page size measuring 4.25 inches by 5.5 inches.

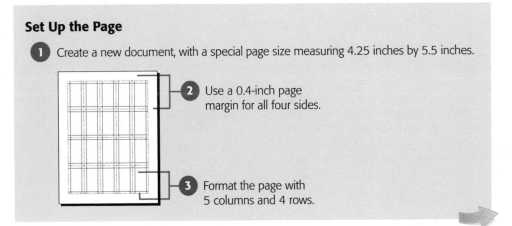

2 Use a 0.4-inch page margin for all four sides.

3 Format the page with 5 columns and 4 rows.

4 Select the printer you will use and confirm that the current paper size is 8.5-by-11-inch letter size, in Portrait orientation. This project was printed on a black-and-white PostScript printer.

5 Because the project will be printed in black-and-white, select the Black And Gray color scheme to limit your color choices.

Why should I use the pink guides instead of the blue guides? The blue guides include a safety margin (or gutter allowance) of 0.10 inch. While this is essential for separating text columns, it isn't appropriate when you are using the guides as a drawing grid, as you are in this exercise. The pink guides provide precise page divisions and allow you to create objects that abut one another.

Search for clip art. Publisher's clip art files do not have descriptive filenames. You might find it easier to locate the appropriate image by inserting a clip art image instead of a picture. On the Insert menu, choose Clip Art from the Picture command's cascading menu. In the Microsoft Clip Gallery 4.0 window, search for the keyword *musicians*.

Creating the First Page

This small postcard has a big design impact, thanks to bold shapes and a few well chosen words.

Create the Background

1 Using the pink guidelines on the underlying grid, create two rectangles.

@ The first rectangle spans columns 1, 2, 3, 4, and 5 and rows 3 and 4.

@ The second rectangle overlaps the first. It spans columns 1 and 2 and row 4.

2 Format the rectangles as indicated.

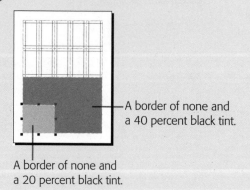

A border of none and a 40 percent black tint.

A border of none and a 20 percent black tint.

Preserve the aspect ratio of an imported image.

Even when you are trying to fit a picture into a layout, you should not distort a picture's aspect ratio. In this exercise, you use two different techniques to preserve the aspect ratio of the musician's image:

- You used the Scale Object command to resize the width and height of the picture equally.

- You used the Crop Picture tool to enlarge the frame without enlarging the picture.

Create groups to separate elements in a design.

Grouping can help you manage and manipulate your designs more efficiently. Once they are grouped, the rectangles, picture, and rules that form the backdrop will now function as a single object, making the text frames you're about to add easier to select. Even if you do accidentally select and move the grouped object, the elements in the group will remain properly aligned to one another.

Import and Recolor the Picture

1 Without drawing a picture frame, insert the picture file PE00737_.wmf (found on the Publisher CD-ROM in the Clipart subfolder).

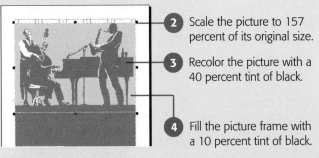

2 Scale the picture to 157 percent of its original size.

3 Recolor the picture with a 40 percent tint of black.

4 Fill the picture frame with a 10 percent tint of black.

5 Position the picture along the top blue row guide. It should span the width of the page.

6 Using the Crop Picture tool, extend the top of the picture frame to the pink margin guide. This provides some breathing room for the sax player's head.

Add Rules

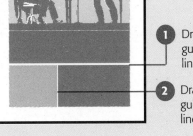

1 Draw a 4-point white line along the pink guide that separates rows 3 and 4. The line should span all 5 columns.

2 Draw a 2-point white line along the pink guide that separates columns 2 and 3. The line should match the height of row 4.

3 Select all the objects on the page and group them together.

For the text of this announcement, see Appendix B.

Use decorative fonts for short text blocks. Because cards—especially announcements and invitations—don't contain a large amount of text, you don't need to consider legibility first when you choose your font. A card is the perfect opportunity to break out with a fun or decorative font. For this project, you should choose Britannic Bold to be consistent with the display type on the first page.

Add Display Type

1 Using the pink guides, draw a text frame that spans columns 1, 2, 3, 4, and 5 and row 3.

2 Change the left, right, top, and bottom text frame margins to 0.1 inch.

3 Format the text frame with a transparent fill and align text vertically at the bottom of the frame.

4 Using the pink guides, draw a second text frame that spans columns 3, 4, and 5 and row 4.

5 Change the left, right, top, and bottom text frame margins to 0.1 inch.

6 Format the text frame with a transparent fill and align text vertically at the top of the frame.

7 Enter the text and format it as indicated.

Britannic Bold font, 70 points, white characters, left alignment, with 1 space of line spacing.

Britannic Bold font, 12 points, white characters, left alignment, with 1 space of line spacing.

Experiment with informal fonts. This announcement is a perfect opportunity to use an informal font. The Britannic Bold font exhibits rhythmic variation in the stroke that is reminiscent of the syncopation in jazz music. But there are a number of decorative alternatives that would work just as well. Look at the single word *Jazz*, formatted with Bauhaus 93 (top), Colonna MT (center), and Forte (bottom). Ask yourself what different flavors of jazz (bebop, big band, fusion) would correspond to each font.

JAZZ

JAZZ

JAZZ

Use typographic characters. When you enter the text for this project, you should insert an accented *é* (from the Symbol dialog box) in the word *Café*. You should also apply the superscript attribute to the letters *th* following each date.

Creating the Message for Page 2

Brevity is the watchword when writing the message for a postcard, because you must be sure to leave an appropriate amount of space for the address information.

Choose a Font for the Text

1 Insert a new page. Create a text frame measuring 2.35 inches wide by 3.45 inches high.

2 Enter the text and format it as Britannic Bold, 12 points, black characters, left alignment, with 1 space of line spacing.

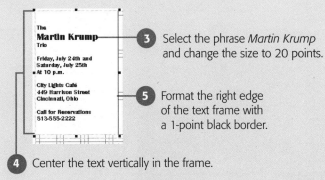

3 Select the phrase *Martin Krump* and change the size to 20 points.

5 Format the right edge of the text frame with a 1-point black border.

4 Center the text vertically in the frame.

6 Rotate the entire text frame to the left 90 degrees and position it at the bottom of the page.

Why do I have to feed the card stock through the printer twice? If you have a standard laser printer, you must feed the card stock through your printer twice in order to print on both sides of the same piece of paper. Notice that you have been instructed to print page 2 of the postcard first. This page contains only text, requires the least amount of toner, and should not cause any problems when you feed the card through the printer for a second pass. If you own a duplex printer, have installed the correct Microsoft Windows 95 driver, and have enabled duplex printing, Publisher can print both sides of the postcard simultaneously.

Use specialty paper stocks. You can improve the quality of your publications by purchasing specialty papers. For this project, you can buy card stock measuring 8.5 inches by 11 inches that has already been divided into four postcards. These cards are produced from heavy stock that is appropriate for mailing. And they are perforated to make the job of trimming them down to size a simple matter of tearing the paper along a dotted line. You can find laser printer–compatible postcards in stationery stores or through mail-order sources, such as Paper Direct.

Completing the Announcement

Print the Document

1 In the Print dialog box, click the Page Options button and select the Multiple Copies per Sheet option. The Sample area shows that four copies of the document will fit on a single sheet of paper.

2 Insert a piece of perforated 8.5-by-11-inch card stock into the printer's manual feed.

3 Deselect the crop mark option and print only page 2 of the document. Publisher prints four instances of page 2.

4 Feed the same piece of card stock through the printer, but invert it in order to print on the opposite side.

5 Print only page 1 of the document.

Publisher prints four instances of page 1.

6 Separate the cards along the perforations to produce the final mailing piece.

Tournament Bikes

Sales ◆ Custom Orders ◆ Expert Repairs

Visit Our
Web Site
www.t_bikes.com

- ◆ Racing Bikes
- ◆ Touring Bikes
- ◆ Mountain Bikes
- ◆ Children's Bikes
- ◆ Jogging Strollers

215-555-8989
1653 Newfield Ave
Norristown, PA 19401

Phone Book Advertisement

By designing ad copy in Microsoft Publisher, you can avoid both the cost of an outside designer and the typesetting fee charged by the publication in which your ad will appear.

Preparing the Publication

This advertisement will ultimately be printed on a page in a phone book, alongside other display ads and company listings. Phone books, magazines, and newspapers typically print partial-page display ads at standard sizes. The size may be a fraction of the overall page size (such as 1/2 page or 1/3 page) or may be measured by the column inch (with a standard column determining the width of the ad). Ultimately, these sizes are relative. The exact dimensions will vary depending on the trim size and column layout of the publication. Call the publication in which you intend to advertise for exact dimensions before you begin your design.

Why are the page margins set to zero? This design will be printed on a sheet of paper that is larger than the dimensions of the ad. You, therefore, can make the page margins as small as you want, and not be in danger of placing objects in the nonprinting margin. Setting a margin of 0 inches for this project creates a 0.1-inch safety area between the pink margin guides and the blue column guides. Normally, when the page size and the paper size are identical, the page margins must be large enough to prevent you from placing text and pictures in the nonprinting area of the paper.

Crop artwork to create a bolder design. You can increase the impact of a picture by cropping it. In this project, cropping the image and placing it at the edge of the advertisement creates the illusion that the biker is riding into the reader's field of view. This refinement adds a sense of movement to the design. Notice how the position of the artwork, which points toward the text, helps to direct the reader's attention to the message.

Set Up the Page

1 Create a new special size publication measuring 5.5 inches wide by 2.5 inches high.

2 Set page margins at 0 for all four sides.

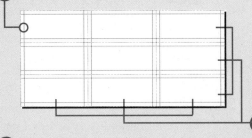

3 Create 3 columns and 3 rows.

4 Select the printer you will use and confirm that the current paper size is 8.5 by 11 inches in Landscape orientation.

Importing and Editing the Clip Art

A well-chosen clip-art image provides instant identification of a business. Look for a picture that has both the right content and the right mood. For example, the picture used in this project conveys the idea of racing, not just biking.

Import and Crop Clip Art

1 Without drawing a picture frame, insert the clip art image SL00286_.wmf found on the Publisher CD. You can easily find the image by searching for the word *bikers*.

2 Scale the picture to 300 percent of its original size.

3 Using the bottom right handle, crop the image to measure 2.36 inches wide by 2.42 inches deep.

4 Move the picture until it aligns with the bottom right edge of the page.

For the text of this advertisement, see Appendix B.

Choose an appropriate font. A bold, modern typeface—like Eras ITC—has a sporty look that is appropriate for a bike shop.

Creating the Ad Copy

Most people don't read the phone book; they skim it. Make sure that your message is clear and concise. Your company name and phone number are the most important pieces of information in a phone book ad. They should jump out at the reader.

Type and Format the Company Name and Contact Information

1 Using the blue column guides, create a text frame that fills columns 1 and 2, and row 1.

2 Draw a second text frame that fills columns 1 and 2, and row 3.

3 Draw a third text frame that fills the intersection of column 1 and row 2.

4 Make all three frames transparent.

Make use of font variants to rank the information from most to least important. In a small design, like this advertisement, you should use only one typeface. But you should choose a typeface with variants. This design employs two different weights of the same font family: Eras Bold ITC and Eras Medium ITC. Notice how the most important information, such as the company name and the phone number, has been set in boldface. The different weights also add visual interest to the type treatment.

Edit the text for a quick read. Short, immediately understood messages are what advertising is all about. If you take the time to edit your text, you'll find that you can communicate your message with just a few words. In this design, three words under the store name sum up the entire scope of the business. And the bulleted list details the wide range of products available, but it does so in a succinct manner.

Type and Format the Company Name and Contact Information *(continued)*

5 Type the contact information and format the text as indicated below:

Eras Bold ITC, 22 points, center alignment

Eras Bold ITC, 11 points, center alignment

Eras Bold ITC, 12 points, center alignment

Eras Medium ITC, 9 points, center alignment

Eras Bold ITC, 10 points, center alignment

Create the Body Copy

1 Draw a text frame that measures 1.63 inches wide by 1.03 inches high. It should fill column 2 and fit snugly against the top and bottom of the existing text frames.

2 Enter the copy, which is a simple list of the kinds of bicycles Tournament Bikes carries. Format the text as indicated.

Eras Medium ITC, 11 points

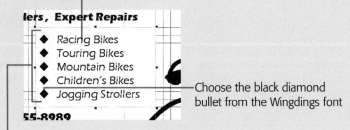

Choose the black diamond bullet from the Wingdings font

Bulleted List, 0.25-inch indent, left alignment

3 Center the text vertically in the text frame.

Fine-Tuning the Design

You can add geometric shapes and symbols to a design to emphasize and organize text. In this project, you'll correct three noticeable shortcomings:

- The subhead identifying the company contains too many commas to be effective as display copy.

- The text inviting readers to visit the company Web site is floating in an awkward white space.

- The ad does not have a boundary to separate it from the other partial-page ads that will appear on the same page in the phone book.

Add Bullets to the Display Copy

1 Highlight the comma and the space after the word *Sales*.

2 Using the Insert Symbol dialog box, replace the highlighted characters with a black diamond-shaped bullet from Wingdings font.

3 Highlight the last letter in the word *Sales*, the bullet, and the first letter in the word *Custom*. Expand the kerning by 1.75 points.

4 Repeat steps 2 and 3 to replace the comma and space after the word *Orders* with a bullet.

White text pops. You can give a simple text element the impact of a picture by reversing the color from black to white. You must be sure to keep the text legible by contrasting it with the background color. In this project, the white text against the black starburst highlights important information and balances the layout.

Why does the display type for the phone number move to the right when I nudge the starburst? The starburst shape is forcing the display type to wrap around its boundary. You can solve the problem and return the display type to the correct position by selecting the starburst-and-text frame group and sending it to the bottom of the stack.

Add a Starburst Background to the Web Address

1 Using the pink guides, draw a starburst shape that spans column 2 and row 2.

2 Fill the starburst with 100 percent black.

3 Send the starburst behind the text frame containing the Web address.

4 Change the color of the text to white, and (using Shift-Enter) break the text on three lines.

5 Center the text over the starburst and group the two objects.

6 Rotate the group by 20 degrees.

7 Nudge the group down and to the right by 0.06 inch.

8 Send the group to the bottom of the stack.

Create the Ad Border

1 Draw a box measuring 5.5 inches wide by 2.5 inches high. Position the box directly over the page edges.

2 Format the box with a 3-point black rule.

Use reproduction-quality paper to generate camera-ready art. To generate printouts that are suitable for reproduction (called camera-ready art), you must print on special paper (called repro paper) that provides a high-contrast white background for black text and black-and-white illustrations. This paper is available from stationery stores and mail-order companies.

Completing the Advertisement

If you are working with a high-resolution printer, with 600 dpi resolution or higher, you can produce either proofs or camera-ready printouts on your laser printer.

Print the Document

1 In the Print dialog box, click the Page Options button and select the One Copy Per Sheet option. The Sample area shows that one copy of the document will be centered on the paper.

2 In the Print dialog box, turn on Print Crop Marks.

3 Insert a sheet of reproduction-quality paper into your printer.

4 Print the document normally.

The crop marks align with the black border that surrounds your advertisement. These crop marks will help the phone book publisher trim and position the ad on the final publication page.

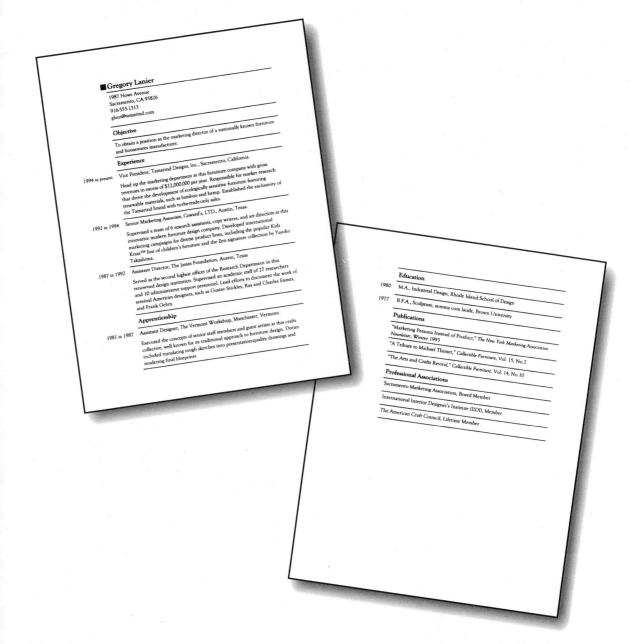

■ **Gregory Lanier**

1987 Howe Avenue
Sacramento, CA 95826
916-555-1313
glani@tamarind.com

Objective

To obtain a position as the marketing director of a nationally known furniture
and housewares manufacturer.

Experience

1994 to present   Vice President, Tamarind Designs, Inc., Sacramento, California.

Head up the marketing department at this furniture company with gross
revenues in excess of $12,000,000 per year. Responsible for market research
that drove the development of ecologically sensitive furniture featuring
renewable materials, such as bamboo and hemp. Established the exclusivity of
the Tamarind brand with to-the-trade-only sales.

1992 to 1994   Senior Marketing Associate, Coward's, LTD., Austin, Texas.

Supervised a team of 6 research assistants, copy writers, and art directors at this
innovative modern furniture design company. Developed international
marketing campaigns for diverse product lines, including the popular Kidz
Kraze™ line of children's furniture and the Zen signature collection by Yasuko
Takashima.

1987 to 1992   Assistant Director, The James Foundation, Austin, Texas

Served as the second highest officer of the Research Department in this
renowned design institution. Supervised an academic staff of 27 researchers
and 10 administrative support personnel. Lead efforts to document the work of
seminal American designers, such as Gustav Stickley, Ray and Charles Eames,
and Frank Gehry.

Apprenticeship

1981 to 1987   Assistant Designer, The Vermont Workshop, Manchester, Vermont.

Executed the concepts of senior staff members and guest artists at this crafts
collective, well known for its traditional approach to furniture design. Duties
included translating rough sketches into presentation-quality drawings and
rendering final blueprints.

Education

1980   M.A., Industrial Design, Rhode Island School of Design

1977   B.F.A., Sculpture, summa cum laude, Brown University

Publications

"Marketing Persona Instead of Product," *The New York Marketing Association
Newsletter*, Winter 1993

"A Tribute to Michael Thonet," *Collectible Furniture*, Vol. 15, No. 2

"The Arts and Crafts Revival," *Collectible Furniture*, Vol. 14, No. 10

Professional Associations

Sacramento Marketing Association, Board Member

International Interior Designer's Institute (IIDI), Member

The American Craft Council, Lifetime Member

Résumé

A well-designed résumé is so distinctive it stands out from the résumés of other job applicants. However, the layout must be uncluttered and have an easily perceived hierarchy of information. In this project, note the use of white space, rules, and headings to organize the elements of the résumé.

Preparing the Publication

Business documents, such as this résumé, use standard paper size and margin settings.

Set Up the Page

1. Create a new full-page document measuring 8.5 by 11 inches.

2. Select the printer you will use and confirm that the current paper size is 8.5-by-11-inch letter size in the Portrait orientation. This project was printed to a PostScript printer.

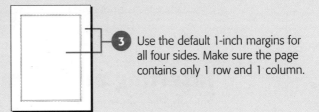

3. Use the default 1-inch margins for all four sides. Make sure the page contains only 1 row and 1 column.

The power of custom cell borders. Custom borders are responsible for the airy, elegant design of this résumé. By applying borders to only the top and bottom margins of a selected range of cells, this design avoids a cramped, boxy design.

Creating a Layout with the Table Tool

You'll create a more flexible layout if you use Microsoft Publisher's Table tool rather than layout guides to create rows and columns. The structure of a résumé, with dates in one column and descriptions in another, makes it ideally suited to a table format.

Set Up the Table Structure

1 Draw a table frame that begins at the 2.5-inch mark on the vertical ruler and that aligns with the left, right, and bottom row and column guides.

2 Set up the table with 19 rows, 2 columns, and the None table format.

3 Holding down the Shift key, move the division between the two columns to 2.5 inches on the horizontal ruler.

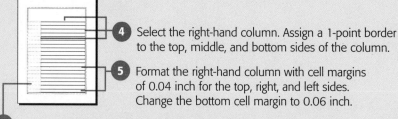

4 Select the right-hand column. Assign a 1-point border to the top, middle, and bottom sides of the column.

5 Format the right-hand column with cell margins of 0.04 inch for the top, right, and left sides. Change the bottom cell margin to 0.06 inch.

6 Select the left-hand column. The top, left, and bottom cell margins can remain at 0.04 inch. Change the right cell margin to 0.15 inch. Increasing this margin will provide an appropriate amount of room between the date information and the text information.

Inserting and Formatting Text

Publisher's powerful tools, such as drag-and-drop text editing and the capability to format all the text in a column at one time, allow you to create a table quickly and easily. Begin by creating text styles for the Description, Date, and Category items.

The résumé text was created in a word processing program and formatted as standard paragraphs. If you insert the text directly into the table, all the copy will be placed in the first cell. For more flexibility, place the text into a temporary text frame on Publisher's Pasteboard.

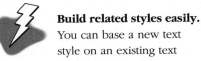

Build related styles easily. You can base a new text style on an existing text style. Simply highlight the style name you want to use as the starting point. Publisher picks up all the formatting attributes when you click the Create A New Style button. You can then make a few changes to create a new style.

Create Text Styles

1. Using the Text Styles dialog box, create a style named Description and specify the following attributes:
   - Goudy Old Style font
   - 11-point size font
   - 14 points of line spacing
   - 7 points after paragraphs
   - Left alignment

2. Create a new text style named Date. Base this style on the Description style, but make the following changes:
   - Italic
   - 0 points after paragraphs
   - Right alignment

3. Create a new text style named Category. Base this style on the Description style, but make the following changes:
   - Bold
   - 13-point size font
   - 0 points after paragraphs

For the text of this résumé, see Appendix B.

Removing predefined formats. When you insert a text file into a document, Publisher attempts to retain any formatting attributes, such as font, point size, and alignment, that were assigned within the word processing program. Assigning the Normal text style to the imported text deletes any associated style names and makes it easier to apply new text styles.

Note that local attributes, such as boldface or italics, are always maintained. In this example, the titles of publications remain italicized even when the Description text style is subsequently applied to the copy.

Insert Text on the Pasteboard

1 Using your favorite word processing program, create and save a file called Resume.

2 Draw a text frame on the Pasteboard that is approximately the same size as the page.

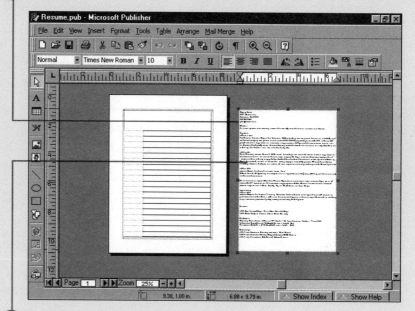

3 Insert the text file called Resume.

4 Highlight the entire story and format it with Publisher's default Normal text style.

**Import a table from another application.** You can bypass many of the procedures in this project—including the creation of the table itself—by importing a table from another Microsoft Office application. For example, if you copy or insert a table from Microsoft Excel or Microsoft Word, Publisher automatically creates a new table object.

Drag the Text to the Résumé

1 Before you move the text into the table, confirm that the Grow To Fit Text command on the Table menu is active.

2 Highlight and then drag each item to an appropriate position in the table. Date items are positioned in the left-hand column. Category and Description items are positioned in the right-hand column. After you enter all the text, the table will extend past the bottom of the page margin.

3 Highlight the entire left-hand column and format it with the Date text style.

4 Highlight the entire right-hand column and format it with the Description text style.

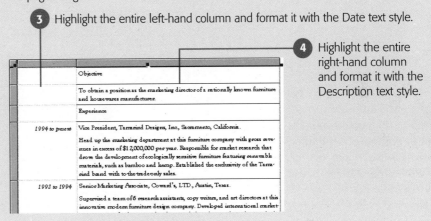

Fine-Tuning the Table

You must address several minor flaws in the table:

- ℮ Assign the correct text style to category headings.

- ℮ Center category headings vertically in each cell.

- ℮ Eliminate bad line breaks by turning off hyphenation.

- ℮ Insert a true trademark symbol to replace typewriter-style characters.

- ℮ Move the portion of the table that extends past the page margins onto a second page.

Format Category Headings

1 Scroll through the text, and assign the Category text style to categories.

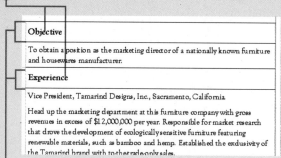

Objective
To obtain a position as the marketing director of a nationally known furniture and housewares manufacturer.
Experience
Vice President, Tamarind Designs, Inc., Sacramento, California
Head up the marketing department at this furniture company with gross revenues in excess of $12,000,000 per year. Responsible for market research that drove the development of ecologically sensitive furniture featuring renewable materials, such as bamboo and hemp. Established the exclusivity of the Tamarind brand with to-the-trade-only sales.

2 With the category items still selected, align the text vertically in the cell.

 Why doesn't Publisher automatically convert the typewriter-style characters to typographic characters when I insert the word processing file? Publisher's AutoCorrect function corrects only characters as you type; it does not automatically correct imported text. There are, however, two very easy ways to change the typewriter-style characters (tm) to a true trademark symbol.

@ Locate and highlight the typewriter-style characters. Retype the same combination of characters—(tm). Publisher's AutoCorrect function will replace the characters you type with a true ™ symbol.

@ Locate and highlight the typewriter-style characters. Use the Symbol command on the Insert menu to insert the trademark symbol.

Adjust Text

1 Select the entire column containing category and description items, and turn off hyphenation.

2 Locate the typewriter-style characters (tm) and replace them with the trademark symbol ™.

Continue the Table on a Second Page

1 Select all the rows beginning with the category *Education*. Cut these rows to the Clipboard.

2 Delete the empty rows from the table.

3 Insert a second page.

4 Select the Paste command on the Edit menu. Publisher retains the format of the table, including borders and text styles.

5 Align the new table with the top, left, and right page guides.

Choose a font that fits your personality and the message. A typeface evokes a particular feeling in a reader. When you choose a font for your résumé, think about the characteristics of the type. Does a particular font match your personality? Is the position you are applying for serious or more relaxed? Goudy Old Style, which is used in this project, is formal and restrained but has a very light touch. Experiment with possible typefaces. Remember that the most important quality of the typeface you choose is its readability.

Adding Name and Address Information

Creating a second table is the easiest way to add the name and address information to this résumé. Duplicating key attributes such as the alignment and the 1-point rule integrates the second table into the design.

Insert and Format the Name

1 Starting at the 2.5-inch mark on the horizontal ruler, draw a table frame that extends to the right column margin. It should measure 1.25 inches deep.

2 Holding down the Shift key, use the Adjust pointer to move the row division to the 1.5-inch mark on the vertical ruler.

3 Drag the name and address from the text frame on the Pasteboard, and format it as shown below.

Goudy Old Style font, 16-point font size, bold, left alignment, aligned at the bottom of the cell

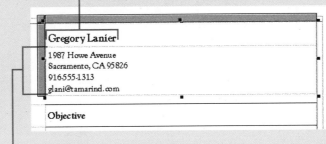

Goudy Old Style font, 11-point font size, left alignment, 14 points of line spacing

Emphasize important information. The most important piece of information in a résumé is the subject's name. In this design, you draw attention to the name with a graphic accent: the black rectangle.

Clean up the PUB file. At the beginning of this project, you created a text frame on the Pasteboard to temporarily store text. Take a moment to delete the now empty text frame. Objects left on the Pasteboard won't print; however, they do increase the file size.

Collate as you copy. If you are mailing your résumé to a long list of recipients, consider duplicating it at a service bureau. Service bureaus often offer high-quality stationery, and today's high-speed copiers can collate and even staple publications faster than you could ever do it by hand.

Add Decorative Elements

2 Pull down two horizontal ruler guides to align with the baseline and ascenders of the name. Make the text frame transparent to view the ruler guides.

1 Assign a 1-point border to the bottom of the top cell.

3 Use the Box tool to draw a square bullet that is exactly as high as the letter G. Format the box with a black fill color.

Printing the Publication

Select Print Options

1 Choose the appropriate options in the Print dialog box. Confirm that you are printing both pages, and turn off crop marks.

2 If you are printing more than one copy, consider turning off collation. Doing so will dramatically speed up the print time, although it will require you to collate by hand.

Flyer

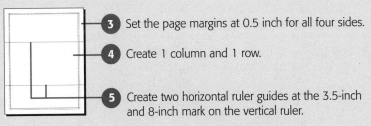

Asuccessful flyer grabs a reader's attention with a strong image and bold headlines. As you work on this flyer for a winter sports festival at the local high school, notice how the various elements—the clip art, the font choice, and graphic accents—work together to create a unified design.

Preparing the Publication

Flyers are typically printed on one side of standard letter-sized paper. Use ruler guides to align objects in the layout and choose a color scheme that complements the design.

Set Up the Page

1. Start a new full-page document.

2. Select the printer you will use and confirm that the current paper size is 8.5-by-11-inch letter size in Portrait orientation.

3. Set the page margins at 0.5 inch for all four sides.

4. Create 1 column and 1 row.

5. Create two horizontal ruler guides at the 3.5-inch and 8-inch mark on the vertical ruler.

6. In the Color Scheme dialog box, select the Floral scheme.

Inserting Artwork

The image of a snowman illustrates one of the events at the festival: a competition to build the best snowman. But the style is equally important. The bright colors and flowing lines create a festive mood.

Resizing vector artwork. If you were to look in the Scale Object dialog box, you would see that you have just enlarged this picture by over 160 percent. However, because this is a vector drawing, you can enlarge it without degrading the image quality. This artwork will print at the highest quality of which your printer is capable.

For more information about vector art, see Chapter 10.

Insert the Picture

1 Draw a clip-art frame that aligns with the two horizontal ruler guides. The frame should span the entire width of the page from the left to the right margin.

2 Insert the picture So00333_.wmf from Publisher's CD clip-art library. You can find the picture by searching for the keyword *snowman*.

Publisher resizes the picture frame to maintain the aspect ratio of the image and centers the picture on the page.

Creating a Background

The picture of the snowman seems to float in space. You can ground him by drawing a background.

Draw and Format a Rectangle

1 Draw a rectangle that aligns with the top, bottom, left, and right pink margin guides.

2 Send the rectangle behind the picture.

Use the background to temporarily hide objects.

When it is visible, the rectangle in this design obscures the layout and ruler guides. In order to see the guides, send the rectangle to the background page and turn off the display of the background.

When you are ready to print the document, simply turn on the display of the background again.

For more information about the background, see Chapter 2.

Draw and Format a Rectangle *(continued)*

3 Format the rectangle with a 4-point black rule.

The transparent background of the vector clip-art image lets you see the fill color of the rectangle lower in the stack.

4 Fill the rectangle with a 40 percent tint of Accent 3 (turquoise).

5 Select the rectangle and send it to the background.

6 Select Ignore Background on the View menu to temporarily hide the rectangle.

Creating the Headline

The text treatment for the headline should complement the image you've chosen. The Forte font contains script letters that echo the bold and casual lines in the drawing. Notice how the free-flowing lines in the drawing don't strictly adhere to the outlines of the shapes. In the same way, the letters in the Forte font don't strictly adhere to the baseline of the text block.

Create the Headline

1 Starting at the top blue row guide, draw a text frame that spans all 3 columns. The text frame should measure 2.9 inches deep. The bottom of the text frame should align with the horizontal ruler guide at the 3.5-inch mark on the vertical ruler.

2 Change the text frame margins to 0 for all four sides.

Use negative line spacing when appropriate.

Microsoft Publisher automatically applies 1 line space to text you type or import. Publisher defines 1 line space as 120 percent of the type's point size—which is too much space for text set at large point sizes. The amount of space between the lines of text in this headline is even more noticeable because the words contain no descenders (letters that fall below the baseline). To make the text look correct, you must use a negative value of 0.65 space to delete the extra leading between the lines.

Create the Headline *(continued)*

3 Enter the text *The 5ᵗʰ Annual Winter Festival.*

4 Highlight the text and assign the following formats:

- @ 0.65 line space
- @ Center alignment
- @ Align text vertically at the bottom of the frame

The 5th Annual——————Forte, 28 points

Winter——————Forte, 120 points

Festival——————Forte, 72 points

Adding a List

The list of events at the festival uses a playful type treatment, where curved text is placed against a snowball. When you add graphic accents to a design, take the time to visually incorporate the drawn elements with the imported artwork. Here, for example, an off-center, partial black outline mimics the line style in the drawing.

Repeat design motifs to create a cohesive design. You can create a visual pattern to hold a layout together by repeating design motifs. In this project, the second snowball creates a sense of perspective. It appears to be in the background, while the larger snowball appears to be in the foreground of the picture.

Create complex drawings by overlapping geometric shapes. The second, smaller snowball is composed of four overlapping shapes that create the illusion of two freely drawn black lines on top of a white circle. The individual objects, shown below, consist of three circles and one oval. Begin by placing the large, white circle on top of the large, black circle, offset slightly up and to the right. Add the smaller black circle, making sure to leave a rim of white on the right edge of the composition. Top it all off with the small oval, leaving an interior crescent of black.

Create the Snowball Drawing

1 Starting at the 7-inch mark on the vertical ruler and the 4.5-inch mark on the horizontal ruler, draw a true circle (shown below) 3.25 inches in diameter.

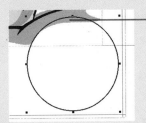

The circle should overlap the clip-art image slightly.

2 Format the circle with a white fill and a border of None.

3 Duplicate the circle.

4 Fill the duplicate with black.

5 Move the black circle 0.1 inch to the left.

6 Using the Send Backward command, send the black circle behind the white circle.

7 Group the two objects.

8 Create another smaller snowball measuring approximately 0.65 inch in diameter.

9 Move the smaller snowball to the left of the snowman's scarf at the 1-inch mark on the horizontal ruler and the 3.75-inch mark on the vertical ruler.

Create the WordArt Elements

1 Draw a WordArt frame measuring 3.5 inches wide by 1.25 inches deep.

2 Type or paste the text *Snowman Competition* in the WordArt text box.

3 Format the text with the Arch Up (Curve) text shape, 28 point size, and an Arc Angle of 110 degrees.

Flyer

For the text for this flyer, see Appendix B.

Use the Size And Position dialog box to increase precision. Instead of moving the grouped WordArt elements with the mouse, take advantage of the Size And Position dialog box. You can't resize a grouped object by using this dialog box, but you can enter exact coordinates (as shown below) to place the object anywhere on the page.

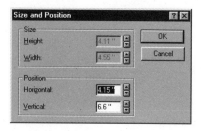

Create the WordArt Elements *(continued)*

4 Duplicate the WordArt frame three times and replace the text, as shown in the following illustration.

5 Overlap the WordArt frames by a 0.5-inch vertical offset.

6 Group the WordArt frames and rotate the entire group to the left by 20 degrees.

7 Position the grouped object at the 4.15-inch mark on the horizontal ruler and the 6.6-inch mark on the vertical ruler.

Entering and Formatting Text

The remaining text in this flyer informs the reader of the festival's location, date and time, and admission. You should continue to use the Forte font to provide consistency with the other text elements.

Type and Format Body Copy

1 Draw a text frame measuring 2.5 inches square. Position the text frame at the 1.15-inch mark on the horizontal ruler and the 7.65-inch mark on the vertical ruler.

2 Insert or type the location, admission, and date and time information.

3 Highlight the text and format it with the Forte font at 14 points.

Format display type at relatively large point sizes. The Forte font is a display typeface. It should always be formatted at a fairly large size, such as 14 points or larger. At smaller points sizes, decorative display fonts are simply not legible. In addition, at the larger points sizes (normally 14 points or above), Publisher will automatically kern letters to improve character spacing.

For more information about character spacing, see Chapter 6.

Type and Format the Body Copy *(continued)*

4 Center the text in the text frame.

5 Fine-tune the text by adjusting the line breaks and by inserting symbols, as shown below.

Create a blank line between each paragraph, and insert the round bullet character from the Wingdings font.

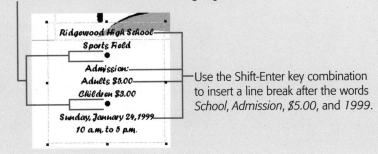

Use the Shift-Enter key combination to insert a line break after the words *School*, *Admission*, *$5.00*, and *1999*.

Completing the Publication

Before you can print the publication, you must make the background page—and the rectangle it contains—visible.

Print the Flyer

1 Deselect Ignore Background on the View menu. The light blue rectangle becomes visible.

2 In the Print dialog box, turn off crop marks.

3 Specify the number of copies you want to print.

4 Print the document normally.

THE CLARK
FAMILY BULLETIN

Patrick Sean Clark II just turned 3. He's big for his age, as you can see in this totally adorable picture taken by cousin Kate. If you want to see more of little Pat, click the picture to view a larger version of the photograph.

Grandma Sylvia just got back from an extended visit with Lori and Mike's family in Minneapolis. Here's her summary of the trip, "The weather was wonderful and the grandchildren were a blast. Oh yeah, Lori and Mike were fun too."

Timmy Dugan (though he prefers Tim these days) is off to college. He's attending Columbia University in New York City. If you want to wish him luck, you can contact him at his new e-mail address, timo5@aol.com.

REUNION TIME

It's time to finalize the plans for our 4th biennial family reunion. Helen and George are lobbying for San Francisco in October. By October the fog has departed, leaving clear skies and warm temperatures. And there are lots of other things to do in San Francisco, like visit museums or take quick trips to the wine country.

Dave wants to go on a cruise. He has found a reasonably priced cruise that sails from Puerto Rico to Aruba. We'd have to change the date, because October is the rainy season in the Caribbean. But in Dave's words, "A cruise is perfect. You can sun or swim, go dancing after dinner, or indulge at the all-you-can-eat buffet!" Dave has agreed to keep track of everyone's vote. So please e-mail him (not me!) with your opinions at dave@t_bikes.com.

WEBMASTER

Contact Margaret Clark Russell at mcr@aol.com.

Family Web Page

This personal Web page contains lots of fun elements, like a confetti background, colorful accents, and a banner created with WordArt. However, the design respects the limitations of the World Wide Web by keeping the pictures small and the text formatting simple.

Preparing the Web Publication

Microsoft Publisher's Web authoring tools appear when you choose the Web Page option in the Catalog dialog box.

Create layouts with no overlapping objects to avoid graphic regions.
When Publisher generates an HTML document, it converts all overlapping objects into graphic regions, which are pictures that take longer to download. As you complete each procedure in this sample project, notice the precise placement of design elements and the use of column guides and ruler guides to prevent objects—especially text frames—from overlapping other objects.

Set Up the Web Page

1 Start a new Web publication

2 In the Page Setup dialog box, choose the Standard (VGA) page layout option. Change the page height to 9 inches.

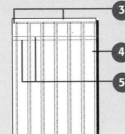

3 Leave the page margins at 0 for the bottom and right sides. Change the top and left page margin to 0.25-inch.

4 Create a grid consisting of 6 columns and 1 row.

5 Move to the background page and create two horizontal ruler guides at the 1.25-inch mark and the 1.5-inch marks on the vertical ruler.

Set Up the Web Page *(continued)*

5 Return to the foreground.

6 In the Web Properties dialog box, click the Site tab. Then type an appropriate keyword (such as *Clark*) and a description (such as *The Clark family Web site*). Specify that the target audience will be using HTML 2.0+ browsers and the US/Western European character set.

7 In the Web Properties dialog box, click the Page tab. Then type an appropriate title for the page, such as *The Clark Family Bulletin*.

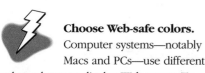

Choose Web-safe colors. Computer systems—notably Macs and PCs—use different color palettes to display Web pages. To be sure that the colors in your Web page display properly on a wide variety of computer systems, you should choose colors from a Web-safe palette. You can find a Web-safe palette by searching graphics sites on the Web or by creating a 256-color file in an image editing or paint program that supports a Web palette.

Create a Custom Background and Color Scheme

1 In the Color and Background Scheme dialog box, select the Custom tab.

2 Click the Texture check box. Click the Browse button, and select the file Wb02072_.gif for the background. (The file is normally found in the /Microsoft Office/Clipart/ Backgrounds folder.)

3 Create a custom color scheme by using the following RGB values, which are listed in order as red, green, blue:

- @ Main: 0, 0, 0
- @ Accent 1: 0, 102, 102
- @ Accent 2: 51, 102, 153
- @ Accent 3: 204, 102, 0
- @ Accent 4: 204, 51, 51
- @ Accent 5: 255, 255, 255
- @ Hyperlink: 0, 51, 153
- @ Followed hyperlink: 102, 0, 102

Choose text colors based on function. When choosing colors for text elements in your Web page, keep the following functional considerations in mind:

@ The text must be legible on a wide variety of monitors, including 16- and 256-color monitors. Choose text colors that contrast with the background in both hue (color) and value (lightness or darkness).

@ Readers must be able to distinguish normal text from hyperlink text or followed hyperlinks. Choose noticeably different colors for the Main, Hyperlink, and Followed Hyperlink items in the Custom Color Scheme dialog box.

Overriding the default body text color. Using Publisher's normal text styles function, you can change the color of text on a case-by-case basis. In the current project, for example, the Web Head text style is formatted as white, not black. Employ this feature sparingly; too many text colors in a Web document can make it difficult to distinguish normal text from hyperlink text.

Creating Text Styles

You should limit your text styles to standard fonts and simple text styles. This will enable Publisher to convert your document to HTML without any loss of formatting.

HTML Text Styles			
Text Style	Character Type and Size	Indents and Lists	Line Spacing
Web Body	Arial, 10 points	Left alignment	1 space
Web Head	Arial, bold, white, 11 points	Center alignment	1 space

Creating the Banner

Though this Web page is intended to disseminate family information, anyone with access to the World Wide Web can read it. Therefore, you should clearly identify the purpose of the Web site with a banner.

Create the First WordArt Element

1 Go to the background.

2 Draw a WordArt frame that measures 4.5 inches wide by 0.9 inch deep. The frame should align with the top pink page guide and the blue guide for column 2.

3 Type the word *CLARK*. Choose the following WordArt formats:

@ Plain Text shape

@ Arial Black font

@ Best Fit size

@ Black characters

Why must I use two separate WordArt elements to create the shadow effect? To have the first word in the banner appear in a Web-safe color (Accent 1), you must recolor the WordArt element using Publisher's Recolor Object command. Unfortunately, this would also recolor the shadow to a pale shade of green. By creating a second WordArt element, you can preserve the more appropriate gray color for the shadow. When you publish this document to the Web, Publisher will combine the two overlapping objects into a single picture.

Create the First WordArt Element *(continued)*

4 Assign a margin of 0.02 inch to all four sides of the WordArt frame.

5 Using Publisher's Recolor Object command, change the color of the text to Accent 1 (green).

6 Duplicate the WordArt object.

7 Recolor the duplicate with a light gray color (use an RGB value of 204, 204, 204).

8 Move the duplicate down 0.1 inch, to the left 0.2 inch, and to the bottom of the stack.

Create the Second and Third WordArt Elements

1 Draw a second WordArt frame that spans columns 2 and 3. The frame should measure 0.25 inch deep and should align with the two horizontal ruler guides.

2 Type *FAMILY.* Apply the following WordArt formats:

      @ Plain Text shape

      @ Arial Black font

      @ Best Fit size

      @ White characters

      @ Letter Justify alignment

Create the Second and Third WordArt Elements *(continued)*

3 Fill the frame with the Accent 2 (blue) color.

4 Assign a margin of 0.05 inch to the top, left, and bottom sides of the WordArt frame. Make the right margin 0.1 inch.

5 Duplicate the WordArt frame.

6 Resize the width of the duplicate to 2.88 inches. It should abut the right edge of the *FAMILY* object and span columns 4, 5, and 6.

7 Change the text to read *BULLETIN*.

8 Change the fill color of the frame to Accent 4 (red).

9 Assign a margin of 0.05 inch to the top, right, and bottom sides of the WordArt frame. Change the left margin to 0.1 inch.

Use the background as a safety zone. This Web project contains only one page. However, you should still place the banner on the background for safety's sake. While you are working on the foreground, you cannot select—and inadvertently change or delete—objects placed on the background.

Add the Final WordArt Element

1 Create another duplicate of the *FAMILY* WordArt object.

2 Change the text to read *THE*.

3 Resize the width of the frame to 0.7 inch.

4 Fill the WordArt frame with the Accent 3 color (orange).

5 Assign a margin of 0.05 inch to all four sides of the WordArt frame.

6 Rotate the frame 90 degrees to the left.

7 Position the frame at the 1.06-inch mark on the horizontal ruler and the 0.25-inch mark on the vertical ruler. It should align with the top and left side of the *CLARK* WordArt frame.

8 Return to the foreground.

Why should I use the Ctrl-Shift-drag method to duplicate the picture frame? Ctrl-drag allows you to copy and move an object in one operation. Shift-drag allows you to constrain the movement of an object to the vertical or horizontal axis. By holding down both Ctrl and Shift as you drag the picture frame, you will create a copy, move it horizontally, and maintain the vertical alignment.

What will happen if I resize bitmapped pictures in Publisher? Resizing a bitmapped picture in Publisher is not normally recommended because it can degrade image quality. In this case, however, you are decreasing the size of the picture, which results in less image degradation than increasing the size of a bitmapped picture. In addition, when Publisher generates the final HTML file, it will take a snapshot of the screen, automatically reducing the high resolution of these images to a resolution appropriate for monitor output.

Adding Pictures to the Web Page

A Web site is a great way to show off the latest crop of family photos. The formatting applied to the picture frame mimics the colors of the WordArt banner.

Import and Format the First Picture

1. Using the Insert menu, import the Clip Gallery picture Ph01499j.jpg. You can find the picture easily by searching for the keyword *baseball players*.

2. Position the picture at the 2-inch mark on the vertical ruler, aligned with the first column guide.

3. Using the lower-right selection handle, resize the picture until it spans columns 1 and 2.

4. Using the Crop Picture tool, hide the bottom of the picture. The cropped picture should measure 1.75 inches deep.

5. Format the picture frame with a 7-point border, using the Accent 3 color (orange).

Insert and Edit Additional Pictures

1. Ctrl-Shift-drag a copy of the picture to columns 3 and 4.

2. Ctrl-Shift-drag a second copy of the picture frame to columns 5 and 6.

Insert and Edit Additional Pictures *(continued)*

3 Insert new pictures and change the border color as follows:

Insert the picture Ph01816j.jpg. You can find the picture by searching the Clip Gallery for the keyword *grandma*.

Change the border color to Accent 1 (green).

Insert Ph01509j.jpg. You can find the picture by searching the Clip Gallery for the keyword *teens*.

Change the border color to Accent 2 (blue).

4 If necessary, adjust the size, crop, and position of the pictures to mimic the size and placement of the first picture frame.

Creating Display Type

Simple text frames filled with accent colors continue the design motif of this Web page. They also add much needed structure to the page.

Create and Format Display Type

1 At the 5.75-inch mark on the vertical ruler, draw a text frame that spans columns 3, 4, 5, and 6 and that measures 0.25 inch deep.

2 Type the text *REUNION TIME* and format it as follows:

REUNION TIME

Assign the Web Head text style.

Fill the frame with Accent 1 (green). Use default text frame margins of 0.04 inch for all four sides.

Design efficiently by reformatting duplicate objects. You can create a layout much more quickly if you duplicate an object, reposition it on the page, and then change one or two of its attributes. In this procedure, for example, duplicating the display type text frame and editing the text is more efficient than creating a new text frame. Likewise, in the previous procedure it is more efficient to insert different pictures into duplicate frames than it would be to draw, scale, and format two additional picture frames.

 For the text of this Web site, see Appendix B.

Turn off automatic hyphenation. HTML does not support automatic hyphenation of any kind. You therefore should select each text frame in your Web publication and disable automatic hyphenation. This guarantees that the line breaks you see in your working version of the document will match the line breaks your readers see when they view the document using a Web browser.

Copy and Modify the Display Copy

1 Place a duplicate of the text frame containing the display copy in columns 1 and 2 at the 8-inch mark on the vertical ruler. Reduce the width of the text frame to 1.72 inches.

2 Change the text to read *WEBMASTER*.

3 Change the fill color to Accent 2 (blue).

Inserting Body Copy

This Web page uses the Arial font for body copy. It's acceptable to use a sans-serif font because the text blocks are relatively short and therefore easy to read. In fact, the text that appears below each photograph functions as an extended caption.

Insert Extended Photo Captions

1 Place a horizontal ruler guide at the 3.88-inch (3 7/8-inch) mark on the vertical ruler.

2 Draw three separate text frames. Each frame should span 2 columns and measure 1.75 inches deep. Position the frames as shown below.

3 Type the extended captions or insert the copy from a text file.

4 Format the text as follows:

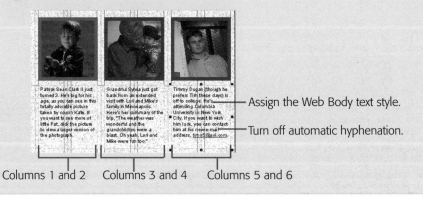

Assign the Web Body text style.

Turn off automatic hyphenation.

Columns 1 and 2   Columns 3 and 4   Columns 5 and 6

Isn't it improper to separate paragraphs with a blank line? When you are designing a print publication, it is considered bad form to separate paragraphs with a blank line. However, HTML doesn't support sophisticated text formats, such as indented paragraphs, tabs, or custom line spacing. Inserting a blank line is the only way to separate paragraphs.

 Why does Publisher force me to highlight a text phrase before I can insert a hyperlink? Publisher allows you to associate a hypertext link with a single word or phrase within a longer text block. Because of this feature, Publisher requires you to specify exactly which word or words within a text frame should be associated with the hyperlink. In the adjacent procedure, for example, you created a hypertext link for a specific email address rather than for the entire text frame.

Insert Body Copy

1 Starting at the 6.13-inch (6 1/8-inch) mark on the vertical ruler, draw a text frame that spans columns 3, 4, 5, and 6. The bottom of the text frame should align with the bottom row guide.

2 Type or insert the text about the family reunion.

3 Assign the Web Body text style and turn off automatic hyphenation.

4 Starting at the 8.39-inch (8 3/8-inch) mark on the vertical ruler, draw a second text frame that spans columns 1 and 2. The bottom of the text frame should align with the bottom row guide.

5 Type or insert Margaret Clark Russell's email address.

6 Assign the Web Body text style and turn off automatic hyphenation.

Creating Hyperlinks

A Web document isn't truly complete until you add interactivity in the form of hyperlinks. Even though this publication contains only a single Web page, you can still add links to email addresses and to an externally stored file.

Create Email Hyperlinks

1 Locate and highlight each email address in the publication, as shown on the following page.

Create Email Hyperlinks *(continued)*

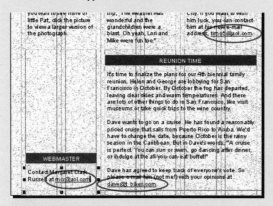

2 In the Hyperlink dialog box, select the Internet E-mail Address option and type the appropriate email address in the text box.

Create a Hyperlink for a Picture

1 Using Windows 95 Explorer, locate the file Ph01499j.jpg in the Clipart folder on Publisher's CD. Copy the file to the folder where you have stored the Web publication.

2 In Publisher, select the picture of the little boy in columns 1 and 2.

3 In the Hyperlink dialog box, choose the option A File On Your Hard Disk. Type the location and filename or use the Browse button to locate the file on your hard disk.

Proofread and fine-tune your Web site using Publisher's automated tools. You should use all of Publisher's standard tools to check your Web site for errors or inconsistencies. Run the spelling checker and the Design Checker to have Publisher alert you to potential problems. You can even print out a paper copy of the Web site to proofread the text.

Use the Web Publishing Wizard to automatically post your documents to the World Wide Web. The Microsoft Web Publishing Wizard, activated when you choose the Publish To Web command on the File menu, walks you through the process of posting an HTML document to the Web.

For more information about the Web Publishing Wizard, see Chapter 12.

Previewing and Producing the Web Site

Before you publish your document to the Web, you should use Publisher's special Preview feature to see what the document will look like when it is viewed using a Web browser. Using a Web browser also allows you to check all the hyperlinks in the document.

Preview the Web Site and Test Hyperlinks

1 Choose the Preview Web Site command on the File menu. Publisher opens your browser and loads the Web page.

2 Proofread and explore the Web page.

The title you typed in the Web Properties dialog box appears in the browser's title bar.

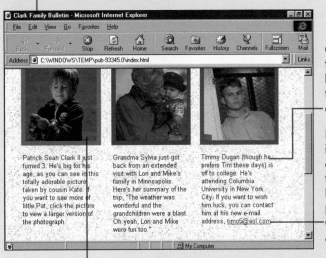

Confirm that the text formatting in the Web browser matches the text formatting you created in Publisher.

Hypertext links appear in the blue color you designated. Position the pointer over a hyperlink. The hand pointer will appear. Click the hyperlink to activate it.

When you click the hyperlinked picture, the full-size JPEG image will appear in your browser. Click the Back button in your browser to return to the Web page.

3 When you are satisfied that the document appears as it should, and that the hyperlinks work as they should, close your Web browser application.

Determine file size restrictions. An Internet Service Provider (ISP) typically provides a limited amount of space on its Web server (its computer) where customers can store a Web site. You should contact your ISP to determine how much space has been allotted for your use—probably 1 or 2 MB. Then design your Web site with that maximum file size in mind. This project, for example, requires only 98 KB of storage space.

Generate an HTML File

1 In the Web Properties dialog box, click the Page tab, and confirm that you are using the filename and the extension required by your ISP.

2 Choose Save As HTML on the File menu. Select or create a folder, and then click OK. Publisher creates an HTML document as shown below.

—Publisher converts all imported pictures and graphic regions to the GIF format at a resolution that is appropriate for on-screen viewing.

Publisher also copies the external JPEG file to the folder to make sure it will be available when your readers try to access it.

3 Contact your ISP for more information about posting your HTML document to its server.

Company Logo

A sophisticated logo can help a small business make a big impression. This logo embellishes the company name with WordArt effects, imported clip art, and drawn shapes. The result is a recognizable symbol that can be used for standard business documents, such as stationery or a business form, and promotional items, such as a shopping bag or baseball cap.

Preparing the Publication

This project focuses on the logo design and, therefore, doesn't require you to set up page guides. However, you should use ruler guides to help you properly align and position elements.

Set Up the Page

1. Start a new full-page document.

2. Select the printer you will use and confirm that the current paper size is 8.5-by-11-inch letter size in Portrait orientation.

3. Leave the page margins at 1 inch for all four sides. The number of rows and columns should remain at one.

Choose the appropriate Snap To function. You'll find this project much easier to complete if you turn off Snap To Guides and turn on Snap To Ruler Marks.

Why should I draw an element from the middle out? Drawing an element from the middle out ensures that it is centered. For each object, start from the intersection of the ruler guides and hold down the Ctrl and Shift keys as you draw.

Vary rule weights to create visual rhythm. You can add interest to a logo design by varying the line weights. In the following illustration, which uses 3-point, 1.5-point, and 6-point rules, the interplay of thick and thin lines creates a visual rhythm. The logo in this letterhead project also makes use of different line weights for the rules and circles.

Set Up the Page *(continued)*

4 Pull a ruler guide down from the horizontal ruler to the 5.5-inch mark on the vertical ruler.

5 Pull a ruler guide out from the vertical ruler to the 4.25-inch mark on the horizontal ruler.

6 Move the zero points of the rulers to align with the intersection of the ruler guides.

Creating the Background Shapes

Draw the Background Shapes

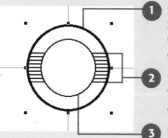

1 Starting from the intersection of the ruler guides (the new zero point), draw—from the middle out—a circle with a 0.75-inch radius (the diameter is 1.5 inches). Format the circle with a solid white fill color and a 3-point black border.

2 Starting in the center of the circle, draw nine parallel rules that intersect the circle. Space the rules 0.063 (1/16) inch apart, and format them with a 2-point line thickness.

3 Draw a second circle—once again, from the center out— with a 0.5-inch radius (the diameter is 1 inch). Format the circle with a solid white fill color and a 2-point black border.

4 Group these elements together.

Create logos quickly with clip art. You can often create a logo quite easily by combining an appropriate piece of clip art with the name of your company. Even when you are simply placing clip art next to text, look for a special visual relationship between the two. In the following logo design, the banner is positioned very close to (and flies high above) the most important word in the company name, *Trophy*.

SPORTING GOODS

Combine multiple WordArt elements. Publisher offers several WordArt shapes that can wrap text around a circle or curve. You could create a version of this logo by using the Circle or Button shapes. But you have much more control over how the words in this logo wrap around a circle if you create two separate WordArt elements by using the Arch Up and Arch Down shapes.

Creating WordArt Elements

You can make text conform to the outline of a drawn shape by creating the text object in Microsoft Publisher's WordArt module.

Create the Main WordArt Element

1 Draw a WordArt frame that is 1.25 inches wide by 1.25 inches high.

2 Type *TROPHY* in uppercase letters in the text box.

3 Assign the following attributes to the text:

- @ Arch Up (Pour) shape
- @ Arial font
- @ 12-point font size
- @ Bold
- @ Center alignment

4 In the Spacing Between Characters dialog box, choose the Very Loose (150 percent) option.

5 In the Special Effects dialog box, change the Arc Angle value to 105 degrees, which will flatten the curve to match the circular background shapes.

6 In the Shadow dialog box, choose the three-dimensional shadow (third option from the right). Assign a shadow color of silver.

Company Logo

Create the Main WordArt Element *(continued)*

7 Click outside the WordArt frame to return to the document.

8 If necessary, reposition the WordArt frame to center it on the upper band of the circular background.

 Why does Publisher keep asking me if I want to resize the WordArt frame?

You've typed a longer text phrase but haven't yet changed the point size. As a result, the WordArt object is—at least temporarily—too large for the frame. In the alert box, click No to maintain the current size of the WordArt frame, and then reduce the size to 8 points.

Create the Second WordArt Element

1 Copy the *TROPHY* WordArt element and paste a duplicate in the publication.

2 Double-click the duplicate to activate WordArt.

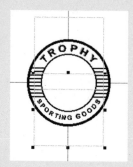

3 Change the text to read *SPORTING GOODS* (in uppercase letters).

4 Change the formatting to Arch Down (Pour) and 8-point font size. Leave the following options unchanged: Arial font, bold, center alignment, and three-dimensional shadow.

5 In the Spacing Between Characters dialog box, choose the Loose (120 percent) option.

6 In the Special Effects dialog box, change the Arc Angle to 120 degrees.

7 Click outside the WordArt frame to return to your document.

8 If necessary, reposition the WordArt frame to center it on the lower band of the circular background.

Crop WordArt to avoid text wrapping problems. When you finish assembling the WordArt elements, you'll notice that the WordArt frames extend past the circle. If you place the logo on top of a text frame, you'll create an undesirable text wrap. You can avoid this problem by using the Crop Picture tool to hide some of the white space in the WordArt frames. Using the Crop Picture tool allows you to resize the frame without changing the size or aspect ratio of the WordArt effect. Don't resize the frames, or you will distort the effect.

When can I change a picture's aspect ratio? Changing a picture's aspect ratio (by scaling the height and the width by different percentages) is not normally recommended. It distorts the picture and (in the case of bitmapped graphics) can degrade the printed quality of the image. There are two circumstances that allow you to change the picture's aspect ratio:

- The image is a vector drawing. You can change the size and the aspect ratio of vector drawings without compromising the printed quality of the image.

- The image is a fairly abstract representation of an object. Making the trophy slightly wider to work within the logo does not create a visual sense of distortion.

Crop the WordArt Frames

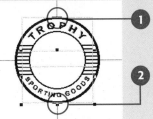

1 Using the Crop Picture tool, move the top selection handle of the Trophy object down. Reduce the height of the WordArt frame to 0.85 inch.

2 Using the Crop Picture tool, move the bottom selection handle of the Sporting Goods object up. Reduce the height of the WordArt frame to 0.9 inch.

3 Group the WordArt elements with the background shapes.

Adding a Picture to the Logo

Simple images, like the silhouette of a trophy used here, are often the best choices for a logo design. They function as immediately recognizable symbols, and they don't distract the reader from the company name.

Insert a Clip-Art Picture

1 Without drawing a frame, import the picture SL01189_.wmf from Publisher's clip-art library. You can find the image easily by searching for the keyword *trophy*.

2 Using the Scale Object dialog box, increase the picture's height to 116 percent and the width to 133 percent.

3 Center the trophy picture over the grouped logo design.

4 Group the objects together.

Company Logo

Create a logo library. As you develop publications for your business, you'll discover that you need variations of the logo. You might require a smaller size for your business card or, as shown below, a tinted logo for use as a watermark (a light image that prints behind text). As you create different versions of the logo, save them as custom Design Gallery objects. Soon you'll have a library of logo-related design effects that you can reuse in all your publications.

Completing the Logo

You should always print your designs to proofread the text and check the design. Once you've developed a strong logo, you should use it in all of your publications. Storing the logo in the Design Gallery makes it easy to access. Whenever you need the logo, you can simply import it from this publication.

Print a Proof of the Design

1. Open the File menu and choose Print.
2. Turn off the Print Crop Marks and Collate check boxes.
3. Click OK.

Add the Logo to the Design Gallery

1. Select the logo.
2. Choose Add Selection To Design Gallery on the Insert menu. In the Add Object dialog box, type an Object Name (such as Trophy) and a Category designation (such as Logo).
3. Save the file to finalize the addition of the logo to the Design Gallery.

Purchase Order

Trophy Sporting Goods
15 Old Country Road
Richardson, TX 75081
Voice: 214-555-1313
Fax: 214-555-1414

#90065-30-421

Vendor:	Date:
Address:	Resale Number:
	Terms:
	Ship Via:
Phone:	Ordered By:
Fax:	Authorized By:

Qty.	Description	Unit Price	Discount	Total
		Subtotal		
		Freight		
		Balance		

Business Form

Awell-designed business form is easy to understand and easy to use. The person who fills out the form should be able to figure out exactly what information is needed and should have enough room to enter text legibly. The person who receives the form should be able to read and process the information without errors.

Determine the number of columns or rows that you need. You should always base the number of column and row guides on the width and height of the smallest element in your layout. In this business form project, for example, the narrowest text block is 1/8 page wide. Therefore, you should divide the page into eight vertical sections—or columns.

Preparing the Publication

Creating an underlying grid for this business form allows you to position and size a wide range of elements—including the internal column divisions of a table—with precision.

Set Up the Page

1 Start a new, blank full-page document.

2 Select the printer you will use and confirm that the current paper size is 8.5-by-11-inch letter size in Portrait orientation.

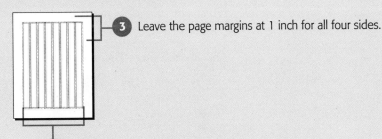

3 Leave the page margins at 1 inch for all four sides.

4 Create a grid consisting of 8 columns and 1 row.

What should I do if I haven't completed the project in Chapter 24?

The following procedures assume that you have already designed the logo in Chapter 24. You can still complete this project by making one simple adjustment. When asked to import the Trophy Sporting Goods logo, substitute a piece of clip art.

Creating the Header

Typically, the top portion of a business form contains the company logo, the title of the form, and contact information, such as an address and telephone number. Inserting the logo gives you an opportunity to take advantage of the Design Gallery.

Insert the Company Logo

1 Open the Design Gallery and click the Your Objects tab.

2 Use the Browse command (accessed via the Options button) to locate the PUB file containing the logo you created in Chapter 24, and insert the logo into the current publication.

3 Align the exterior circle of the logo with the leftmost column guide and the top row guide.

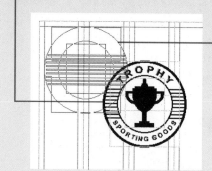

Publisher always shows you a gray outline of the elements in a group to help you position objects precisely.

Draw the Page Division

1 Starting at the 2.75-inch mark on the vertical ruler, draw a horizontal line that spans all 8 columns.

2 Change the line width to 2 points.

Draw the Page Division *(continued)*

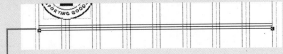

3 Create two duplicates of the line. Position the rules 0.063 (1/16) inch apart.

4 Group the three lines together.

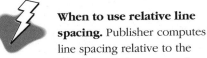

When to use relative line spacing. Publisher computes line spacing relative to the point size of the font. In this project, for example, the line spacing for all text lines is set at the default of 1 space. Publisher computes the line spacing for the 24-point text as 28.8 points, for the 12-point text as 14.4 points, and for the 9.5-point text as 11.4 points.

Use relative line spacing so that you can mix font sizes in a single text frame without worrying about the descenders on one line of text crashing into the ascenders on the next line.

Insert the Address and Phone Information

1 Draw a text frame that spans columns 3, 4, 5, and 6 and measures 1.5 inches high. Align the top of the text frame with the top row guide.

2 Enter the text in the illustration and format it as indicated.

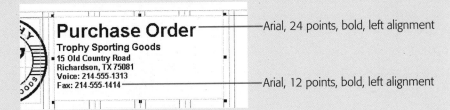

Arial, 24 points, bold, left alignment

Arial, 12 points, bold, left alignment

Purchase Order
Trophy Sporting Goods
15 Old Country Road
Richardson, TX 75081
Voice: 214-555-1313
Fax: 214-555-1414

3 Draw a second text frame that spans columns 7 and 8 and measures 0.5 inches high. Align the top of the text frame with the top row guide.

4 Enter the order number *#90065-30-421*. Format it with the following attributes:

- Arial font
- 12-point font size
- Bold
- Right alignment

Creating the Vendor and General Information Items

When you create an order form, think about who will be relying on it for information. For example, if you don't want a vendor to charge you sales tax, you must leave room to enter your resale number. If all orders require approval, you need to include a place for a supervisor's signature.

You can expedite your work in this section of the form by duplicating individual frames and groups of frames, and then by moving them to the proper positions.

Sometimes Snap To Objects provides the best alignment. If you're having trouble aligning a duplicate text frame with the frame below it, turn on Snap To Objects. This command enables you to quickly snap each frame into the proper alignment.

Create the Vendor Information Area

1 Pull down a horizontal ruler guide. Position it at the 4.5-inch mark on the vertical ruler.

2 Draw a text frame that spans columns 1, 2, 3, and 4 and measures 0.25 inch high. The bottom of the text frame should align with the horizontal ruler guide.

3 Type *Fax:* in the text box.

4 Format the text with the following attributes:

- @ Arial font
- @ 8-point font size
- @ Bold

5 Format the text frame with a clear fill color and a 1-point border at the bottom of the frame.

6 Duplicate this text frame five times. Move each duplicate up so that the bottom of the copied frame aligns with the top of the previous frame.

Consider design alternatives. In this purchase order project, you create the vendor and general information items using standard text frames. However, you could create these elements using a table instead. By using Publisher's capability to apply custom borders to table cells, you could create a single table that looks exactly like the group of six text frames in the adjacent procedure.

How to edit text within groups. You don't have to ungroup objects in order to edit text. Simply subselect the text frame. Publisher indicates the subselected frame with a red outline. Then highlight the existing text and type the new text.

Create the Vendor Information Area *(continued)*

7. Enter labels for address and phone information as shown.

8. Select these six text frames and group them together.

Create the Order Information Area

1. Create a duplicate of the group, and position it so that it spans columns 5, 6, 7, and 8. The bottom of the group should align with the horizontal ruler guide at the 4.5-inch mark on the vertical ruler.

2. Enter the labels shown here.

Creating the Order Table

Use a table to ensure consistent alignment of rules and text.

Draw and Format the Table

1 Starting at the 4.75-inch mark on the vertical ruler, draw a table frame that spans all 8 columns and aligns with the bottom column guide.

2 In the Create Table dialog box, specify 16 rows, 5 columns, and the Checkbook Register table format.

3 Select the entire table. In the Border Style dialog box, select the Line Border tab and assign a 1-point rule to the grid.

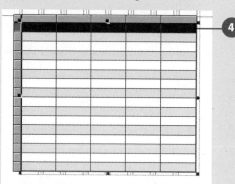

4 Select the top row and format it with the following attributes:

- Arial font
- 10-point font size
- Bold
- Center alignment

5 Select a range of cells comprising all the rows in columns 1 and 2 except the first row. Format them with the following attributes:

- Arial font
- 10-point font size
- Left alignment

How do I align the numbers in the table along the decimal point?
Publisher's table tools don't offer decimal alignment, but you can create this effect by choosing right alignment and then entering all numbers in a consistent format. For example, you might enter each number with a decimal point and two trailing zeros: *$00.00*.

Column guides versus page guides. Publisher distinguishes between column guides (shown in blue) and page guides (shown in pink). Whenever you use the layout guides as a grid, align objects to the pink guidelines instead of the blue guidelines.

Draw and Format the Table *(continued)*

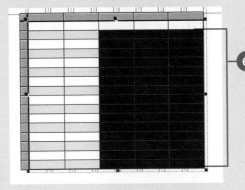

6 Select a range of cells comprising all the rows in columns 3, 4, and 5 except the first row. Format them with the following attributes:

- ◉ Arial font
- ◉ 10-point font size
- ◉ Right alignment

7 Holding down the Shift key, use the Adjust pointer to resize the columns of the table in relation to the underlying grid as indicated below.

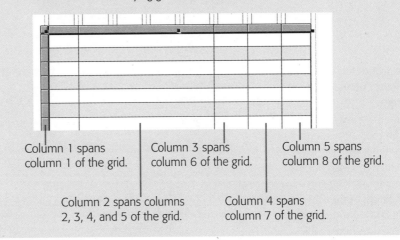

Column 1 spans column 1 of the grid.

Column 3 spans column 6 of the grid.

Column 5 spans column 8 of the grid.

Column 2 spans columns 2, 3, 4, and 5 of the grid.

Column 4 spans column 7 of the grid.

Enter the Table Labels

1 Type the labels into each cell of the first row of the table, as shown below.

Qty.	Description	Unit Price	Discount	Total

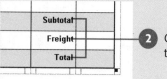

2 Create summary labels in the bottom three cells of table column 4.

3 As you type, Publisher will format the text with the 10-point Arial font. Select each label and boldface the text.

Can I delete the cells I won't be using in the table? If you want to maintain the alignment of text in the table, don't delete the cells at the bottom of columns 1, 2, and 3. Instead, make this section of the table invisible by changing the formatting attributes. Doing so won't change the structure of the table, but it will produce the illusion that the cells have been deleted from the table.

Hide Unneeded Cells and Customize the Table Border

1 Select the bottom three rows in columns 1, 2, and 3 of the table.

2 Fill the selected cells with a solid white color.

3 Select the Line Border tab in the Border Style dialog box. Select the left edge, the bottom edge, and the interior vertical and horizontal dividers (but not the top or right edges), and format them with no rule. The selected section looks like the following illustration.

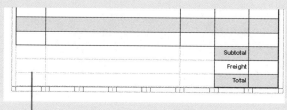

Though dotted cell boundaries appear on screen, they will not print.

Forms built from tables are easy to fill out electronically. When you design a form with Publisher, you can print it out and enter the information by hand. Alternatively, you can fill out the form electronically, using Publisher as a forms processor. Using the Table tool to build a form makes the form easier to fill out electronically, because the Tab key will move you from cell to cell in the table. If you create a table using text frames, you must lift your hands from the keyboard and use the mouse to select the next text frame.

Completing the Purchase Order

Save this file as a template so that you can use the form over and over again.

Save the File As a Template

1 In the Save As dialog box, turn on the Template check box.

2 Type an appropriate filename, such as Purchase Order, in the text box.

Print the Document

1 Open the File menu and choose Print.

2 Turn off the Print Crop Marks check box.

3 Enter the number of copies you want to print. Click OK.

Horseman
Antiques

984 Patriots Way
Concord, MA 01742

Voice: 508-555-6768
Fax: 508-555-6779
Sales: 800-555-5656
Email: horseman@msn.com

Horseman
Antiques

984 Patriots Way
Concord, MA 01742

Horseman
Antiques

984 Patriots Way
Concord MA 01742

Voice: 508-555-6768
Fax: 508-555-6779
Sales: 800-555-5656
Email: horseman@msn.com

Alison Chamberlain
Proprietor

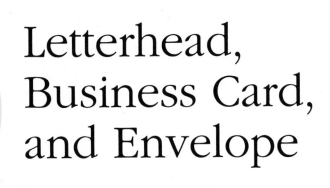

Letterhead, Business Card, and Envelope

No matter how large or small your company, stationery is a necessity. With a strong logo design and an elegant typeface, this letterhead design makes a wonderful first impression on prospective customers. The matching envelope and business card complete the package.

Preparing the Letterhead Publication

You should set up page and column guides for this document as you would for any standard business document. Here, a narrow column on the left side of the page will contain the logo and address information.

Set Up the Page

1 Start a new, blank full-page publication.

2 Select the printer you will use. Confirm that the current paper size is 8.5 by 11 inches in Portrait orientation.

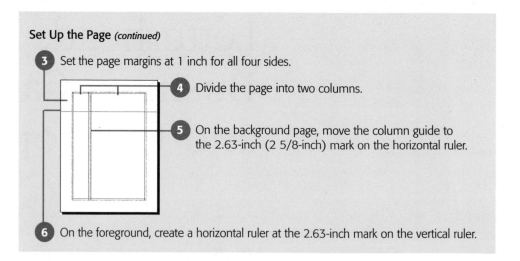

3 Set the page margins at 1 inch for all four sides.

4 Divide the page into two columns.

5 On the background page, move the column guide to the 2.63-inch (2 5/8-inch) mark on the horizontal ruler.

6 On the foreground, create a horizontal ruler at the 2.63-inch mark on the vertical ruler.

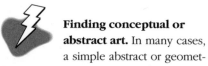

Finding conceptual or abstract art. In many cases, a simple abstract or geometric shape is the best choice for a logo design. You can find appropriate images quite easily in Publisher's Clip Gallery, because in addition to literal descriptions, like *cat* or *house*, images are identified by conceptual descriptions, such as *silhouette* or *symbol*. For example, you can find the two images shown below by searching for the keyword *logo*.

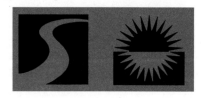

Creating the Logo

When you design a logo, you should first look for inspiration in the company name. Here, a picture of a rider on horseback echoes the store's name. Once you've chosen an appropriate image, you must develop a framing device that will tie the picture and the company name together in a cohesive logo design.

Insert a Clip-Art Image

1 Insert the picture An01157_.wmf from Publisher's clip-art library. You can easily find the picture in the Clip Gallery by searching for the keyword *horses*.

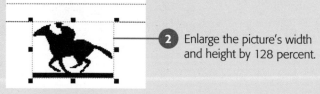

2 Enlarge the picture's width and height by 128 percent.

3 Position the image in the center of the first column, aligned with the top row guide.

Use compound rules. The clip-art image in this project sports a heavy black line as a base. The simple design solution would extend that heavy shape across the width of the address column. The resulting design would be too dark for the font choice (Garamond) and visually boring. Instead of a single heavy rule, create a compound rule (composed of two overlapping and grouped lines) that lighten up the design and add rhythm and variety to the logo.

Add a Compound Rule

1 Draw a 2.5-point black line that measures 0.5 inch horizontally.

2 Draw a 0.25-point horizontal black line that spans the width of the first column.

3 Center the two lines vertically and horizontally.

4 Group the lines together.

5 Position the group in column 1 at the 2.63-inch (2 5/8-inch) mark on the vertical ruler.

6 Place a duplicate of the compound rule over the clip-art picture. The compound rule should completely hide the horizontal base of the image.

7 Group the clip-art picture and the compound rule together.

8 Place another duplicate of the compound rule in column 1 at the 8.5-inch mark on the vertical ruler.

Add Organization and Address Personal Information Components

1 Confirm that this document is associated with the Primary Business personal information set.

2 Insert the Organization Name personal information component.

3 Align the frame with the first column guide and the 1.5-inch mark on the vertical ruler.

Will the text I type into the Primary Business personal information components appear in other documents? If you have previously created a document with Primary Business personal information components, you don't need to worry. The documents will continue to display the correct information.

However, when you insert a Primary Business personal information component into any documents you subsequently create, Publisher will display the information for Horseman Antiques. This is no cause for alarm. In a new document, simply type the name, address, and phone/fax/email for your business (replacing the copy from this project) to reestablish the correct information.

Add Organization and Address Personal Information Components *(continued)*

4 Resize the frame to the width of column 1 and a height of 0.5 inch.

5 Replace the default text with *Horseman Antiques.* Type each word on a separate line.

6 Insert the Address personal information component.

7 Align the frame with the first column guide and the 2-inch mark on the vertical ruler.

8 Resize the frame to the width of column 1 and a height of 0.5 inch.

9 Replace the default text with the following text, separated on two lines:

984 Patriots Way
Concord, MA 01742

10 Format the text elements as indicated below:

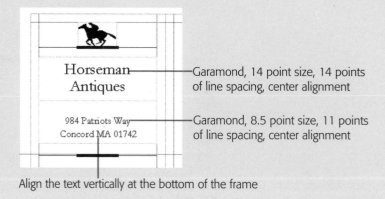

Garamond, 14 point size, 14 points of line spacing, center alignment

Garamond, 8.5 point size, 11 points of line spacing, center alignment

Align the text vertically at the bottom of the frame

Add the Phone/Fax/Email Personal Information Component

1 Insert the Phone/Fax/Email personal information component.

2 Align the frame with the first column guide and with the 8.63-inch (8 5/8-inch) mark on the vertical ruler.

Accommodate multiple phone numbers and email addresses. Today's business climate requires a company to have at least two phone numbers (one for voice communication and one for faxes) and an email or Web address. Stores often add toll-free numbers for phone orders. When you design stationery, you must leave a sufficient amount of room to accommodate all of these numbers. In the current project, a separate column contains the current contact information and can easily accommodate more phone numbers as the business grows.

Add the Phone/Fax/Email Personal Information Component *(continued)*

3 Resize the frame to the width of column 1. The frame should measure 0.75 inch deep.

4 Replace the default text with the copy in the following illustration.

5 Using the Format Painter, copy the formatting from the Address personal information component to all the text in this object.

Formatting the Body of the Letter

To ensure visual consistency, you should create text styles for the greeting and body of the letter that work with the logo design. You can even finalize the position of the letter by drawing and formatting an empty text frame.

Letterhead Text Styles			
Text Style	**Character Type and Size**	**Indents and Lists**	**Line Spacing**
Address/Signature	Garamond, 11 points	Left alignment	14 points
Body/Date	Garamond, 11 points	Left alignment	14 points, 10 points of space after paragraphs
Greeting	Garamond, 11 points	Left alignment	14 points, 10 points of space before and after paragraphs
Closing	Garamond, 11 points	Left alignment	14 points, 30 points of space after paragraphs

Use descriptive text style names. Publisher allows you to type a lot of information in a text style name—up to 32 characters' worth. Take advantage of that by truly describing the purpose of the text style. In this project, the text style names identify the components to which they should be applied. For example, the Body/Date text style should be assigned to the dateline and the actual message of the letter.

Create an Empty Text Frame

1 Draw a text frame that spans column 2. The text frame should align with the horizontal ruler guide at the 2.63-inch (2 5/8-inch) mark on the vertical ruler and the bottom row guide.

2 Select the text frame and turn off automatic hyphenation.

Saving a Template

You should save the letterhead design as a template to protect the layout from inadvertent changes.

Save a Template

1 In the Save As dialog box, turn on the Template check box.

2 Type an appropriate filename, such as Letterhead, in the text box.

3 Click Save.

Publisher stores the file in the ../Templates/Publications folder. Each time you start a new publication based on this template, Publisher opens a copy of the file, leaving the original file intact.

Creating a Matching Business Card and Envelope

You can easily create a matching business card and envelope by copying essential elements of the Letterhead design to the Clipboard.

Create an Envelope

1 Open the Letterhead template, or start a new publication based on the Letterhead template.

Consider postal regulations when designing envelopes. The United States Postal Service will have no trouble delivering letters mailed in this envelope design. However, the design does not meet postal specifications for automated handling. The serif Garamond font is too delicate for the high speed machines that perform optical character recognition (OCR). In addition, the return address extends into the area reserved for the mailing address.

If you're planning a large mailing and you want to take advantage of the reduced mailing rates for automated handling, you should use a sans-serif, monospaced font to address letters. The last line of the return address should be positioned in the top 1.25 inches of a number 10 envelope. Contact your local post office for more information about automated handling specifications.

Why can't I choose the Business Card page layout to create this publication? Publisher's Business Card page layout has a horizontal orientation; it measures 3.5 inches wide by 2 inches deep. You can't change the orientation of the layout. In order to create a vertically oriented card, you must enter custom values in the Width and Height text boxes in the Page Setup dialog box.

Create an Envelope *(continued)*

2 Copy the clip-art picture, the compound rules, and the Organization and Address personal information components to the Clipboard.

3 Start a new, blank publication based on the Envelope page layout.

4 Choose the Envelope #10 (4 1/8 by 9 1/2 inches) option.

5 Confirm that this document is associated with the Primary Business Personal Information Set.

6 Paste the elements into the document, group them together, and align the group along the top and left margin guides.

7 Save the publication as a template with an appropriate name, such as Envelope.

Create a Business Card

1 Open the Letterhead template, or start a new publication based on the Letterhead template.

2 Select all of the objects in the left column and copy them to the Clipboard.

3 Start a new, blank publication with a custom page size of 2 inches wide by 3.5 inches deep.

4 Create margins of 0.19 inch for the left and right side of the page. Create margins of 0.15 inch for the top and bottom of the page.

Why do all of the objects overlap one another when I try to align them?

If you want to align a group of selected objects horizontally on a page, you must choose the following options in the Align Objects dialog box:

- In the Left To Right area, select Centers.

- In the Top To Bottom area, select No Change.

- Select the Align Along Margins option.

Create a Business Card *(continued)*

5 The business card should contain only one column and one row.

6 Confirm that this document is associated with the Primary Business Personal Information set.

7 Paste all of the elements from the Clipboard into the Publication.

8 Reposition all of the objects as shown in the following illustration.

Align the group containing the clip-art picture and the compound rule with the top row guide.

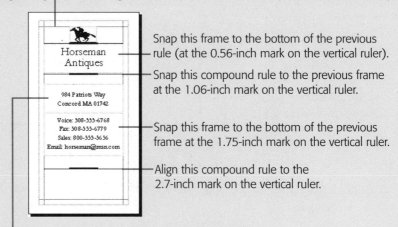

Snap this frame to the bottom of the previous rule (at the 0.56-inch mark on the vertical ruler).

Snap this compound rule to the previous frame at the 1.06-inch mark on the vertical ruler.

Snap this frame to the bottom of the previous frame at the 1.75-inch mark on the vertical ruler.

Align this compound rule to the 2.7-inch mark on the vertical ruler.

Align this frame at the 1.25-inch mark on the vertical ruler. Align the text vertically in the center of the frame.

9 Select all of the objects on the page, and center them left to right on the page.

10 Insert a Job Title personal information component. Align it at the bottom row guide, and resize the frame to the width of the business card. The frame should measure 0.25 inch deep.

11 Insert a Personal Name personal information component. Align the bottom of the frame with the top of the Job Title frame. Resize the frame to the width of the business card. The frame should measure 0.25 inch deep.

Create a Business Card *(continued)*

12 Replace the default information, and format the text as shown in the following illustration.

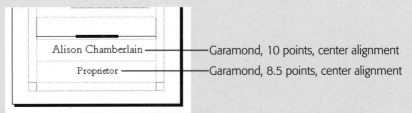

Alison Chamberlain —————— Garamond, 10 points, center alignment

Proprietor —————— Garamond, 8.5 points, center alignment

13 Save the file as a template with an appropriate name, such as *Business Card*.

Completing the Stationery Set

Though the stationery contains a minimal amount of text, you should still print the letterhead, envelope, and business card in order to proofread the copy.

Print a Proof of the Letterhead

1 Begin a new document based on the Letterhead template.

2 In the Print dialog box, turn off the Print Crop Marks check box.

3 Click OK.

4 Close the document without saving the publication.

Print multiple copies of the business card. You can produce business cards efficiently and use less paper by printing multiple copies of the publication on a single piece of card stock. In the Print dialog box, select Page Options, and choose Print Multiple Copies Per Sheet.

 For more information about the Page Options dialog box, see Chapter 16.

Print a Proof of the Envelope

1. Begin a new document based on the Envelope template.

2. In the Print dialog box, turn off the Print Crop Marks check box.

3. Click OK. When prompted, manually feed a #10 envelope to your printer.

4. Close the document without saving the publication.

Print a Proof of the Business Card

1. Begin a new document based on the Business Card template.

2. In the Print dialog box, click the Page Options button, and select the Print One Copy Per Sheet option.

3. In the Print dialog box, turn on the Print Crop Marks check box.

4. Click OK.

5. Close the document without saving the publication.

Horseman Antiques

984 Patriots Way
Concord, MA 01742

April 22, 1998

Edward Stern
18 Hollingswood Drive
Concord, MA 01742

Dear Edward,

As an avid collector of Shaker furniture, I'm sure you will want to attend an upcoming estate sale here at Horseman Antiques. This unique event will place no fewer than 40 museum-quality pieces on the auction block. Of course, a substantial collection such as this includes classic Shaker chairs and tables. But it also contains rare items, such as a tailoring counter valued at $85,000. You'll also find utilitarian objects like butter churns, pegged chair railings, and farm tools.

You will have an opportunity to inspect all of the items for sale at our warehouse, which we will open at 10 A.M. and close promptly at 4 P.M. on Saturday, May 23, 1998. If you wish, you can also arrange a private viewing during the week of May 18th through the 22nd by contacting my assistant, Esther Schmindler, at our toll-free number.

We will accept blind bids by mail or fax until 5 P.M. on Friday, May 29th. We will telephone to notify you if your bid has been accepted.

As always, it is a privilege to do business with you.

Sincerely,

Alison Chamberlain
Proprietor

Voice: 508-555-6768
Fax: 508-555-6779
Sales: 800-555-5656
Email: horseman@msn.com

Mail Merge Letter

After you've designed a letterhead, you can use Microsoft Publisher's mail merge functions to generate business correspondence efficiently. This project employs the entire range of Publisher's mail merge functions, including personalizing a letter and using a filter to select only a portion of the address list for the current mailing.

Preparing the Publication

Using a custom template can greatly simplify document setup.

Open a Template

1. Select New on the File menu.
2. On the Existing Publications tab, click the Templates button.
3. Open the Letterhead template you created in Chapter 26.

Creating the Address List

Setting up a basic address list in Publisher is as easy as filling in the blanks, because the address list already contains fields for general information such as names, addresses, and phone numbers. You can make the address list even more powerful by creating custom fields for data that relates specifically to your business.

 Double-check the current printer settings. When you open a template, many document settings—including the choice of printer and paper—are loaded along with the publication. It's always a good idea to open the Print Setup dialog box and confirm that the printer and paper choices are correct. In this case, the printer is a PostScript device, and the paper is standard 8.5-by-11-inch letter-sized paper in Portrait orientation.

For the text of this mail merge project, see Appendix B.

Is it okay to misspell words when entering data in the address list? No, you must be sure that you have spelled the information you enter into the address list correctly and consistently. Publisher's spelling checker does not work within dialog boxes—only within the actual publication file. In addition, when you create filters for your data, Publisher looks for exact spelling matches.

Is it okay to leave fields blank in the address list? Yes, it's perfectly okay to leave blank fields in the address list. The blank fields will not appear in your publication when you merge it with the address list. If you find the blank fields distracting, however, you can always delete them by clicking the Customize button in the address list dialog box.

Customize the Address List

1 Choose Create Publisher Address List on the Mail Merge menu.

2 In the Customize Address List dialog box, delete the following fields:

- Title
- Company Name
- Address Line 2
- Country
- Work Phone
- E-mail Address

3 Highlight the last item on the list, Home Phone.

4 Add a field called Period after the Home Phone field.

5 Return to the address list dialog box.

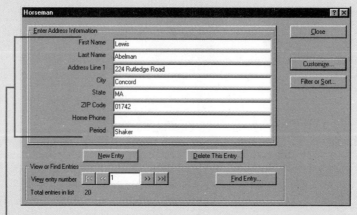

6 Enter the information for the address list, including names, addresses, and the period style that interests each customer.

7 When you've finished entering the names and addresses, save the address list to a file called Customers.mdb.

Why should I type general descriptions such as "First" and "Last" instead of a person's name? You're typing dummy text to designate the position of a person's given name and surname. Later in this project, you'll replace this text with live field codes that link the letter to the address list. When you print the final version of the letter, the field codes will be replaced with the actual names from the address list.

Use typographic-style characters instead of typewriter-style characters. You can make your documents—even a simple letter—look much more professional by replacing typewriter-style characters with typographic-style characters. In this letter, for example, the days of the month—May 18th, May 22nd and May 29th—are followed by superscript characters. You must use the Font dialog box to apply the Superscript attribute to selected text. You should likewise format the letters A.M. and P.M. as small caps.

Creating the Letter

Because you created text styles and saved them as part of the letterhead template, generating this letter is basically a matter of inserting the text. You can even enter the date automatically using the Date And Time command on the Insert menu.

Type and Format Text

1 Select the blank text frame.

2 Type or import the text of the letter. Create separate paragraphs, but don't insert extra line spaces between paragraphs.

3 Assign text styles as indicated in the following illustration.

Body/Date

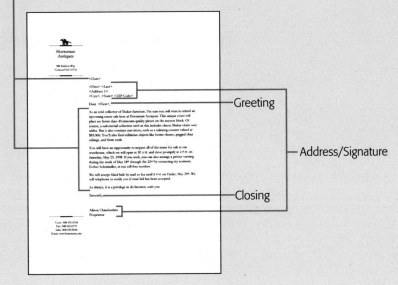

Greeting

Address/Signature

Closing

Insert the Date

1 Highlight the placeholder text for the date.

2 Select Date And Time from the Insert menu.

3 In the Date and Time dialog box, select the appropriate (Month, Day, Year) format. Instruct Publisher to insert the date as plain text.

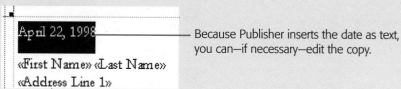

Because Publisher inserts the date as text, you can—if necessary—edit the copy.

Inserting Field Codes into the Letter

Before you can take advantage of an address list, you must associate the current document with a data source. Once the connection has been made, you can insert field codes that point to specific information in the address list.

Open a Data Source and Insert Field Codes

1 Choose Open Data Source on the Mail Merge menu.

2 Locate and select the file Customers.mdb that you created earlier. When you click Open, the Insert Fields dialog box appears.

Use filters to find information in an address list.

If you create an address list within Publisher (rather than connecting the publication to a data source created with another application), you can use filters to find information. In this letter project, for example, you can apply a filter to see how many people are interested in Mission furniture. Simply apply a filter where the Period field is equal to *Mission*. After you've viewed the results of the search, which show that only four people like Mission furniture, click the Remove Filter button.

Open a Data Source and Insert Field Codes *(continued)*

③ Use the following table to replace dummy text in your document with live field codes that point to the address list.

Text to Be Replaced by Field Codes	
Highlight This Text	**Insert This Field Code**
<First>*	First Name
<Last>	Last Name
<Address 1>	Address Line 1
<City>	City
<State>	State
<ZIP Code>	ZIP Code

* *Appears in the address and the greeting of the letter.*

④ When you've finished entering field codes, click the Close button. Your publication should resemble the following illustration.

Within the working view of a publication, field codes are identified with surrounding double brackets.

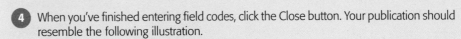

Field codes can be formatted with Publisher's full range of character and paragraph formats.

Filtering and Sorting the Address List

Publisher allows you to manipulate an address list in two important ways. You can apply a filter, which uses the selection criteria you specify to create a subset of information from the address list. In this project, for example, you will use a filter to select only the entries of those people who are interested in Shaker-style furniture.

You can also sort an address list to determine the order in which entries will be viewed or printed. Although you can sort on any field in the address list, you will probably most often sort on the ZIP Code field so that you can presort a mailing to qualify for reduced postal rates.

You can't filter or sort an address list until you've merged it with the current publication.

Merge the Address List and the Publication

1 Choose Merge on the Mail Merge menu. The Preview Data dialog box appears, and the first entry in the address list appears in place of the field codes.

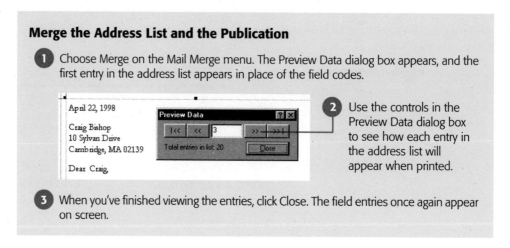

2 Use the controls in the Preview Data dialog box to see how each entry in the address list will appear when printed.

3 When you've finished viewing the entries, click Close. The field entries once again appear on screen.

Use Publisher's on-screen preview to check the results of filtering and sorting operations. If you've applied filtering or sorting criteria to an address list, you can see the results on screen by selecting the Show Merge Results command on the Mail Merge menu. The Preview Data dialog box appears. Only those entries from the address list that meet your selection criteria appear on screen, replacing the field codes in your text. In this mail merge project, for example, only eight entries from the address list meet the selection criteria you specified earlier.

Filter and Sort the Address List

1 Select Filter or Sort on the Mail Merge menu to open the Filtering And Sorting dialog box.

2 On the Filter tab, apply a filter with the following selection criteria:

- ◉ For Field, choose Period.
- ◉ For Comparison, choose Is Equal To.
- ◉ For Compare To, type *Shaker*.

3 On the Sort tab in the Filtering And Sorting dialog box, create an ascending sort order based on the ZIP Code field.

Printing a Merged Document

Before you print the multiple copies that constitute a merged document, you should test the results of the filtering and sorting criteria you specified by using special mail merge options that appear in the Print Merge dialog box.

Print a Test of the Merged Document

1 Choose Print Merge on the File menu.

2 In the Print Merge dialog box, click the Test button to print a single instance of the mail merge letter.

Print the Merged Document

1 Choose Print Merge on the File menu.

2 Turn off the Print Crop Marks check box.

3 Choose one of the following options:

  ◉ Select All Entries to print a copy of the publication for each entry in the address list that meets the selection criteria.

  ◉ Select Entries. Enter numbers in the From and To text boxes to print a copy of the publication for a subset of the entries in the address list that meet the selection criteria.

4 Click OK.

Panel 1 (top left)

SCUBA CURRENTS

Current Tidings
Dive Destinations
Shark School
Request Form

Current Tidings

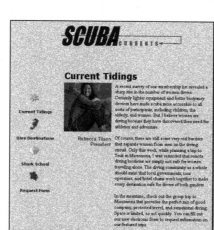

Rebecca Tilson
President

A recent survey of our membership list revealed a sharp rise in the number of women divers. Certainly lighter equipment and better buoyancy devices have made scuba more accessible to all sorts of participants, including children, the elderly, and women. But I believe women are diving because they have discovered their need for athletics and adventure.

Of course, there are still some very real barriers that separate women from men on the diving circuit. Only this week, while planning a trip to Truk in Micronesia, I was reminded that remote diving locations are simply not safe for women traveling alone. The diving community as a whole should insist that local governments, tour operators, and hotel chains work together to make every destination safe for divers of both genders.

In the meantime, check out the group trip to Micronesia that provides the perfect mix of good company, protected travel, and sensational diving. Space is limited, so act quickly. You can fill out our new electronic form to request information on our featured trips.

Panel 2 (top right)

SCUBA CURRENTS

Current Tidings
Dive Destinations
Shark School
Request Form

Palau, Truk, and Yap

Sponsored by Scuba Currents, this trip makes three stops on different islands known for their rich marine life and stunning reef formations. Imagine yourself snapping underwater photos of the grey reef sharks at Blue Corner in Palau, swimming with mantas in the Goofnuw channel of Yap, or wreck diving among the Japanese battleships sunk off the coast of Truk. Experienced tour guides and scuba masters make these adventures accessible and safe.

Saba Island

Scuba Currents is now booking a group excursion to Saba, the magical island in the Netherlands Antilles. The all-inclusive dive and travel package features low airfares, a rain forest trek, sea kayaking, and dive certification courses. Experienced dive masters and hiking guides with a personal knowledge of the island's flora and fauna make this an ideal trip for the entire family. The weeklong adventure is scheduled for the last week of November.

Panel 3 (bottom left)

SCUBA CURRENTS

Current Tidings
Dive Destinations
Shark School
Request Form

Shark School

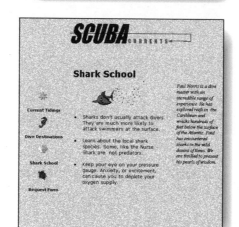

- Sharks don't usually attack divers. They are much more likely to attack swimmers at the surface.

- Learn about the local shark species. Some, like the Nurse Shark, are not predators.

- Keep your eye on your pressure gauge. Anxiety, or excitement, can cause you to deplete your oxygen supply.

Paul Harris is a dive master with an incredible range of experience. He has explored reefs in the Caribbean and wrecks hundreds of feet below the surface of the Atlantic. Paul has encountered sharks in the wild dozens of times. We are thrilled to present his pearls of wisdom.

Panel 4 (bottom right)

SCUBA CURRENTS

Current Tidings
Dive Destinations
Shark School
Request Form

Request For Information

Fill out the following form to receive more information about our featured dive destinations.

Name/Membership I.D.

First Name [ ]
Last Name [ ]
Membership I.D. [ ]

Send information about:

☐ Palau, Truk, and Yap
☐ Saba Island

Send information by:

○ Fax [Fax number]
○ E-mail [E-mail address]

[Submit] [Reset]

Professional Web Site

Using Microsoft Publisher's special Web publishing tools, you can design a multipage Web site complete with hyperlinks and multimedia events. Objects inserted using the Design Gallery or Publisher's Form Control tool can automate complex tasks, such as creating an interactive table of contents or programming an electronic reader response form.

Preparing the Web Publication

When you set up a Web publication, you must determine the general appearance of each page by specifying a page size and background. However, you must also specify other more sophisticated attributes. For example, you should associate searchable keywords with your publication to make your site easier to find on the World Wide Web. And you should choose the appropriate character set and HTML version for your target audience.

Determine the appropriate size for your Web pages. The width and height of your Web pages are determined by two different factors. The width should be based on the display resolution most likely to be used by your readers. In this case, choosing the Standard option guarantees that even those readers with standard VGA 640-by-480-pixel screens will be able to see the entire width of the page.

The height should be based on the amount of information you intend to place on each Web page. In this project, for example, the page height is reduced to only 6 inches, because each page contains a relatively small amount of information. Instead of scrolling down one long page, readers can click hyperlinks to move from page to page.

Set Up the Web Page

1. Start a new, blank Web page publication.

2. In the Page Setup dialog box, choose the Standard (VGA) option. Change the page height to 6 inches.

3. Set the page margins to 0 for all four sides.

4. Create a grid consisting of 4 columns and 1 row.

Set Up the Web Page *(continued)*

5 On the background, create four horizontal ruler guides positioned as shown in the following illustration.

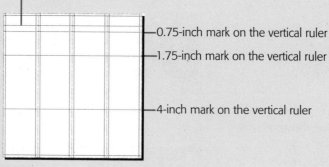

0.5-inch mark on the vertical ruler

—0.75-inch mark on the vertical ruler

—1.75-inch mark on the vertical ruler

—4-inch mark on the vertical ruler

6 Return to the foreground.

Choose Web-safe colors.
Computer systems—notably Macs and PCs—use different color palettes to display Web pages. To be sure that the colors in your Web page display properly on a wide variety of computer systems, you should choose colors from a Web-safe palette. You can find a Web-safe palette by searching graphics sites on the Web or by creating a 256-color file in an image editing or paint program that supports a Web palette.

Create a Custom Color and Background Scheme

1 In the Color And Background Scheme dialog box, select the Custom tab.

2 Click the Texture check box, then click the Browse button, and select the file Wb007601.gif for the background. (The file is normally found in the /Microsoft Office/Clipart/Backgrounds folder.)

3 Create a custom color scheme using the following RGB values, which are listed in order as red, green, blue:

- ℮ Main: 0, 0, 0
- ℮ Accent 1: 0, 0, 153
- ℮ Accent 2: 255, 0, 0
- ℮ Accent 3: 255, 255, 0
- ℮ Accent 4: 153, 204, 255
- ℮ Accent 5: 255, 255, 255
- ℮ Hyperlink: 0, 102, 51
- ℮ Followed hyperlink: 102, 0, 102

Confirm file naming conventions with your Internet Service Provider.

When you generate the final HTML document, Publisher will create a separate file for each page in the publication using the filenames and file extension you specify in the Web Properties dialog box. You should contact your Internet Service Provider (ISP) to determine the required file naming conventions and file extensions. Once you have this information, enter it in the File Name text box and File Extension drop-down list on the Page tab of the Web Properties dialog box.

Should I use Verdana in my Web publications?

Microsoft has approved the Verdana font and its variations (italic, bold, and bold italic) for use on the Web. However, there is always the chance that a reader with an older system or a Mac might not have the Verdana font available. If that should happen, Arial or Helvetica will most likely appear on screen in place of Verdana. In this design, Verdana is used exclusively for display type. So even if substitution should occur, it will not change the layout significantly.

Assign Web Site and Web Page Properties

1. In the Web Properties dialog box, click the Site tab. Then type appropriate keywords (such as *scuba, diving, water sports, vacation, travel*) and a description (such as *Scuba Currents is a club for professional and amateur scuba divers*). Specify that the target audience will be using HTML 2.0+ browsers and the US/Western European character set.

2. Click the Page tab in the Web Properties dialog box. Then type an appropriate title for the page, such as *Scuba Currents*.

3. Add three blank pages to the publication. In the Insert Page dialog box, be sure to check Add Hyperlink To Web Navigation Bar.

4. Make sure that page 2 is the currently displayed page. Open the Web Properties dialog box, click the Page tab, and type an appropriate title for the page, such as *Dive Destinations*.

5. Repeat step 4 for pages 3 and 4, typing appropriate titles each time, such as *Shark School* and *Request for Information*, respectively.

Creating Text Styles

Publisher ships with several fonts that are appropriate for use on the Web. In this publication, Times New Roman (a serif font) and Verdana (a sans-serif font) are combined to provide visual variety.

HTML Text Styles			
Text Style	Character Type and Size	Indents and Lists	Line Spacing
Web Body	Times New Roman, 10 points	Left alignment	1 space
Web Head	Verdana, bold, Accent 1 (blue), 18 points	Left alignment	1 space
Web Contents	Verdana, bold, Accent 1 (blue), 8 points	Left alignment	1 space
Web Form	Arial, 10 points	Right alignment	1 space
Web Bullet	Verdana, round, 10 points	Bulleted, indented 0.25-inch, left alignment	1 space

Create simple text styles.
If you create complex text styles, there's a good chance that the formatting will be lost or changed when Publisher converts your document to the simpler structure of an HTML document. Protect your designs by creating simple text styles. Doing so gives Publisher the best chance of converting the document to HTML without any loss of formatting.

What is the difference between a document's background and the Color And Background Scheme dialog box?
The Color And Background Scheme dialog box is a Web publishing tool that allows you to specify a background color or texture for all the pages in your document. Think of this dialog box as a formatting option.

The background is a standard Publisher feature that allows you to create a layout for elements (such as type, pictures, or logos) that will repeat on every page of the document. Think of the background as a layout function.

Creating the Repeating Elements

Like traditional desktop publishing documents, Web documents contain repeating elements, such as a running header containing the company logo. Instead of a table of contents or footer that displays page numbers, however, Web documents contain hyperlinked navigation bars to move you forward or backward through a multipage document. Objects and hyperlinks placed on the background are duplicated and function identically on each page of the Web site.

Create a WordArt Logo

1 Move to the background.

2 Starting at the pink guide that divides columns 1 and 2, draw a WordArt frame measuring 1.8 inches wide by 0.65 inch high. The frame should align with the top row guide and the ruler guide at the 0.75-inch mark on the vertical ruler.

3 Type *SCUBA* into the WordArt text box, and format it as follows:

- @ Impact font
- @ Plain text shape
- @ Stretch
- @ Best Fit size
- @ Black characters

4 Select the WordArt frame, and create margins of 0.05 inch for all four sides.

5 Recolor the WordArt text with Accent 1 (blue).

Use WordArt to incorporate unique fonts into a Web document. The logo employs a nonstandard font, Impact. To be sure that the correct font appears on screen when a reader views this document with a Web browser, create the object as a WordArt element. Publisher automatically converts WordArt elements to pictures when it generates an HTML file.

 Why should I use the Recolor Object command to choose colors for WordArt? Publisher's WordArt module allows you to choose colors from a limited palette. There is no guarantee that these are Web-safe colors. To apply a Web-safe color from your color scheme to a WordArt object, you must use the Recolor Object command.

 Why should I use a box to connect the two horizontal lines in the logo? If you zoom in on the rules in the logo, you'll see that the box with the 3-sided border has perfectly sharp corners. Aligning the top and bottom (horizontal) edges of the box with the horizontal rules in the logo takes a small amount of effort. While you certainly can create the same effect by connecting the two horizontal lines in the logo with a third (vertical) line, you'll find it is much more difficult to achieve the same level of precision.

Add a Second WordArt Element

1 Starting at the blue guide for column 3, draw a WordArt frame measuring 1.4 inches wide by 0.25 inch high. Position the frame between the ruler guides at the 0.5- and 0.75-inch marks on the vertical ruler.

2 Type *CURRENTS* into the WordArt text box, and format it as follows:

- @ Impact font
- @ Plain text shape
- @ Best Fit size
- @ Letter justify
- @ Black characters

3 Select the WordArt frame, and create margins of 0.1 inch for all four sides.

4 Recolor the WordArt text with Accent 2 (red).

Add Supporting Rules to the Logo

1 Starting at the 0.43-inch mark on the vertical ruler, draw a line that measures 3.45 inches wide. The left point of the line should align with the left edge of the SCUBA WordArt frame.

2 Format the rule with Accent 2 (red) and a line weight of 2 points.

3 Send the line to the bottom of the stack.

4 Draw a second rule measuring 0.55 inch wide at the 0.62-inch mark on the vertical ruler. The left point of the rule should align with the pink guide between columns 3 and 4.

5 Format the rule with Accent 2 (red), a 2-point line weight, and a left-pointing arrowhead.

Include pages in the Web navigation bar automatically. Publisher can automatically add pages (and the appropriate hyperlinks) to a Web navigation bar. If you decide to delete a page from your Web site, Publisher can automatically delete the reference in the Web navigation bar. To take advantage of this feature, you must select the Add Hyperlink To Web Navigation Bar option in either the Web Properties dialog box (on the Page tab) or the Insert Pages dialog box. In this project, when you inserted the Web navigation bar, Publisher automatically created four hyperlink buttons—one for each page in the publication.

Can I use the Wizard to alter the Web navigation bar? Yes, you can click the Wizard button, located at the lower right-hand corner of the Web navigation bar, in order to choose a different design from the Design Gallery. However, the Wizard merely changes the layout. You must still subselect individual frames and use Publisher's standard tools to insert new text and pictures.

For the text of this Web site, see Appendix B.

Add Supporting Rules to the Logo *(continued)*

6 Zoom in to a 400 percent view, and draw a box that measures 0.22-inch square. The box should align with the two red lines.

7 Format the box with a 2-point, Accent 2 (red) border on the top, right, and bottom sides. The left side should have no border.

8 Group all of these objects together.

Insert a Web Navigation Bar

1 Insert the Summer Web navigation bar from the Design Gallery.

2 Position the object in the first column, at the 2-inch mark on the vertical ruler.

3 Reduce the width of the navigation bar to span column 1.

4 Subselect each text frame in the Web navigation bar, format the text with the Web Contents text style, and type the text shown in the following illustration.

5 Double-click each picture frame to invoke Publisher's Clip Gallery. Insert the images shown in the following illustration. You can easily find these images by searching for the keyword *ocean*.

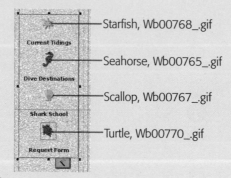

Starfish, Wb00768_.gif

Seahorse, Wb00765_.gif

Scallop, Wb00767_.gif

Turtle, Wb00770_.gif

6 Return to the foreground.

Create layouts with no overlapping objects to avoid graphic regions. When Publisher generates an HTML document, it converts all overlapping objects into graphic regions, which are pictures that take longer to download. As you complete each procedure in this sample project, notice the precise placement of design elements and the use of column guides and ruler guides to prevent objects from overlapping. Frames are allowed to abut one another, but they never overlap.

What does a flashing red box mean? If you overlap two or more objects, Publisher alerts you to the fact that these objects will be converted to a graphic region when you generate the HTML document. Resize or reposition the objects to create a layout in which objects do not overlap one another.

Decrease download times by decreasing the size of pictures. The pictures in this sample Web publication are less than 2 inches square. Keeping the pictures (and their respective file sizes) small will allow your readers to download this page as quickly as possible.

Creating the Home Page

The first page of a Web site is often referred to as the home page. It's an opportunity to introduce the company to your readers, and to inform them of the kinds of information they will find on subsequent pages of the Web site.

Insert a Photograph

1 Insert the portrait Ph01789j.jpg from Publisher's Clip Gallery. You can easily find this picture by searching on the keyword *woman*.

2 Holding down the Ctrl key, use the Crop Picture tool to move a side selection handle toward the middle of the picture. Publisher will crop the picture equally from the left and right sides. Stop when the picture measures 2.31 inches wide by 2.31 inches high.

3 Align the top of the picture with the ruler guide at the 1.75-inch mark on the vertical ruler.

4 Reduce the picture's size to 1.4 inches wide by 1.4 inches deep. It should align with the blue row guide between columns 1 and 2, and the pink row guide between columns 2 and 3.

Insert Text

1 First, change the default text frame attributes. Select the Text tool, but don't draw a text frame. In the Text Frame Properties dialog box, set margins of 0 for all four sides.

2 Draw a text frame that spans columns 2, 3, and 4 and measures 0.35 inch high. Align the bottom of the text frame with the ruler guide at the 1.75-inch mark on the vertical ruler.

Current Tidings

Turn off automatic hyphenation. HTML does not support automatic hyphenation of any kind. You, therefore, should select each text frame in your Web publication and disable automatic hyphenation. This guarantees that the line breaks you see in your working version of the document will match the line breaks your readers see when they view the document using a Web browser.

Insert Text *(continued)*

3 Enter the text *Current Tidings*, and format it with the Web Head text style.

4 Draw a second text frame spanning columns 3 and 4 and measuring 4.15 inches deep. The top of the text frame should align with the horizontal ruler guide at the 1.75-inch mark on the vertical ruler.

5 Draw a third text frame spanning column 2. The text frame should measure 1.4 inches wide and 0.5 inch deep. The top of the text frame should align with the 3.25-inch mark on the vertical ruler.

6 Enter the text and format it as shown in the following illustration.

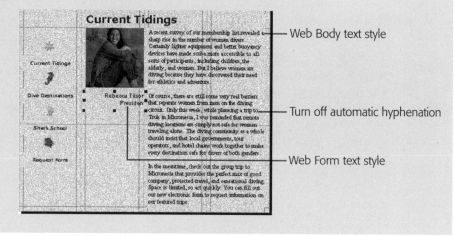

Creating the Second Web Page

In a traditional newsletter, you routinely jump stories from page to page because it's easy for readers to turn the page. In a Web document, however, it's important for each page to be a self-contained unit. The second page for this sample Web document contains short text blocks that are easy to read on screen.

The power of duplication. When you duplicate and reuse objects, you work more efficiently. In this project, for example, when you copy the Web Body text frame from the first page to the second page, you duplicate a text frame that is the correct width, is associated with the correct text style, and has hyphenation already disabled.

Duplicate and Modify Text Frames

1 On page 1 of the publication, copy the Web Head and Web Body text frames to the Clipboard.

2 Paste the duplicates onto page 2. Position them exactly as they appear on page 1.

3 Replace the heading text with *Palau, Truk, and Yap*. Make sure that Publisher retains the Web Head text style.

4 Replace the text in the larger text frame with the copy about Palau, Truk, and Yap.

Palau, Truk, and Yap

Sponsored by Scuba Currents, this trip makes three stops on different islands known for their rich marine life and stunning reef formations. Imagine yourself snapping underwater photos of the gray reef sharks at Blue Corner in Palau, swimming with mantas in the Goofnuw channel of Yap, or wreck diving among the Japanese battleships sunk off the coast of Truk. Experienced tour guides and scuba masters make these adventures accessible and safe.

5 Format the copy with the Web Body text style.

6 Using the bottom selection handle, resize the frame to 1.75 inches deep.

7 Create a duplicate of the text frame containing the heading. Align the bottom of the text frame with the ruler guide at the 4-inch mark on the vertical ruler. Replace the existing text with *Saba Island*.

8 Create a duplicate of the text frame containing the descriptive copy. Align the top of the text frame with the ruler guide at the 4-inch mark on the vertical ruler. Replace the text with the appropriate copy about Saba.

Insert Photographs

1 Insert the photograph Ph01293j.jpg from Publisher's clip-art library. You can find the picture by searching on the keyword *beach*.

2 Scale the image to 76 percent of its original size.

3 Using the Crop Picture tool, crop the left and bottom edges of the picture until it measures 1.4 inches square.

Create text descriptions for Web pictures. When a reader accesses your Web site, he or she may not see the pictures you've inserted into the document. The reader may have chosen to view only text in order to speed up performance, or heavy Internet usage may slow down the transmission of graphics files.

You can assign a label to any picture in a Web publication by typing a phrase into the Alternate Text Representation text box in the Object Properties dialog box. If the picture itself doesn't appear on the reader's screen, the text label will appear. This feature is especially important if you've used pictures to create hyperlinks in your Web site, because it allows the reader to navigate the site without viewing the images.

Don't overlap GIF animations with other objects. If you overlap a GIF animation with another object, Publisher will convert it to a graphic region (a static picture) when you generate the HTML document. Though the first frame of the animation will appear in the Web site, the animation will not play when viewed with a browser.

Insert Photographs *(continued)*

4 Position the picture in column 2, aligned with the ruler at the 1.75-inch mark on the vertical ruler.

5 Insert the photograph Ph01317j.jpg from Publisher's clip-art library. You can find the picture by searching on the keyword *beach*.

6 Scale the image to 61 percent of its original size.

7 Using the Crop Picture tool, crop the top, left, and right edges of the picture until it measures 1.4 inches square.

8 Position the picture in column 2, aligned with the ruler guide at the 4-inch mark on the vertical ruler.

Creating a Multimedia Experience

Web publishing allows you to entertain your readers with sounds and movement. Using the Web Properties dialog box and Publisher's support of the animated GIF format, you can create Web pages that continuously play music and motion clips.

Insert an Animated GIF File

1 Move to page 3.

2 Insert the file AG00179_.gif from Publisher's Clip Gallery. You can find it by clicking the Motion Clips tab and searching on the keyword *swimming*.

3 Align the animation with the ruler guide at the 1.75-inch mark on the vertical ruler. Center it in columns 2 and 3 at the 2.18-inch mark on the horizontal ruler.

Preview multimedia files. When you're working on a publication, you can't play motion clips or listen to sound files. Publisher displays only the first frame of an animation and represents sound files with an icon (on the publication page) or with a filename (in the Web Properties dialog box). You can, however, preview the files in the Clip Gallery. Open the Clip Gallery (by choosing Clip Art from the Picture cascading menu on the Insert menu), locate the multimedia file, and click the Play button.

Associate a Sound File with a Web Page

1 Confirm that you are on page 3 of the publication. In the Web Properties dialog box, click the Page tab.

2 In the Background Sound area, click the Browse button, and locate the file Safri_01.mid. It's normally stored in the /Program Files/Microsoft Office/Clip Art/Publisher folder.

3 Click the Loop Forever option.

Insert and Format Text

1 Draw a text frame spanning columns 2, 3, and 4 and measuring 0.35 inch deep. Align the bottom of the text frame with the ruler guide at the 1.75-inch mark on the vertical ruler.

2 Draw a second text frame spanning columns 2 and 3 and measuring 2.5 inches deep. Align the top of the text frame with the bottom of the animated GIF frame.

3 Draw a third text frame spanning column 4 and measuring 3 inches deep. Align the top of the text frame with the ruler guide at the 1.75-inch mark on the vertical ruler.

4 Select the second and third text frames and turn off automatic hyphenation.

5 Type or insert the text, and format it as shown in the following illustration.

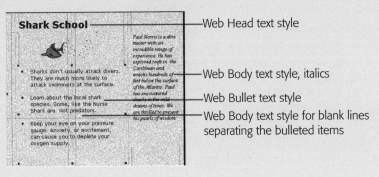

Web Head text style

Web Body text style, italics

Web Bullet text style

Web Body text style for blank lines separating the bulleted items

Why should I use the Arial font instead of the Verdana font for the response form? Certain objects in the response form, specifically the drop-down list and the Fax and E-mail text boxes, contain default text. Publisher automatically formats default text with the Arial font set at 10 points. You cannot change these formats. Use the Arial font for the remainder of the form to produce a consistent document.

Creating a Response Form

The fourth and final page of this Web site contains a response form. Using Publisher's form control objects, you can create a response form that includes text boxes, option buttons, check boxes, and drop-down lists. You should combine form control objects with standard text elements that explain the form's purpose and that clearly identify each section.

Create Supporting Text Elements

1. Move to page 4.

2. Draw a text frame spanning columns 2, 3, and 4 and measuring 0.35 inch deep. Align the bottom of the text frame with the ruler guide at the 1.75-inch mark on the vertical ruler.

3. Enter the text *Request For Information*, and format it with the Web Head text style.

4. Draw a second text frame, spanning columns 2 and 3 and measuring 0.5 inch deep. Align the top of the text frame with the ruler guide at the 1.75-inch mark on the vertical ruler.

5. Select the text frame and turn off automatic hyphenation.

6. Type or insert the following text:

   Fill out the following form to receive more information about our featured dive destinations.

7. Format the text with the Web Body text style.

8. Create three text frames that span columns 2, 3, and 4. Each text frame should measure 0.25 inch deep.

Assign data processing properties to form control objects. Remember to assign useful data processing properties to each form control object in your response form. Form control properties can affect the way an object behaves in the reader's Web browser. In the current project, for example, the Membership I.D. item will be a mandatory field, will limit users to a total of 15 characters (the length of a legitimate I.D. number), and will hide the membership number with asterisks. More importantly, form control properties allow you to structure and identify the information returned to you. In the dialog box below, the phrase *Member_ID* will be returned as the identifying label for the Membership I.D. text box.

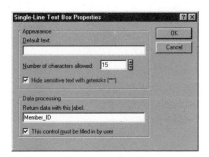

Create Supporting Text Elements *(continued)*

9 Enter the text for each section of the form; position and format the text as shown in the following illustration.

Arial font, bold, 10 points, right alignment

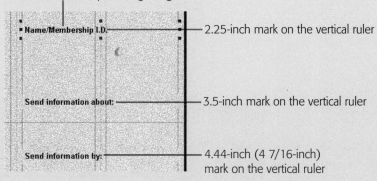

- Name/Membership I.D. → 2.25-inch mark on the vertical ruler
- Send information about: → 3.5-inch mark on the vertical ruler
- Send information by: → 4.44-inch (4 7/16-inch) mark on the vertical ruler

Create Text Box Form Control Objects

1 Using the Form Control tool, draw a single-line text box that spans columns 3 and 4. A single-line text box is always 0.25 inch deep.

2 Draw a text frame that spans column 2 and measures 0.25 inch deep.

3 Select both objects, and align their bottom edges.

4 Group the objects and position them at the 2.55-inch mark on the vertical ruler (which is 0.063 (1/16) inch below the bottom of the text frame containing the first section heading).

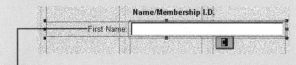

5 Type the phrase *First Name*, and format it with the Web Form text style.

Create Text Box Form Control Objects *(continued)*

6 Create two duplicates of the group and position them 0.063 inch apart.

7 Replace the existing text with the phrases *Last Name* and *Membership I.D.*, as shown below.

 Allow multiple selections. If you want the reader to choose more than one item in a group, you must create form control objects that permit multiple selections. Both the Check Box and the List Box form control objects are appropriate. In this project, for example, check boxes allow the reader to request information for both of the featured dive destinations.

Create Check Box Form Control Objects

1 Create two check box form control objects that span columns 3 and 4 and measure 0.25 inch deep.

2 Position the objects beneath the second section heading, leaving 0.063 (1/16) inch between each object.

3 Enter the text as shown in the following illustration and format it as:

@ Web Form text style

@ Left alignment

Send information about:

☐ Palau, Truk, and Yap

☐ Saba Island

Create mutually exclusive choices. Publisher can return only one value for each data processing label. When you assign more than one option button the same data processing label, you are actually creating mutually exclusive items. In the current project, a reader will be able to select only one delivery method—fax or e-mail—not both.

Create Option Button Form Control Objects

1 Create two option button form control objects that span column 3 and measure 0.25 inch deep.

2 Position the objects beneath the third section head, leaving 0.063 (1/16) inch of space between each object.

3 Enter the text shown in the following illustration and format it as:

> ◎ Web Form text style
>
> ◎ Left alignment

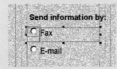

4 Right-click the actual button (not the label text frame) for the Fax item, and select the Option Button Properties command from the shortcut menu.

5 In the Option Button Properties dialog box, enter a data processing label, such as *Send_by*, and a data processing value, such as *Fax*.

6 Repeat steps 4 and 5 for the E-mail item, selecting the same data processing label (*Send_by*) from the drop-down list, and entering a data processing value of *E-mail.*

7 Create two single-line text-box form control objects that span column 4 and measure 0.25 inch deep.

8 Position the objects beneath the third section head, leaving 0.063 inch of space between each object. The text boxes should align with the option buttons in column 3.

9 Double-click each single-line text box to open the Single-Line Text Box Properties dialog box. Enter the default text shown in the following illustration.

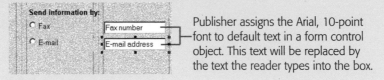

Publisher assigns the Arial, 10-point font to default text in a form control object. This text will be replaced by the text the reader types into the box.

Choose a data retrieval method. Before you publish your Web site, contact your ISP to determine the correct data retrieval method. If your ISP supports Microsoft FrontPage Server Extensions, you can save the submitted form in an appropriate format (such as HTML) or have the responses delivered to your email address.

Test the functionality of form control objects. When you fill out the reader response form, test the behind-the-scenes function of the objects. For example, in this project you defined the Membership I.D. text item as a mandatory field with a maximum of 15 characters. Try entering an I.D. number that exceeds 15 characters to see if the field is truly capped. Or try to submit the form without filling in an I.D. number. Your Web browser should display an appropriate error message, such as the one shown below.

Create Command Button Form Control Objects

1 Create a command button to submit the form.

2 Align the button at the left of column 3. Align the bottom of the button with the bottom row guide.

3 Create a command button to reset the form.

4 Align the button at the left of column 4. Align the bottom of the button with the bottom row guide.

Previewing and Producing the Web Site

A preview of this Web site allows you to confirm that the hyperlinks work, the multimedia objects play correctly, and the electronic response form can be completed.

Preview and Test the Web Site

1 Choose the Preview Web Site command on the File menu.

2 In the Preview Web Site dialog box that appears, click Web Site.

3 Check to be sure that the text formatting in the Web browser matches the text formatting you created in Publisher.

4 Position the pointer over a hyperlink in the Web navigation bar. The Hand pointer will appear. Click the hyperlink to move from page to page.

5 Move to page 3. Confirm that the GIF animation and the associated sound file play continuously while the page is displayed.

Look for hyperlink opportunities. Inserting hyperlinks in a Web document delivers tangible benefits to your reader. You can make your Web site easier to navigate by providing links to other pages in the HTML document at convenient locations. You can even direct your readers to useful information by inserting hyperlinks that point to other Web sites on the World Wide Web.

Use the Microsoft Web Publishing Wizard to automatically post your documents to the World Wide Web. Instead of saving the Web site to a folder on your local hard disk, you can publish directly to the World Wide Web. The Web Publishing Wizard, activated when you choose the Publish To Web command on the File menu, walks you through the process of posting an HTML document to the Web.

For more information about the Web Publishing Wizard, see Chapter 12.

Preview and Test the Web Site *(continued)*

6 Move to page 4. Complete the response form, as shown below.

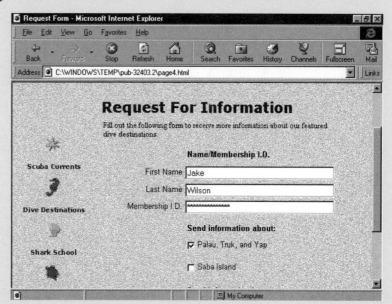

7 When you're satisfied that the document appears and works as it should, close your Web browser application.

Generate an HTML File

1 Choose Save As HTML on the File menu.

2 In the Save As HTML dialog box, specify or create a folder.

3 When you click OK, Publisher creates an HTML document.

4 Contact your ISP for more information about posting your HTML document to its server.

Edible Flowers

Sweet Violet

A nosegay of *Viola odorata* is a gift of sweet affection. The purple blooms are, quite appropriately, a symbol of Venus. The Romans fermented crushed flowers to make a sweet wine, but modern-day cooks use crystallized blossoms as an edible decoration for desserts. Herbalists use an infusion made from flowers to cure insomnia.

Rather than offer seeds, we offer Violet seedlings instead, which can be transplanted to an outdoor site in spring. Once rooted, these perennials will return to bloom year after year. Indeed, you may find that the runners which Sweet Violets use for natural propagation invade other parts of your garden.

Seedlings (24)	#4234	2.50
Fresh flowers (1 lb.)	#4235	15.00
Plant in bloom	#4236	35.00

4

Edible Flowers

Spring 1999

Edible Flowers

Johnny-Jump-Up

Although these bright purple and yellow blooms look quite a lot like Pansies, Johnny Jump-Ups are totally edible. The mild flavor is slightly sweet, making Johnny Jump-Ups a perfect decoration for soft cheeses or cold fruit soups. Try combining goat cheese with Johnny Jump-Ups and watercress.

You should plant Johnny Jump-Ups in either full or partial sun at the first sign of thaw. And you can plan to enjoy both the sight and taste of the flowers in early spring. After the warm weather is over, you can still harvest these edible flowers. Simply order the potted plant instead of seeds. Our hothouse grown plants will bloom even in the dead of winter.

Seedlings (24)	#2234	2.50
Fresh flowers (1 lb.)	#2235	15.00
Plant in bloom	#2236	35.00

2

Edible Flowers

Nasturtium

Only in recent times has Nasturtium, or *Tropaeolum minus*, been considered a purely ornamental plant. Persians nibbled Nasturtium petals as early as 400 B.C. Nasturtiums reached their peak of popularity in the kitchens of 17th century Europe. The flowers, stems, and young leaves of this plant are edible. The flavor is peppery and has a marked similarity to watercress. Indeed, Nasturtium's tangy, slightly hot taste has made it a favorite salad ingredient of Nouvelle-cuisine chefs.

Plant Nasturtium in the spring. The plants will begin to bloom in summer, but the harvest will last through fall. You can keep picked flowers fresh by floating them in a bowl of cold water.

Seedlings (24)	#3234	2.50
Fresh flowers (1 lb.)	#3235	15.00
Plant in bloom	#3236	35.00

3

Mail-Order Catalog

This project meets the basic criteria of good catalog design: the page layout is uncluttered, and the critical ordering information is easy to find and scan. The design reflects the nature of the products sold in its pages. The delicate text styles and a spring-green spot color complement the copy about edible flowers.

Preparing the Publication

This project takes advantage of Microsoft Publisher's spot-color functions, which require you to set up the publication for a printing service.

Select Printing Service Options

1. Choose Prepare File For Printing Service on the File menu. From the cascading menu, select Set Up Publication. Complete the setup procedure with the following choices:

   - Select Green as Spot Color 1. Don't select a second spot color.

   - Select the MS Publisher Imagesetter as the printer for final output.

   - Select Extra Paper Sizes.

   - Show all printer marks.

2. Choose the Book Fold layout in the Page Setup dialog box.

3. Set up the page in Landscape orientation, with a custom page size of 4.5 inches wide by 7.5 inches high.

4. When Publisher asks whether you want to automatically insert additional pages, click No.

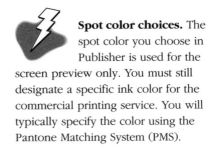

Spot color choices. The spot color you choose in Publisher is used for the screen preview only. You must still designate a specific ink color for the commercial printing service. You will typically specify the color using the Pantone Matching System (PMS).

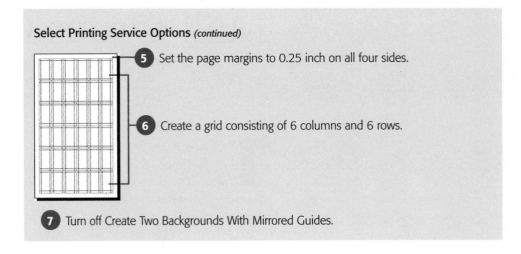

Select Printing Service Options *(continued)*

5 Set the page margins to 0.25 inch on all four sides.

6 Create a grid consisting of 6 columns and 6 rows.

7 Turn off Create Two Backgrounds With Mirrored Guides.

Creating Text Styles

This document utilizes only two fonts: Lucida Calligraphy and Perpetua. Lucida Calligraphy serves a purely decorative function and is limited to display type. Perpetua serves the practical function and is used for all the body copy. Nevertheless, Perpetua's small x-height and long, delicate ascenders and descenders add the perfect typographic touch to this catalog. Use the table that follows to create the text styles you will apply to the copy you type or import.

Catalog Text Styles			
Text Style	**Character Type and Size**	**Indents and Lists**	**Line Spacing**
Body Copy	Perpetua, 10.5 points	First line indent of 1 pica, justified alignment	12.5 points
Box Numbers	Perpetua, bold, 10 points	Right alignment	12.5 points
Box Text	Perpetua, bold, 10 points	Left alignment	12.5 points
First Paragraph	Perpetua, 10.5 points	Justified alignment	12.5 points
Subhead	Lucida Calligraphy, italic (default), 10 points, Spot Color 1 (green)	Left alignment	12.5 points

Alternative font choices.
The design in this chapter uses the Perpetua and Lucida Calligraphy fonts, but other font combinations would work equally well. You should experiment with alternative font choices, such as the Garamond and Edwardian Script ITC combination or the Calisto MT and Viner Hand ITC combination shown below.

Creating the Repeating Elements

You should place repeating elements, such as the headers and page numbers, on the background page. Objects placed on the background are automatically duplicated on each page.

Create the Header

1 Move to the background.

2 Draw a text frame that spans columns 2, 3, 4, and 5. Align the top of the frame with the top of the first row. The frame should measure 0.25 inch high.

3 Type *Epicurean Delights* in the frame.

4 Highlight the text and format it with the following attributes:

Perpetua font
Small capitals
12-point font size
Center alignment
Vertical alignment in text frame

Lucida Calligraphy font
16-point font size
Center alignment
Vertical alignment in text frame

5 Select the text and assign Loose spacing between characters.

6 Starting at the 0.75-inch mark on the vertical ruler, draw a second text frame. The text frame should span columns 2, 3, 4, and 5 and should measure 0.57 inch high. It will align with the first row guide.

7 Type *Edible Flowers*.

8 Format the text as shown in the previous illustration.

Why can't I center the rule between the text lines? If you have difficulty centering the BorderArt rule between the two text boxes, turn off Snap To Guides and Snap To Objects.

 How can I be sure that the size of my text frame is correct? You have two options:

@ Keep your eye on the status line at the bottom of the screen to double-check the size of the text frame as you create it.

@ Use the Size And Position dialog box to enter explicit values for the width and height of the text frame.

Add a Decorative Rule

1 Draw a box between the two text frames.

2 Collapse the box to a single line by moving the top and bottom selection handles together until they overlap.

3 Format the collapsed box with the Vine BorderArt pattern at 15 points.

4 Center the rule between the text lines.

Insert Page Numbers As a Footer

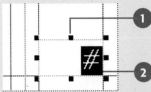

1 Draw a text frame at the bottom of the page. The frame should span the rightmost column and measure 0.25 inch high.

2 Insert a page-number mark (#).

3 Highlight the page-number mark and format it with the following attributes:

@ Lucida Calligraphy font

@ 14-point font size

@ 15 points of line spacing

@ Right alignment

@ Centered vertically in text frame

When you eventually return to the foreground, Publisher will replace this symbol with the correct page number on each page.

When should I use the mirrored guides option?

When you created the layout guides at the beginning of a project, you turned off Create Two Backgrounds With Mirrored Guides because mirroring an empty background is inefficient. After you add repeating elements (such as the page number and header), you should turn on this check box.

Copy Background Elements to the Left-Hand Page

1 Switch to Full Page view.

2 In the Layout Guides dialog box, turn on Create Two Backgrounds With Mirrored Guides.

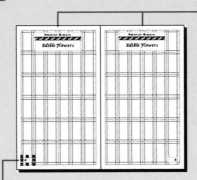

When you view the background, you see backgrounds for left-hand and right-hand pages.

The background for the left-hand page now contains the same elements as the background for the right-hand page, except that the page-number text frame has been moved to its mirror position at the outside of the page.

3 Select the text frame containing the page-number mark on the background for the left-hand page.

4 Click the Left alignment button on the Format toolbar.

5 Return to the foreground.

Creating, Importing, and Formatting Catalog Text

Catalog copy doesn't have to be a hard sell. These sometimes historical, often whimsical descriptions of edible flowers create a mood that is supported by the delicate type treatment. Pricing information, on the other hand, should always be presented in a clear format that's easy to locate and read. Presenting the pricing information in a different format, such as a table, adds visual interest to a page.

Clean up word processing files before you import your text. Before you insert the text into the Publisher document, use your word processing program to check for errors: run the spelling checker and the grammar checker. Proofread the copy for errors such as double words, dropped words, double spaces, and incorrect punctuation. But most importantly, read the text for sense.

 For the text of this catalog, see Appendix B.

Type the Text

1 In a word processing application; type the text for the body copy. Create three separate files.

2 Save the files as Johnny, Nasturtium, and Violet.

Import and Format the Johnny-Jump-Up Article

1 Draw a text frame that spans columns 2, 3, 4, and 5. Vertically, the text frame should span rows 2, 3, 4, and 5.

2 Insert the file Johnny.

3 Click in the first line (which happens to be an entire paragraph), and format it with the Subhead style.

4 Click in the next paragraph, and format it with the First Paragraph style.

5 Click in the next paragraph, and format it as Body Copy.

Use tables instead of tabs. Price lists contain tabular material. However, you shouldn't structure tabular data with tabs that can easily become misaligned. Instead, use Publisher's Table tool. Tables automatically adjust row height to maintain the horizontal alignment of elements, even multiline elements.

Create a Fancy First Letter

1 Select the subhead.

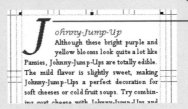

2 Create a custom fancy first letter with the following attributes:

- Lucida Calligraphy font
- 4 lines high
- Combination letter position of 1 line above the paragraph and 3 dropped lines
- Spot color 1 (solid green)

Create the Pricing Table

1 Draw a table frame that spans columns 2, 3, 4, and 5. The frame should measure 0.75 inch high. The top of the frame should align with the top of the last row.

2 In the Create Table dialog box, create a table with three rows and three columns. Leave the Default table format selected.

3 Enter the text for Johnny-Jump-Up prices.

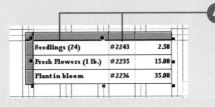

4 Using the Adjust pointer and the Shift key, widen the first column in the table until it spans columns 2 and 3 and stretches across the gutter between columns 3 and 4. Using the Shift-Adjust pointer combination, widen the second column of the table to span column 4.

5 Select the entire table. Format the top, center, and bottom of the table with a hairline black border.

6 Format columns 1 and 2 of the table with the Box Text style. Format column 3 with the Box Numbers style.

7 Select the entire table, and assign margins of 0.02 inch to all four sides of each cell in the table.

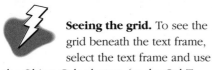

Seeing the grid. To see the grid beneath the text frame, select the text frame and use the Object Color button (or the Ctrl-T keyboard shortcut) to make the frame transparent.

Adding a Picture to the Catalog

In a mail order catalog, pictures are a key sales tool. People rarely buy something they've never seen, and an attractive picture can often convince someone to make an impulse purchase.

Import and Modify a Picture

1 Starting at the guide for row 4, draw a square clip-art frame that spans columns 4, 5, and 6.

2 Insert the clip-art picture NA00043_.wmf from Publisher's CD clip-art library. You can easily find this picture by searching on the keyword *dogwoods*.

3 Recolor the picture using a 100 percent tint of the green spot color.

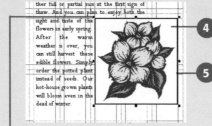

4 Assign picture frame margins of 0.05 inch to all four sides of the image.

5 Assign a 1-point black border to the frame.

6 Align the upper left corner of the picture frame with the intersection of the guides for row 4 and column 4.

When should I insert new pages into my design? If you wait until you've completed the layout for an entire page before inserting new pages, you can instantly duplicate the completed layout on each new page.

Completing the Catalog Pages

When you insert pages into a publication, you have the option of adding blank pages or duplicating an existing layout. In this sample project, you'll duplicate the objects on page 1 to quickly assemble the remaining catalog pages.

Insert Pages

1 Insert two pages. Be sure to add the pages after the current page and select the Duplicate All Objects on Page Number 1 option.

2 When Publisher asks whether you want to automatically insert the correct number of pages for a booklet, click No.

Can I add custom fancy first letters to a library of designs? When you create or customize a drop cap, Publisher automatically adds the design to the choices in the Drop Cap dialog box. This makes it easy for you to apply the fancy first letter format to subsequent paragraphs in the current documents. However, the custom drop cap will not be available in other publications. If you want to use a custom drop cap in several publications, add the text frame containing the drop cap to the Design Gallery and save the file. You can then import the custom Design Gallery object into any other publication.

For more information about customizing the Design Gallery, see Chapter 14.

Replace the Duplicated Text with New Text

1 Move to page 2.

2 Select the large text frame containing the duplicate text about Johnny-Jump-Ups, and highlight the entire story.

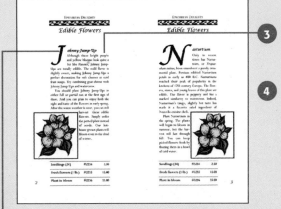

3 Insert the file Nasturtium. The new text will replace the highlighted text.

4 When Publisher asks whether you want to use Autoflow, click No.

5 Format the first line with the Subhead style and the drop cap you created earlier.

6 Format the first paragraph after the subhead with the First Paragraph style.

7 Format the final paragraph with the Body Copy style.

8 Move to page 3, and repeat steps 2 through 7 using the file Violet.

Reuse design motifs.
One way to minimize your workload is to copy an element from another page and then reformat it. For example, in this project, the front cover mimics the header design. Instead of creating the individual elements again, copy the header from the background. Then resize and reformat them.

Type New Table Text

1 Select the table containing the pricing information for Nasturtiums.

2 Enter the correct ID numbers.

3 Repeat steps 1 and 2 for Sweet Violets.

Creating the Cover Page

The exercises in this chapter have all stressed the importance of consistency in a publication, but every publication contains pages that are unique, such as the cover or title page.

Insert a Cover Page

1 Move back to page 1, and insert a new blank page before the current page.

2 In the alert box that appears, click OK to insert the page.

3 Toggle on Ignore Background. This command hides the header and page number on the cover. It affects only the currently displayed page.

Add and Format the Cover Text

1 Copy the three objects in the header design (found on the background) to the foreground of the cover page (page 1).

2 Reformat the design to match the following illustration.

Use gradients to enhance clip art. Many of the vector images in Publisher's clip-art library have transparent backgrounds. You can fill the background with a gradient. In this catalog, for example, you could repeat the design motif of the front cover by adding a gradient background to the picture of the flower, as shown below.

Add and Format the Cover Text *(continued)*

Change the point size of *Epicurean Delights* to 20 points. Increase the height of the text frame to 0.44 inch. Stretch the frame across the width of the page. Center the text vertically in the frame.

The decorative rule remains at a 15-point size, but it is stretched across the entire width of the page. It aligns with the top of the main text frame.

Edible Flowers fills the entire third row. Increase the size to 32 points. Center the text vertically in the frame.

The text frame is filled with a symmetrical horizontal gradient. The base color is a 20 percent tint of the green spot color. Color 2 is a 50 percent tint of the green spot color.

3 Draw a text frame at the bottom of the page. The frame should span the page horizontally and measure 0.35 inch high.

4 Type *Spring 1999*.

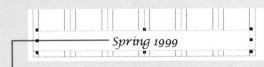

5 Format the text with the following attributes:

- Lucida Calligraphy font
- 14-point font size
- Center alignment
- Vertical alignment at the bottom of frame

Viewing facing pages enables you to create a balanced design. Whenever you use the Book Fold layout, use the Two-Page Spread option (found on the View menu). As you work on your design, look at it the way the reader will—as a spread rather than one page at a time. In the current project, doing so will help you rearrange the elements in the spread so that the two pages form a mirror image of each other.

Use only true italics and boldface. You should apply italic and boldface formats only when you have the appropriate versions of a font installed on your system. In this project, the Perpetua font comes in four different versions: normal, bold, italic, and bold italic.

However, if you do not have the appropriate version of the font installed, Microsoft Windows 95 will fake the effect by slanting a normal font at an oblique angle (to simulate italics) and stretching a normal font (to simulate boldface). The results are less than ideal.

Fine-Tuning the Layout and the Text

You should always scrutinize the layout and the text to discover and fix problem areas before you send the document to a service bureau or commercial printer. At this point in the design process, there are two problem areas:

@ The picture on page 2 is not balanced with the layout on page 3.

@ Typewriter-style text should be replaced with typographic-style text. For example, Latin names should be italicized, and the abbreviation *B.C.* should appear in small caps.

Balance the Pages

1 Move to pages 2 and 3.

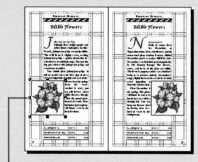

2 Select the picture frame on page 2, and move it to the outside of the page.

Proofread the Text and Adjust Formatting

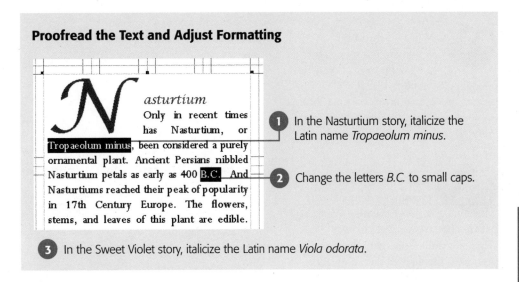

1 In the Nasturtium story, italicize the Latin name *Tropaeolum minus*.

2 Change the letters *B.C.* to small caps.

3 In the Sweet Violet story, italicize the Latin name *Viola odorata*.

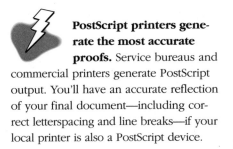 **PostScript printers generate the most accurate proofs.** Service bureaus and commercial printers generate PostScript output. You'll have an accurate reflection of your final document—including correct letterspacing and line breaks—if your local printer is also a PostScript device.

Printing a Proof and Producing the Catalog

When you print a publication created with the Book Fold layout, Publisher positions two pages of the publication on each sheet of paper. This page imposition (the arrangement of pages on a larger piece of paper) guarantees that the pages will be in the correct order when you assemble the finished catalog.

Print a Proof of the Catalog to a Local Printer

1 In the Print Proof dialog box, turn on Collate and Show All Print Marks.

2 Turn off Print Color Separations.

What's a dummy?
A dummy is a mock-up of the final printed, trimmed, folded, and bound publication. You can use the proofs you create on your local printer to collate, trim, and assemble a dummy catalog by hand.

Why does the file size change so dramatically when I create a PostScript printer file? When you create a PostScript printer file, Publisher must produce a file with all the information necessary to generate the printout. Images are converted to the PostScript format, and font information for non-standard fonts (such as Lucida Calligraphy and Perpetua) is embedded in the file. As a result, the printer file can grow quite large. In this sample, the PostScript printer file requires 1.9 MB of disk space. Compare that to Publisher's format, which requires only 104 KB.

For more information about preparing files for a printing service, see Chapter 17.

Assemble the Catalog As a Dummy

1 Photocopy pages 2 and 3 right side up onto the back of the sheet with pages 4 and 1.

2 Fold the paper down the center to form the spine of the catalog.

3 Use the crop marks as a guide to trim away the excess paper.

Transfer the Publication to a Printing Service for Output

1 Before you send a file to the service bureau, generate an InfoSheet. This report contains important information about your publication, such as paper size and font usage.

2 Check with the printing service to see which of the following file formats you should generate:

- Publisher's native format. This requires the service bureau to have a current copy of Publisher 98 and the fonts you've used in the document.

- A PostScript printer file, which you've generated using the Create File In PostScript command (found on the Prepare File For Printing Service cascading menu).

3 Transfer the file to your printing service.

4 The printing service will generate printing plates and reproduce the catalog on an offset press, using black ink and a color ink that closely approximates Spot Color 1.

New World Wines
194 Cardinal Lane
Redwood City, CA 94065

When we first opened New World Wine in 1972, everyone laughed. Imagine... an entire store devoted exclusively to American wine. Now, 26 years later, many people—but especially our customers—applaud our decision. The relationships we've developed in the larger wine community allow us to procure the best of today's premier wines, especially sought-after estate bottlings and limited releases. Our deep knowledge of small producers helps us to discover the great wines of tomorrow.

The staff here at New World Wines participates in regular wine tastings, both to educate our collective palette and to investigate wines as they are released to the market. Occasionally we discover an exceptional wine at an exceptional price. Our new Discovery program allows us to share both the wines and the savings with you by offering a 30% discount on selected wines when they are purchased by the case.

A shared discovery is a precious gift.

...red wine from the San Joaquin valley of California. The wine is not identified by a varietal name because, in the classic French tradition, it blends the juice of several different grapes, including Cabernet Sauvignon, Merlot, and Malbec. Our tasters found the classic berry aromas of ripe cherries and blueberries, with a spicy accent of black pepper.

With a balance of fruit flavors and soft tannins, Stonehill Heritage is ready to drink right now. But this full-bodied wine can also be cellared for the next 3 to 5 years and will only improve with age.

Our enthusiasm for this wine led us to order 200 cases. But, even with a per bottle price of $20, we expect it to fly off the store shelves. Don't miss this incredible bargain. Place your order today.

Rating 87

Joshua Creek   Gewürztraminer 1996

The Pacific Northwest now produces fine Rieslings and Gewürztraminers in the German style. So our expectations were high when we opened our first bottle of the Joshua Creek Gewürztraminer from the Yakima Valley in Washington State. We weren't disappointed.

Though light-bodied, this wine is a pale yellow gem. It is packed with fruit accents that include green apple and fresh grapefruit aromas. The youthful, pleasantly tart finish makes it a refreshing summer aperitif or the perfect compliment to spicy Asian food.

The Joshua Creek Gewürztraminer is at its peak right now, and ideally should be consumed in the next year. Because Joshua Creek is a relatively unknown vineyard, we can offer the wine at an unbelievably low price. Don't let this remarkable value slip through your fingers.

Rating 90

Order Form

Item	Quantity	Price Per Case	Total
Stonehill Vineyards Heritage 1994		$149	
Joshua Creek Gewürztraminer 1996		$105	
		Subtotal:	
		Tax:	
		Shipping:	
		Total:	

Delivery

Name:

Address:

City, State, ZIP:

Daytime Phone:

Payment

Payment Method: ☐ Check ☐ Mastercard ☐ Visa ☐ American Express

Credit Card #:

Expiration Date:

Signature:
"I certify that I am at least 21 years of age."

Three-Fold Brochure

Using Microsoft Publisher and a laser printer, you can produce a three-fold brochure entirely on the desktop. This self-mailing brochure is ideal as an inexpensive sales tool. You can avoid the cost of outside printing services—and the address area on the outside of the brochure eliminates the cost of envelopes!

Preparing the Publication

The layout of a three-fold brochure is determined by the two folds. It's important that you divide the page into three equal sections, called panels. You must also accommodate normal page margins for your printer's nonprinting area. You can accomplish both goals by using a combination of page guides and ruler guides.

Set Up the Page

1 Start a blank, full-page document. In the Catalog dialog box, click the Custom Page button and change the orientation to Landscape.

2 Select the printer you will use, and confirm that the current paper size is 8.5 by 11 inches.

3 Set the page margins at 0 for all four sides.

4 Create a grid consisting of 3 columns and 1 row.

Can I really divide an 11-inch page into three equal sections? No. There is no easy way to divide a standard 11-inch page into three equal sections. Do the math, and the result will be the infinite fraction of 3.6666666 inches. But by having Publisher divide the page with column guides, the page divisions will be as accurate as possible.

 Why must I create separate text styles for the rules? When you assign the underline attribute in the Font dialog box, Publisher doesn't allow you to determine the position of the rule in relation to the text above it. The result is a rule that is simply too close to the text (shown below). As you can see, underlining can make text illegible by obscuring the descenders of the letters. When you create a separate text style for a rule, you can specify indents and line spacing to control the position of the underline.

Stonehill Vineyards

Set Up the Page *(continued)*

5 On the background, create ruler guides at the following positions:

7.88-inch (7 7/8-inch) mark on the horizontal ruler

—0.5-inch mark on the vertical ruler

—7.75-inch mark on the vertical ruler

—8-inch mark on the vertical ruler

10.5-inch mark on the horizontal ruler

6 Return to the foreground.

Creating Text Styles

The following table specifies the formatting attributes of the text in this project. Notice how paragraph indents add white space around the text. You can also control the position of text by adjusting the spacing before or after a paragraph. For example, the Body Copy text style includes left and right indents of 0.25 inch and 15 points of space after each paragraph.

In addition, there are three text styles that take advantage of Publisher's new character underlining options. These text styles combine underlining, paragraph indents, and line spacing formats to precisely position rules between paragraphs.

Text Attributes for the Three-Fold Brochure				
Text Style	**Character Type and Size**	**Indents and Lists**	**Line Spacing**	**Tabs**
Body Copy	Times New Roman, 10 points	Left indent of 0.25 inch, right indent of 0.25 inch, justified alignment	18 points, 15 points of space after paragraphs	None
Heading	Tw Cent MT Condensed Extra Bold, 10 points	Left alignment	12 points, 15 points of space before paragraphs	2.94 inches, right alignment
Rating	Tw Cent MT Condensed Extra Bold, 8 points	Center alignment	10 points, 15 points of space after paragraphs	None
Rule Above Rating	Tw Cent MT Condensed Extra Bold, 4 points, thick underline	Left indent of 1 inch, right indent of 1 inch, left alignment	5 points, 10 points of space before paragraphs, 5 points of space after paragraphs	1.94 inches, left alignment
Rule With Space After	Tw Cent MT Condensed Extra Bold, 4 points, thick underline	Left alignment	5 points, 30 points of space after paragraphs	2.94 inches, left alignment
Rule With Space Before	Tw Cent MT Condensed Extra Bold, 4 points, thick underline	Left alignment	5 points, 15 points of space before paragraphs	2.94 inches, left alignment
Order Form	Tw Cent MT, medium, 10 points	Left alignment	12 points	None

Creating the Front Cover

The front cover sets the mood for the entire document. Publisher's WordArt tool is used to create a unique headline treatment.

Draw the Background

1. Draw a box on the right panel. The box should measure 2.63 inches wide by 7.5 inches deep. It should align with the ruler guides.

2. Assign a black fill.

Extend the background of a picture. By placing the photograph on a black box, you are merging its edges (which are also black) with the larger background. The result is a much more dramatic presentation, where the single wine glass stands out against a stark backdrop.

Insert a Photograph

1 Insert the picture Ph02262j.jpg from Publisher's Clip Gallery. You can easily find the image by searching on the keyword *wine*.

2 Scale both the width and the height of the picture to 70 percent.

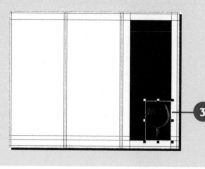

3 Align the picture with the right and bottom edges of the black box.

Add the Title

1 Draw a WordArt frame measuring 2.8 inches wide by 1.25 inches deep.

2 Type the text *A shared discovery is a precious gift.*

3 Assign the following WordArt formats:

- Arch Up (Curve)
- Tw Cent Condensed Extra Bold font
- Best Fit size
- Letter Justify
- White characters

4 Close the WordArt dialog box. Select the WordArt frame.

Use WordArt to animate headlines. Instead of printing headlines as straight, horizontal lines of text, consider using WordArt to flow the text into unique shapes. Here, placing the headline along a curve creates a sense of movement. And because the curve mimics the general shape of the wine glass, the WordArt effect also sets up an interesting visual interaction between the text and the picture.

Add the Title *(continued)*

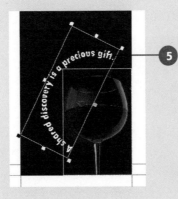

5. Rotate the WordArt frame by 64 degrees and position it to surround the wine glass.

Add a Logo

1. Draw a text frame measuring 1.5 inches wide by 0.5 inch deep.

2. Type the text *New World Wines,* and format the text and text frame as:

- Tw Cent Condensed Extra Bold, 12 points
- White
- Transparent fill

3. Draw a clip-art frame measuring 0.25 inch wide by 0.25 inch deep. It should align with the left edge of the text frame containing the store name.

4. Insert the image Sy00905_.wmf. You can easily find the symbol by searching on the keyword *logo.*

Use picture frame margins to resize artwork. When creating the logo for New World Wines, it is best to draw the picture frame at 0.25 inch square. Doing so allows you to easily align the picture frame with the text frame. If you need to further resize the picture, just create picture frame margins. The larger the picture frame margin, the smaller the picture.

Add a Logo *(continued)*

5 Recolor the picture to make it white.

6 Create picture frame margins of 0.04 inch for all four sides.

7 Group the two elements together, and position them at the 0.75-inch mark on the vertical ruler and the 8.13-inch (8 1/8-inch) mark on the horizontal ruler.

Creating the Return Address

The center panel on a three-fold brochure typically contains the address information. You'll leave most of the panel blank in anticipation of the mailing address, but you should take this opportunity to create the return address. You can save time by editing a duplicate of the logo design you just created.

Copy and Reformat the Logo

1 Copy the logo from the first panel.

2 Restore the clip-art image to its original color—black.

3 Change the font color to black.

Use Publisher's mail merge feature to address the brochures. You can address these brochures by using Publisher's mail merge feature. Simply create a text frame where a mailing label would normally be positioned, and then insert field codes from an address list you've created. When you print the document, Publisher will print multiple copies of the brochure, each copy containing a different entry from the address list.

 For more information about Publisher's mail merge functions, see Chapter 13.

Insert Address Information

1 Draw a text frame measuring 1.5 inches wide by 0.5 inch deep. The top of this text frame should align with the bottom of the text frame containing the store name.

2 Enter the text shown in the following illustration, and format it as follows:

3 Group the text frame together with the logo, and use the Rotate Right command to rotate the group 90 degrees to the right.

4 Position the group at the upper right-hand corner of the middle panel, aligned with the horizontal ruler guide and the blue column guide.

Creating the Second Panel

When the brochure is finished and folded, the left panel becomes the second panel, because it is the "page" that the reader will see immediately after the front cover. It is therefore the best position for general, introductory text.

Insert Introductory Text

1 Draw a text frame on the left panel that measures 3.47 inches wide by 8.3 inches deep. The text frame should align with the top and bottom blue row guides and the left and right blue column guides.

2 In the Text Frame Properties dialog box, create margins of 0.25 inch on all four sides. Turn off text wrap.

Three-Fold Brochure

For the text of this brochure, see Appendix B.

Why don't the rules appear in my publication? To have the rules appear, you must press the Tab key. This forces the current text insertion point to the right margin of the text frame and applies the underlining to the width of the text column.

Insert Introductory Text *(continued)*

3 Insert the introductory text, and format it as shown in the following illustration.

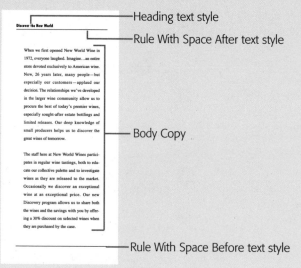

————Heading text style

————Rule With Space After text style

————Body Copy

————Rule With Space Before text style

4 Place the text insertion point in the first Body Copy paragraph, and add a custom drop cap with the following format:

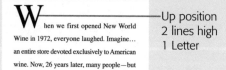

————Up position
2 lines high
1 Letter

Insert Clip Art

1 Temporarily ungroup the logo on the first panel, and make a copy of the clip-art picture. (Be sure to regroup the logo.)

2 Restore the picture to its original colors.

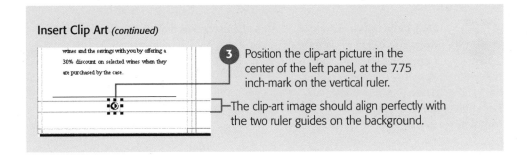

wines and the savings with you by offering a
30% discount on selected wines when they
are purchased by the case.

3 Position the clip-art picture in the center of the left panel, at the 7.75 inch-mark on the vertical ruler.

The clip-art image should align perfectly with the two ruler guides on the background.

Use special typographic characters. When you create this text in your word processing program, you should carefully proofread the text and insert the appropriate typographic characters. This project requires you to insert three different typographic characters.

- You should use a true em dash when separating phrases in a sentence—like this.

- You should insert a true ellipsis (which is different than three periods in a row).

- Finally, you should insert the letter *u* that includes a diacritical mark (called an umlaut) for the name of one of the wine varietals, as shown below.

Gewürztraminer

Creating the Interior of the Brochure

The interior of the brochure contains descriptions of the wines for sale, as well as an order form. By duplicating the text frame from the second panel, you can quickly insert the descriptive text.

Insert Descriptive Text

1 Select the text frame and the clip-art image on the left panel, group them together, and copy them to the Clipboard.

2 Insert a new page.

3 Paste two copies of the group, and position them in the left and center panel.

4 Select all of the text in the left text frame, and insert the descriptive copy for Stonehill Vineyards.

5 Duplicate the formatting from the second panel as follows:

- Assign the Heading text style to the first paragraph.

- Assign the Rule With Space After text style to the following blank line. Remember to press the tab key to have the rule appear.

- Assign the Body Copy text style to the next three paragraphs.

- Create a custom drop cap for the first Body Copy paragraph.

Do I have to re-create the drop cap effect each time I apply it? No. Publisher stores the custom drop cap you created earlier in the Drop Cap dialog box. You can apply it as many times as you like within this publication only.

Insert Descriptive Text *(continued)*

6 Assign the following text styles to the remaining text:

Rating: 87 ————— Rule Above Rating text style
————— Rating text style

7 Repeat steps 4 through 6 with the text frame in the center panel, inserting the descriptive copy for Joshua Creek.

Fine-Tuning Text Formats

1 Place the text insertion point immediately before the word *Heritage* in the heading on the left panel.

2 Insert a tab to align the text at the right edge of the frame.

3 Highlight the wine style and vintage, and change the formatting as follows:

Stonehill Vineyards Heritage 1994 ——— Tw Cent MT, italic

4 Repeat steps 1 through 3 for the phrase *Gewürztraminer 1996* in the center panel.

Creating the Order Form

You can create this complex order form within a single table frame. The custom borders organize the information into easily understood sections. And minor adjustments to the text formatting highlight section headings.

Insert Text into a Table

1 On the right panel, draw a table frame measuring 2.63 inches wide by 7.5 inches deep. It should align with the green ruler guides.

2 Set up the table with 20 rows and 4 columns. Choose the None style.

3 Holding down the Shift key, reposition the division between columns as indicated below.

The 8.94-inch (8 15/16-inch) mark on the horizontal ruler

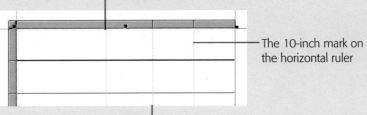

The 10-inch mark on the horizontal ruler

The 9.5-inch mark on the horizontal ruler

4 Select the entire table and assign the following formatting attributes:

@ In the Cell Properties dialog box, set cell margins at 0 for the top, left, and right sides. Leave the bottom margin value at 0.04.

@ In the Border Style dialog box, choose a hairline rule for the bottom and center horizontal sides of each cell.

@ Use the Order Form text style.

@ On the Format menu, align the text at the bottom of each cell.

Create order forms that can be completed by hand. If you expect your readers to fill out an order form by hand, leave enough space for their entries. Check boxes, which need only a simple mark, require the least amount of space. But fill-in-the-blank items, such as name and street address, should accommodate the average person's handwriting and names of varying length. Ask yourself if someone named Alexander Rodchenko living in Worthington Springs, Florida, could fit his name and address into your order form. If you cram a complex order form into a tiny table frame, be prepared to have illegible answers returned to you.

Insert Text into a Table *(continued)*

5 Enter the text as shown in the following illustration; change the formatting as indicated:

Order Form

Item	Quantity	Price Per Case	Total
Stonehill Vineyards Heritage 1994		$149	
Joshua Creek Gewürztraminer 1996		$105	

	Subtotal:
	Tax:
	Shipping:
	Total:

Delivery

Name:

Address:

City, State, ZIP:

Daytime Phone:

Payment

Payment Method: ☐ Check ☐ Mastercard ☐ Visa ⊙ American Express

Credit Card #:

Expiration Date:

Signature:

I certify that I am at least 21 years of age.

Select the rows containing category headings. Merge the cells together. Increase the size to 10 points. Boldface and center each of the headings. Change the custom border at the bottom of the cell to 1 point.

Select the row 2 and the cells containing the actual prices, and center the text.

Select the cells in the intersection of rows 5 through 8 and column 3; align the text at the right.

Select the cells in the intersection of rows 5 through 8 and columns 1, 2, and 3. Remove the borders.

Select the cell containing the word *Mastercard*, and merge it with the last cell in the row. Select the cell containing the phrase *American Express*, and merge it with the last cell in the row.

Insert the open square bullet, from the Wingdings 2 font, immediately before each payment method.

Select the last row and merge the cells together. Italicize the text. Align the text at the top of the cell. Remove the border from the bottom of the cell.

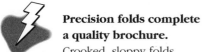

Precision folds complete a quality brochure.

Crooked, sloppy folds can ruin the appearance of a folded brochure. Use one of these methods to guarantee crisp, straight creases in your three-fold brochure:

@ Purchase special prescored paper from stationery stores or paper companies (such as Paper Direct). To fold your brochures, simply follow an existing crease in the paper.

@ Create a guide (also called a template) to help you fold the brochures manually. Draw a table frame that completely covers an 8.5-by-11-inch page in Landscape orientation. Divide the table into three columns and one row. Format the table grid with a 1-point rule. When printed, this document will show you the exact location of each fold.

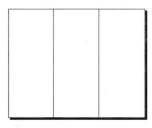

Printing and Folding the Brochure

The two different ways to fold a three-fold brochure are referred to by the shape that the edge of the paper makes. A Z-fold is an accordion fold, which is unsuitable for a self-mailer because the left and right edges of the folded document are open. A C-fold is the correct choice for a self-mailer because the second fold encloses the first fold so that only one edge has to be sealed for mailing.

Z-fold   C-fold

Print the Brochure

1 In the Print dialog box, turn off crop marks. Click OK.

Copy and Fold the Brochure

1 Copy page 2 of the publication on the back of page 1.

2 Fold the publication in a C-fold so that the brochure can be taped shut.

March 2, 1998
Volume 8, Issue 3

Broad*sides*

An inside look at architecture and interior design at Broadside Associates

Broadside Associates Acquires Integrated Space

By Trisha Armstead

On January 30th of this year, Broadside Associates acquired Integrated Space, a cutting-edge interior design firm located here in Redwood City, California. The eight-year-old company grossed over $7 million in commissions last year and has projected billings of $11 million this year. That success is directly attributable to Dick Hunter—the firm's founder and current President.

Hunter established his reputation for innovation with a series of boardroom and executive-suite projects that go beyond utilitarian issues and use interior design to establish the client's corporate identity. He furnished an office with Frank Gehry cardboard chairs for the president of International Corrugated. And in what is perhaps his best known commission, the boardroom at Ridder Labs, Hunter created an eye-popping glass environment inspired by the retorts, condensation coils, and Erlenmeyer flasks found in a laboratory.

Known as something of a visionary in the industry, Hunter's most recent commissions tran-

Dick Hunter of Integrated Space

scend aesthetics and attempt to create a truly beneficial workplace for a company's employees. In recent years, Integrated

Space has focused on creating healthier office environments for both new and existing buildings. When asked about this latest crusade, Hunter answered bluntly, "Research has proven that improved ventilation systems, natural light simulations, and ergonomic furniture can substantially reduce absenteeism and significantly increase productivity. Ignoring the office environment is bad business."

CEO Logan Broadside summed up Broadside Associates' strategy in these words.

(Continued on page 2)

Hometown Boy Does Good

As part of a state funded sweat equity project, Lewis Balthazar, a senior designer here at Broadside Associates, recently helped restore a small 6-story apartment building. Coincidentally, the building is located in Shorehaven, the part of town where Balthazar himself grew up.

Balthazar was involved in every aspect of the design and construction. His innovative floor plan brings light and a de-

ceptive sense of space to these small, 600-square-foot apartments. What were once cold-water railroad flats are now modern duplex apartments.

Though I'm extremely proud of the many commercial buildings I've designed, this project gave me a unique sense of personal satisfaction. I feel I've given something back to the community that nourished me."—Donald Neuman

Newsletter

Newsletters are a great promotional tool for small businesses. You can use newsletters to provide valuable information to customers, such as the impending release of a new product or a change in company strategy. In this project, you'll learn how to structure the first page of a newsletter.

Preparing the Publication

Newsletters come in all shapes and sizes. This newsletter takes advantage of the low cost and availability of standard letter-sized paper. The design is based on a three-column grid, which gives you the flexibility to size stories according to their importance. Notice that the lead story spans all three columns, while the secondary lead occupies only two columns.

Set Up the Page

1 Start a new, blank full-page document.

2 Select the printer you'll use and confirm that the current paper size is 8.5 by 11 inches, in Portrait orientation.

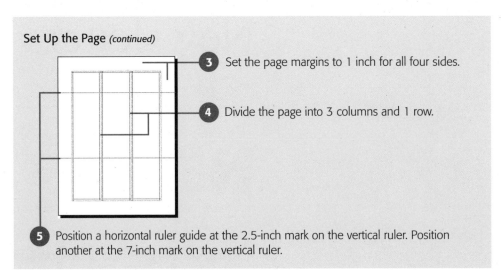

3 Set the page margins to 1 inch for all four sides.

4 Divide the page into 3 columns and 1 row.

5 Position a horizontal ruler guide at the 2.5-inch mark on the vertical ruler. Position another at the 7-inch mark on the vertical ruler.

Use line spacing consistently. In this project, many text elements are formatted with different point sizes, but all of the elements appearing in the body of a story—including body copy, captions, and bylines—are formatted with the same amount of line spacing. Consistent line spacing helps you align the baselines of text across columns for a professional look.

Creating Text Styles

Newsletters typically contain many different text styles for elements such as bylines, headlines, photo captions, and table of contents entries. The following table summarizes the text styles you should create for this project.

Newsletter Text Styles				
Text Style	**Character Type and Size**	**Indents and Lists**	**Line Spacing**	**Tabs**
Body Copy	Bell MT, 10.5 points	First line indent of	13 points 1 pica, justified alignment	None
Byline	Franklin Gothic Book, 10 points	Left alignment	13 points	None
Caption	Franklin Gothic Book, italic, 8 points	Left alignment	13 points	None
First Paragraph	Bell MT, 10.5 points	Justified alignment	13 points (no first line indent)	None
Headline 1	Bell MT, bold, 32 points	Left alignment	32 points	None

Text Style	Character Type and Size	Indents and Lists	Line Spacing	Tabs
Headline 2	Bell MT, bold, 24 points	Left alignment	24 points	None
TOC Entry	Franklin Gothic Book, 9 points	Left alignment	13 points	None
TOC Number	Franklin Gothic Book, 9 points	Left alignment	13 points	None

Creating a Template

Magazines, newspapers, and newsletters are published in cycles; any publication issued on a regular basis (daily, weekly, monthly, bimonthly, or quarterly) is called a periodical. The structure of a periodical involves two kinds of repeating elements, which together should be saved as a template:

@ Elements that repeat on every page, such as page numbers and running headers and footers, and are placed on the background of a publication.

@ Elements that appear in every issue, such as the logo, the date, and the table of contents. The volume number, date, and words in the table of contents change from issue to issue, but the placement and style of these elements remain consistent.

Perfecting both the appearance and the placement of these elements in a template streamlines the production of subsequent issues of the publication.

Create the Masthead

1. Draw a text frame that spans columns 1 and 2. Extend the frame to the pink column division between rows 2 and 3. The text frame should align with the top row guide and the horizontal ruler guide at the 2.5-inch mark on the vertical ruler.

2. Create left and top text frame margins of 0. Create a bottom text frame margin of 0.04 inch, and a right text frame margin of 0.07 inch.

3. In the Text Frame Properties dialog box, turn off text wrap.

Create the Masthead *(continued)*

4 Type the publication name *Broadsides*. Format the text as indicated:

@ Best Fit copyfitting option

@ Vertical alignment at the bottom of frame

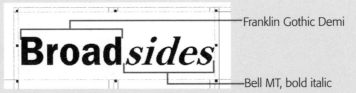
Franklin Gothic Demi

Bell MT, bold italic

5 Starting at the top row guide, draw a second text frame overlapping the existing text frame. It should span column 1 and measure 0.4 inch deep.

6 Leave the top, bottom, and right text frame margins set to 0.04 inch. Change the left margin to 0.07 inch.

7 Type the text shown in the following illustration and format it as follows:

Franklin Gothic Demi, 8 points

8 Starting at the 2.25-inch mark on the vertical ruler, draw another text frame overlapping the main text frame. It should span columns 2 and 3 and measure 0.25 inch deep.

9 Leave the top, bottom, and right text frame margins set to 0.04 inch. Change the left margin to 0.07 inch.

10 Type the text shown in the following illustration and format it as follows:

Franklin Gothic Book, 8 points

Character spacing with expanded kerning of 0.6 point

Why should I be concerned about small margin values such as 0.07 inch? Type is normally measured in points. There are 72 points to an inch. So what appears to be a small measurement, such as 0.07 inch, is actually a significant value when it influences the size or placement of text. In this project, increasing the left text frame margin to 0.07 inch correctly aligns the masthead's text elements along the left side.

Repeat elements of the masthead in the header and footer. Once you've created the masthead, you can easily generate a header and footer for subsequent pages in the publication. To create a header, simply copy the *Broadsides* text frame to the background, resize it to 1 column wide by 0.5 inch deep, and position it at the top of the page. Because you created this element using the Best Fit copyfitting option, Publisher will automatically adjust the point size of text based on the size of the text frame, as shown below.

Broad*sides*

To create the footer, copy the issue number and volume text frame to the background, resize it to 3 columns wide by 0.25 inch deep, and position it at the bottom of the page.

Create the Table of Contents

1 Starting at the top row guide, draw a table frame that spans column 3. The bottom of the table frame should align with the horizontal ruler guide at the 2.5-inch mark on the vertical ruler.

2 Create a table with 2 columns, 5 rows, and a style of None.

3 Enter the text shown in the following illustration and format it as follows:

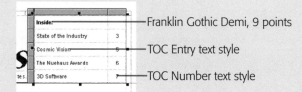

———Franklin Gothic Demi, 9 points

———TOC Entry text style

———TOC Number text style

Create Rules for the Masthead and Table of Contents

1 Select rows 2 through 5 in the table containing the table of contents. In the Border Style dialog box, format the row divisions only with a hairline rule.

Inside:	
State of the Industry	3
Cosmic Vision	5
The Nuehaus Awards	6
3D Software	7

2 Select row 1 in the table. Format the bottom of the row with a 1-point rule.

3 Using the Line tool, draw a 2-point black line that aligns with the horizontal ruler guide at the 2.5-inch mark on the vertical ruler and that spans all 3 columns.

4 Draw a 1-point black line that aligns with the bottom pink page guide and that spans all 3 columns.

For the text of this newsletter, see Appendix B.

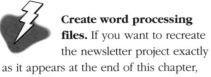

Create word processing files. If you want to recreate the newsletter project exactly as it appears at the end of this chapter, you must create two files—one for each story—using your favorite word processing application. Enter the text, and follow these guidelines.

@ As you create the text, press Enter after each paragraph, but don't add extra line spaces. Don't press Tab to insert paragraph indents. The Body Copy text style creates indents.

@ Type only one space after a period or colon.

@ Run the spelling checker and proofread the text before importing it.

@ Save the files with names that will be easy to identify, such as *Interior* and *Hometown*.

Save the Newsletter As a Template

1 Choose Save As from the File menu. The Save As dialog box appears.

2 Turn on the Template check box.

3 Turn on Save Preview to save a thumbnail version of the file.

4 Enter a descriptive filename, such as *Newsletter*, in the File Name text box.

Create a New Publication from the Template

1 Choose New on the File menu.

2 On the Existing Publications tab of the Catalog dialog box, click the Templates button.

3 Open the Newsletter template. The file that Publisher brings up is not the template but a copy of it called *Unsaved Publication*.

Importing the Newsletter Text

Microsoft Publisher automatically inserts white space, called a gutter, between column guides, so the default margins of a text frame are unnecessary. Before drawing text frames, change the default text frame margin values.

Set Default Text Frame Margins

1 Select the Text tool, but don't draw a text frame.

2 In the Text Frame Properties dialog box, create a left, right, and top margin of 0. Set the bottom frame margin to 0.03 inch.

Select text in the overflow area. When you use the Ctrl-A keyboard shortcut or the Highlight Entire Story command on the Edit menu, you're selecting all of the text in the story—even if it is temporarily stored in the overflow area. Doing so allows you to assign the correct text style to the entire story, even though the text in the overflow area remains hidden.

Insert the Lead Story

1 Draw a text frame that spans all 3 columns. The frame should align with the horizontal ruler guide at the 2.5-inch mark on the vertical ruler and measure 1 inch deep.

2 Type or insert the text shown in the following illustration and format it as follows:

- @ Headline 1 text style
- @ Vertical alignment at the bottom of frame

An inside look at architecture and interior design at Broadside Associates | 3D Software | 7

**Broadside Associates
Acquires Integrated Space**

Use Shift-Enter to force a line break after the word *Associates*.

3 Starting at the 3.5-inch mark on the vertical ruler, draw a text frame that spans all 3 columns and measures 0.25 inch deep. This frame should abut the text frame containing the headline.

4 Type or insert the text in the following illustration and format it as follows:

- @ Byline text style
- @ Vertical alignment in the center of frame

Acquires I

By Trisha Armstead

5 Starting at the 3.75-inch mark on the vertical ruler, draw a text frame that spans column 1 and extends to the bottom row guide.

6 Insert the lead story. When Publisher asks if you want to autoflow the text, click No.

7 Using the Ctrl-A keyboard shortcut, highlight all of the text and assign the Body Copy text style.

8 Place the insertion point in the first paragraph and change the text style to First Paragraph.

Draw a series of text frames. Clicking the Text tool while holding down the Ctrl key keeps the Text tool active, allowing you to draw a series of text frames without having to choose the Text tool repeatedly. When you want to return to the normal work mode, select the Pointer tool.

Why should I align headlines at the bottom of the text frame? Readers are sensitive to small amounts of white space. By aligning a headline at the bottom of a text frame, you are creating a strong visual relationship between the headline and the text that follows it.

Insert the Lead Story *(continued)*

9 Draw two more text frames in columns 2 and 3. Position the top of the text frames at the 3.75-inch mark on the vertical ruler. Align the bottom of each text frame with the 6.88-inch (6 7/8-inch) mark on the vertical ruler.

10 Connect the text frame in column 1 to the text frame in column 2. Then connect the text frame in column 2 to the text frame in column 3.

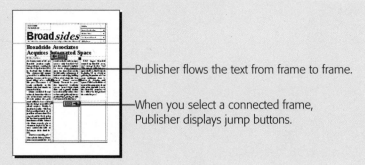

—Publisher flows the text from frame to frame.

—When you select a connected frame, Publisher displays jump buttons.

Insert the Second Lead

1 Starting at the horizontal ruler guide located at the 7-inch mark on the vertical ruler, draw a text frame that spans columns 2 and 3 and measures 0.52 inch deep.

2 Type or insert the text shown in the following illustration and format it as follows:

@ Headline 2 text style

@ Vertical alignment at the bottom of frame

3 Starting at the 7.52-inch mark on the vertical ruler, draw a text frame that spans column 2 and extends down to the bottom row guide.

4 Duplicate this frame and move it to column 3.

Insert the Second Lead *(continued)*

5 Link the two text frames together.

6 Insert the second story and format it as follows:

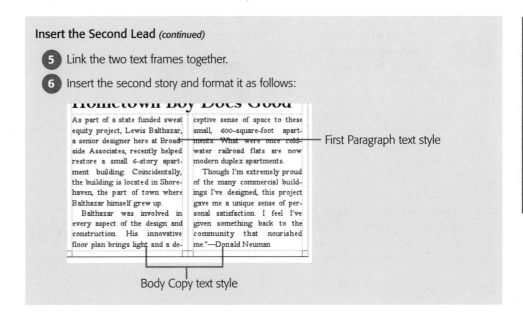

Hometown Boy Does Good ———— First Paragraph text style

Body Copy text style

Inserting and Editing a Photograph

Publisher's Clip Art Gallery contains a number of business-oriented portraits. You'll have to make a few minor adjustments to the size and position of the photo to integrate it into the layout.

Insert, Position, and Crop the Picture

1 Without drawing a frame, insert the picture Ph01617j.jpg from Publisher's Clip Art Gallery. You can easily find the picture by searching on the keyword *businessman*.

2 Position the picture in column 2 at the 3.75-inch mark on the vertical ruler. Align the right side of the picture with the right column guide for column 2.

3 Using the Crop Picture tool, select the left center handle and reduce the picture's width to the width of column 2.

Speed up printing times by trimming portions of a picture in an image editing program. Publisher's cropping function doesn't actually trim away parts of the picture; it merely hides them. Although the hidden part of the picture won't print, your printer still has to process the information, which slows down the print job. This performance hit can be significant if your document contains lots of scanned or bitmapped pictures. To speed up printing time, cut away unwanted portions of a photograph using your scanning or image editing software.

Insert, Position, and Crop the Picture *(continued)*

4 Using the Crop Picture tool, select the bottom center handle and reduce the picture's height to 1.96 inches, making it a perfect square.

Fine-Tuning the Layout

Whenever you create a complex layout, you must take the time to review and adjust the various elements. At this stage of the project, there are two design problems:

@ The photograph isn't identified with a caption.

@ The second story should be separated from the main story with a rule.

Insert a Caption

1 Draw a text frame that spans column 2. The frame should abut the bottom of the picture frame and should measure 0.25 inch deep.

2 Type the text shown in the following illustration and format it as follows:

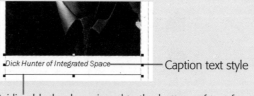

Dick Hunter of Integrated Space ——— Caption text style

Hairline black rule assigned to the bottom of text frame

Fix typographic problems like a pro. Professional production editors always try to fix typographic problems that can occur in a complex layout, such as widows and orphans. In this story, a ladder (multiple consecutive hyphens) forms a distracting pattern. You can use the same basic techniques professionals do:

- Add or delete words.

- Alter the character spacing, specifically the tracking values.

- Use Ctrl-Enter to force a line break without starting a new paragraph.

- Change the hyphenation zone.

 Should I create a Continued On text style? No. Publisher automatically creates a Continued-On text style when you assign the Continued On Page property to a text frame and link it to a text frame on a different page. Publisher always creates Continued-On text with a default style: Times New Roman, 8 points, italic, right alignment.

Draw a Rule

1 Draw a 2-point black rule spanning columns 2 and 3. The rule should align with the horizontal ruler guide at the 7-inch mark on the vertical ruler.

Fine-Tuning the Text

Once you've finalized the layout, you can turn your attention to the particulars of the text. You should always use Publisher's spelling checker and carefully proofread the document for sense. In addition, you should make adjustments so that the copy fits the layout. At this point in the project, there are two noticeable problems:

- Text remains in the overflow area of the "Integrated Space" lead story.

- There are four consecutive hyphens in the lead story.

Jump Text to Another Page

1 Insert a second page in the publication.

2 Draw a text frame anywhere on the second page.

3 Return to page 1, and select the third text frame of the lead story.

4 In the Text Frame Properties dialog box, select the Include Continued On Page option.

5 Link this text frame to the text frame on page 2. Publisher automatically inserts a Continued notice into the text frame on page 1.

6 In the Text Style dialog box, change the font of the Continued-On Text style to Franklin Gothic Book.

environment is bad business."
CEO Logan Broadside summed up Broadside Associates' strategy in these words.
(Continued on page 2)

Publisher updates the appearance of this Continued notice (and any other Continued notices in the publication) with the new text style format.

Use a photocopier as a replacement for a printing press. Because this newsletter was designed to fit on a standard 8.5-by-11-inch page, it can be reproduced easily by a local copy shop or graphics service bureau. So instead of paying a premium for offset printing, you can create a large number of newsletters for pennies a copy. If you do decide to use a photocopier as a replacement printing press, prepare the file in one of the following ways:

@ Send an electronic version of the file (in either PUB or PostScript format) to the copy shop or service bureau. Printing directly to a photocopier from a computer network delivers the highest quality output.

@ Print a reproduction-quality version of the newsletter on your desktop laser printer. Consult with your copy shop concerning the resolution of bitmapped images. You may find that reducing the halftone resolution of your laser printer output results in cleaner, crisper photocopies.

For more information about working with a commercial printing service, see Chapter 17. For more information about changing halftone resolution, see Chapter 16.

Adjust Line Breaks

1 Zoom in on the second paragraph in the lead story. You should see four consecutive hyphens as shown in the following illustration.

> rectly attributable to Dick Hunter—the firm's founder and current President.
>   Hunter established his reputation for innovation with a series of boardroom and executive-suite projects that go beyond utilitarian issues and use

2 Place the text insertion point before the word *reputation*, and press Shift-Enter to force a line break without starting a new paragraph.

3 Check the entire story again for too many consecutive hyphens or other typographic problems.

Completing the Newsletter

Print Page 1 of the Newsletter

1 Open the File menu and choose Print.

2 Select the Current Page option.

3 Turn off Print Crop Marks.

Microsoft Draw 98

Microsoft Draw 98 is a separate drawing program that is shipped with several Microsoft applications, including Microsoft Publisher. Publisher's drawing tools and Draw's drawing tools work identically—meaning that you select a tool and drag to create an object. However, Draw employs a new, more intuitive interface. For example, most of the program's functions are available from easy-to-access toolbars and flyout menus. In addition, Draw offers more advanced drawing functions, including:

Access Draw as an OLE application. You can also insert a new drawing using the Insert Object dialog box (found on the Insert menu). Choose Microsoft Draw 98 Drawing from the Object Type list box. The Object Type list box contains an index of all the OLE applications installed on your system.

For more information about OLE, see Chapter 11.

@ AutoShapes, a wide variety of shapes and lines

@ The capability to create and edit free-form shapes

@ A sophisticated WordArt tool that includes a gallery of preformatted designs

@ More robust formatting options, including new fill types, a wider choice of line attributes, custom shadows, and three-dimensional effects

@ The capability to change the contents of an imported picture

Although Draw is not a part of Publisher, you can access it as though it were through a feature called OLE (Object Linking and Embedding). Any drawing you create in Draw is really an object embedded in a Publisher document. When you save the Publisher document, you also save the embedded object.

Why don't I see the New Drawing option on the Picture command's flyout menu? You did not install Draw when you installed Publisher. Run the Publisher Setup program, choose the Custom installation, and select the Office Art option.

Open Draw

1 To predetermine the size of the Draw object, draw a picture frame. Or if you want to create a new drawing at the default size, proceed to step 2.

2 Choose Picture on the Insert menu. On the cascading menu, select New Drawing. The Microsoft Draw 98 application appears, replacing Publisher's menus and toolbars. A gray frame appears around the Draw picture.

Draw uses Microsoft Office–style menus and formatting toolbars, which replace Publisher's menus and toolbars. Toolbars, such as the Format toolbar shown here, can be docked at the top or bottom of the work area.

Resize handles indicate that an object or a group of objects is selected.

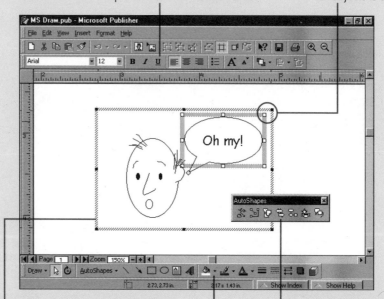

The gray frame indicates that the Draw object is active and can be edited.

Draw also includes specialized toolbars, such as the AutoShapes toolbar.

The Draw toolbar, docked at the bottom of the work area, contains standard functions, such as a rotate tool and quick access to frequently used formatting commands like Fill Color and Line Style. It also contains tools to create WordArt objects, custom shadows, and three-dimensional effects.

Creating AutoShapes

AutoShapes are drawn objects that *look* similar to Publisher's drawn objects. But AutoShapes have built-in functions that make them much more powerful than Publisher's drawn object, as shown below.

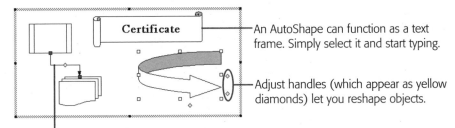

An AutoShape can function as a text frame. Simply select it and start typing.

Adjust handles (which appear as yellow diamonds) let you reshape objects.

You can draw special connectors between shapes that remain attached when you rearrange the shapes.

Microsoft Draw 98 AutoShapes		
Shape	**Description**	**Sample**
Lines	6 tools to create straight lines, lines with arrowheads, curved lines, free-form shapes, and scribbles.	
Connectors	9 tools to create straight, bent, or curved lines that connect two shapes. Connectors attach to special points (shown in blue) on the outlines of shapes and remain attached when you move the shapes.	

Microsoft Draw 98 AutoShapes *(continued)*		
Shape	**Description**	**Sample**
Basic shapes	28 tools to draw geometric and picture shapes.	
Block arrows	24 tools to draw arrow shapes.	
Flow chart	24 tools to draw standard flow chart symbols. Publisher identifies each tool with the function it normally represents, such as Predefined Process, Or, Collate, Stored Data, and Terminator.	
Stars and banners	16 tools to draw scrolls, banners, simple stars, and starbursts.	
Callouts	20 tools to create speech and thought balloons and text frames with built-in pointers.	

 Why aren't the curved lines and shapes in my drawing smooth when I print them? Draw simulates curves with small line segments. At larger sizes and with heavy line weights, the line segments become more noticeable. If you have drawn a curve or a free-form shape, you can add more points (creating smaller line segments) to smooth the curve.

Create an AutoShape

1 Open Draw.

2 Select a category from the AutoShapes toolbar. On the cascading menu, select the shape you want to create.

3 Within the Draw frame (not shown), drag to draw an AutoShape.

Use menu commands to create a WordArt object. You can invoke the WordArt Gallery by selecting WordArt from Draw's Insert menu.

Combine multiple WordArt objects. As you can see in the following illustration, you can create multiple WordArt objects within a Draw picture frame. Each word or phrase is a separate object. However, when you exit Draw and return to your Publisher document, Publisher treats the collection of objects as a single drawing.

Creating a WordArt Object

Draw offers a WordArt tool that is similar to, but more powerful than, Publisher's WordArt tool. WordArt objects created in Draw are treated like any other shape. The sophisticated formatting options available for AutoShapes are also available for WordArt objects.

Create and Format a WordArt Element in Draw

1 Open Draw.

2 On the Draw toolbar, click the Insert WordArt tool (shown below). The WordArt Gallery appears.

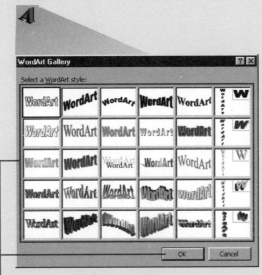

3 Choose one of the 30 designs in the WordArt gallery. Don't worry if the effect isn't exactly what you want; you can easily change the formatting attributes later.

4 Click OK. The Edit WordArt Text dialog box appears.

Why can't I enter a point size of my choosing into the Size box in the Edit WordArt Text dialog box? Within the Edit WordArt Text dialog box, you must choose one of the predetermined point sizes from the Size drop-down list. You cannot type a point size of your choosing. However, once you have clicked OK, you can use the resize handles on the WordArt object to adjust the size.

Can I use a Special Effects dialog box to adjust the angle and arc of a Draw WordArt shape? No. Instead of using a separate dialog box to adjust the angle or arc of a WordArt shape, you drag the special Adjust handle that appears on the boundary of a Draw WordArt object.

Create and Format a WordArt Element in Draw *(continued)*

5 Type a word or phrase in the Text box.

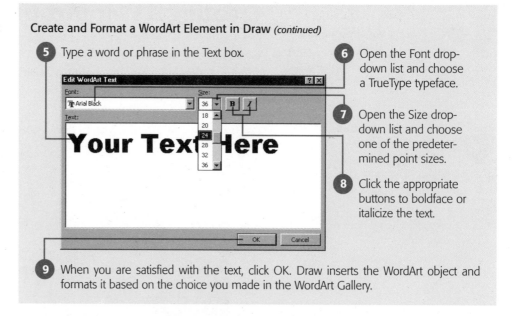

6 Open the Font drop-down list and choose a TrueType typeface.

7 Open the Size drop-down list and choose one of the predetermined point sizes.

8 Click the appropriate buttons to boldface or italicize the text.

9 When you are satisfied with the text, click OK. Draw inserts the WordArt object and formats it based on the choice you made in the WordArt Gallery.

Resize or Reshape a WordArt Object in Draw

1 Select the WordArt element you want to change. Resize and Adjust handles appear around the WordArt element, and the WordArt toolbar appears.

To change the size of the WordArt object, drag a Resize handle.

To fine-tune the shape of the WordArt object, drag an Adjust handle.

Why can't I see the WordArt toolbar? You may have inadvertently closed the WordArt toolbar. To open it again, choose Toolbars on the View menu. From the cascading menu, select WordArt. Alternatively, you may have docked the WordArt toolbar. Look for it at the top of the screen (above the Office Standard toolbar). Double-click the toolbar's Move icon (the double gray bars at the left) to create a floating palette.

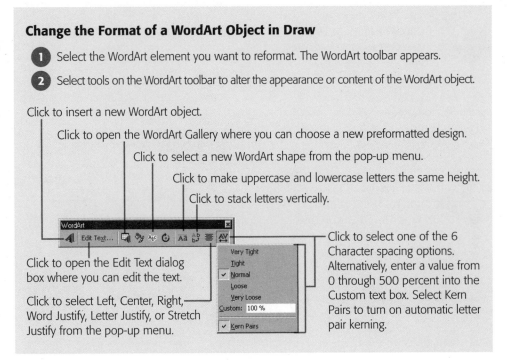

Change the Format of a WordArt Object in Draw

1 Select the WordArt element you want to reformat. The WordArt toolbar appears.

2 Select tools on the WordArt toolbar to alter the appearance or content of the WordArt object.

Click to insert a new WordArt object.

Click to open the WordArt Gallery where you can choose a new preformatted design.

Click to select a new WordArt shape from the pop-up menu.

Click to make uppercase and lowercase letters the same height.

Click to stack letters vertically.

Click to open the Edit Text dialog box where you can edit the text.

Click to select Left, Center, Right, Word Justify, Letter Justify, or Stretch Justify from the pop-up menu.

Click to select one of the 6 Character spacing options. Alternatively, enter a value from 0 through 500 percent into the Custom text box. Select Kern Pairs to turn on automatic letter pair kerning.

Very Tight
Tight
✓ Normal
Loose
Very Loose
Custom: 100 %
✓ Kern Pairs

Alternate access to formatting dialog boxes. You can also access all of Draw's formatting dialog boxes (for colors and lines, size, position, shadow settings, and three-dimensional settings) by choosing the appropriate command on the Format menu.

Formatting Options

The formatting options in Draw are much more powerful than the equivalent tools in Publisher. As an example, in Publisher you can fill an object with a two-color gradient. In Draw you can fill objects with a one-color, two-color, or multi-color gradient. Draw also provides some unique tools, such as the capability to customize a shadow effect, extrude an object into the third dimension, or fill an object with a picture.

Choose colors in Draw that will match the colors you use in Publisher.

There is only one way to guarantee that the colors you choose in Draw will match the colors you use in Publisher. You must use custom colors, and specify exact RGB (or HSL) values.

Why can't I choose a scheme color for an object in a Draw picture?

You cannot access Publisher's color scheme within Draw. However, once you have closed the Draw application, you can use Publisher's Recolor Object command to assign a scheme color to the object.

Choosing Colors in Draw

1 Select the AutoShape or WordArt object you want to color.

2 Select the Fill Color or the Line Color tool, and choose one of 40 basic colors from the drop-down palette. Alternatively, click More Fill Colors to open the Colors dialog box.

3 Click the Custom tab to specify colors using the HSL or RGB color model.

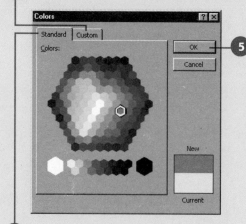

5 Click OK.

4 Alternatively, click the Standard tab, and choose one of 127 colors or 14 percentages of black.

Choose or Customize a Line or Outline in Draw

1 Create or select an AutoShape or WordArt element.

2 Click the Line Style button on the Format toolbar. On the cascading menu, select one of 13 predefined line styles, or click the More Lines command to customize the outline or line.

3 On the Colors And Lines tab (of the Format dialog box) specify the color, dash pattern, arrowhead, and weight of the line.

4 Click OK.

What is the difference between a picture fill and a texture fill? Textures are small, seamless bitmapped pictures that fill objects with a repeating pattern to simulate surfaces like marble or wood. Pictures are images stored in any graphics format Draw supports. When used as a fill, the picture is clipped to the outline of the shape.

Create Fill Effects in Draw

1 Select the AutoShape or WordArt object you want to fill.

2 With the object selected, click the Fill Color button on the Format toolbar. Select Fill Effects from the cascading menu. The Fill Effects dialog box appears.

3 Click one of the four tabs.

Click the Gradient tab to choose one of 24 predefined multi-color gradients, a one-color gradient, or a two-color gradient.

Click the Texture tab to choose one of 24 predefined bitmapped textures, such as White Marble or Oak. Alternatively, you can import a bitmapped picture to use as a repeating texture pattern.

Click the Pattern tab to select one of 48 patterns.

Click the Picture tab to import a picture in any format Draw supports. The picture will appear inside the shape or WordArt text.

4 Click OK.

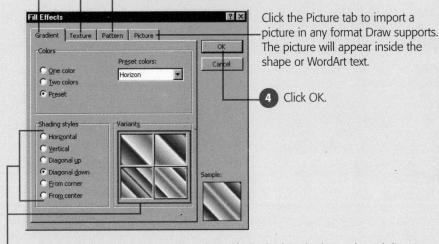

You can choose a variant for each gradient that includes both a shading style and direction.

Choose or Customize a Shadow in Draw

1 Create or select an AutoShape or WordArt element.

2 Click the Shadow button on the Format toolbar. On the flyout menu, select one of 20 predefined shadows, or click the Shadow Settings button to customize the shadow. The Shadow Setting toolbar appears.

Click to toggle the shadow on or off.

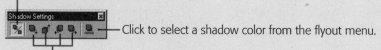

Click to select a shadow color from the flyout menu.

Click these four buttons to nudge the shadow up, down, left, or right.

Why doesn't the front of the three-dimensional object change color when I select a new color from the 3-D Setting toolbar? When you select a color from the 3-D Settings toolbar, you change the color of the three-dimensional extrusion—meaning the sides of the object. In order to change the color for the face of the object, use the normal Fill Color tool on the Format toolbar.

Choose or Customize a 3-D Extrusion in Draw

1 Create or select an AutoShape or WordArt element.

2 Click the 3-D button on the Format toolbar. On the flyout menu, select one of 20 predefined three-dimensional effects, or click the 3-D Settings button to customize the extrusion. The 3-D Settings toolbar appears.

Click to toggle the three-dimensional extrusion on or off.

Click to select one of 6 preset depths from the flyout menu, or enter a value from −600 to 9600 points in the Custom text box.

Click to select one of 9 directional views from the flyout menu, and to toggle between Perspective and Parallel (isometric) views.

Click these four buttons to tilt the extrusion up, down, left, or right.

Click to select a color for the three-dimensional sides of the object.

Click to choose one of four surfaces from the flyout menu: Wireframe (a three-dimensional outline), Matte (no shine), Plastic (slight shine), and Metal (high shine).

Click to select one of eight lighting directions and to toggle between Bright, Normal, and Dim lighting.

For more information about picture file formats, inserting pictures, and using the Microsoft Clip Gallery, see Chapter 10.

Why can't I use Publisher's Crop Picture tool to delete part of an imported picture? You can use Publisher's Crop Picture tool (or Draw's Crop tool) to hide part of an imported picture. But you can only adjust the picture frame, which hides outer horizontal and vertical portions of the image, as seen below. You cannot delete an element that overlaps another part of the picture without deleting the underlying element.

When you use Draw to delete part of an imported picture, you can select and delete individual objects within the picture, as shown below. The changes you make are not limited to the straight edges of the picture. In fact, you can delete elements even when they overlap others in the picture.

Altering Imported Pictures

Just like Publisher, Draw lets you change the appearance of a picture by moving it, cropping it, resizing it, applying a border, or filling the background with a color. In addition, Draw offers tools to edit the individual elements within an imported picture. For example, you can reshape the outlines of shapes in a vector drawing or change the brightness and contrast of a bitmapped picture.

Import a Picture into Draw

1 Open Draw.

2 On the Insert menu, select Clip Art to open the Microsoft Clip Gallery 4.0 or select Picture From File to open the Insert Picture dialog box.

3 Using either the Clip Gallery dialog box or the Insert Picture dialog box, locate and import a picture in any format that Draw supports. The imported image appears in the document and is treated as a single object.

Edit an Imported Vector Image

1 Select a vector (or draw-type) imported image.

2 Click the Ungroup button on the Standard toolbar, or select the Ungroup command from the Draw flyout menu on the Format toolbar.

3 Publisher asks if you want to convert the imported object to a Draw object. Click Yes.

4 Click away from the image to deselect all the individual objects.

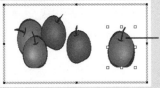

Use the pointer to select one object, or Shift-click to select a number of objects.

5 Use any of Draw's tools to edit the object. You can move, delete, resize, or rotate the object. You can change any of the formatting attributes for the object's outline and fill.

Adding and deleting control handles. To add a new control handle, hold down the Ctrl key and click the outline of the object. To delete an existing control handle, hold down the Ctrl key while you click the handle.

Use Draw to mirror imported vector images. Sometimes the clip-art picture you want to use in a layout is simply facing the wrong way. While Publisher can flip drawn objects horizontally or vertically to create a mirror image, it cannot flip imported pictures. You can circumvent this shortcoming by using Draw to flip imported vector pictures. After you've inserted the vector drawing, Ungroup and then Group the picture. This converts the picture (and all of the shapes it contains) to Draw objects that can still be selected as a single element. Select the Rotate Or Flip command on the Draw menu. From the flyout menu, select Flip Horizontal to create a left-to-right mirror image or Flip Vertical to create a top-to-bottom mirror image.

Alter the Outline of an Object in an Imported Vector Picture

1 Select a vector (or draw-type) imported image.

2 Click the Ungroup button on the Standard toolbar, or select the Ungroup command from the Draw flyout menu on the Format toolbar.

3 Publisher asks if you want to convert the imported object to an Draw object. Click Yes.

4 Click away from the image to deselect all the individual objects.

5 Use the pointer to select one object.

6 Open the Draw menu and choose Edit Points.

—The object is now surrounded by control handles that appear at the vertex of each curve or line segment.

7 Use Publisher's Zoom box to increase the magnification level until you can clearly see the control handles and select them with precision.

8 Use the pointer to grab a control handle and drag it to a new location, which changes the shape of the object.

Change the Picture Quality of an Imported Bitmapped Image

1 Select an imported bitmapped picture. The Picture toolbar appears.

2 Click the Ungroup button on the Standard toolbar, or select the Ungroup command from the Draw flyout menu on the Format toolbar.

3 Publisher asks if you want to convert the imported object to a Draw object. Click Yes. The Picture toolbar appears.

Why would I want to make a color in a bitmapped image transparent? Web pages often include silhouette effects with a bitmapped picture, where the irregular outlines of the picture's subject appear against the background texture you've chosen for your Web site. Unfortunately, most bitmapped pictures are rectangular and opaque. In order to create a silhouette, the color that surrounds the picture's subject must be transparent, as in the picture of the globe shown below.

A bitmapped picture silhouetted against a Web background texture

Draw can make only one selected color transparent. This technique does not work well when multiple colors surround the photograph's subject.

 For more information about transparent GIF images, see Chapter 10.

Change the Picture Quality of an Imported Bitmapped Image *(continued)*

4 Adjust the picture by clicking the appropriate tools on the Picture toolbar.

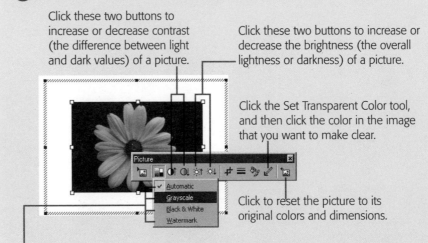

Click these two buttons to increase or decrease contrast (the difference between light and dark values) of a picture.

Click these two buttons to increase or decrease the brightness (the overall lightness or darkness) of a picture.

Click the Set Transparent Color tool, and then click the color in the image that you want to make clear.

Click to reset the picture to its original colors and dimensions.

Click the Image Control button. On the flyout menu, select one of the four options:

@ Automatic displays the picture's original colors.

@ Grayscale converts a color picture to shades of gray.

@ Black-and-white converts a color or grayscale image to a high contrast picture.

@ Watermark lightens the colors in a picture, making it a suitable background for text.

Text for Design Projects

The text that you will need to complete the design projects in Part 2 appears below. For line spacing, indentation, and other formatting, refer to the design chapters.

You can also download this text from the Microsoft Press Web site at http://mspress.microsoft.com/mspress/products/1426.

Chapter 19 Post Card Announcement

Jazz
The Martin Krump Trio
At City Lights Café
Saturday and Sunday
July 24th and 25th

The Martin Krump Trio
Friday, July 24th and
Saturday, July 25th
At 10 p.m.
City Lights Café
449 Harrison Street
Cincinnati, Ohio
Call for Reservations
513-555-2222

Chapter 20 Phone Book Advertisement

Tournament Bikes
Sales, Custom Orders, Expert Repairs

Racing Bikes
Touring Bikes
Mountain Bikes
Children's Bikes
Jogging Strollers

Visit Our
Web Site
www.t_bikes.com

215-555-8989
1653 Newfield Ave.
Norristown, PA 19401

Chapter 21 Résumé

Gregory Lanier
1987 Howe Avenue
Sacramento, CA 95826
916-555-1313
glani@tamarind.com

Objective
To obtain a position as the marketing director of a nationally known furniture and housewares manufacturer.

Experience
1994 to present
Vice President, Tamarind Designs, Inc., Sacramento, California.
Head up the marketing department at this furniture company with gross revenues in excess of $12,000,000 per year. Responsible for market research that drove the development of ecologically sensitive furniture featuring renewable materials, such as bamboo and hemp. Established the exclusivity of the Tamarind brand with to-the-trade-only sales.

1992 to 1994
Senior Marketing Associate, Coward's, LTD., Austin, Texas.
Supervised a team of 6 research assistants, copy writers, and art directors at this innovative modern furniture design company. Developed international marketing campaigns for diverse product lines, including the popular Kidz Kraze(tm) line of children's furniture and the Zen signature collection by Yasuko Takashima.

1987 to 1992
Assistant Director, The James Foundation, Austin, Texas.
Served as the second highest officer of the Research Department in this renowned design institution. Supervised an academic staff of 27 researchers and 10 administrative support personnel. Led efforts to document the work of seminal American designers, such as Gustav Stickley, Ray and Charles Eames, and Frank Gehry.

Apprenticeship
1981 to 1987
Assistant Designer, The Vermont Workshop, Manchester, Vermont.
Executed the concepts of senior staff members and guest artists at this crafts collective, well known for its tradi-tional approach to furniture design. Duties included translating rough sketches into presentation-quality drawings and rendering final blueprints.

Education
1980
M.A., Industrial Design, Rhode Island School of Design
1977
B.F.A., Sculpture, summa cum laude, Brown University

Publications
"Marketing Persona Instead of Product," *The New York Marketing Association Newsletter*, Winter 1993
"A Tribute to Michael Thonet," *Collectible Furniture*, Vol. 15, No.2
"The Arts and Crafts Revival," *Collectible Furniture*, Vol. 14, No.10

Professional Associations
Sacramento Marketing Association, Board Member
International Interior Designer's Institute (IIDI), Member
The American Craft Council, Lifetime Member

Chapter 22 School Flyer

The 5th Annual
Winter
Festival

Snowman Competition
Toboggan Rides
Snowboarding
Ice Skating

Ridgewood High School Sports Field
Admission: Adults $5.00 Children $3.00
Sunday January 24, 1999
10 a.m. to 5 p.m.

Chapter 23 Family Web Page

The Clark Family Bulletin

Webmaster
Contact Margaret Clark Russell at mcr@aol.com.

Patrick Sean Clark II just turned 3. He's big for his age, as you can see in this totally adorable picture taken by cousin Kate. If you want to see more of little Pat, click the picture to view a larger version of the photograph.

Grandma Sylvia just got back from an extended visit with Lori and Mike's family in Minneapolis. Here's her summary of the trip, "The weather was wonderful and the grandchildren were a blast. Oh yeah, Lori and Mike were fun too."

Timmy Dugan (though he prefers Tim these days) is off to college. He's attending Columbia University in New York City. If you want to wish him luck, you can contact him at his new e-mail address, timo5@aol.com.

Reunion Time
It's time to finalize the plans for our 4th biennial family reunion. Helen and George are lobbying for San Francisco in October. By October the fog has departed, leaving clear skies and warm temperatures. And there are lots of other things to do in San Francisco, like visit museums or take quick trips to the wine country.

Dave wants to go on a cruise. He has found a reasonably priced cruise that sails from Puerto Rico to Aruba. We'd have to change the date, because October is the rainy season in the Caribbean. But in Dave's words, "A cruise is perfect. You can sun or swim, go dancing after dinner, or indulge at the all-you-can-eat buffet!"

Dave has agreed to keep track of everyone's vote. So please e-mail him (not me!) with your opinions at dave@t_bikes.com.

Chapter 24 Company Logo

Trophy Sporting Goods

Chapter 25 Business Form

Purchase Order
Trophy Sporting Goods
15 Old Country Road
Richardson, TX 75081
Voice: 214-555-1313
Fax: 214-555-1414

#90065-30-421
Vendor:
Address:
Phone:
Fax:

Date:
Resale Number:
Terms:
Ship Via:
Ordered By:
Authorized By:

Qty.
Description
Unit Price
Discount
Total

Subtotal
Freight
Total

Chapter 26 Letterhead,
Business Card, and Envelope

Horseman Antiques
984 Patriots Way
Concord, MA 01742

Voice: 508-555-6768
Fax: 508-555-6779
Sales: 800-555-5656
Email: horseman@msn.com

Chapter 27 Mail Merge Letter

Address List

First	Last	Address	City	State	ZIP	Style
Lewis	Abelman	224 Rutledge Road	Concord	MA	01742	Shaker
Joan	Anderson	1440 Cactus Tree Road	Concord	MA	01742	Mission
Craig	Bishop	10 Sylvan Drive	Cambridge	MA	02139	Colonial
Jim	Brown	19 Kings Point Rd.	Concord	MA	01742	Shaker
Roscoe	Chandler	1850 Ingersoll Way	Cambridge	MA	02139	Mission
Sandra	Clark	2246 Boulevard East	Concord	MA	01742	Colonial
Ken	Diamond	159 Mulholland Drive	Cambridge	MA	02142	Art Deco
Margaret	Dumont	12 Rittenhouse Avenue	Cambridge	MA	02142	Shaker
Joe	Ehrlich	1625 Mesa Street	Concord	MA	01742	Mission
Howard	Friedman	200 Ocean Circle	Cambridge	MA	02139	Art Deco
Amy	Harte	36 Fortuna Avenue	Cambridge	MA	02142	Shaker
Dave	Howard	289 Olean Street	Concord	MA	01742	Colonial
Steven	Jackson	153 Palm Court	Cambridge	MA	02139	Shaker
Charles	Jones	19 Emerson Circle	Concord	MA	01742	Art Deco
Jackie	Prescott	1536 Windsor Circle	Cambridge	MA	02142	Colonial
Scott	Resnick	619 Albemarle Road	Concord	MA	01742	Shaker
Edward	Stern	18 Hollingswood Drive	Concord	MA	01742	Shaker
Bob	Taylor	4239 Cardinal Street	Cambridge	MA	02139	Colonial
Judy	Williams	7 Summer Street	Concord	MA	01742	Mission
Steve	Young	114 Franklin Avenue	Concord	MA	01742	Shaker

Letter

\<Date\>
\<First\>\<Last\>

\<Address 1\>
\<City\>, \<State\> \<ZIP Code\>

Dear \<First\>,

As an avid collector of Shaker furniture, I'm sure you will want to attend an upcoming estate sale here at Horseman Antiques. This unique event will place no fewer than 40 museum-quality pieces on the auction block. Of course, a substantial collection such as this includes classic Shaker chairs and tables. But it also contains rare items, such as a tailoring counter valued at $85,000. You'll also find utilitarian objects like butter churns, pegged chair railings, and farm tools.

You will have an opportunity to inspect all of the items for sale at our warehouse, which we will open at 10 A.M. and close promptly at 4 P.M. on Saturday, May 23, 1998. If you wish, you can also arrange a private viewing during the week of May 18th through the 22nd by contacting my assistant, Esther Schmindler, at our toll-free number.

We will accept blind bids by mail or fax until 5 P.M. on Friday, May 29th. We will telephone to notify you if your bid has been accepted.

As always, it is a privilege to do business with you.

Sincerely,
Alison Chamberlain
Proprietor

Chapter 28 Professional Web Site

Scuba Currents

Current Tidings
Dive Destinations
Shark School
Request Form

Current Tidings
A recent survey of our membership list revealed a sharp rise in the number of women divers. Certainly lighter equipment and better buoyancy devices have made scuba more accessible to all sorts of participants, including children, the elderly, and women. But I believe women are diving because they have discovered their need for athletics and adventure.

Of course, there are still some very real barriers that separate women from men on the diving circuit. Only this week, while planning a trip to Truk in Micronesia, I was reminded that remote diving locations are simply not safe for women traveling alone. The diving community as a whole should insist that local governments, tour operators, and hotel chains work together to make every destination safe for divers of both genders.

In the meantime, check out the group trip to Micronesia that provides the perfect mix of good company, protected travel, and sensational diving. Space is limited, so act quickly. You can fill out our new electronic form to request information on our featured trips.

Rebecca Tilson
President

Palau, Truk, and Yap

Sponsored by Scuba Currents, this trip makes three stops on different islands known for their rich marine life and stunning reef formations. Imagine yourself snapping underwater photos of the gray reef sharks at Blue Corner in Palau, swimming with mantas in the Goofnuw channel of Yap, or wreck diving among the Japanese battleships sunk off the coast of Truk. Experienced tour guides and scuba masters make these adventures accessible and safe.

Saba Island

Scuba Currents is now booking a group excursion to Saba, the magical island in the Netherlands Antilles. The all-inclusive dive and travel package features low airfares, a rain forest trek, sea kayaking, and dive certification courses. Experienced dive masters and hiking guides with a personal knowledge of the island's flora and fauna make this an ideal trip for the entire family. The weeklong adventure is scheduled for the last week of November.

Shark School

Sharks don't usually attack divers. They are much more likely to attack swimmers at the surface.

Learn about the local shark species. Some, like the Nurse Shark, are not predators.

Keep your eye on your pressure gauge. Anxiety, or excitement, can cause you to deplete your oxygen supply.

Paul Norris is a dive master with an incredible range of experience. He has explored reefs in the Caribbean and wrecks deep below the surface of the Atlantic. Paul has encountered sharks in the wild dozens of times. We are thrilled to present his pearls of wisdom.

Request for Information

Fill out the following form to receive more information about our featured dive destinations.

Name/Membership I.D.
First Name
Last Name
Membership I.D.

Send information about:
Palau, Truk, and Yap
Saba Island

Send information by:
Fax
Fax number
E-mail
E-mail address

Chapter 29 Mail-Order Catalog

Epicurean Delights
Edible Flowers
Spring 1999

Johnny-Jump-Up
Although these bright purple and yellow blooms look quite a lot like Pansies, Johnny-Jump-Ups are totally edible. The mild flavor is slightly sweet, making Johnny-Jump-Ups a perfect decoration for soft cheeses or cold fruit soups. Try combining goat cheese with Johnny-Jump-Ups and watercress or endive.

You should plant Johnny-Jump-Ups in full or partial sun at the first sign of thaw. You can enjoy both the sight and taste of the flowers in early spring. After the warm weather is over, you can still harvest these edible flowers. Simply order the potted plant instead of seeds.

Our hot-house grown plants will bloom even in the dead of winter.

Johnny-Jump-Up Pricing Table Text

Seedlings (24)	#2243	2.50
Fresh Flowers (1 lb.)	#2235	15.00
Plant in bloom	#2236	35.00

Nasturtium

Only in recent times has Nasturtium, or Tropaeolum minus, been considered a purely ornamental plant. Ancient Persians nibbled Nasturtium petals as early as 400 B.C. And Nasturtiums reached their peak of popularity in 17th Century Europe. The flowers, stems, and leaves of this plant are edible. The flavor is peppery and has a marked similarity to watercress. Indeed, Nasturtium's tangy, slightly hot taste has made it a favorite salad ingredient of Nouvelle-cuisine chefs.

Plant Nasturtium in the spring. The plants will bloom in summer, but the harvest will last through fall. You can keep cut flowers fresh by floating them in a bowl of water in the refrigerator.

Nasturtium Pricing Table Text

Seedlings (24)	#3243	2.50
Fresh Flowers (1 lb.)	#3235	15.00
Plant in bloom	#3236	35.00

Sweet Violet

A nosegay of Viola odorata is a gift of sweet affection. These tiny purple blooms are, quite appropriately, a symbol of Venus. The Romans fermented crushed flowers to make a sweet wine, but modern-day cooks use crystallized blossoms as an edible decoration for desserts. And herbalists use an infusion made from flowers to cure insomnia.

Rather than offer seeds, we offer Violet seedlings, which can be transplanted to an outdoor site in spring. Once rooted, these perennials will return to bloom year after year. Indeed, you may find that the runners which Sweet Violets use for natural propagation invade other parts of your garden.

Sweet Violet Pricing Table Text

Seedlings (24)	#4243	2.50
Fresh Flowers (1 lb.)	#4235	15.00
Plant in bloom	#4236	35.00

Chapter 30 Three-Fold Brochure

New World Wines

A shared discovery is a precious gift.

New World Wines
984 Cardinal Lane
Redwood City, CA 94061

Discover The New World

When we first opened New World Wines in 1972, everyone laughed. Imagine...an entire store devoted exclusively to American wine. Now, 26 years later, many people—but especially our customers—applaud our decision. The relationships we've developed in the larger wine community allow us to procure the best of today's premier wines, especially sought-after estate bottlings and limited releases. Our deep knowledge of small producers helps us to discover the great wines of tomorrow.

The staff here at New World Wines participates in regular wine tastings, both to educate our collective palette and to investigate wines as they are released to the market. Occasionally we discover an exceptional wine at an exceptional price. Our new Discovery program allows us to share both the wines and the savings with you by offering a 30% discount on selected wines when they are purchased by the case.

Stonehill Vineyards Heritage 1994

Stonehill Vineyards Heritage is a Bordeaux-style red wine from the San Joaquin valley of California. The wine is not identified by a varietal name because, in the classic French tradition, it blends the juice of several different grapes, including Cabernet Sauvignon, Merlot, and Malbec. Our tasters found the classic berry aromas of ripe cherries and blueberries, with a spicy accent of black pepper.

With a balance of fruit flavors and soft tannins, Stonehill Heritage is ready to drink right now. But this full-bodied wine can also be cellared for the next 3 to 5 years and will only improve with age.

Our enthusiasm for this wine led us to order 200 cases. But, even with a per-bottle price of $20, we expect it to fly off the store shelves. Don't miss this incredible bargain. Place your order today.

Rating: 87

Joshua Creek Gewürztraminer 1996

The Pacific Northwest now produces fine Rieslings and Gewürztraminers in the German style. So our expectations were high when we opened our first bottle of the Joshua Creek Gewürztraminer from the Yakima Valley in Washington State. We weren't disappointed.

Though light-bodied, this wine is a pale yellow gem. It is packed with fruit accents that include green apple and fresh grapefruit aromas. The youthful, pleasantly tart finish makes it a refreshing summer aperitif or the perfect complement to spicy Asian food.

The Joshua Creek Gewürztraminer is at its peak right now, and ideally should be consumed in the next year. Because Joshua Creek is a relatively unknown vineyard, we can offer the wine at an unbelievably low price. Don't let this remarkable value slip through your fingers.

Rating: 90

Order Form
Item
Quantity
Price Per Case
Total
Stonehill Vineyards Heritage 1994

$149

Joshua Creek
Gewürztraminer 1996

$105

Subtotal:
Tax:
Shipping:
Total:

Delivery
Name:
Address:
City, State ZIP:
Daytime Phone:

Payment
Payment Method:
Check
Mastercard
Visa
American Express
Credit Card #:
Expiration Date:

Signature:
*I certify that I am over 21 years of age.

Chapter 31 Business Newsletter

Broadsides
An inside look at architecture and interior design at
Broadside Associates.
March 2, 1998
Volume 8, Issue 3

Inside:

Broadside Associates Acquires Integrated Space
By Trisha Armstead

On January 30th of this year, Broadside Associates acquired Integrated Space, a cutting-edge interior design firm located here in Redwood City, California. The eight-year-old company grossed over $7 million in commissions last year and has projected billings of $11 million this year. That success is directly attributable to Dick Hunter—the firm's founder and current President.

Hunter established his reputation for innovation with a series of boardroom and executive-suite projects that go beyond utilitarian issues and use interior design to establish the client's corporate identity. He furnished an office with Frank Gehry cardboard chairs for the president of International Corrugated. And in what is perhaps his best known commission, the boardroom at Ridder Labs, Hunter created an eye-popping glass environment inspired by the retorts, condensation coils, and Erlenmeyer flasks found in a laboratory.

Known as something of a visionary in the industry, Hunter's most recent commissions transcend aesthetics and attempt to create a truly beneficial workplace for a company's employees. In recent years, Integrated Space has focused on creating healthier office environments for both new and existing buildings. When asked about this latest crusade, Hunter answered bluntly, "Research has proven that improved ventilation systems, natural light simulations, and ergonomic furniture can substantially reduce absenteeism and significantly increase productivity. Ignoring the office environment is bad business."

CEO Logan Broadside summed up Broadside Associates' strategy in these words. "The merger with Integrated Space thrills us. But it's just the beginning. We are already negotiating the purchase of a landscape architecture firm well known for designing public spaces. While I can't disclose the name of the company or the specifics of our timetable, I can say that Broadside Associates will be a full-service design firm by the end of the year."

Hometown Boy Does Good

As part of a state funded sweat equity project, Lewis Balthazar, a senior designer here at Broadside Associates, recently helped restore a small 6-story apartment building. Coincidentally, the building is located in Shorehaven, the part of town where Balthazar himself grew up.

Balthazar was involved in every aspect of the design and construction. His innovative floor plan brings light and a deceptive sense of space to these small, 600-square-foot apartments. What were once cold-water railroad flats are now modern duplex apartments.

"Though I'm extremely proud of the many commercial buildings I've designed, this project gave me a unique sense of personal satisfaction. I feel I've given something back to the community that nourished me."—Donald Neuman

Index

Page numbers in italics refer to figures and tables.

Publications By Wizard tab, 18, 190, 248
Publish To Web command, *230*
Publisher 98, new features, 17–20, 247
publishing Web sites, 227–231

Question mark (?) wildcard character, 22, *74*
Question Mark icon, 8
quotation marks
double (" "), *79*
single (' '), *79*
straight (" "), 80

Radio buttons, *5*
raster images. *See* bitmapped images
ratings, *459*
recent publications, *20*
Recolor Object command, 178–179, 185, 427
recoloring
pictures, *179*
postcard announcements, 337
rectangles, 138, *362–363*
Redo command, 9
registered symbol (®), *79*
relative URLs, 224
Remind To Save Publication option, 38
Reminders, disabling, 7
Remove Filter button, 417
removing. *See* deleting
Replace command, 72–73
replacing. *See also* editing
special characters, 74–75
text, *70–74*
typewriter-style characters, 74, 79–81, 452

Reset Design dialog box, *252*
Reset Tippages button, 6
resizing. *See also* sizing
command buttons, 222
objects, 51
aspect ratio, 52
from its center, 52
numerically, *53*
selection handles, *52*
tables, 127
pictures, 53, 462
vector images, 362
WordArt frames, 386, *488*
resolution
bitmapped images, 168
color, 168, 269
grayscale, 168
images
GIF, *195*
scanned, 168
monitors, *168*
printers, *168,* 291–292
Web sites, 190–191, 423
response forms, Web sites, 434
check boxes, 436
command buttons, 438
control properties, 435–436
option buttons, 437
text boxes, 435
résumé
categories, 356
fonts, 357
page setup, 352
printing, 358
sample text, 497–498
tables, 355
text, 353–354
return address, three-fold brochures, *462–463*

reverse text, 348
RGB (red, green, blue). *See* color
Rich Text Format (RTF), *71*
right-clicking shortcut menus, 4
right-hand pages, 34
RMI sound files, 158
rotating
objects, 55–56
text, *205*
rows, 105
borders, 134–135
deleting, 129
guides, 45–46
sizing, *127–128*
Web sites, 193
RTF (Rich Text Format), *71*
rulers, 39
alignment, 48
displaying, 40
guides, 44, 46
horizontal, *40, 43, 49*
indents, *105–106*
tabs, 105–106
objects, 47, 49
points, 41
positioning, *43, 47*
special indents, *40*
status, 45
tabs, *40*
vertical, *40, 43, 49*
zero points, *40,* 42
Rulers command, *40*
rules. *See also* borders
adding, 337, *459*
alignment, 444
arrowheads, 143
decorative, *444*
drawing, 481, 485
formatting, 142

About the Author

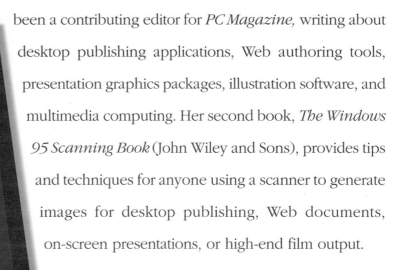

Luisa Simone is a New York–based consultant, teacher, and journalist specializing in computer graphics. For the past nine years, she has been a contributing editor for *PC Magazine,* writing about desktop publishing applications, Web authoring tools, presentation graphics packages, illustration software, and multimedia computing. Her second book, *The Windows 95 Scanning Book* (John Wiley and Sons), provides tips and techniques for anyone using a scanner to generate images for desktop publishing, Web documents, on-screen presentations, or high-end film output.

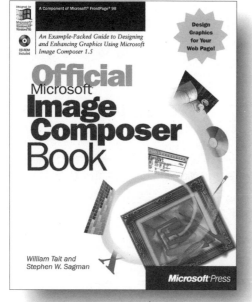

Take the
whole family
siteseeing!

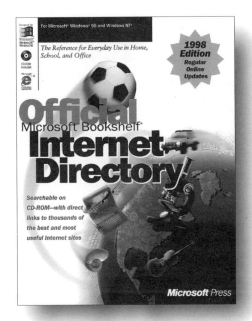